TEA WITH SOCIALISTS

TEA WITH SOCIALISTS

GOVERNMENT IN YOUR PANTIES

BLAINE BROWN

PLOUGHMAN'S PRESS

NEW YORK MMXII

PLOUGHMAN'S PRESS

Released Oct. 31, 2012

The Ploughman's Press Speakers Bureau can bring authors to your live event. For more information or to book an event, contact the Ploughman's Press Speakers Bureau at: www.ploughmanspeakers.com.

First Edition, October 2012.

ISBN 978-0-9885-1994-7 (paper-b)
ISBN 978-0-9885-1993-0 (e-book)

Printed in the United States of America

To Amanda—
Who lifted when I could not

To Vanessa—
Who challenged me to open my mouth

Contents

Acknowledgments

I wish to thank Brenda Brown, Julie Richardson, Angela Richards, Allison Tidwell, MariLouise Harrow, Jeremy Fullmer, Cameron Stewart, Beverly Giroux, Benjamin Richardson, Joshua Parker, and Amy Cosby for their suggestions and support. Without their encouragement this book would never have been completed; and without their input it would be a very different book.

I also wish to thank Bo Davis, the most understanding of legal clients, without whose patience this project would never have been concluded.

1

Prologue

It would be comforting if a clear political diagnosis of the Tea Party movement were available—if we knew precisely what political events had inspired the fierce anger that pervades its meetings and rallies, what policy proposals its backers advocate, and, most obviously, what political ideals and values are orienting its members.

—J. M. Bernstein[i]

SINCE SHORTLY AFTER THE WALL Street Bailout of October, 2008, American citizens have been increasingly preoccupied with politics.

In a startling turn for incumbent politicians and establishment political commentators alike, newly-activated citizens have begun attending congressional recess town hall meetings in droves—to question the motivations, legislative decisions, and loyalty of their representatives to the federal government. At town hall meetings nationwide, the refrain is uniform and relentless: "Why does Washington continue legislating policies we abhor? Can't Washington hear us? What must we do to be heard?"

Such close encounters with the electorate have left federal legislators uneasy about conducting unscripted interviews with constituents.[1] Many legislators responded to town-hall tumults by abolishing town hall meetings altogether, and by replacing them with the far more antiseptic "tele-town-hall"—combining the twin virtues of physical separation from angry constituents and susceptibility to complete agenda-setting control.[2] Other legislators simply moved meetings to private settings at banks, credit unions, and places of businesses—where they can dictate which constituents (if any)

[i] J.M. Bernstein, *The Very Angry Tea Party*, THE NEW YORK TIMES (June 13, 2010).

attend, supervise what questions (if any) are asked, serve guests fine catered meals, sip a cocktail, and enjoy the ensuing applause.[3]

But town hall meetings are not the only venue at which American citizens have been conspicuous as of late. Demonstrations, protests, and rallies organized under varying mottos—many strongly reminiscent of slogans from or incidents to the American Revolution—have materialized spontaneously on the initiative of citizens themselves. They are organized primarily by word of mouth. They form in small towns and large metropolises alike. They are ubiquitous on tax day. And while occasionally overlooked by network media, such bottom-up political activity cannot be forecast to ebb anytime soon. Indeed, the nation appears to be undergoing another Great Awakening—this time in a political sense.

Adherents to such protests have no identifiable leadership or hierarchy.[4] Adherents do not hail from any single socio-economic strata, religion, ethnicity, gender, or sexual orientation. Instead they are bound only by common political concerns and coincident worldviews.[5] The political groundswell is, in a word, grass-roots. For convenience we shall refer to the amalgamation of similarly-situated movements of politically energized citizens as the "Tea Movement."

In only a few short years, the leaderless Tea Movement has exploded onto the national political stage. More than 40% of the adult U.S. population now consistently self identify as Tea Movement supporters.[6] And coinciding precisely with the Tea Movement's emergence in 2008, citizens are dumping former affiliations with Democrat and Republican Parties in droves.[ii]

Yes, the Tea Movement is proving to be a serious headache for establishmentarians in both camps:

On the one hand, Left-leaning pundits label Tea Movement protesters (and their demonstrations) dangerous, violent, anti-government, and both racially and politically subversive. Democratic representatives to Congress specifically complain that the Tea Movement is comprised of *terrorists*: "We have negotiated with terrorists! This small group of terrorists have [sic] made it impossible to spend any money."[7] (By which Democrats mean the Tea Movement has made it more difficult *for the federal government* to spend *citizens'* money.) Vice President Biden concurs: "They have acted like terrorists." Indeed, the Tea Movement has put "guns to [Democrats'] heads" during congressional debt ceiling negotiations.[iii]

[ii] "More than 2.5 million voters have left the Democratic and Republican parties since the 2008 elections, while the number of independent voters continues to grow. . . . [R]egistered Democrats declined in 25 of the 28 states that register voters by party. Republicans dipped in 21 states, while independents increased in 18 states." Richard Wolf, *Voters Leaving Republican, Democratic Parties in Droves*, USA TODAY (Dec. 22, 2011).

[iii] Again, this is Vice President Biden's turn of phrase. Jonathan Allen & John Bresnahan, *Sources: Joe Biden Likened Tea Partiers to Terrorists*, POLITICO (Aug. 2, 2011).

In Senate Majority Leader Harry Reid's estimation, the Tea Movement has pushed the federal government to the threshold of default: As "a result of the Tea Party direction of this Congress the last few months has [sic] been very, very disconcerting, and very unfair to the American people. It stopped us from arriving at a conclusion [to Congress' 2011 debt ceiling debacle] much earlier."[8] Wherever federal spending is concerned, Democratic representatives proclaim that "Tea Partiers . . . have made their slash and burn lunacy clear . . . . The arsonists must be stopped."[9]

On the other hand, Tea Movement adherents have specifically rejected advice, participation, administration, and direction from interested political parties and media figures on the Right—who would love nothing more than to take the reins of this fledgling movement and direct its fervor into paths more favorable to themselves[iv] While Tea Movement adherents do not conduct business under the banner of any one party, they have supported the candidacy of certain Republican congresspersons. Yet they have also proudly targeted and openly destroyed the candidacy of Republican incumbents during Party primaries.[10] (As thirty-six-year incumbent Republican Senator Orrin Hatch admitted in 2012, when facing a primary challenge from a Tea Party upstart, "I despise these people."[11]) Tea Movement adherents have brazenly (and sincerely!) requested senior Republican Senators currently serving as powerful, ranking members of Senate Committees *to retire*.[12] (And certain multi-term Republican Senators have complied with their request![13]) They have dismayed G.O.P. leadership time and again with congressional insurrections at the most politically inopportune occasions.[14]

Tea Movement adherents have been repeatedly censured by Republican Congressional leadership for such strident breaches of party discipline. In the words of Speaker of the House John Boehner, "Get your ass in line!"[15] Republican insiders do not appreciate Tea Movement mutinies in Congress. And while Tea Movement Republicans now represent a large and growing congressional caucus, establishment Republicans admonish them in no uncertain terms: "This ain't your party."[16]

Yes, the Tea Movement has proven disagreeable to Republicans and Democrats alike. For this reason both Parties intend to stamp out the Tea Movement. Admittedly, they have not yet "disarmed the bomb"[17]—but party insiders on both sides of the aisle comfort themselves with hopes that Tea Movement influence and autonomy will soon fade. Immediately after the

---

[iv] When asked if the Republican Party was "slowly co-opting" the Tea Movement, Republican insider, strategist, and lobbyist Scott Reed candidly responded: "Trying to. And that's the secret to politics: trying to control a segment of people without those people recognizing that you're trying to control them." Matt Bai, *Does Anyone Have a Grip on the G.O.P.?*, THE NEW YORK TIMES (Oct. 12, 2011).

2010 midterm elections, for example, polls showed a full 70% of Washington, D.C. elites already believed the Tea Movement to be a passing fad.[18] Democratic Congressional leaders speak of the Tea Movement in the past tense, and opine that the Movement is merely a passing craze occasioned by a poor economy.[19] And today Republican insiders fancy that presidential primaries—and the general elections which follow—provide political processes which will allow them to root out the remaining "Tea Party zaniness" within their midst.[20]

(Meanwhile, members of the Tea Movement are independently contemplating whether to go to the polls and cast a ballot for the Republican Establishment's candidate on November 6—or whether to just stay home. And the Tea Movement's rudimentary, bottom-up machinery is again targeting and torpedoing the candidacy of establishment Republican Senate hopefuls—this time in Indiana, Texas, Nebraska, Florida, Michigan, Wisconsin, Utah, and elsewhere.[21])

Political scientists regale us with empirical studies illustrating that political polarization is at an all-time high in modern America.[22] And they explain that polarization with reference to the emergent Tea Movement.[23] But that is where establishment thinkers' powers of explanation end.

Political commentators are baffled by the "seething anger" of the Tea Movement.[24] Not only do commentators profess ignorance of the source of such anger, they are also at a loss to coherently explain either the Tea Movement's policy aims or the values animating those aims.[25] Commentators like J. M. Bernstein publicly lament the lack of a "clear political diagnosis" of the Tea movement.[26]

And while maintaining that Tea Movement "policy proposals" are unclear, establishment political commentary nevertheless simultaneously condemns those few "concrete policy proposals" made by the Tea Movement as "contradictory" or "paradoxical."[27] As an example of such contradictions, J. M. Bernstein cites a Tea Movement proposal to "balance the budget, but don't raise taxes."[28]

Establishment political thought also struggles to understand Tea Movement political strategy. As establishment commentary astutely observes, the Tea Movement is *not* directed at achieving political power for making new demands upon government.[29] Rather, the Tea Movement strives to "neutralize . . . political power,"[30] and to be "left alone" by government.[31] Consequently, establishment political thought concludes that the Tea Movement "has no constructive political agenda."[32] And establishment political thought finds a political movement bent on *less* government frightening in the extreme: "In truth, there is nothing that the Tea Party movement wants; terrifyingly, it wants *nothing*. . . . [T]hey are nihilists."[v]

Yes, the Tea Movement not only frustrates both major electoral Parties, but also bewilders establishment political thought.

It is unclear whether establishment commentators struggle more with arithmetic or with finance; but when they call proposals to "balance the budget without raising taxes" contradictory, they are not thinking outside the establishmentarian box. A simple solution to Mr. Bernstein's "paradox" is, of course, to balance the budget *by cutting government expenditures while leaving taxes unchanged*. This is what, for example, families in Middle America do when family budgets exceed family income. The fact that this solution does not occur to Mr. Bernstein is symptomatic of the wide and deepening divide between establishment political thought and Middle Americans—a divide which defines the Tea Movement.

Similar observations may be made regarding establishment commentators' analysis of Tea Movement political strategy. Contrary to commentators' assertions, an agenda to "neutralize political power" does not signify "lack of a constructive political agenda." Nor does the Tea Movement's desire for less government suggest it "wants *nothing*." A longing for *less* of something is certainly a want, just as a fat man who wishes to eat less food wants *something*—and for the fat man such a want represents a constructive nutritional agenda. In any case, when one wants less of something—in this case government—it certainly doesn't make one a "nihilist"! (As a professor of philosophy Mr. Bernstein surely knows this. But perhaps Mr. Bernstein's political ideology clouds his philosophical vision?)

The fact that establishment political thinkers find Tea Movement political strategy incomprehensible evinces the growing chasm separating establishment political thought and Middle America. Establishment political thinkers and Middle Americans live in orthogonal universes, and when they convene to discuss grievances they talk past one another.

This treatise examines the growing disconnect between politician and plebian, between establishment political thought and Middle American worldview, and the growing distrust and animosity which result. Its thesis provides that socialism is key to understanding this divide; that while socialism is embraced by Washington politicians and bureaucrats, establishment academics, coastal professionals, and political commentators

---

[v] J.M. Bernstein, *The Very Angry Tea Party*, THE NEW YORK TIMES (June 13, 2010) (emphasis original). At more rhetorically charged moments, Pulitzer Prize-winning commentators describe Tea Movement adherents as "a maniacal gang with knives held high," "cannibals," "vampires," and "zombies"—within a single piece! *See, e.g.*, Pulitzer Prize-winning political columnist Maureen Dowd, *Washington Chain Saw Massacre*, THE NEW YORK TIMES (Aug. 2, 2011).

alike, it is rejected in equal measure by Middle Americans. Indeed, the witting or unwitting adoption of socialism by social and political elites—and its wholesale rejection by Middle Americans—underlies the divide between rulers and ruled on issues as far ranging as federal debt; federal taxation; federal economic "stimuli;" federal bailouts of large corporations and banking institutions; federalized health care; federalized mortgage relief; debauchery of the dollar; inflation; immigration; federal energy policy; national defense; TSA's manhandling of airport passengers; deficit spending for social programs; and multiple re-extensions of unemployment benefits.

In examining the growing rift between American socialism and Middle America, this treatise also explains the "inscrutable" Tea Movement. Inspecting the divide between American socialism and Middle America exposes the Tea Movement in high relief: It illustrates *what* the Movement is—what political ideals inspire its members, what policies motivate its actions, and what political aspirations it holds. It also delineates *why* the Tea Movement arose in the first place.

This treatise's examination of the rift between American Socialism and Middle America, and the Tea Movement it produced, proceeds as follows:

Book I outlines socialist thought. It begins by describing socialist premises and first principles. It follows socialist principles' maturation into practical political aims and explicit programs. It reflects on the consequences of socialist thought—both calculated policies and unintentional effects. Book I also expounds the reasons behind Middle American resistance to socialist thought and policy.

Book II, the present volume, analyzes socialist method. In particular, it explores the contemporary method by which socialism establishes itself within the United States—against the wishes of the Middle American majority.

Book III examines Socialist America. It illustrates how contemporary federal policy specifically implements the socialist premises, principles, policies, and goals explored in Book I by means of the modern socialist method described in Book II. In other words, Book III shows that establishment political policy—both Republican and Democrat—*is socialism.* Book III analyzes federal taxation, federal debt, federal bailouts, federalized health care, federalized mortgage relief, federal energy policy, quantitative easing, inflation, immigration, banking regulation, unemployment insurance, and national defense *in the context of socialist thought*—and concludes that Washington policy on these issues provoked a Middle American backlash we call the Tea Movement.

Book IV discusses the future of the chasm separating American socialism and Middle America. It examines the contemporary relationship between government and governed, between ruler and ruled, between "Representative" and "constituent." It closes with a sincere warning regarding the consequences of irrepresentative government—and a plea to those in positions of influence on both sides of the divide to reconcile while yet they may.

In summary, this treatise aims to provide a "political diagnosis" of the Tea Movement so earnestly solicited by Mr. Bernstein and his establishmentarian comrades. Its examination of socialist theory and method appeals to the human experience in an effort to illuminate what are, at first perusal, mere political abstractions. It may thus be of assistance to many establishmentarians who do not understand the foundations of their own political creed. It may also be helpful to members of the political class who, while consciously or unconsciously subscribing to the tenets of socialist thought, remain uncertain why their "seething" constituents reject the socialist benefits continuously lavished upon them from Washington.

This treatise may also prove helpful to Middle Americans who, while outraged at Washington policy and practice, nonetheless fail to recognize with precision the socialist principles undergirding those policies they deplore. That is, it may help Middle Americans better understand the origin and theory of policies they denounce, focus their political dialog, and better articulate their displeasure with Washington policy. (Assuming, of course, that Middle Americans' representatives to Washington care to grant them audience.)

Before we begin, two disclaimers are in order.

First, the subject of this book is *mere socialism*—i.e., *those premises, policies, and goals common to all sects of socialism*—and Middle American opposition thereto. For this reason, an effort has been made *not* to distinguish between the myriad socialist factions, including Democratic Socialism, National Socialism, Libertarian Socialism, Utopian Socialism, Guild Socialism, Syndicalism, Communism, Anarchism, De Leonism, Leninism, Trotskyism, Marxism, Maoism, Bureaucratic Collectivism, etc., except where absolutely necessary. The various branches of socialism are in general agreement on the premises, principles, policies, and goals of socialist life—their differences lie primarily in the niceties of getting from here to there. Their narrow sectarian disputes over method are not a subject of this volume. Instead, the subject of this volume is the generalized dispute between Middle America on the one hand and the common premises, policies, and goals of all socialist sects on the other. For this reason the various socialist factions have been subsumed herein under one, uncapitalized appellation: *socialism.*

Second, an important distinction must be drawn at the outset between secular socialism on the one hand (which *is* a subject of this treatise), and religious organizations which may superficially resemble socialist society on the other (which are *not*). Many religious orders take vows of poverty, strict material equality, and submission of individual will—in even the most personal of matters—to that of the religious community. Such vows may be strictly enforced. Despite superficial similarities, however, religious communities represent an entirely different species of political organization. The key difference between secular socialism and religious orders, and the reason that such religious organizations are not analyzed here, is that participation in religious communities is *strictly voluntary*: If you should decide you don't like living as a nun, you simply leave the convent.

The secular socialism with which this treatise concerns itself furnishes no "opt out" provision. It is not a voluntary political system. It seeks instead to impose its own order *upon all.*

Further Notes to Chapter 1

[1] *See, e.g.*, Jeff Zeleny, *Democrats Skip Town Halls to Avoid Voter Rage*, THE NEW YORK TIMES (June 6, 2010); J.M. Bernstein, *The Very Angry Tea Party*, THE NEW YORK TIMES (June 13, 2010).
[2] Jeff Zeleny, *Democrats Skip Town Halls to Avoid Voter Rage*, THE NEW YORK TIMES (June 6, 2010).
[3] *Ibid.*
[4] Mark Lilla, The Tea Party Jacobins, THE NEW YORK REVIEW OF BOOKS (April 29, 2010) ("[T]hey still have no identifiable leadership.").
[5] *See, e.g.*, Study, *Partisan Polarization Surge in Bush, Obama Years: Trends in American Values, 1987-2012*, PEW RESEARCH CENTER (June 4, 2012) ("Unlike in 1987, when this series of surveys began, the values gap between Republicans and Democrats is now greater than gender, age, race or class divides.").
[6] *See* Tea Party Support Polls produced for ABC News and The Washington Post, LANGER RESEARCH ASSOCIATES (04/08/2012 [41%]; 03/10/2012 [44%]; 02/04/2012 [43%]; 01/15/2012 [40%]; 12/18/2011 [42%]; 11/03/2011 [43%]; 10/02/2011 [42%]; 09/01/2011 [47%]; 07/17/2011 [44%]; 06/05/2011 [46%]; 04/07/2011 [42%]). Copy on file with author.
[7] Michael F. Doyle, Representative for Pennsylvania's 14th congressional district, provided us with this metaphor. Jonathan Allen & John Bresnahan, *Sources: Joe Biden Likened Tea Partiers to Terrorists*, POLITICO (Aug. 2, 2011).
[8] Josiah Ryan, *Reid: Tea Party Has Pushed Congress in a 'Very, Very Disconcerting' Direction*, THE HILL (Aug. 2, 2011).
[9] Credit for this metaphor goes to Luis Vicente Gutiérrez, Representative for Illinois' 4th congressional district. Jonathan Allen & John Bresnahan, *Sources: Joe Biden Likened Tea Partiers to Terrorists*, POLITICO (Aug. 2, 2011).
[10] Including Senators Bob Bennett (R Utah, defeated by relative unknown Mike Lee) and Lisa Murkowski (R Alaska, defeated by complete unknown Joe Miller). This is to say nothing of protesters' disruption of Republican's handpicked, non-incumbent candidates for Senator—like, for example, KY Sec. of State Trey Greyson (R, Kentucky, defeated by opthalmologist Rand Paul). *See, e.g.*, Chris Cillizza, *Utah Senator Bob Bennett Loses Convention Fight*, THE WASHINGTON POST (May 8, 2010); Dan Joling, *Senator Murkowski's Defeat Marks Major Tea Party Win*, ASSOCIATED PRESS (Sept. 1, 2010).
[11] Steven Nelson, *Orrin Hatch 'Dogonne Offended' by 'Radical Libertarians' Trying to Take Away His Senate Seat*, THE DAILY CALLER (April 13, 2012).
[12] Paul Steinhauser, *Major Conservative Group Urging Hatch to Retire*, CNN POLITICAL TICKER (June 16, 2011).
[13] "The tea party movement has become the dead bad-luck bird hanging around the GOP establishment's neck. . . . [It] so badgered Maine Sen. Olympia Snowe that the Republican Moderate—a shoo-in for re-election—has decided to leave the Senate." Froma Harrop, *Radical Tea Partiers Won't Negotiate*, REAL CLEAR POLITICS (Aug. 7, 2012).
[14] For example, for breaking ranks with Congressional Republican leadership and (1) failing to support extensions of the debt ceiling; and (2) failing to support extensions of the The Patriot Act. *See, e.g.*, Deirdre Walsh, *Boehner to GOP Members: 'Get Your Ass in Line'*, CNN POLITICAL TICKER (July 27, 2011); David R. Sands, *Patriot Act Reverse Surprises House Republicans*, THE WASHINGTON TIMES (Feb. 8, 2011).
[15] This pithy line was delivered by Speaker of the House John Boehner to mutinous Tea Movement House members. Jake Sherman & John Bresnahan, *Boehner Tries to Tame GOP on Debt Ceiling Plan*, POLITICO (July 27, 2011); Deirdre Walsh, *Boehner to GOP Members: 'Get Your Ass in Line'*, CNN POLITICAL TICKER (July 27, 2011).
[16] John Feehery, Republican insider, lobbyist, and former senior House aide puts it thus: "The thing I get a kick out of is these Tea Party folks calling me a RINO [i.e., a Republican In Name

Only]. No, guys, I've been a Republican all along. You go off into your own little world and then come back and say it's your party. This ain't your party." Matt Bai, *Does Anyone Have a Grip on the G.O.P.?*, THE NEW YORK TIMES (Oct. 12, 2011).

[17] In the words of Republican veteran, strategist, and (now) lobbyist Don Fierce, "We have not disarmed the bomb." *Ibid.*

[18] *Power and the People*, A Politico Poll Series Sponsored by Qualcomm, POLITICO (Nov. 16, 2010). Survey on file with author.

[19] Senate Majority Leader Harry Reid confidently states that, "The Tea Party was the result of a terrible economy. I've said that many times, and I believe that. . . . [The Tea Party] will pass. They will lose a number of seats next year." Glenn Cook, *Reid Expects Tea Party to Fade Away*, LAS VEGAS REVIEW-JOURNAL (Aug. 14, 2011).

[20] Matt Bai, *Does Anyone Have a Grip on the G.O.P.?*, THE NEW YORK TIMES (Oct. 12, 2011):

> Soon enough, however, all heads will swivel to Iowa and New Hampshire, where a Republican nominee will emerge at last to put his or her stamp on the party's image. And this is where, the [Republican] establishment presumes, the long season of Tea Party zaniness will finally recede into the background, subsumed into some more enlightened, and more practical approach. . . .
>
> In other words, while some strange things can happen when the Republican faithful get restless in the off years, the presidential process is the means by which the party establishment has traditionally reasserted control.

[21] *See, e.g., ibid.*

[22] "As Americans head to the polls this November, their values and basic beliefs are more polarized along partisan lines than at any point in the past 25 years. Unlike in 1987, when this series of surveys began, the values gap between Republicans and Democrats is now greater than gender, age, race or class divides. . . . [T]he average partisan gap has nearly doubled over this 25-year period—from 10 percentage points in 1987 to 18 percentage points in the new study." Study, *Partisan Polarization Surges in Bush, Obama Years: Trends in American Values, 1987-2012*, PEW RESEARCH CENTER (June 4, 2012).

[23] *See, e.g.*, Alan Abramowitz, *Partisan Polarization and the Rise of the Tea Party Movement*, AMERICAN POLITICAL SCIENCE ASSOCIATION 2011 ANNUAL MEETING PAPER (2011), available at the Social Science Research Network, http://ssrn.com/abstract=1903153; *see also* CNN's favorite plagiarizer, Fareed Zakaria, *Why Political Polarization Has Gone Wild in America (And What To Do About It)*, CNN (July 24, 2011) ("Watching the extraordinary polarization in Washington today, many people have pointed the finger at the Tea Party saying it's ideologically extreme, refuses to compromise and cares more about purity than problem solving. I happen to agree with much of that critique . . . .").

[24] J.M. Bernstein, *The Very Angry Tea Party*, THE NEW YORK TIMES (June 13, 2010).

[25] *Ibid.*

[26] *See, supra* note i and accompanying text.

[27] J.M. Bernstein, *The Very Angry Tea Party*, THE NEW YORK TIMES (June 13, 2010).

[28] *Ibid.*

[29] Mark Lilla, *The Tea Party Jacobins*, THE NEW YORK REVIEW OF BOOKS (April 29, 2010).

[30] *Ibid.*

[31] *Ibid.* As with so many other features of the Tea Movement, "resentment for government" is yet another aspect which "positively baffle[s]" Republican insiders. Matt Bai, *Does Anyone Have a Grip on the G.O.P.?*, THE NEW YORK TIMES (Oct. 12, 2011).

[32] Mark Lilla, *The Tea Party Jacobins*, THE NEW YORK REVIEW OF BOOKS (April 29, 2010).

2

Incrementalism

[W]e must proceed from one step to the next. If you say to anyone in the United States today, "What we want is socialism and the expropriation of private property in the means of production and collective control," then people run away from you. That does not mean that the idea of socialism is false—to the contrary!

—Herbert Marcuse[i]

We have said that, in order to judge a government, it is not so important to consider the pace at which it advances as the direction it is taking. This goal, this direction, has been defined by several of our governments as "twenty-first century socialism."

—Marta Harnecker[ii]

VIRUSES ARE CURIOUS LITTLE ORGANISMS.

For all time, their ultimate endeavor remains the same: *replication.*

But the poor little buggers cannot replicate on their own. Being acellular, they possess neither an independent metabolism nor the cellular machinery necessary to multiply. So in order to accomplish their ultimate design, viruses must attach themselves to living cells within a host organism. Viruses must penetrate previously healthy cells, commandeer their cellular machinery and metabolisms, and trick *them*—the host's cells—into assembling and giving birth to new viruses.

---

[i] Socialist theorist Herbert Marcuse, *Das Problem der Gewalt in der Opposition*, Questions and Answers to Lecture at Free University of West Berlin (July 1967), as published in HERBERT MARCUSE, FIVE LECTURES: PSYCHOANALYSIS, POLITICS AND UTOPIA 98 (Beacon Press, 1970).

[ii] Marta Harnecker, *Latin America & Twenty-First Century Socialism: II. Twenty-First Century Socialism*, MONTHLY REVIEW: AN INDEPENDENT SOCIALIST MAGAZINE, vol. 62 issue 3 (July-August, 2010).

It is a sad procedure for the host and his cells. Prognosis for the commandeered cells is generally death. Prognosis for the host is, at best, suffering. If the host's immune system learns how to disrupt virus replication in time, the host may survive. And if the host survives, its immune system will forever remember how to defend against those viral attacks over which it triumphed in the past. (Thank heavens I only had the chicken pox once . . . .)

If this were the end of the story, life would be terribly difficult for viruses.

But this is not the end of the story.

While virus' eternal goals remain replication and the domination of host cells necessary to that end, their methods for accomplishing these goals are constantly changing. The replication process invites occasional mistakes, and new strains of viruses are occasionally produced. These new strains are organized somewhat differently, function somewhat differently, and employ slightly different methods of cellular subterfuge, attachment, penetration, and usurpation than their parent viruses. They therefore appear differently to a host's immune system. Indeed, new viral strains may be *invisible* to it. As a result, new strains may have success where their parent virus can no longer find a foothold—even amongst host cells protected by an experienced and attentive immune system.

Viruses are highly adaptable. And viruses do not diagnose themselves. These are the keys to their success. As a result, viruses are both the most numerous and the most genetically diverse biological entity on earth.[1]

Certain other organisms share viruses' adaptability and opportunism.

One of these is socialism.

Like a virus, socialism's ultimate endeavors also remain constant through time. Socialism plans to implement proactive redistributive injustice through "moral" government. It intends to invoke group "rights" at the expense of the individual. It aims to make local decisions for individuals, families, and communities (including—yes—even your toilet's flush volume). It endeavors to administer these policies via the coercive might of monolithic political power.

Socialism, like a virus, is also incapable of reproducing on its own—i.e., outside of developed, host societies. Socialism has always recognized this.[2] Socialism operates by redistributing private wealth from one citizen to another, and outside highly developed host societies there is not enough private wealth to cover the costs of redistribution. So socialism must attach itself to productive persons within a functioning host nation in order to successfully replicate. Historically speaking, socialist replication has meant socialist revolution; that is, remaking society according to socialist ideals. And historically speaking, this has been ruinous for those persons and nations which socialism successfully penetrates. (As we have already seen in Book I, socialist revolution leads to a very specific socio-economic condition which capitalists refer to as "famine.")

If a host nation successfully thwarts socialist revolution, it learns—much like a viral host's immune system. Persons and nations which have endured and rebuffed socialist revolutionary onslaught learn to defend themselves against the particular organizations, ideas, and methods of attack against which they previously prevailed. Should socialism attempt revolution again, using the same methods amongst the same people within the same host nation, it generally fails.[iii]

Yet this is not the end of socialism.

Like a virus, Socialism is also adaptable and opportunistic: The organization itself, portions of its underlying theory, practice of its social policies, and methods employed to realize its goals are ever shifting, adapting, re-balancing, and re-branding to match temporal and political realities.[iv] Indeed, socialist organization ossifies only within those host nations where socialism formally takes the reins of power. In countries where socialism has *not* formally ascended, socialism continues to tinker with shifting strategies—trying to find one that will put it over the top. The chimerical nature of socialist method affords little surprise when one recognizes socialism's material "morality"[v] and the generalized policy of coercion by which socialism intends to reach its material aims.[vi] Based on those principles, socialism's battle-cry is that the end justifies *all* means. And in order to have success, those means are constantly shifting.

Avoiding socialism is akin to avoiding a virus: one can't rely on last-year's flu shot. One must vaccinate oneself against *this year's* flu bug. One must remain vigilant to recognize symptoms, to identify newer strains, to recognize their designs upon the host, and to monitor illness' progress.

Doing anything less only invites infection.

[iii] There are too many examples to list here. But consider, for example, Syndicalism and Anarchism in America; Communism in South Korea; Communism in the Philippines; etc. Such organizations made organized attempts at socialist revolution in the host countries listed and utterly failed. While they were very close to completing socialist revolutions in the twentieth century, they would be laughed out national assemblies in their respective host countries today.

[iv] "[O]ur theory is based on materialism. The issues addressed by Marxism *are bound to adapt* when it encounters new material, the method with which to address them remains true." Jean Paul Holmes, *Defeating the Ultra-Right: Know Your Enemy*, POLITICAL AFFAIRS (June 2, 2010) (emphasis added).

[v] *See* TEA WITH SOCIALISTS, Book I (The Hive Mentality), chap. 3 *Redistributive Injustice*; chap. 6 *The Amorality of Moral Government.*

[vi] *See* TEA WITH SOCIALISTS, Book I (The Hive Mentality), chap. 8 *Liberty and Coercion.*

Hunting Squirrels

Socialism's adaptability cannot be appreciated apart from a temporal frame of reference. Nor can socialism's current revolutionary method be understood outside its historical context. And so, we must briefly survey socialism's past.

Socialist thinkers originally assumed that "workers" (as they condescendingly refer to those beneath them in the hive hierarchy) would rise up and violently establish international socialism during the next major "imperialist war"—if only given a nudge in that direction by the socialist vanguard. So naturally, early socialist revolutionary strategy hinged upon waiting for the right moment—preferably during wartime—to spring a violent revolutionary trap. *Worldwide.*[3] Simultaneously. In a twinkling.

But when international socialism failed to achieve planetary conquest during World War I,[vii] some socialists started backing away from their original creed of violent, worldwide, wartime revolution.[4] They began to argue instead that imperialist war was neither a sufficient nor even a necessary condition for socialist revolution.

And after international socialism again failed to achieve worldwide supremacy during World War II,[viii] more socialists abandoned the old strategy of explosive, planetary, socialist revolution. They began to theorize that while multinational crises were juicy opportunities, socialist revolution *need not wait for war.* They began to contend that instead of attempting instantaneous planetary scale, socialism should focus on shepherding socialist revolutions in piecemeal fashion—*one nation at a time.* And they began to argue that to have success, socialist revolution must *harmonize its form and pace with temporal and political realities found within those individual nations.*[5]

In some territories this new, reformed revolution might require uncommon patience. In certain places, it might necessitate abandoning

---

[vii] It is only fair to admit while *not all* workers of the world united against capitalism during WWI, socialism nevertheless had fabulous successes during that period. The Bolsheviks overthrew Russian government and created the USSR. German sailors and soldiers rebelled and established *Arbeiter- und Soldatenräte* modeled on Bolshevik soviets (i.e., socialist councils), and military and civil institutions were seized by socialists across Germany. Germany's *Rat der Volksbeauftragten* ("Council of People's Commissioners") was established, consisting of four socialist party members (three taken from the Majority Social Democrats party, and one from the Independent Social Democratic Party). Social welfare, wage agreement regulation, and national health insurance were immediately established. The table was set for the National Socialist German Workers Party in 1918.

[viii] Of course, socialism did well during WWII, too. By waiting out the war of attrition between Chiang Kai-shek's Chinese National army and Imperial Japanese forces, Mao and his Communist followers saved their strength for the coming contest with the winner. When Imperial Japan finally surrendered in 1945, Mao and his People's Liberation Army pounced. And hundreds of millions of new host cells were successfully penetrated.

violent uprisings altogether. It would most certainly require new tactics, new organizations, and new terminology. But these were costs socialism was willing to pay in exchange for ultimate success.

So socialism adapted.

In a few short years socialist revolutionary methods transformed dramatically. The old socialist dogma of a rapid, violent, worldwide, wartime, workers' revolution was discarded.[6] In its place socialists set pragmatic, adaptive, nationally-tailored goals for revolution.[7] As a result of this strategic refinement those persons, parties, and nations seeking symptoms of the old, explosive brand of socialist revolution were caught—like patients with last year's flu shot—clutching an obsolete vaccine.

The new, nationally tailored, temporally responsive, adaptive revolutionary strain of socialism currently operates across the globe. No doubt socialism's revolutionary method may change again at some future date, but for now its plans for adaptive revolution are quite explicit and can be identified in most any contemporary socialist publication.[8]

While socialism's new revolutionary method is intended for general, worldwide application, it has special significance for America. Indeed, socialism's new, adaptive revolution developed largely as a response to socialist setbacks *in America*. You see, socialism is as foreign to American political thought as monarchy. Its theoretical development took place far across the sea. The conclusions at which socialism arrived present antitheses to Americans' heritage of individual emancipation from monolithic government. As a result, socialism appeared to Middle Americans remarkably like the monolithic English Parliament—from which Americans had only recently freed themselves.

These were impossible differences, and they were made painfully apparent during elections. After stiff electoral defeats early in the twentieth century, socialists discovered that Middle Americans would never embrace the hive mentality, group rights, materialist morality, "moral" government, or monolithic domination *so long as Middle Americans knew what they were voting for.* Middle Americans were certainly never going to vote for someone from the "Socialist Party of America." At least Middle Americans were never going to vote for Socialist Party members, as socialists found to their dismay, *in large numbers.*[ix]

But socialists in America had an even bigger problem. Wherever electoral victories were not forthcoming, socialists had become accustomed to achieving decisive victory through assassination and armed conflict. This

---

[ix] The Socialist Party of America was established in 1901. The high water marks for socialist electoral success occurred in 1912 (greatest percentage of popular vote, at 5.99%) and again in 1920 (greatest number of popular votes, at 913,693). But even *then*, its Presidential candidate Eugene V. Debs failed to garner a single electoral vote. And electoral "successes" for American socialists dropped off precipitously after 1920.

technique had been used to successfully establish socialism in Russia, China, North Korea, Cuba, Laos, Vietnam, and Cambodia. *In America*, however, socialists found assassination quite ineffective.[x] And socialists recognized that, *in America*, armed conflict could never lead to socialist victory, either. *In America*, an armed uprising would be crushed overnight—by Middle Americans themselves. And so American socialism has scrupulously avoided any possibility of a decisive, Bolshevik-style revolution (i.e., warfare) in America.

This last point cannot be overemphasized. Socialists, it is true, do not lose sleep over metaphysical questions. They do not, during quiet moments, consider their moral standing in the universe. They are not troubled by the possibility of a later, transcendental accounting. They subscribe instead to the epicurean comforts of the hive mentality. (In a deterministic universe devoid of free will, one need not disquiet oneself with such bourgeois superstitions!)

Yet socialists nevertheless *do fear*. Like all fears, socialists' fears relate to those things they value most. What socialists value most are *material considerations*. And for socialists, one material consideration is more alarming than all others. It consists in a concrete scenario envisioned by socialists to be a very real possibility. It may be sketched as follows:

> Hillbillies, rednecks, and country boys across America confer via short-wave radio. They organize hunting parties. They simultaneously call in sick at the coal mine, auto-body repair shop, or dry farm. They drive out of the hills and across the plains in 4x4 pick-ups—with the windows down so they can periodically spit a wad of Red Man chaw on the road. They crank up Creedence Clearwater Revival.
>
> They drive to the East and West Coasts, where they rendezvous at pre-arranged RV campsites, local bowling alleys, and Hooters establishments. They slip into one of the many camouflage jumpers or gillie suits hung in their ample deer-season wardrobes. They spread out through costal cities at squad level. They hide themselves in the shadows of trees, in briar patches, and behind natural blinds to break up their silhouettes—as all hillbillies, rednecks, and country-boys are wont to do. They wait for the predetermined signal.
>
> At the appointed hour, the signal is given. And the nation's hillbillies, rednecks, and country-boys simultaneously begin to *hunt socialists like they hunt squirrels*. With a little help from the Second Amendment.[9]

Such an outlandish idea sounds comically far-fetched to mainstream *non*-socialists. But for American socialists, the thought of inspired, organized, liberty-loving hicks hiding under every bush and behind every blade of grass with a rifle in hand is one material possibility that cannot be ignored. The thought causes socialists to shudder. Every day. (Indeed, Left-leaning

---

[x] *E.g.*, the assassination of Presidents William McKinley (by avowed anarcho-socialist and Emma Goldman fanatic Leon Czolgosz) and John F. Kennedy (by Soviet defector, pro-Castro agitator, and avowed communist Lee Harvey Oswald).

colonels war-game this very scenario: Employing the U.S. Army to violently put down Tea Movement "insurrection" (!).[10] Meanwhile Left-leaning journalists irresponsibly and incorrectly suggest that mass murderers are Tea Movement adherents.[11])

Above all other revolutionary considerations, this one takes precedence: *Socialists do not wish to awaken Middle America.* As dearly as socialists pine for revolution, they do not want to play squirrel for backwoodsmen. At all costs socialists wish to avoid a Middle American insurrection.

Squirrel hunting is the single most important reason behind socialism's adoption of adaptive revolution in America—a careful revolution premised on matching revolutionary pace to national, temporal, and political realities. Probably squirrel hunting should serve as the cover art on this volume. It is an image which must never be forgotten.

Because socialists cannot forget it.

The Middle American Problem

Despite stunning successes elsewhere during the past century, socialists suffered serious setbacks implementing their program here in America. Socialists couldn't win American elections while candidly admitting their platform. And socialist panic over the prospect of squirrel hunting precluded violent workarounds. Socialists recognized that their American difficulties, in both electoral and armed conflicts, sprung from a single obstacle: *the American middle class.*

Socialists' problem with Middle America came in two flavors:

First, socialists' difficulties were due to a *lack of support for socialist theory, goals, and practice within the American middle class.* That is, Middle Americans would never knowingly support proactive redistributive injustice, group rights, "moral" government, and monolithic coercion. Instead, Middle Americans tenaciously upheld traditional American liberties; every peon wished to make his or her own choices.

Second, socialists' difficulties were due to the *U.S. Constitution, which codified Middle American political and cultural liberties* by fragmenting government power and thereby outlawing socialist practice.

It was this lack of support among the American middle class—i.e., the *first* flavor—which prevented socialist successes at the American ballot box and on the American battle field. Numerically speaking, Middle Americans comprised the great majority of American citizens. Middle Americans' numerical superiority and staunch anti-socialism meant socialists could never be victorious through *explicit* revolution of any sort. Middle Americans would notice an explicit revolution. And Middle Americans would crush it.

Socialists' adaptive solution to Middle American opposition was simple: Socialism would avoid direct conflicts with Middle America. It would do so by *abandoning explicit revolution altogether*. Socialism would thus avoid lasting referenda on its policies—both electorally and militarily.

In America, socialist revolution would not proceed along the lines of successful, explicit revolutions in other countries and at other times. It would not issue as an explosion, overnight—or even overyear. It would not proceed openly. Instead, it would be carefully adapted to temporal and political realities *here*. It would be adapted to *sidestep* the Middle American problem.

Yes, the socialist revolution in America would be a silent one. It would operate stepwise, and so slowly between steps as to be almost imperceptible. Gains would be incremental, and would be consolidated only over time. Socialist revolution in America would rarely make conspicuous fits or starts; instead, it would put the frog in the pot and turn up the heat—*ever* so slowly. It would proceed steadily, unrelenting. It would no longer rely exclusively on the working class; it would seek out new and diverse revolutionary groups.[12] (Like "women, indigenous peoples, black people, young people, children, pensioners, people of diverse sexual orientations, people with disabilities, and others."[13] And also "the nationally and racially oppressed, . . . seniors, family farmers, professional[s] and intellectuals."[14])

Eventually—and here socialists had to be patient!—American politics, government, and culture could be transformed into socialist ones. A mountain of overlapping socialist institutions, programs, dependents, ideas, regulations, societies, and historical revisions would be constructed. Given sufficient time, the socialist Ararat would become insuperable. Even a Deluge of ferocious little Middle Americans would be powerless to surmount its heights. (Squirrel hunting would be defeated before it had begun!) In the meantime—while the socialist mountain was being built—it would go safely unnoticed. Until it was too late. Until American socialism was inescapable. This strategy of stepwise, tacit socialist revolution we may call *Incrementalism*.

Incrementalism has been described at length by socialist thinkers, American and otherwise. Amongst comrades, Incrementalism may be described simply as avoiding "false oppositions between . . . gradual and radical change."[15] In other words, over time, gradual changes can lead to more desirable, radical ones. At other times, Incrementalism may be described as "Revolution not when the time is right, but revolution here and now."[16] By which socialists mean small changes should be made today, instead of waiting for a perfect opportunity to overthrow national government.

But Incrementalism is often sketched with bolder strokes. When it is, it is often described by way of contrast to the antique socialist stratagem of instantaneous, violent, international revolution. So for example Sam Webb, National Chair of a prominent American socialist party, explained the "lengthy process"[17] of Incrementalism as follows:

> [T]here is no direct or smooth path to socialism or a "Great Revolutionary Day" on which the economy breaks down, the workers revolt and seize power, the state, economy and civil society are smashed and remade from top to bottom in one fell swoop, and socialism springs up full grown, like Minerva from the head of Zeus [sic] . . . .
>
> The . . . vision of the revolutionary process, which [sic] I embrace, is that the struggle for socialism goes through different phases during which the configuration of contending class and social forces changes, requiring, in turn, new strategic policies and forms of transition to match the new alignment of forces and new level of mass political consciousness. . . . Electoral and legislative forms of struggles will interact with various forms of extra-parliamentary mass action. . . .
>
> In seeking forms of transition to socialism and in considering its main tasks in our country, we should be unabashed proponents of our own nationally specific path."[18]

At other times, Incrementalism is described not only in contrast to coup d'état, but more directly—as a quiet revolution which lives and works *within* the capitalist body. Again the formula is small, unobtrusive, unnoticed, socialist advances over time. And so we find prominent socialist philosopher and professor at the Meritorious Autonomous University of Puebla (Mexico), John Holloway, describing Incrementalism as follows:

> [I]t becomes more and more clear that capitalism is a catastrophe for humanity. A radical change in the organisation [sic] of society, that is, revolution, is more urgent than ever. And this revolution can only be world revolution if it is to be effective.
>
> But it is unlikely that world revolution can be achieved in one single blow. This means that the only way in which we can conceive of revolution is as interstitial revolution, as a revolution that takes place in the interstices of capitalism, a revolution that occupies spaces in the world while capitalism still exists.[19]

Incrementalism is called by many names. Some socialists call it "twenty-first century socialism,"[20] by which they mean to emphasize Incrementalism's currency and fashionability. Other socialists refer to Incrementalism as "socialism with red wine and empanadas,"[21] by which they mean to spotlight the pleasant and refreshing non-violence of Incrementalism's new revolutionary method. Others yet call it "visionary gradualism,"[22] by which they mean to underscore its cautious and deliberate chronology. Some socialists designate it "quiet revolution,"[23] by which they mean to indicate its stealth. On other occasions, socialists name Incrementalism "Indoamerican socialism,"[24] by which they mean to emphasize Incrementalism's geographic origin.

However it is characterized and whatever its name, Incrementalism is *exceedingly* patient.[xi] It does not insist on creating the United Socialist States of America tomorrow. Instead, Incrementalism contents itself with taking a step in that direction today—by organizing coalitions of special interests which can agree to one piece of the socialist pie *now*.[25]

Incrementalism contents itself with establishing a new institution dedicated to proactive redistributive injustice here (remember the Social Security Administration? The *one hundred plus new federal agencies* chartered under Obamacare?[26]); creating a new "group right" to mollify an agitated section of the population there (remember the "Homeowners Affordability and Stability Plan" for mortgage relief? Unemployment benefit extensions? Prescription drug benefit for seniors, a.k.a. Medicare Part D?). It circumscribes choice in the name of "social justice," "mandatory spending," "entitlements"—always terminology suggesting a moral (and therefore a political) imperative—but *never* in the name of federal coercion. And especially never in the name of socialism.

Incrementalism contents itself with regulating a new industry here (remember the Dodd-Frank Wall Street Reform and Consumer Protection Act of 2010? The Patient Protection and Affordable Care Act of 2010?); with nationalizing a section of the free market there (remember the federal government's buyout of Chrysler and General Motors? Nationalization of airport security under TSA?). It does such things in the name of crisis—sometimes financial, sometimes environmental, often security-related, and *always* an imminent emergency!—but *never* in the name of socialism. Socialism contents itself with encroaching upon a little State power here (by prohibiting States from developing energy reserves within their own territories); usurping another State power there (by dictating State criminal law); controlling State policies through bribery (by openly conditioning grants of vast federal monies upon States' capitulation to *federal* policy); in sum, with consolidating federal power. It does such things in the name of uniformity, order, and equality—but *never* in the name of establishing a government of sufficient coercive power to administer socialist policy.

Incrementalism picks battles socialism can win today under cover of *non*-socialist virtues—in hopes of avoiding an explicit and decisive battle with Middle America which it would surely lose. It takes baby steps toward socialism on all fronts. It then allows institutional creep do the rest of the

---

[xi] Just how patient? According to Incrementalist theorists, achieving socialist revolution by Incrementalist strategy could take decades, centuries, or perhaps longer: "Some talk in terms of decades, others in terms of hundreds of years, still others think that socialism is the goal we must pursue but that perhaps we may never completely reach." Marta Harnecker, *Latin America & Twenty-First Century Socialism: II. Twenty-First Century Socialism*, MONTHLY REVIEW: AN INDEPENDENT SOCIALIST MAGAZINE, vol. 62 issue 3 (July-August, 2010) (emphasis added).

work, expanding the number and scope of socialist programs, institutions, and policies over time.

This is Incrementalism.

Rebranding

Incrementalism was the perfect answer to squirrel hunting: A smooth, silent, patient, unrelenting revolution was the way to go. Before those hillbillies recognized what was happening—before they had time to organize—socialism in America would be fait accompli.

Still, Incrementalism would require some modicum of quiet electoral success. Candid elections had proven calamitous.[xii] But perhaps Middle Americans could be bamboozled? After all, many companies and products formerly rejected by Middle America had been profitably rebranded, repackaged, remarketed, and resold. They were well-accepted by Middle America the second time around. Why not socialism, too?

So Incrementalism commenced its adaptive American revolution with rebranding campaigns. When socialists discovered the term "socialist" revealed too much and was not admired in the American heartland, they changed their appellation to "progressive"—which both obscured socialism's aims and sounded like a philosophy no one could rationally resist. (Who would advocate being "*regressive*"?) When Middle Americans discovered what socialists meant by the term "progressive," socialists redefined the term "liberal" (from its original meaning of legal equality and free-markets, to material parity and command markets (!)) and applied it to themselves. And Incrementalists remain acutely sensitive about socialism's *nom de publique* today: They do not wish to scare off potential proselytes. They continue to debate socialism's proper appellation. Some go so far as to suggest that socialism be referred to simply as "living well" (!).[27]

Incrementalism was well aware that Middle America possessed a special love for its *own* heritage of liberty, its *own* political traditions, and its *own* American institutions. As noted in a 1936 symposium exploring "the means required to build . . . a specifically American vision" of socialism, Theodore Dreiser suggested that

> [I]f "this powerful emotional force of Americanism" will aid in the expected transition from capitalism to socialism, then [socialist] *Party policy should immediately adapt and make specific use of terminology and form seen as commonplace and avoid all connections to foreign associations.*[28]

Following Dreiser's lead, and through repeated misuse, Incrementalism has commandeered both connotation and denotation of English words related to American conceptions of liberty, American institutions, and

---

xii *See supra* n. ix (Socialist Party presidential candidates have never garnered a single electoral vote).

American traditions. Incrementalism's linguistic adaptation campaign prominently features words like "freedom," "justice," "democracy," "equality," "social," "moral," "progress," "fairness," "investment," "middle class," and "American Dream."[xiii] By changing the meaning of beloved English words and applying them to socialist theory and institutions, Incrementalism expropriates Middle American goodwill to its own, foreign, socialist purposes.

Incrementalism was also keen to eliminate foreign terminology that might alert Middle Americans to the socialist origins of those ideas it was peddling. So Incrementalism purged foreign words from the American socialist lexicon altogether—even those words with the longest and proudest of socialist pedigrees. "Proletariat," "bourgeoisie," and "solidarity" are out. "Working class," "upper class" and "unity" are in. (And when socialists seek rhetorical flourish, "the poor," "the rich," "capitalists," "tycoons", "compromise," and "non-partisan" are freely substituted.)

Incrementalism's linguistic campaign—and the abuse of English language which necessarily attends it—continues full-throttle today.[29] Leading Incrementalists like Mr. Webb tell us plainly that socialism's task is to "transform the meaning of freedom."[30] Mr. Webb goes further, stating that for an American socialist revolution to occur, "a revolution in the meaning of freedom, culture and values is absolutely necessary."[31] You know the game: freedom no longer means individual liberty to choose. It means trading individual liberty today for a promise of material equality tomorrow.[32]

More recently Mr. Webb has also opined that socialists should "retire" the term "Marxism-Leninism" in favor of simply "Marxism." Mr. Webb's reasoning is simple: Leninism "has a negative connotation among ordinary Americans, even in left and progressive circles. Depending on whom you ask, it either sounds foreign or dogmatic or undemocratic or all of these together."[33] (*Shhhhhh!*—Don't let's scare the sheep! Instead, let's conceal all foreign-, dogmatic-, and undemocratic-sounding parts of our platform . . . .)

Incrementalism's rebranding did not end with commandeering American English. As noted by Herr Dreiser, socialist revolution requires not only use of American political terminology, but also use of American political *form*[34]—meaning political organizations and institutions. Like Incrementalism's linguistic campaign, its institutional campaign intended to simultaneously (1) avoid associations with foreign forms, and (2) hijack forms viewed by Middle Americans as being commonplace, American, and patriotic.[35]

To avoid identification with foreign forms, Incrementalism minimized the previously visible role of *The Party*. Red flags and May Day parades were

---

[xiii] Socialists have a fondness for commandeering not only the meaning of words, but also symbols. For example, socialists observed the popularity of the ubiquitous, two-fingered, "V-is-for-victory" salute during post-World War II celebrations—and quickly repackaged it as the ubiquitous, international, *anti-war* symbol for socialist rallies.

officially out. (Aside from their use at the occasional Occupy protest or immigrant rally, where that memo was regularly ignored.) Mao suits and ratty pea coats were out, too. Spending big money to elect candid members of Socialist Parties to high political office, which had been tried and found stupendously ineffective,[36] was also out. Instead, Incrementalism would support members of *any party* who furthered socialist policy in fact.

In truth, socialists needed a political vehicle they could ride to electoral victories. Vehicles using various permutations of "socialist," "international," "worker," "anarchist," "syndicalist," and "communist" in their titles weren't working. In America's two-party, winner-takes-all political system, socialists would never have success running as The Party. To have electoral success, socialists were going to have to participate like everyone else—as Republicans or Democrats. And so, in the name of Incrementalism, socialists encouraged themselves to do just that:

> We must all become Republicans and Democrats . . . shaking hands with the worst of them, frequenting their speakeasies, gambling in their dens, attending their churches, patronizing their brothels. We must join Rotary Clubs; we must play checkers at the Y.M.C.A. We must demand unceasingly the expulsion of the Reds [i.e., socialists]. We must be conformity itself. And occasionally, over drinks and a cigar, we must say lightly to our boon companions . . . "Why don't the big fellows have to part with a little more of their incomes in times like these?"[37]

Incrementalism toyed with expressing itself variously under Republican and Democratic banners for years.[xiv] But when Franklin Delano Roosevelt (FDR) arrived on the scene in 1932—with campaign promises of "a new deal for the American people," premised upon a "*more equitable opportunity to share in the distribution of national wealth*,"[38]—Incrementalism knew it had found its Party and its Man. Incrementalism had found a vehicle for implementing socialist policy in America: the Democratic Party.

(Because it is so often denied by Incrementalist journalists and historians, we must be clear on this point: *FDR's New Deal was socialism in America.* This was recognized by socialists at the time.[xv] And it is recognized by socialists

---

[xiv] Incrementalism became particularly active under the name "Progressive Party," under Presidents Teddy Roosevelt (Republican) and Woodrow Wilson (Democrat).

[xv] "The New Deal is plainly an attempt to achieve a working socialism and avert a social collapse in America; it is extraordinarily parallel to the successive 'policies' and 'Plans' of the Russian experiment. Americans shirk the word 'socialism', but what else can one call it? . . . There is a strong opposition on the part of great interests in America to the President [Franklin Delano Roosevelt], who has made himself the spear-head of the collectivizing drive; they want to put the brake now on his progressive socialisation [sic] of the nation, and quite possibly, at the cost of increasing social friction, they may slow down the drift to socialism very considerably." H. G. WELLS, THE NEW WORLD ORDER 61-62; 70 (The Mayflower Press, Plymouth England 1940).

today.[xvi] This remains, however, a sensitive subject where Incrementalist public relations are concerned. To publicly speak of FDR's New Deal as socialist would frustrate the closeted purposes of Incrementalism! So this fact remains painfully taboo . . . .)

And so, as soon as FDR revealed his domestic policy, Incrementalism immediately jumped onboard the Democrat Bus—early in the 1930s.[39] And Incrementalism has never quit that vehicle since. In the words of the AMERICAN SOCIALIST VOTER, Oct., 2009,

> In the United States, socialists joined with others on the Left to build a broad-based, anti-corporate coalition [shout out to Communists!], with the unions at the center [shout out to Syndicalists!], to address the needs of the majority by opposing the excesses of private enterprise [shout out to all Marxists!].
>
> Many socialists have seen the Democratic Party, since at least the New Deal, as the key political arena in which to consolidate this coalition, because the Democratic Party held the allegiance of our natural allies. Through control of the government by the Democratic Party coalition, led by anti-corporate forces, a progressive program regulating the corporations, redistributing income, fostering economic growth [LOL!] and expanding social programs could be realized.[40]

The Democrat Party remains the electoral vehicle for American socialism today. Over the years, there have occasionally been debates among socialists regarding exactly how to drive the Democrat Bus, and where on the Democrat Bus everyone should sit. Sometimes these debates have created

---

[xvi] "[Y]ears of communist-led unemployed council campaigns and union activism put huge grassroots pressure on the New Deal government to enact far-reaching labor and social legislation. . . . Communists stood in the forefront of the working-class struggle for much of this [New Deal] legislation, from labor law reform to Social Security and assistance for the unemployed. . . . [W]ithout the CPUSA, the mass organizations it created and led, the campaigns it initiated, and its defeats and victories, these [New Deal] achievements would not have been possible." Norman Markowitz, *Fighting for Change: The Great Depression, the New Deal and the CPUSA*, POLITICAL AFFAIRS (Sept. 2, 2009).

"The Left's involvement in Popular Front activities both led and complimented the rise of the Americanism [LOL!] which accompanied the Roosevelt Administration's gains . . . . An indication of the impact of the Popular Front on radicals and on the Communist Party's support of President Roosevelt was the fact that Charles Seeger, by 1936, was already an employee of the federal government, director of the Music Unit section of the Resettlement Administration, aiding migrating Southerners as they moved up and out of the Dustbowl." John Pietaro, *Out of the Red Megaphone: The Modernist Protest Music of a Lost Age*, POLITICAL AFFAIRS (Dec. 14, 2010).

See also Marilyn Bechtel, *Jobs, Labor and WPA's Living Legacy*, PEOPLE'S WORLD (July 29, 2010); People's World Editorial Board, *New Deal 2.0*, PEOPLE'S WORLD (Dec. 11, 2009); John Wojcik, *Economic Meltdown: We Need a New, Green New Deal!*, PEOPLE'S WORLD (July 23, 2008); People's World Editorial Board, *Needed: a new New Deal*, PEOPLE'S WORLD (Mar. 21, 2008); Simon Rosenberg and Peter Leyden, *The 50-Year Strategy—Beyond '08: Can Progressives Play for Keeps?*, MOTHER JONES 67 (Nov., Dec. 2007).

schisms among American socialists.[xvii] But ever since FDR, the Democratic Party has pitched by far the most successful brand of American socialism. This remains true today.

How true, you ask?

Well, pretty damn true. For example, the Congressional Progressive Caucus is the largest (and therefore controlling) caucus among Democratic Congresspersons.[41] As of the 112th Congress (i.e., through Jan. 3, 2013), it comprises a full seventy-seven Representatives in the House (and one Senator).[42] Members of the Congressional Progressive Caucus chaired a full ten of the twenty standing committees in the House of Representatives through January 3, 2011 (i.e., the 111th Congress). During the same period a full seventy-six Congresspersons—all Democrats—were avowed socialists and named members of Democratic Socialists of America.[43] (*Nota bene*: None of these Congresspersons, of course, disclosed their affiliation with the Democratic Socialists of America *when first running for election*. And therein lies the crux of the Incrementalist game.)

Occasionally someone will point out the fact that Congressional Progressive Caucus members are socialists.[44] Caucus members will dub such accusations "outrageous."[45] They will complain of "witch hunts."[46] They will make plaintive references to McCarthyism.[47] They will allege their accusers have "no ideals or principles."[48] They don't want Middle Americans to know they are socialists, after all—that would leave Incrementalism in ruins! But even when publicly challenged as avowed socialists, they will skirt the issue: They will refuse to engage in "base and childish" debates about ideological orientation.[49] They will argue that any accusation of socialism "denigrates the millions of Americans who voted to elect Congressional Progressive Caucus members."[50] Remarkably, they will eschew the simplest means to deflect that accusation: *They will never deny they are socialists*.[51] Because outright denial would discourage knowing socialist supporters!

And so it is that prior to the November 2010 midterm elections, former Communist Party USA (Ohio) Chairman Rick Nagin counseled us that "only if Democrats are elected will the progressive movement have the time and space to grow."[52] And so it is that in 2011, Mr. Webb can proudly (and rightly!) affirm that the "main forces" of socialism "continue to work within

---

[xvii] Explicitly using the Democratic Party as a vehicle for socialist revolution was the strategy of two of the three branches of the Socialist Party of America (SPA) in the 1960s. One branch, under the leadership of Michael Harrington, wished to have the SPA work from inside the Democratic Party and—over time—pull it leftward. This was the explicitly Incrementalist approach. Another branch, under the leadership of Max Shachtman, found the Promised Land in Lyndon Johnson's Great Society—and wished simply to merge with Lyndon Johnson's wing of the Democratic Party in its present form. (With as far left as the Democratic Party moved under Lyndon Johnson, this second faction of the SPA saw little reason to modify Democratic Party policy: the Democratic Party was *already implementing the socialist vision of its own accord!*) Both of these factions of the SPA sent delegates to the 1968 Democratic Convention.

the Democratic Party." And so it is that in 2011, Mr. Webb can also look hopefully forward to that great day when socialist elements may completely "tak[e] over the Democratic Party."[53]

Once Incrementalism had taken a seat on the Democrat Bus it was time to return to electioneering. (Tacitly, of course.) And what began as an effort to fool Middle Americans just long enough to get a foothold in American politics has, today, become a primary objective of Incrementalism. Rather than participating reluctantly or intermittently in elections, "A party of socialism in the 21st [sic] century . . . *will elevate electoral and legislative struggle to a primary arena of struggle; it will see such participation as absolutely essential at every phase of struggle.*"[54] And with good reason: "A party of socialism in the 21st [sic] century believes that majoritarian political movements are the midwives of reforms, radical and otherwise, and eco-socialist transformations."[55]

In 2011 Sam Webb clarified the vital role elections play for Incrementalism. In doing so he again contrasted Incrementalism with the old socialist tactic of violent, instantaneous, worldwide revolution, and also provided a fine summary of the reasons for socialism's contemporary Incrementalist approach:

> The traditional imagery of the revolutionary process—economic breakdown, insurrection, dual power, violence and bloody clashes, smash the state, and the quick rollout of socialism—provides few insights. In fact, I would argue that it is an analytical deadweight; it favors simplicity over complexity; it dulls and dumbs down the socialist imagination; and it's disabling strategically and tactically. . . .
>
> Thus the nature of the struggle isn't simply the people against the state, but the people *winning positions and influence in the state and then utilizing them to make changes (within and outside of the state) in a highly contested political environment*—an environment of sharp clashes, uncertain outcomes, and an engaged people.
>
> Now some will say that this is highly unlikely, even utopian. But one has to ask: is the seizure of power and the quick dismantlement of the existing state in favor of a new "out of the ashes" socialist state any less utopian? The latter model has been ascendant for nearly a century and still socialism is only a wish among communists in the advanced capitalist world. Of course, the reasons for this are many, but I don't believe the insurrectionary model of revolution makes the road any easier or is any more realistic as a reading of the future.[56]

We must make one careful distinction. The fact that socialists recognize the Democratic Party as "home" must never be misunderstood to mean that Incrementalism refuses to work with representatives or agents having *other* party affiliations. On the contrary, Incrementalism explicitly works with anyone, from any party, with any special interest, who is willing to implement a piece of socialism *today*—whether or not such persons or groups are believed by socialists to be reliable allies in the long term.[57] If Incrementalism should be able to work from within the Green Party (which it has done since the beginning), all the better! If Incrementalism should be able to accomplish its aims under the Republican banner (which it does all the time—Remember President George W. Bush's prescription drug benefit for seniors [Medicare Schedule D]? No Child Left Behind? TARP? The Department of Homeland Security? TSA? Expanding the federal budget 30% over eight years?), better still! The rebranding campaign is thus greatly improved. Incrementalism is more convincingly disguised. Cutting "non-partisan" deals is business as usual in Washington; and all works together to thwart squirrel hunting.

And so it is today that those people, parties, and nations hunting for socialism in red flags; foreign terminology; foreign form; nineteenth century dogma; or political parties using "socialist," "international," "workers," or "syndicalist," in their titles; are looking in all the wrong places. Such people, parties, and nations are clinging to last year's flu shot.

They will pay the full measure of their obsolescence.

Closeting Impotence

You protest.

You haven't heard of Incrementalism, you say?

But of course you haven't.

You won't hear socialists publicly expound Incrementalist strategy on the nightly news. You won't hear them bemoan fears of squirrel hunting on talk radio. You won't hear them admit that Middle Americans don't want socialism, so socialists took the revolution underground. You won't hear them float plans to replace representative government with monolithic socialism slowly—imperceptibly—over time. To do so would betray the whole purpose of Incrementalism.

And so, as with certain other tenets of socialism, the subject of Incrementalism remains permanently closeted.

What you *will* hear socialists declare is how any insinuation of stealth-socialism is a reactionary conspiracy theory of the first order. Like Bush-Cheney plotting 9/11. Yes, yes!—talk of tacit revolution is unmitigated paranoia; the product of a disordered mind.

However, if you listen to socialists' private conversations—when they speak freely among comrades—you will hear something very different.

You will hear what you read in this chapter.

Further Notes to Chapter 2

[1] *See, e.g.*, Curtis A. Suttle, *Marine Viruses—Major Players in the Global Ecosystem*, 5 NATIONAL REVIEW OF MICROBIOLOGY 801 (Oct. 2007); Rotem Sorek et al., *CRISPR—A Widespread System that Provides Acquired Resistance Against Phages in Bacteria and Archaea*, 6 NATURE REVIEWS MICROBIOLOGY 181 (March 2008).

[2] *See, e.g.*, Friedrich Engels, *On Social Relations in Russia* (transcribed by Andy Blunden) (pamphlet 1875) ("The revolution that modern socialism strives to achieve is, briefly, the victory of the proletariat over the bourgeoisie and the establishment of a new organisation [sic] of society by the destruction of all class distinctions. This requires not only a proletariat to carry out this revolution, but also a bourgeoisie in whose hands the social productive forces have developed so far that they permit the final destruction of class distinctions. Among savages and semi-savages there likewise often exist no class distinctions, and every people has passed through such a state. It could not occur to us to re-establish this state, for the simple reason that class distinctions necessarily emerge from it as the social productive forces develop. Only at a certain level of development of these social productive forces, even a very high level for our modern conditions, does it become possible to raise production to such an extent that the abolition of class distinctions can constitute real progress, can be lasting without bringing about stagnation or even decline in the mode of social production. But the productive forces have reached this level of development only in the hands of the bourgeoisie. The bourgeoisie, therefore, in this respect also is just as necessary a precondition for the socialist revolution as is the proletariat itself. Hence a man who says that this revolution can be more easily carried out in a country where, *although* there is no proletariat, there is no bourgeoisie *either*, only proves that he has still to learn the ABC of socialism.") (emphasis original). http://www.marxists.org/archive/marx/works/1874/refugee-literature/ch05.htm.

[3] *See, e.g.*, Frederick Engels, *The Principles of Communism*, No. 19 (1847) ("19. *Will it be possible for this revolution to take place in one country alone? No.* By creating the world market, big industry has already brought all the peoples of the Earth, and especially the civilized peoples, into such close relation with one another that none is independent of what happens to the others. Further, it has co-ordinated [sic] the social development of the civilized countries to such an extent that, in all of them, bourgeoisie and proletariat have become the decisive classes, and the struggle between them the great struggle of the day. It follows that the communist revolution will not merely be a national phenomenon but must take place simultaneously in all civilized countries—that is to say, at least in England, America, France, and Germany. . . . *It is a universal revolution and will, accordingly, have a universal range. . . .*") (as published in KARL MARX & FREDERICK ENGELS, SELECTED WORKS, Vol. 1, 81-97 (Progress Publishers, 1969), http://www.marxists.org/archive/marx/works/1847/11/prin-com.htm).

[4] Even prior to WWI, a minority of the more insightful socialist thinkers had abandoned the idea of violent, international, wartime socialist revolution. *See, e.g.*, Wilhelm Liebknecht, *How It Could Be Done*, Published in JUSTICE, Sept. 7 1901, p. 3 (Jacques Bonhomme, trans.) ("But we shall not pass at once into Socialism. The transition takes place gradually, and it is not our duty to draw a picture of the future (which would be useless labour [sic]), but to determine a practical programme [sic] for the period of transition, to formulate and to justify measures which may be immediately applicable to the present state of society . . . .") http://www.marxists.org/archive/liebknecht-w/1901/09/how.htm.

[5] *E.g.*, Georgi Dimitrov, *Main Report Delivered to the 7th congress of the Communist International* (Aug. 2, 1935) ("We would not be revolutionary Marxists . . . if we did not suitably *reconstruct* our policies and tactics in accordance with the changing situation and the changes occurring in the world labor movement. . . . We want to take into account the concrete situation at each moment, in each place, and not act according to *a fixed, stereotyped form* anywhere . . . . We want to eradicate from our ranks all *self-satisfied sectarianism*, which above all blocks our road to the masses and impedes the carrying out of a truly Bolshevik mass policy.") (emphasis original). http://www.marxists.org/reference/archive/dimitrov/works/1935/08_02.htm; Vladimir I. Lenin, *Left Wing Communism: An Infantile Disorder*, (June 1920) (pamphlet), as republished in VLADIMIR LENIN, 31

LENIN'S COLLECTED WORKS 17-118 (Julius Katzer trans., Progress Publishers 1964) (*see* in particular the chapter entitled *Several Conclusions*).
[6] *See, e.g.*, Marta Harnecker, *Latin America & Twenty-First Century Socialism: Inventing to Avoid Mistakes*, MONTHLY REVIEW: AN INDEPENDENT SOCIALIST MAGAZINE, vol. 62 issue 3 (July-August, 2010).
[7] Socialism's new revolutionary method is "not a matter of copying foreign models or of exporting ours; it's about building a model of *socialism tailored for each country*." *Ibid.* (emphasis added).
[8] *Ibid.* Often socialists signal their embrace of the new, adaptive, nationally-tailored revolutionary method by simply rejecting the old, instantaneous, violent, worldwide revolutionary one. For example, Fidel Castro summarizes socialism's commitment to the new, adaptive revolutionary method as follows:

> There will be new tactics: not the Bolshevik style and not even our [Cuban] style, because these belong to a different world. That should not discourage anyone. We need to see and to analyze, with the greatest possible objectivity, the current setting in which the struggle will have to unfold . . . There will be other roads and other ways by which the conditions will be created for transforming this world into another one.

Fidel Castro, *El Mundo Caótico al que Conduce la Globalización Neoliberal No Puede Sobrevivir*, GRANMA (June 25, 1998) (quoted by István Mészáros, *Cuba: The Next Forty-Five Years?*, 55 MONTHLY REVIEW 8 (Jan. 2004).
[9] An essential point which socialists intentionally obscure and which non-socialists too often forget is that rural populations in Russia, China, North Korea, Cuba, and Vietnam desperately resisted socialist revolution *even without the advantages conferred by a Second Amendment.* Speaking of this phenomenon in Russia, we are told:

> And if those scrolls—of both the *extrajudicial* executions and those by tribunal—are unrolled for us someday, the most surprising thing will be the number of ordinary peasants we find on them. Because there was no end to the number of peasant uprisings and revolts from 1918 to 1921, even though they did not adorn the colored pages of the official *History of the Civil War*, and even though no one photographed them, and no one filmed motion pictures of those furious crowds attacking machine guns with clubs, pitchforks, and axes and, later, lined up for execution with their arms tied behind their backs . . . . The revolt in Sapozhok is remembered only in Sapozhok; the one in Pitelino only in Pitelino. We learn from Latsis the number of peasant rebellions that were suppressed during that same year and a half in twenty provinces—344.

ALEKSANDR I. SOLZHENITSYN, THE GULAG ARCHIPELAGO Book I, 302-3 (Thomas P. Whitney trans., Harper & Row 1973) (1968) (citing MARTIN I. LATSIS' "popular review of the Cheka's activity" for 1918 and half of 1919, DVA GODA BORBY NA VNUTRENNOM FRONTE 75 (Moscow, 1920)).

And so we are left to ask: *What would the outcome have been had American hillbillies, rednecks, and country boys' foreign counterparts had access to firearms?* Socialists cringe when confronted with this hypothetical.
[10] For example, Colonel Benson details a hypothetical scenario in which armed Tea Partiers:

> [T]ake[] over the government of Darlington, South Carolina, occupying City Hall, disbanding the city council, and placing the mayor under house arrest. Activists remove the chief of police and either disarm local police and county sheriff departments or discourage them from interfering. . . . With Darlington under their control, militia members quickly move beyond the city limits to establish "check points"—in reality, something more like choke points—on major transportation lines. Traffic on I-95, the East Coast's main north-south artery; I-20; and commercial and passenger rail lines are stopped and searched, allegedly for "illegal aliens."

This is the sort of scenario that keeps Leftists up late at night. You have to read it to believe it.

And why war-game such a scenario? According to Colonel Benson, "A key . . . aspect of full spectrum operations is *how to conduct these operations within American borders. . . . Army officers are professionally obligated to consider the conduct of operations on U.S. soil.*"

Colonel Benson's piece expressly applies the principles of *The Army Operating Concept 2016-2028*, US ARMY TRAINING AND DOCTRINE COMMAND, Pamphlet 525-3-1 (Aug. 19, 2010), which similarly considers domestic "contingencies." *Ibid.* at 27-29. Colonel Benson's Tea Party insurrection scenario is expressly intended as a conflict simulation on "War, and the use of federal military force on U.S. soil," against U.S. citizens. Incredibly, it appears in the highly regarded Small Wars Journal. And it concludes ominously: In a Tea Party insurrection, "Americans will expect the military *to execute without pause and as professionally as if it were acting overseas.*" Just take a minute to let that sink in. Kevin Benson & Jennifer Weber, *Full Spectrum Operations in the Homeland: A "Vision" of the Future*, SMALL WARS JOURNAL (July 25, 2012) (emphasis added).

[11] Readers will remember that Brian Ross of ABC News suggested, on-air, that the Aurora, Colorado theater killer was a "Tea Party" member. *See, e.g.*, Dylan Byers, *ABC News Apologizes for 'Incorrect' Tea Party Report*, POLITICO (July 20, 2012); Dylan Byers, *ABC President: Ross Report Hurts Coverage*, POLITICO (July 24, 2012).

[12] While "workers," especially industrial workers and peasants, represent the familiar and traditional revolutionary class of socialism, they are no longer alone. The new, adaptive socialist revolution seeks other revolutionaries:

> A communist Salvadoran guerrilla comandante, Jorge Schafik Handal, was the first to insist that the new Latin American revolutionary subject could not be just the working class, that there were new revolutionary social subjects, and that, therefore, the revolutionary process could not be led by communists alone—that all these new subjects had to be included.

Marta Harnecker, *Latin America & Twenty-First Century Socialism: Inventing to Avoid Mistakes*, MONTHLY REVIEW: AN INDEPENDENT SOCIALIST MAGAZINE, vol. 62 issue 3 (July-August, 2010). And who would these new socialist revolutionaries be? *See, infra*, n. 13 - 14 and accompanying text.

[13] According to socialist thinker Marta Harnecker, socialism's new revolutionaries consist of "women, indigenous peoples, black people, young people, children, pensioners, people of diverse sexual orientations, people with disabilities, and others." *Ibid.*

[14] According to Sam Webb, Chairman of the Communist Party USA, the new socialist revolutionary class consists of "the working class . . . coupled [to] communities of the nationally and racially oppressed, women, . . . youth[,] . . . seniors, family farmers, professional[s] and intellectuals, gays and lesbians, etc. . . ." Sam Webb, *Reflections on Socialism*, 14 (Communist Party USA, June 4, 2005).

[15] Sam Webb, *A Party of Socialism in the 21st Century: What It Looks Like, What It Says, and What It Does*, POLITICAL AFFAIRS (Feb. 3, 2011).

[16] John Holloway, *Can We Change the World Without Taking Power?: A World Social Forum Debate*, 106 INTERNATIONAL SOCIALISM (April 5, 2005).

[17] Sam Webb, *Reflections on Socialism* 16 (published by cpusa.com).

[18] Sam Webb, *Socialism Revisited, Part 1*, paper presented to a panel entitled "Imaginings of Socialism," at the Left forum sponsored by Global Left Dialogue (New York City, April 17, 2005), as published by POLITICAL AFFAIRS MAGAZINE (April 21, 2005). *See also* Sam Webb, *A Party of Socialism in the 21st Century: What It Looks Like, What It Says, and What It Does*, POLITICAL AFFAIRS (Feb. 3, 2011) ("A party of socialism in the 21st [sic] century elaborates a strategic policy at each stage of struggle. After all, there is no direct or inevitable path to socialism. Nor is the working class going to simply 'rise up' at some appointed time and fight for a society of justice. The struggle for socialism goes through phases and stages, probably more than we allow for in our current writings and program.").

[19] John Holloway, *Can We Change the World Without Taking Power?: A World Social Forum Debate*, 106 INTERNATIONAL SOCIALISM (April 5, 2005).

[20] This label for Incrementalism was popularized in 2005 by Hugo Chávez, leader of the United Socialist Party of Venezuela—though it was apparently coined in 2000 by Tomás Moulian, a prominent Chilean socialist. *See, e.g.*, Marta Harnecker, *Latin America & Twenty-First Century Socialism: II. Twenty-First Century Socialism*, MONTHLY REVIEW: AN INDEPENDENT SOCIALIST MAGAZINE, vol. 62 issue 3 (July-August, 2010).
[21] A term coined by Salvador Allende Gossens, the first Marxist to become president of a Latin American country *by way of democratic election*. See, e.g., *Ibid.*
[22] An insightful phrase invented by the Milton Friedman of socialism, Michael Harrington. MICHAEL HARRINGTON, SOCIALISM: PAST AND FUTURE 248-49, 278 (Arcade Publishing 2011) (1989).
[23] A frank description by Howard Zinn, the socialist historian and playwright. *See* Catherine Parayre, *The Conscience of the Past: An Interview with Historian Howard Zinn*, FLAGPOLE (Feb. 18, 1998).
[24] Another title for Incrementalism popularized by Hugo Chávez, leader of the United Socialist Party of Venezuela. Marta Harnecker, *Latin America & Twenty-First Century Socialism: II. Twenty-First Century Socialism*, MONTHLY REVIEW: AN INDEPENDENT SOCIALIST MAGAZINE, vol. 62 issue 3 (July-August, 2010).
[25] Organizing coalitions of special interests (a.k.a. "popular movements") is an explicit key to Incrementalist socialism. Marta Harnecker, a distinguished Chilean socialist who lives in Cuba, described this aspect of Incrementalism as follows:

> The left matured, as well, in its relationship with the popular movements when it understood that they [i.e., the popular movements] must not be treated simply as transmission belts for party decisions but must have increasing autonomy, so they can develop their own agendas for struggle. The left also began to understand that *its role is to coordinate various agendas* and not to elaborate one single agenda from above.

Ibid. (emphasis added).
[26] I will not bore the reader by citing all the new federal agencies required under the so-called "Patient Protection and Affordable Care Act," and the "Health Care and Education Reconciliation Act of 2010," together referred to more colloquially as simply "Obamacare." What we are talking about are new federal institutions like the Committee to Review Administrative Simplification Standards, the State American Health Benefit Exchange, the Advisory Board for State Cooperatives, the Federal Coordinated Health Care Office for Dual Eligible Beneficiaries, the Center for Medicare and Medicaid Innovation, the Independent Payment Advisory Board, etc., etc. But they are all there. Have a look for yourself.
[27] In Marta Harnecker's formulation:

> When one talks of socialism, one is talking of something quite different from what we are experiencing. We could give it a different name. If someone doesn't like the word socialism, they can call it communitarianism, if they don't like communitarianism, they can give it the name "living well," that's no problem, we won't fight over names. . . .
>
> Marx and some of his followers called it communism, others have called it socialism, and I agree with García Linera that it doesn't really matter what term we use. What *does* matter is the content.

Marta Harnecker, *Latin America & Twenty-First Century Socialism: II. Twenty-First Century Socialism*, MONTHLY REVIEW: AN INDEPENDENT SOCIALIST MAGAZINE, vol. 62 issue 3 (July-August, 2010) (emphasis original).
[28] The 1936 symposium at which Dreiser spoke convened in New York City, and was entitled *What is Americanism? A Symposium on Marxism and the American Tradition.* John Pietaro, *Out of the Red Megaphone: The Modernist Protest Music of a Lost Age*, POLITICAL AFFAIRS (Dec. 14, 2010).
[29] Incrementalism "implied changing the language used, adapting the content and varying the form for different [revolutionary] subjects [i.e., people], and . . . today, in the information and image era, audiovisual language is extremely important." Marta Harnecker, *Latin America & Twenty-First Century Socialism: Inventing to Avoid Mistakes*, MONTHLY REVIEW: AN INDEPENDENT SOCIALIST MAGAZINE, vol. 62 issue 3 (July-August, 2010).

[30] Sam Webb, *Socialism Revisited*, Paper presented at a panel entitled "Imaginings of Socialism" at the Left Forum sponsored by Global Left Dialogue (New York City, April 17, 2005). http://www.politicalaffairs.net/article/articleview/984/1/89/.
[31] *Ibid.*
[32] Lenin summarized the socialist concept of "freedom" nicely:

> The old bourgeois-democratic constitutions waxed eloquent about formal equality and right of assembly; but our proletarian and peasant Soviet Constitution casts aside the hypocrisy of formal equality. . . . When it is a matter of overthrowing the bourgeoisie, only traitors or idiots can demand formal equality of rights for the bourgeoisie. "Freedom of assembly" for workers and peasants is not worth a farthing when the best buildings belong to the bourgeoisie. Our Soviets have *confiscated* all the good buildings in town and country from the rich and have *transferred* all of them to the workers and peasants for *their* unions and meetings. This is our *freedom* of assembly—for the working people! This is the meaning and content of our Soviet, our socialist Constitution!

Vladimir Lenin, *Letter to American Workers*, published in Pravda No. 178 (August 22, 1918); source: LENIN'S COLLECTED WORKS pp. 62-75, vol. 28 (Jim Riordan, trans., Progress Publishers, Moscow 1965).
[33] Sam Webb, *A Party of Socialism in the 21st Century: What It Looks Like, What It Says, and What It Does*, POLITICAL AFFAIRS (Feb. 3, 2011).
[34] *See supra* n. 28 and accompanying text.
[35] *E.g.*, democratic elections. *See* Marta Harnecker, *Latin America & Twenty-First Century Socialism: Inventing to Avoid Mistakes*, MONTHLY REVIEW: AN INDEPENDENT SOCIALIST MAGAZINE, vol. 62 issue 3 (July-August, 2010) (Incrementalism "underst[ands] that democracy is one of the most beloved banners of the people, and that the struggle for democracy cannot be separated from the struggle for socialism because it is only under socialism that democracy can develop fully."); *see also supra* n. 28 and accompanying text.
[36] *See supra* n. ix (Socialist Party presidential candidates have never garnered a single electoral vote).
[37] Kenneth Burke, *Boring from Within*, 65 THE NEW REPUBLIC 328 (Feb. 4, 1931). Incrementalist enthusiasm for working alongside anyone (and from within any party) willing to support socialist policy is not entirely an American innovation. In fact, it was official Komintern policy that socialists ally themselves with left-leaning parties, nation-by-nation, as circumstances permitted—starting in 1921 (under the Komintern's "United Front" policy) and again, more broadly, from the early 1930s on (under the Komintern's "Popular Front" policy). *See, e.g.*, Fourth Congress of the Komintern, *Theses on the United Front*, Nos. 8 and 15 (adopted by the Executive Committee Dec. 1921) http://ciml.250x.com/archive/comintern/ci_forth_congress_united_front.html; Fourth Congress of the Komintern, *Theses on Komintern Tactics*, No. 10 (Dec. 5, 1922) http://ciml.250x.com/archive/comintern/ci_forth_congress_theses_ tactics.html.

Whatever the source of the idea—American conditions or Komintern communiqués—American socialists were looking to advance socialist policies via alliances with representatives from other political parties. When Stalin no longer favored the Popular Front tactic, it was ridiculed by international socialists as "Browderism" (after Earl Browder, the General Secretary of the Communist Party USA, who continued to direct leftists along this tactic though it had fallen into disfavor with his soviet masters during the Cold War). Yet American Incrementalist enthusiasm for working alongside anyone willing to support socialist policy thrived despite Stalin's ridicule. It remains American socialism's strategy today.
[38] FDR, *Acceptance Speech* delivered at the Democratic National Convention in Chicago (July 2, 1932). *See, e.g.*, *THE PRESIDENCY: The Roosevelt Week*, TIME (Jul. 11, 1932).
[39] *See, e.g.*, Marilyn Bechtel, *Jobs, Labor and WPA's Living Legacy*, PEOPLE'S WORLD (July 29, 2010); People's World Editorial Board, *New Deal 2.0*, PEOPLE'S WORLD (Dec. 11, 2009); John Wojcik, *Economic Meltdown: We Need a New, Green New Deal!*, PEOPLE'S WORLD (July 23, 2008); People's World Editorial Board, *Needed: a new New Deal*, PEOPLE'S WORLD (Mar. 21, 2008);

Simon Rosenberg and Peter Leyden, *The 50-Year Strategy—Beyond '08: Can Progressives Play for Keeps?*, MOTHER JONES 67 (Nov., Dec. 2007).
40 AMERICAN SOCIALIST VOTER, 9 (Oct. 1, 2009). http://www.scribd.com/doc/35733956/DSA-Members-American-Socialist-Voter-Democratic-Socialists-of-America-10-1-09.
41 *See, e.g.*, *About CPC*, at the official website of the Congressional Progressive Caucus: http://cpc.grijalva.house.gov/index.cfm?SectionID=2&ParentID=0&SectionTypeID=2&SectionTree=2.
42 *See, e.g.*, the Congressional Progressive Caucus' website. Under the tab "About CPC," select "Caucus Members." http://cpc.grijalva.house.gov/index.cfm?sectionid=71§iontree=2,71.
43 AMERICAN SOCIALIST VOTER, 2 (Oct. 1, 2009) (mentioning only "seventy" congresspersons (p. 2), but listing by name seventy-six (pp. 2-4). http://www.scribd.com/doc/35733956/DSA-Members-American-Socialist-Voter-Democratic-Socialists-of-America-10-1-09.
44 *See, e.g.*, Aaron Blake, *Republican Rep. Allen West Says Many Congressional Democrats Are Communists*, THE WASHINGTON POST (April 11, 2012); Jonathan Mattise, *Allen West Hears Cheers, Jeers at Town-Hall Meetings in Palm City, Jensen Beach*, THE PALM BEACH POST (April 10, 2012).
45 Raúl M. Grijalva & Keith Ellison, *Progressive Caucus Co-Chairs Dispel Outrageous Allen West Claims*, CONGRESSIONAL PROGRESSIVE CAUCUS PRESS RELEASE (April 11, 2012).
46 *Ibid.*
47 *Ibid.*
48 *Ibid.*
49 *Ibid.*
50 *Ibid.*
51 *Ibid.*
52 Rick Nagin, *Progressive Challenge: Defeat GOP in November Elections*, PEOPLE'S WORLD (July 5, 2010).
53 Unfortunately, when describing such a sensitive subject even Sam Webb—who is normally transparently outspoken—must be translated in order to be understood by the uninitiated. "[T]he main social forces and organizations of political independence [i.e., socialists] and the necessary base of an independent political party [i.e., socialist party] continue to work within the Democratic Party. But with this twist: they operate independently of the organizational structures of that party [i.e., independently of the organizational structures of the Democratic Party]. And that is likely to continue; in fact, as their [i.e., socialists'] dissatisfaction grows they will attempt to enlarge their voice and power. In other words, the main and necessary forces of an independent [i.e., socialist] political party will likely exhaust all or nearly all of the possibilities to reform the Democratic Party, including attempts to take it over, before looking for an exit. Our tactics should take this into account. One final observation: we say too definitively that the independent [i.e., socialist] forces stand no chance whatever of taking over the Democratic Party. That still may be the case, but it is a mistake to rule it out completely at this point." Sam Webb, *A Party of Socialism in the 21st Century: What It Looks Like, What It Says, and What It Does*, POLITICAL AFFAIRS (Feb. 3, 2011). *See also supra* n. 40 and accompanying quote.
54 *Ibid.* (emphasis added).
55 ". . . . Militant minorities comprised of progressive and left forces make a big difference, but they can't and shouldn't try to substitute for broader masses of people. The cause may be righteous and the agitation compelling, but only when righteousness rhetoric is joined by a material force does change happen." *Ibid.*
56 *Ibid.* (emphasis added).
57 *See supra* n. 25; *see also, e.g.*, Sam Webb, *A Party of Socialism in the 21st Century: What It Looks Like, What It Says, and What It Does*, POLITICAL AFFAIRS (Feb. 3, 2011) ("A party of socialism in the 21st century doesn't turn—liberals, advocates of identity politics, single issue movements, centrist and progressive leaders of major social organizations, social democrats, community based non-profits, NGOs, unreliable allies, and the "people" (according to some, a classless category concealing class, racial, and gender oppression)—into enemies. Nor does [a party of socialism in the 21st century] withdraw from participation in capitalist democratic institutions.").

3

The Fourth Head

Bureaucracy is not an obstacle to democracy but an inevitable compliment to it.

—Joseph A. Schumpeter[i]

It required, therefore, a long and slow development, through decades blotted with innumerable instances of helpless poverty and social injustice, to raise political thinking above the standard of freedom from regulation of any kind to a higher standard. This higher standard of the present age is freedom under regulation designed to safeguard the general welfare.

—John A. Vieg[ii]

PROFITABLY ENSCONCED IN AMERICAN ENGLISH terminology and traditional American forms, seated comfortably on the Democrat Bus and enjoying the fruits of electoral success, Incrementalism was poised to make political hay.

But how to make political gains *last?*—that was the question!

It was sufficiently difficult to prepare socialism under the watchful eye of meddling Middle Americans in the first place. They could be fooled for a season, but they were always looking over government's shoulder, and eventually those impudent little Americans would vote someone else into office—someone exhibiting less than exemplary solidarity. The effect was an undesirable and periodic rollback of socialist progress. (Eisenhower and

---

[i] JOSEPH A. SCHUMPETER, CAPITALISM, SOCIALISM, AND DEMOCRACY 206 (Harper Perennial Modern Thought Edition 2008) (1942).

[ii] John A. Vieg, *The Growth of Public Administration*, as printed in JAMES W. FESLER ET AL., ELEMENTS OF PUBLIC ADMINISTRATION 13 (Fritz Morstein Marx [!] ed., Prentice-Hall, Inc. 1946).

Reagan are oft-cited examples among socialists, but rollbacks recurred at a far more disturbing pace at the congressional level.)

This periodic rollback of socialist progress was due not only to Middle Americans themselves, but also to the structure of constitutional government. You see, the very first line of the Constitution requires that "All legislative Powers herein granted shall be vested in a Congress of the United States, which shall consist of a Senate and House of Representatives."[iii] Which means Congress *writes all federal laws*. And the Constitution further insists that "The Congress shall have Power To . . . provide for the . . . general Welfare of the United States."[iv] Meaning Congress *spends all federal money*. And it further demands that Congress possess power "To coin Money, [and] regulate the Value thereof."[v] Meaning Congress *creates money*. And "To borrow Money on the credit of the United States."[vi] Meaning Congress *sets the national debt*. Yes, the Constitution cedes the greatest federal powers to Congress. And herein lies socialists' problem: The Constitution gives Middle Americans power over Congress! It does so by upholding Middle Americans' prerogative to regularly choose (and re-choose) their Congresspersons.[vii]

Incrementalism wanted all that congressional power—but without any strings attached. Incrementalism wanted complete federal authority, but without Middle American oversight. To make political gains last, Incrementalism needed to find a way to *distance government from Middle Americans*.

Yes, Incrementalism needed a way to distance government from Middle Americans' vigilance in the first place; and it needed a way to protect government decisions from Middle American's electoral retaliation thereafter. In this way Incrementalist laws could be written; Incrementalist welfare programs could be funded; Incrementalist debts could be secured; Incrementalist monetary policy could be adopted; and Incrementalist gains could be made politically durable. (And bonus points would be awarded to any plan further providing a scapegoat for unpopular Incrementalist decisions. That way, no matter how unpopular the decision, Incrementalist politicians would remain free from blame—and active in politics!)

It required some thought.

But Incrementalists solved this political riddle.

To further the silent revolution, a new division of the federal government would be created. Or rather, a new *type* of government altogether would be constructed. A *Fourth* Head of federal government. (*Viz.*, fourth to the constitutionally-mandated three: Congress, the Presidency, and the federal

---

iii U.S. CONST. art. 1, § 1.
iv U.S. CONST. art. 1, § 8, cl. 1.
v U.S. CONST. art. 1, § 8, cl. 5.
vi U.S. CONST. art. 1, § 8, cl. 2.
vii U.S. CONST. art. 1, § 2, cl. 1; art. 1, § 3, cl. 1; amend. XVII.

Judiciary.) And this Fourth Head would not be hypothetical; it would not consist merely in intellectual exercise—it would be very, very real.

Institutions within the Fourth Head would be, unlike Congress and the Presidency, *safely insulated from Middle American oversight.* That is to say, *safely insulated from Middle American voting.* Yes, yes! Power within the Fourth Head would be granted to Commissioners or Board Members who would be *safely appointed from above*—never elected from below! Should Middle Americans dislike decisions made by these new federal institutions, they could no longer reach the levers of power—they could never recall Commissioners or Board Members in the next election! At last a little distance could be had between government and governed. Finally, government could function outside the electoral purview of Middle American voters. Within the Fourth Head, irrepresentative, monolithic government would become reality.

But electoral immunity was not all the Fourth Head offered. There were further advantages. This new, Incrementalist division of government would also be free from Constitutional constraints like the separation of powers. Unlike the Legislative, Executive, and Judicial branches of the federal government, the Fourth Head would *mix all powers*—legislative, judicial, and executive—in a single body. For example, unelected Commissioners of the Fourth Head would have the power to *make law*—simply by publishing new "rules" or "regulations" in a government periodical (aptly entitled the "Federal Register"). Conveniently, such "rules" would have *equal authority with federal statutory laws passed by a vote in both houses of Congress and executed by the President.* (Legislative authority.) Furthermore, institutions within the Fourth Head would have the power to *adjudicate disputes* concerning those rules and regulations—or rather, of those federal laws—they published. (Judicial authority.) And finally, the Fourth Head would also have the power to *enforce* those rules and regulations—or rather, those federal laws—they promulgated. (Executive authority.)

Incrementalism would dub these new divisions of the federal government "Independent Administrative Agencies." Taken together they would form an entirely new, fourth branch of the federal government: a federal bureaucracy.

True, the Fourth Head was (and still is) unmentioned in the Constitution. But then, there were plenty of special interests and causes willing to assist in the creation of independent administrative agencies. After all, as Incrementalists noted, whether or not such an unelected bureaucracy is authorized under the Constitution, the services provided by independent administrative agencies are *all for you*—yes you, helpless citizens! The Fourth Head is simply the means necessary to implement *good government. Moral government.*

Modern life is increasingly complex, you know; so many competing interests, so many new technological possibilities. The world shrinks; all are interconnected in a dazzling and ever-growing tangle of inscrutable social, economic, legal, and environmental interrelationships. Indeed, life has become *too* complex for the average fellow! If government is to do all it can for its citizens, then government requires some apparatus to perform those public works. Congress is gridlocked and overworked; the President is busy managing international affairs. Independent administrative agencies are just the ticket to pick up the slack. They are, after all, composed of bona fide *experts*! Why, administrative agencies are veritable brain trusts! If experts don't make those important decisions necessitated by the increasingly complex world we live in—who will?

When Incrementalists got around to grading themselves for the independent-agency-solution, bonus points were in fact warranted. According to Incrementalist plan, the Fourth Head's loyal-yet-election-proof Commissioners—i.e., the new makers of federal law—*could take full blame for political decisions that were unpopular with Middle Americans.* After all, it was the Commissioners themselves who composed and published agency regulations! Not the Incrementalist politicians who appointed them, who privately campaigned for their commissions, or who confirmed their nomination quite anonymously during an obscure Senate vote. Incrementalist politicians could not be blamed; how could they have known what exactly Commissioners would do once placed in power? Besides, once appointed, Commissioners and Board Members could only be removed *for cause*—meaning they broke the law or became criminally insane. Hence Incrementalist politicians could not be blamed for failing to remove a rogue Commissioner, either!

So the Commissioners of independent agencies remained safe from Middle American votes. And so did the Incrementalist politicians who placed them there.

What are these independent administrative agencies? There are so many—literally scores—that they are difficult to keep track of. (But of course this is just the point! To diversify ownership of monolithic government, to create modular redundancy in administration, to spawn multi-agency overlap—so that the origin of Incrementalist gains is obscured, and Incrementalist advances cannot be rolled back.) To list each independent administrative agency here would be futile. Suffice it to say they are legion.

Yet a few of them are familiar enough; their influence is so pervasive we know them even by acronym or abbreviation: The Fed (or FED, the Board of Governors of the Federal Reserve System, established by Act of Congress in 1913). The FDIC (Federal Deposit Insurance Corporation, established by Act of Congress in 1933). The FCC (Federal Communications Commission, established by Act of Congress in 1934). The NLRB (National Labor Relations Board, established by Act of Congress in 1934). The SSA (Social Security Administration, established in 1935 by Congressional Act).

It is no accident that the establishment of so many of the largest, most familiar, and most influential independent administrative agencies occurred during the thirties. Such agencies were, of course, the apparati necessary to implement FDR's New (Socialist) Deal. And with those agencies required to implement the New Deal, Incrementalism got a solid foothold. After the thirties, Incrementalism simply *expanded* independent agency oversight into new areas of interest. It did so by expanding old agencies' authority into new areas, and by creating new agencies altogether. (For example, the EPA [the Environmental Protection Agency, established in 1970 *by Nixon's executive order!*]).

Over time, Incrementalism extended independent agency control over most every aspect of health, safety, redistribution, entertainment, education, economic activity, law, and social relations. Everything from sub-Saharan African business development (yes, the federal government is in charge of that, too!)[1] to television programming;[2] from transportation safety[3] to union elections;[4] from national boiler efficiency standards[5] to criminal sentencing guidelines.[6] The unconstitutional Fourth Head of the federal government has grown far beyond most Americans' comprehension: Why, the SSA *alone* employs 62,000 full-time, federal employees—and administers (i.e., redistributes) 7% of U.S. GDP (!).

Parable of the Locomotive

And what do these independent administrative agencies do? Why, these colossal federal bureaucracies do as they please. Which is, in general, to implement socialist policies (especially those particularly unpopular with Middle America) in a quiet, careful, step-wise manner.

Consider the railroad: It is emblematic of federal methods.

As you have probably noticed, government invents nothing new. Instead, government waits for individual inventors to take career risks, engineering perils, financial gambles, and bodily hazards to design and perfect the steam engine. The sleepless nights. The boiler disasters. Bodies maimed. Investments lost, never to be recouped.

Take Oliver Evans, for example: An enterprising American inventor and engineer, he obtains a patent for a steam-powered wagon in 1789. The idea is so novel he cannot fabricate a working prototype for over a decade thereafter. By 1812, while steam locomotives are still mere imbalanced fairground curiosities, Evans already envisions the day when steam power will forever revolutionize freight transport and human travel, connecting American cities in a network of rails, and traveling at average speeds "almost as fast as birds fly." He even publishes his vision! But few can believe it. And government least of all.

Yet steam engine technology progresses much as Evans predicts. Wood. Coal. Simple expansion engines. High pressure steam engines. Double expansion, and then triple expansion, compound engines. V-hook motion valve gear. Stephenson valve gear. Gooch valve gear. Allen straight link valve gear. Walschaerts valve gear. Explosive technological advances in little time.

Government observes—but does not yet see profit. So far as government is concerned, the locomotive arts are in their infancy; they show no proof of the earth-shattering force they will become.

Government waits for businessmen and bankers to perform due diligence, to recognize the potential of steam locomotion, to form Railroad Companies, and to risk their personal fortunes to invest in the infrastructure (tracks, switching yards, stations, locomotives, and rail cars) essential to steam locomotion. Private Railroad Companies race tracks from one coast to the other—careening over every mountain pass, building around and over every raging river, tunneling through granite mountains, grading hills and valleys. Dynamite and pickaxe, against impossible odds. Shovel and wheelbarrow in the hot sun. Miraculously, within only a few decades time, a copious network of rails crisscrosses the entire nation.

Government observes, but still does not recognize the locomotive's importance.

Eventually—by the latter part of the nineteenth century—American economy is premised upon steam locomotion. The mechanical efficiencies of the steam locomotive, foreseen decades ago by Oliver Evans, are realized. Freight is shipped by rail. People travel by rail. East and West Coasts are united, and the trackless frontier vanishes. Freight and people alike move as fast as birds fly. An unprecedented economic explosion shakes America.

And now—*only now*—government notices the steam locomotive.

And suddenly government has big plans for the railroad!

Redistributional plans.

It seems that Railroad Companies charge lower rates to large shippers than to small ones. And they occasionally offer rebates to larger shippers. And they occasionally charge more for short trips than for long, cross-country passages.

Is this not suspicious?! Why, this is *predatory* pricing! Taking *advantage* of the poor! A *market failure!* A more *equitable distribution* must be made! Or so Incrementalists in the federal government told us. (Perhaps the federal government had never heard of economies of scale? Or had never considered that while long, overland journeys by rail were common, and proceeded by multiply-redundant tracks operated by competing Railroads, short distance travels *did not*? Or that the greatest expense in shipping freight inheres in (1) *loading and unloading the train*, and (2) *overcoming trains' immense inertia* in taking trains from a stand-still up to operating speed—while traveling cross-country at speed is quite efficient? The rolling resistance of smooth, rigid steel wheels on smooth, rigid steel tracks is pretty low, after all . . . .)

The Pullman strike confirms good government's suspicions. Socialist extraordinaire Eugene V. Debs (President of the American Railroad Union, later Chairman of the National Executive Board of the Socialist Democratic

Party of the United States, cofounder of the Social Democracy of America, cofounder of the International Workers of the World, and four-time U.S. presidential candidate on the Socialist Party of America ticket) orchestrates a nationwide strike. Syndicalist strikers attack African American strikebreakers, derail locomotives, damage seven hundred railcars, and set Railroad buildings on fire. Havoc is wrought. The economy stumbles. The Pullman strike proves once and for all how unjustly railways are operated: Railroad tycoons are out of control; good government must intervene![7]

So the federal government goes right to work and creates the *first ever independent administrative agency*—the ICC (Interstate Commerce Commission)—to get Railroads under control. The ICC manages *Railroad redistribution*: i.e., the ICC sets "reasonable and just" shipping rates *as determined by the ICC's sole discretion*. Which means, among other things, setting maximum shipping rates, outlawing rebates, and prohibiting price discrimination. (Thereby making the Railroads unprofitable. Which in turn precipitously devalues Railroad stocks, thereby invigorating the Banker's Panic of 1907[8]—an unforeseen consequence of the ICC which the federal government "solves" by creating the FED (!)).

The ICC also oversees Railroad Companies' financial operations. It allows or disallows acquisitions and mergers. It allows or disallows new line construction and old line abandonment. It grants or denies certificates to operate a rail line. It reviews the financial records of railroads. It settles labor disputes between Railroad Companies and their employees. It manages rail terminals, rail bridges, and rail sleeping cars. It hires a proto-eugenicist from Harvard[viii] to dictate railway consolidation plans *for private railways*.

Once the ICC is firmly in place, Railroads can make no business decisions at all without ICC approval. For all practical purposes, privately-owned locomotives and rail infrastructure have become federal property.

But even this is deemed insufficient control.

The ICC works so well, the federal government decides to establish further independent administrative agencies to regulate Railroads. Like the USRA (United States Railway Association), to operate defunct Railroads which ICC regulations had forced into bankruptcy. The RLB (Railroad Labor Board), to *better* settle labor disputes. The FRA (Federal Railroad

---

[viii] Professor William Ripley, famed creator of the eponymous "Ripley Plan" for railway consolidation, and author of a favorite progressive-era eugenics text, THE RACES OF EUROPE: A SOCIOLOGICAL STUDY (D. Appleton and Co. 1899). The following furnishes a representative sampling: "Slavery also always produces a terrific death rate which vitiates all comparison between the statistics for the white and the negro. It should be noted, moreover, that such an institution exercises a selective choice upon the negro; for the survivors of such severe treatment will generally be a picked lot, which ought to exhibit vitality to a marked degree, all the weaklings having been removed. Racial comparisons are also invalidated by the fact that hygiene and sanitation are generally confined to the European populations, so that, other things being equal, a higher death rate among the natives would be most natural." *Ibid.* at 564.

Administration), to regulate railroad safety. The SACP (Safety Assurance and Compliance Program), which does the same—but more! The RRB (Railroad Retirement Board)—which administers "comprehensive retirement-survivor and unemployment-sickness benefit programs for the nation's railroad workers and their families . . . . Their activities and responsibilities are similar to those of the Social Security Administration"[9]—but specifically for rail workers! And also the STB (Surface Transportation Board), which replaces the ICC in 1996.

Or like the EPA (Environmental Protection Agency), which creates tome upon tome of new regulations for rail transportation. Decreasing the level of sulfur used in locomotive fuel *by 99 percent* (2004). Decreasing particulate matter emissions from all types of locomotive *by 90 percent* (2004). Decreasing nitrogen oxide emissions *by 80 percent* (2009-10). Demanding high efficiency catalytic converter technology for all newly-built locomotives (slated for 2015).[10]

True, even with the myriad of new EPA fuel and emissions regulations it is still difficult to compete with the fuel efficiency of rail transport—which achieves, on average, *greater than 400 ton-miles per gallon of diesel* (!). Which means with one gallon of gas, you can move two thousand pounds of freight, on average, more than 400 miles. *If* you are using a train. This is approximately 400% more efficient than truck transport (100 ton-miles per gallon of diesel on average), for example.[11] Even the Malthusian Eco-caucus of The Party admits as much.[12]

One would think such mind-boggling fuel efficiency would appeal to Incrementalists. But it does not. At least, not enough to deregulate Railroads to the point rail transport becomes similarly *cost efficient* (like it was at the time of its invention and construction by private individuals, and like it remained until independent administrative agencies got involved). So we continue to ship American freight primarily by truck—a method which gobbles diesel, pollutes the atmosphere, and clogs the highways. Trucking may not be fuel efficient, but it sure is cost efficient in comparison to an impossibly overregulated railroad. (Which is why the freight trucking industry developed in the first place.)

What happened to the rail industry? Well, stripped of its inherent efficiencies by independent administrative agencies' overregulation, it doesn't do nearly what it used to. Probably you can think of places in your own town where rotting ties and rusting rails still run—but where trains no longer pass. This is the heritage of the Fourth Head: Business decisions are taken away from the private individuals and companies which developed an industry. They are handed over to a hodgepodge of overlapping independent administrative agencies. Thereafter, business decisions in the industry are poorly made. The industry crumbles. (And with it, industry infrastructure.)

Let us remember: While the Fourth Head rules every rail decision today, it was not the federal government who took career, financial, and bodily risks to invent the steam locomotive. Or the diesel locomotive. It was not the federal government who painstakingly developed and improved locomotive designs. It was not the federal government who manufactured the locomotives. It was not the federal government who maintained locomotive engines in working order. It was not the federal government who financed those massive investments in tracks, switching yards, and stations necessary to make railway locomotion feasible. It was not the federal government who blasted the tops off mountains, who bored through granite, who built bridges over chasms and rivers, who sawed through impenetrable woodlands, who leveled hills and raised valleys to make rail transport a reality. It was not the federal government who took risked life and limb to lay those tracks. And it was not the federal government who maintained that complex network of tracks—spike by spike, tie by tie, wheelbarrow of ballast by wheelbarrow of ballast.

No, it was not the federal government who took these risks. It was not the federal government who took upon itself these labors. But it was, nevertheless, the federal government who *took the railroad.* As soon as the system of rail transport was fully formed; as soon as the locomotive arts were in full flower; as soon as all the tracks were laid; once the earth-shattering importance of railways was undeniable; *then* the federal government must have it. (*My precioussss!*) *Then* the federal government must redistribute it.

And let us remember: Federal expropriation (and redistribution, and eventual destruction) of the Railroads was carried out by the Fourth Head. It was carried out by the mechanism of independent administrative agencies.[ix]

[ix] Incrementalists still look back with fondness upon the Fourth Head's expropriation and redistribution of private Railroads. For example, President Obama—stumping for reelection in Osawatomie Kansas—provided a brilliant recapitulation (and endorsement!) of these events on Dec. 6, 2011:

> You see, this isn't the first time America has faced this choice. At the turn of the last century, when a nation of farmers was transitioning to become the world's industrial giant, we had to decide: *Would we settle for a country where most of the new* ***railroads*** *and factories were being controlled by a few giant monopolies* that kept prices high and wages low? Would we allow our citizens and even our children to work ungodly hours in conditions that were unsafe and unsanitary? Would we restrict education to the privileged few? Because there were people who thought massive inequality and exploitation of people was just the price you pay for progress.
>
> Theodore Roosevelt disagreed. . . . And *so he busted up monopolies,* forcing those companies to compete for consumers with better services and better prices. . . .
>
> Now, for this, Roosevelt was called a radical. He was called a socialist—[laughter from the audience]—even a communist. But today, we are a richer nation and a stronger democracy because of what he fought for in his last campaign.

Barack Obama, *Remarks by the President on the Economy in Osawatomie, Kansas*, OFFICE OF THE PRESS SECRETARY, WHITE HOUSE (Dec. 6, 2011) (emphasis added).

Yes, the locomotive proffers a cautionary tale—one profitable to recall as we explore the Fourth Head's contemporary work. The ICC was, after all, the first independent administrative agency! As such it set the pattern for future agencies' redistributive goals,[13] political independence, industrial overregulation, and technological expropriation. Indeed we may say that the railroad presents a microcosm of Incrementalism as administered by the Fourth Head.

One which will be repeated again,

and again,

and again,

and again . . . .

Agencies at Work

But you protest:

The railroad is ancient history, you say! A primitive technology, and a primitive business model.

Well, don't be overheard saying that by the French or the Japanese—whose high-speed rail can run at speeds of over 300 miles per hour.

Still, the point is well taken.

So let's discuss the Internet.

Many economic and social benefits accrue from the Internet's ability to widely and cheaply disseminate information.

Like the efficiencies of the steam locomotive, the benefits of the Internet can be realized only in combination with vast networks of essential and outrageously expensive infrastructure. In the case of the Internet, essential infrastructure does not consist in ballast, tracks, ties, rail spikes, and rail stations. It consists instead in an impossibly complex network of thousands of miles of high-speed fiber optic cables, thousands of wired links, thousands of microwave links, thousands of core routers, and thousands of enterprise routers.

Like the steam locomotive, the Internet's infrastructure was laid by private (telecommunications) companies—which spent millions of dollars installing, and still spend millions of dollars managing, that impossibly complex network of high-speed fiber optic cables, wired links, microwave links, core routers, and enterprise routers. Can we be clear? *Without those cables, links, and routers the Internet ceases to exist.*

Private companies—like Comcast, for instance—performed the due diligence on Internet technology. Private companies accepted the risk of betting on a fledgling technology. Private companies made gigantic Internet infrastructure investments. And private companies now manage that network so as to minimize network congestion. Private companies do all this at their own expense, in order to sell Internet network access (bandwidth) to customers—like you and me. Such companies are called Internet Service Providers (ISPs).

Incrementalists within the federal government were slow to recognize the reach of this new technology—the Internet. Just like they had been with the locomotive. But once the Internet had swallowed up old methods of communication and economy, Incrementalists envied those private individuals who controlled the Internet. Just like they had envied those who controlled the locomotive. They didn't appreciate such power in the hands of the plebs. They didn't like private companies determining how to partition their own bandwidth across thousands of miles of cable, thousands of microwave links, and thousands of routers. They wished to control who had access to which content and at what speeds across that entire network—the Internet—themselves.[14] They were certain, after all, that a "serious effort to reform the media system would have to necessarily be part of a revolutionary program to overthrow the capitalist political economy."[15,16]

And what could Incrementalists call their Internet expropriation initiative? "Independent Administrative Agency Partitioning of Private Internet Networks" just didn't have a ring to it. That would be a hard sell in Middle America. So Incrementalists coined a new term for commandeering privately owned and operated Internet infrastructure: "Network Neutrality." Now that sounded good! A little alliteration never hurts when composing a mantra for the mindless masses to ape.

So Incrementalist politicians introduced bill after bill in Congress to make "network neutrality" federal law. [x] (That is, to tell private ISPs—who built, and who own and manage all Internet cable, micro links, and routers—just how to partition bandwidth between users.) Such bills were not popular with Middle Americans, of course; the Internet ran very well, and federal bandwidth control smacked of political machinations. Middle Americans and ISPs made their intentions known to congresspersons time and again. And career politicians didn't wish to scuttle political careers over silly "network neutrality" votes. So, time and again, congressional "network neutrality" bills were roundly defeated in Congress.[xi]

But so what if *Congress* couldn't pass a "network neutrality" law? After years of skirting Constitutional limitations on federal lawmaking there were other options! Incrementalists simply shipped the "network neutrality" hot potato over to an electorally-safe branch of the federal government: The

---

[x] There are too many bills to mention them all here. And aside from the few computer geeks who may read this footnote, most will not find the congressional saga of network neutrality terribly interesting. But a few of the more important bills deserve mention: There was the Internet Freedom and Nondiscrimination Act of 2006 (introduced in the Senate); the Communications Opportunity, Promotion and Enhancement Act of 2006 (introduced in the House); the Network Neutrality Act of 2006 (introduced in the House); the Snowe-Dorgan-Obama Internet Freedom Preservation Act of 2007 (introduced in the Senate); the Internet Freedom Preservation Act of 2008 (introduced in the House); etc. The "network neutrality" elements of all were soundly defeated.

[xi] *Ibid.*

Fourth Head. Specifically, Incrementalists shipped "network neutrality" from Congress to an independent administrative agency called the Federal Communications Commission. Decisions at the FCC are made at a safe distance from Middle Americans by a board of five commissioners—who are all *appointed* by the President in staggered terms of five years, and from that five-year term until a replacement has been appointed and confirmed by the Senate.[17] Even a notion as unpopular as "network neutrality" was safe within the electorally insensitive FCC.

Incrementalist appointees at the FCC promptly ruled in August 2008 that Comcast—a privately owned and operated ISP—must partition its bandwidth in a certain way. A redistributive way. Specifically, Comcast must stop delaying BitTorrent uploads in deference to other network traffic, the FCC said.[18] Comcast must maintain a "network neutral" Internet infrastructure. No matter that BitTorrent uploads were hogging Comcast bandwidth. No matter that the FCC's ruling would cause network congestion, delaying and degrading other data transfers on Comcast's network. No matter that the wires, fiber optic cables, micro links, and routers belonged to Comcast. No matter. Incrementalists within the FCC demanded control of Comcast's network![19]

There was only one problem—the FCC received its statutory authority from the Communications Act of 1934.[20] The Communications Act of 1934 did not give the FCC authority to tell Comcast how to partition bandwidth over its private network—and the FCC knew it.[xii] Nor could the FCC show it possessed ancillary jurisdiction[21] to instruct Comcast how to partition its bandwidth. So on April 6, 2010 the United States Court of Appeals for the District of Columbia Circuit vacated the FCC's illegal Comcast-network-partitioning-rule in *Comcast Corp. v. FCC*.[22]

But Incrementalists were not dismayed. Chairman Genachowski and the rest of the FCC Commissioners had bigger plans than conquering Comcast alone. The FCC intended to regulate the *entire* Internet. (The FCC's motto, after all, is to "[p]romote the availability of quality services at *just, reasonable,* and *affordable rates* for all consumers," including "those in low income . . . areas."[23] Which is to say, the FCC intends to redistribute the Internet.) So the FCC would simply wait for an opportune moment to spring new and comprehensive "net neutrality" regulations on the entire ISP industry.

What the FCC needed was a lull in Middle American scrutiny. A recess from political opposition. And a lethargic media cycle. So the FCC wrote up the new Internet partition regulations—knowing they possessed no authority

---

[xii] The FCC itself classifies ISPs (like Comcast) as neither a "telecommunications service" (i.e., telephone network) under Title II, nor a "cable service" (i.e., cable TV) under Title VI of the Communications Act. *In re High-Speed Access to the Internet Over Cable and Other Facilities*, 17 F.C.C.F. 4798, 4802, P 7 (2002). So the FCC knew it was reaching far beyond the limits of its own jurisdiction.

to do so after the Court of Appeals' recent ruling—and they waited. . . . For Christmas Break! Pardon me, I mean Holiday Break. I mean, Mid-Winter Break. I mean, Yule. I mean, Mōdraniht. I mean, Winter Solstice. Whatever. On December 21, 2010, as Middle American families carefully selected Yule logs in preparation for upcoming Winter Solstice celebrations, and politicians flew home on Winter Solstice Recess, and media outlets prepared to operate through the Solstice on skeleton crews—the FCC sprung their regulatory trap: They officially "adopted" the new, privily-written regulations, which purported to establish "net neutrality" for the entire Internet. The President immediately issued a statement praising the FCC for its courage in making horrifically unpopular federal laws, laws which implemented his own Presidential vision for the Internet, and for simultaneously protecting his Presidency from electoral jeopardy.[24] And on December 23, 2010, the FCC quietly released their new and comprehensive "net neutrality" regulations.[25] (Sorry, private ISPs—you laid all the cable, installed all those micro links, networked all those routers—you paid for it all, and you managed it so as to prevent congestion—but The Revolution can't wait.)

With a prolixity achievable only by unelected organs of monolithic government, the FCC detailed—for a full 194 pages—its illegal new "net neutrality" rules. And the reasoning behind its Solstice Grab.[26] The FCC calmly explained that "broadband providers should not pick winners and losers on the Internet."[27] Instead, monolithic government—in the form of the FCC—should do that. Monolithic government had decided that Skype, Google, and P2P should be the winners. And everyone else the losers. So the FCC ruled:

> A person engaged in the provision of fixed broadband Internet access service, insofar as such person is so engaged, shall not block[xiii] lawful content, applications, services, or non-harmful devices, *subject to reasonable network management.*[28]

What exactly did the FCC mean by "*reasonable* network management"? Why, that was just the key! Because the FCC does not define this term—because the FCC alone will adjudicate what is *reasonable* network management—it means the FCC claims *absolute discretion over all fixed broadband network management.* Like FIFA refs' absolute discretion in scoring soccer matches. The FCC simply divested all ISPs of their right to manage their own networks. Their own cables. Their own links. Their own routers.

Of course, the new "network neutrality" rules could cause network congestion, and therefore degradation of Internet traffic generally. The FCC

[xiii] The FCC broadened this rule further by explaining that "in some circumstances the distinction between blocking and degrading (such as by delaying) traffic is merely 'semantic.'" *In re Preserving the Open Internet Broadband Industry Practices*, GN Dkt. 09-191, WC Dkt. 07-52, FCC Dkt. 10-201, ¶ 66 (Dec. 23, 2010). In other words, don't interfere with any signals on your network, ISPs.

knew that, too: "we recognize that some network congestion may be unavoidable."[29] But the FCC didn't care about that. It wished to redistribute the Internet.

Now, only 21% of Americans want the FCC regulating the Internet.[30] A majority of Americans fear that the FCC will use Internet regulation to promote a political agenda.[31] But because the "net neutrality" decision was made under the electorally unyielding Fourth Head of government, Americans can't really do anything about FCC Commissioners' decisions. It is not as though Chairman Genachowski is going to be up for reelection! Besides, Incrementalists *do* want the FCC regulating the Internet—and the FCC is all too happy to comply.

And so another barrow of dirt is dumped at the summit of the socialist Ararat. The silent revolution ascends.

Agencies at Play

The FCC's Solstice Grab was nothing extraordinary. On the contrary, hostile takeover by the Fourth Head is how contemporary, federal lawmaking is ordinarily performed. Especially where unpopular, Incrementalist measures are required.

Today federal dismemberment, redistribution, overregulation, and destruction of Internet networks continues—like Railroad networks before them—at the direction of multiple federal agencies, and at both source and user ends. So while the FCC partitions private Internet Service Providers' networks and dictates what type of rate schedules they may use, other federal agencies are divvying up end user rights. (For example, the DOC [U.S. Department of Commerce, a cabinet-administered agency] is currently developing a comprehensive Internet I.D. system for all Americans.[32] And DHS [the Department of Homeland Security, another cabinet-administered agency] has been surreptitiously monitoring and keeping records of your visits and posts to Facebook, Twitter, YouTube, Hulu, Flickr, and the Drudge Report.[33] Oh, yes—and the FCC is also assisting by means of a separate program, the so-called "Lifeline Program for Low-Income Consumers," which specifically redistributes broadband internet from those who pay for it [consumers] to those who do not [program beneficiaries].[xiv]

[xiv] The FCC's "Lifeline" program provides not only broadband internet, but also provides free cell phone minutes, and free cell phone connection fees. (*See* FCC FAQ, *Lifeline Program for Low-Income Consumers*, (Feb. 16, 2012), http://www.fcc.gov/encyclopedia/lifeline-program-low-income-consumers.) The FCC provides these freebies by imposing a "Universal Service Fund" fee on all internet and phone service providers. (*See, e.g.*, FCC FAQ, *Universal Service*, (Feb. 16, 2012), http://www.fcc.gov/encyclopedia/universal-service.) Service providers pass this fee on to you, the paying consumer, in your monthly broadband internet or phone bill. (Brad Tuttle, *How to Get the Government to Cover Your Cell Phone Bills*), TIME (Feb. 8, 2012)). The freebies are then distributed by yet *another* independent administrative agency, the so-called USAC (Universal Service Administrative

And the FCC is making plans to tax broadband Internet service so as to more easily redistribute it via the FCC's $4.5 billion "Connect America" subsidy.[34] The FCC plans to tax Internet service in spite of the Internet Tax Freedom Act of 1998![35] The FCC has adopted "an express goal," after all: "ensuring availability of broadband for all low-income Americans."[36])

Wherever administrative agencies are employed, Incrementalist strategy has two foci: (1) To transfer implementation of unpopular socialist policies to election-proof bureaucracies, and (2) To extend bureaucratic authority from those limited objects which Americans originally approved to other, further objects which Americans did not. If these foci were imperceptible under the FCC's Internet takeover, they become increasingly obvious with exposure:

For example, the Federal Reserve (FED) was created in response to the 1907 Bankers' Panic. (Which, as we have already seen, was caused in part by the ICC's fixing of railroad fares.[37]) The FED's purpose was to reduce the likelihood of American runs *on American banks* through the "establishment of Federal reserve banks, . . . to establish a more effective supervision of *banking in the United States*."[38] The existence of the FED was, in 1913—and remains today—a contentious issue. But there were at least some Americans in 1913 who supported the FED's creation for the limited purposes of its charter: more effective supervision of banking *in the United States*. Creating a sufficient *reserve* of currency or specie for injection into *American banks* during liquidity crises. In sum, "to furnish an elastic currency"[39] *in America*, and thereby to avoid another Bankers' Panic *in the United States*.

However, almost no Americans wanted in 1913—or want today—the FED loaning billions of dollars of its reserves to *foreign* banks, to shore up *foreign* banks' balance sheets during liquidity crises. Much less would Americans support the FED making the *vast majority* of its discount window loans during a liquidity crisis (say, 70% of $110.7 billion dollars) to *foreign* banks. But that is precisely what the FED did at the zenith of the 2008 liquidity crisis.[40] And so, while Americans were unable to get loans from American banks at any price, the FED was shoveling *billions* of dollars to banks overseas. So foreign banks could avoid runs. So foreign banks could loan money. The FED knew Middle Americans would be outraged, so the FED categorically refused to disclose whom it loaned money to during the 2008 crisis. But after three years of FOIA requests, legal challenges, and court orders—long after the money had been loaned (and hopefully recouped?), and long after the public outcry had simmered down—the FED was forced to admit it.[41]

So, yeah—the FED has both Incrementalist foci covered.

Company). (FCC, *Lifeline Program for Low-Income Consumers* (Feb. 16, 2012), http://www.fcc.gov/encyclopedia/lifeline-program-low-income-consumers). The freebies are available to anyone who receives federal welfare, as well as anyone who earns up to 135% of the current federal poverty level. (Brad Tuttle, *How to Get the Government to Cover Your Cell Phone Bill(s)*, TIME (Feb. 8, 2012)).

And so do other administrative agencies. In fact, Incrementalism has effectively spread the conventions of administrative law, of agency independence, and of institutional proliferation from formally *independent* administrative agencies to traditional, Cabinet-administered, executive agencies as well. So for example:

The United States Department of Homeland Security (DHS) was created in response to three thousand civilian deaths during the terrorist attacks of 9-11. DHS was tasked with improving national security—i.e., making American citizens safer from terrorist attacks going forward. But by 2010—less than a decade after its creation!—"DHS determined it needed to take a proactive approach to climate adaptation."[42] So now DHS has proudly undertaken a "collaborative, department-wide initiative [to] raise awareness of impacts of climate change and risks to DHS mission and operations; identify and prioritize major impact of climate change and risks to DHS; identify potential adaptation strategies; make recommendations for incorporating climate change adaptation into ongoing Departmental planning processes," etc., etc.[43] While DHS' chartered purpose (to protect American citizens from terrorist attacks) was generally supported by the American public, DHS has since gone off the reservation in pursuit of tasks it finds more compelling. And so, while al-Qaeda is currently instructing Muslims living in America to purchase firearms and go on shooting sprees to kill American infidels,[44] DHS is zealously pursuing anthropogenic climate change.

Feel safer?

Or consider the National Institute of Mental Health (NIMH). Based on the agency's name, one might expect its purpose to be related to *Americans'* mental health. After all, its title is the *National* Institute of Mental Health—not the *International* Institute of Mental Health. But as is typical of administrative agencies, the NIMH is like a teensy matryoshka doll: it is nested within other, larger administrative agencies—each of whose decisions are similarly protected from electoral recall by Middle Americans. The NIMH is one of twenty seven agencies comprising the National Institutes of Health (NIH), which is further nested within the United States Department of Health and Human Services (HHS). And like the NIMH, the HHS's motto is boldly domestic: "Improving the health, safety, and well-being *of America.*"

But with the inviolability of decisions made by telescoping agencies, the NIMH—the teensy matryoshka we started with—can undertake more than mere *domestic* health initiatives. And more than *mental* health initiatives, too. Much more! It is so well insulated from Middle American votes that it can throw down a million dollars here and a million dollars there—not for the mental health, safety, and well-being *of Americans*, but rather "to evaluate the feasibility and acceptability of a post-coital male genital hygiene procedure" among Sub-Saharan Africans, "which participants will be asked to practice immediately post-coitus or at least 12 hours after."[45] (Yes—you read that right: the NIMH wants to see if it can convince Sub-Saharan Africans to wash their penises within twelve hours following sex.) So in 2009—at the very nadir of worldwide economic collapse—the well-insulated NIMH went right ahead and spent approximately a million dollars[46] of American tax-payers' money to study whether Africans could be convinced to wash their penises.

Why try to teach Africans to wash their penises after sex? Well, both penile hygiene and HIV are big problems in Sub-Saharan Africa. And it is just possible—not actually known, but merely *possible*—that washing one's penis after sex may decrease the likelihood of contracting HIV. (So even if the NIMH *can* convince Africans to wash their penises after sex, this habit may just as likely *not* decrease the likelihood of contracting HIV! The NIMH is unsure.) Whether penile hygiene actually *reduces the incidence of HIV* is thus a threshold inquiry—a logical prerequisite to spending a million dollars to see if Africans can be persuaded to wash their penises. But not at the NIMH: "If we find that men are able to practice consistent washing practices after sex, we will plan to test whether this might protect men from becoming HIV infected in a later study."[47] In other words, the NIMH is planning a *follow-up* study to determine whether penile hygiene actually lowers the risk of contracting HIV—but in the meantime, they are going to go ahead and spend a million dollars to see if they can convince Africans to wash their dicks. Now that is brilliant! The scientific method flourishes within the halls of monolithic government . . . .

Meanwhile, the National Science Foundation (NSF, a sister organization to the NIMH) is spending approximately 43% of its $6.9 billion annual research budget on YouTube rap videos; Jell-O wrestling and skinny dipping in Antarctica; alcohol; amusement park outings; on-the-job pornography surfing;[xv] digital cameras, surveillance cameras, lenses, and an oversized printer for capturing and printing pornographic photographs; proving that sick shrimp don't run as energetically as healthy shrimp on underwater shrimp treadmills ($3 million for this last project alone!); and other scientifically barren endeavors.[48] While many dispute the *scientific* value of such projects—not to mention the wisdom of their multi-billion dollar expense during the greatest economic downturn since the Great Depression—Incrementalism merrily wends its way through our federal bureaucracy.

And what of the National Aeronautics and Space Administration (NASA)? Its charter is *to boldly go where no woman has gone before*, is it not? To encourage aeronautical engineering and the exploration of space? "To

---

[xv] "[S]ome employees at NSF were spending more time viewing pornography than doing their jobs. The porn viewing was so pervasive that the cases overwhelmed the agency's [Inspector General] and undermined the watchdog's ability to investigate other misspent funds or fraudulent activities." Tom Coburn, *The National Science Foundation: Under the Microscope*, 15 (April 2011).

provide for research into problems of flight within and outside the earth's atmosphere"? At least, that is what the National Aeronautics and Space Act of 1958 declared NASA's purpose to be.[49] And that is what NASA's title plainly suggests. But after fifty some years, NASA's focus has changed. In the words of NASA chief administrator Charles Bolden, NASA's "foremost" aim is to "find a way to reach out to the Muslim world and, uh, engage much more with dominantly Muslim nations, uh, to help them, uh, feel good about, uh, their historic contribution to science and engineering."[50]

So the original purpose of NASA—to encourage exploration of "flight within and outside the earth's atmosphere," a purpose which the vast majority of Americans supported in 1958 and still support today—has been abandoned. (In fact, American astronauts no longer have any way to get into space. NASA has shuttered the space shuttle program. The last shuttle launch took place on July 8, 2011. There will be no more launches. Ever. Henceforth we shall be forced to call NASA's intrepid explorers *geonauts*. Or perhaps they could hitch a ride in Russian space capsules going forward?)

Yet NASA itself does not go away! It lives on. In place of its original aim of aeronautical and space exploration, NASA's purpose is now reduced to a Muslim outreach campaign designed to conciliate belligerent Islamic pride for ancient contributions to science and engineering. Contributions which have been conspicuously absent from "dominantly Muslim nations" for the past 800 years. This latter purpose—the new and "foremost" aim of NASA—is quite unpopular with the vast majority of Americans. But how well-hidden this latter purpose is, originating as it does from *within NASA*! Middle Americans would never think to look *there!*

Then there is the Bureau of Alcohol, Tobacco, Firearms, and Explosives (ATF). Today the ATF is safely nested within the Department of Justice (DOJ).[xvi] Like other agencies, the ATF's original purpose can be inferred from its title: It is supposed to keep firearms out of the hands of violent American criminals, so as to improve U.S. security. But at some point the ATF decided that keeping firearms away from violent criminals in the U.S. just wasn't sufficiently stimulating. So in October, 2009, the ATF started a little operation entitled "Fast and Furious," by which it encouraged licensed firearms dealers to illegally sell guns to straw purchasers in hopes those guns would find their way into the hands of violent Mexican drug cartels.[51] And then the ATF proactively refused to interdict either the straw purchasers or the million and a half dollars of firearms they purchased (!).[52] Just take a minute to let that soak in.

[xvi] Over its storied history, the ATF has bounced around between the Department of the Treasury, the Bureau of Internal Revenue (BIR), the Bureau of Prohibition (BOP), the Internal Revenue Service (IRS), and others. But as of October, 2012, the ATF is nested within the DOJ.

Officially, the ATF's gunrunning scheme might possibly allow the ATF to trace cartel hierarchies all the way to their Mexican kingpins. But the ATF never told Mexico about its plan. And after over 2,000 illegal firearms sales during Operation Fast and Furious, the ATF never uncovered any kingpins. What is more, once those firearms made their way to the cartels they were used to kill people on both sides of the border.[53] So ATF's original function—to keep Americans safe by keeping guns out of violent criminals' hands—has been turned upside down:[54] Now the ATF actively seeks out violent criminal offenders, not to apprehend them, but *to sell them guns*.[xvii]

And the Social Security Administration's (SSA's) original purpose was to mail social security checks to senior citizens. The SSA still does that. But at some point the SSA determined that mailing welfare checks to the elderly wasn't as sexy a job as they might have liked. They decided to branch out into other areas. So in 2012, they are purchasing 174,000 bullets.[55] Not just any bullets, but jacketed hollow-point, .357 magnum bullets.[56] For faster expansion, superior tissue destruction, and improved lethality.

The SSA was a little embarrassed when people noticed its purchase request for 174,000 hollow-point bullets. So it published a prepared statement arguing that the SSA employs "special agents" who need those bullets.[57] Which makes one wonder: What exactly do SSA "special agents" do? Between runs to the post office to mail welfare checks, why do they need so many bullets annually? And if the SSA has armed investigators, what is the FBI for?

Parliamentary Mischief

It is difficult to overlook the fact that administrative agencies appear curiously similar to those Parliamentary agencies which Americans violently rejected in the War for Independence.[xviii] Like Parliament's Board of Customs Commissioners in America. Indeed, organizationally and strategically speaking, they function in precisely the same way: (1) *Appoint* a board of Commissioners who are loyal to the cause; (2) so Commissioners cannot be recalled by popular election; (3) thereby establishing governmental independence from electoral reprisals; (4) give Commissioners a full mixture of legislative, executive, and judicial powers in their domain; (5) when agencies publish unpopular laws, let agency Commissioners take the blame for Parliament; (6) repeat.

[xvii] The ATF's paradoxical behavior is difficult to understand, but it can be explained. Apparently the ATF deplores the Second Amendment: The ATF had hoped Operation Fast and Furious would yield *stricter firearm purchase laws for law-abiding American citizens*. Like a multiple-sales reporting requirement for rifles. *See, e.g.*, Sharyl Attkinsson, *Documents: ATF Used 'Fast and Furious' to Make the Case for Gun Regulations*, CBS NEWS (Dec. 7, 2011).

[xviii] *See, e.g.*, THE DECLARATION OF INDEPENDENCE, ¶¶ 12; 18; 23-24; 15 (U.S. 1776).

And we must concede that in efficacy, administrative agencies today are equals of their historical Parliamentary counterparts. Consider how well administrative agencies work to shelter Incrementalist politicians: Without independent administrative agencies, actual politicians—men and women running for reelection to Congress or to the Presidency—would be forced every few years to explain to Middle Americans why they are employing magisterial discretion to regulate the Internet. (Why is nationwide coercion required when the Internet runs beautifully without it, and when American citizens don't support federal Internet regulation?) And why they are loaning billions of Middle Americans' dollars to foreign banks during liquidity crises. (Why can't Middle Americans get loans from undercapitalized American banks?) And why they are spending millions of taxpayers' dollars annually to fund Sub-Saharan African businesses. (Why the unauthorized, international, redistributive *in*-justice?) And why they are spending billions to test whether sick shrimp run slower than well shrimp. (Why the pork-barrel spending on monolithic government's pet projects during the greatest economic downturn in the past seventy years?)

But no matter! Such questions are now moot: Most of the more unpopular decisions have been shifted to invulnerable Incrementalist bureaucrats, who are well-insulated from electoral retribution or recall. In this bureaucratic alphabet stew—with its hundreds of agencies, acronyms, and overlapping responsibilities—no voter can possibly keep track of which federal organ is doing what within the body politic. Why, over the past ten years alone the Fourth Head has generated *38,000 new federal laws*.[58] That is more than ten new federal laws every single day—far more than any Congress could generate. And these laws are not succinct; they do not resemble, "Thou shalt not steal." They are absurdly detailed and verbose. As of December, 2011, the Fourth Head has generated 169,301 pages of federal laws.[59] And that corpus is growing by the hour.

Many citizens are completely unaware of the existence of the Fourth, Unelected Head of government. When citizens do become aware of the federal bureaucracy's direct interference in their lives, there is little they can do. Tracking down the source of an undesirable regulation is, within an administrative agency, a wild goose chase of epic proportions. When administrative agencies promulgate multi-thousand-page codices of regulations, they don't insert a footnote stating "Sec. 2133.03(a)(II)(A)(4) of these regulations was Chairman Kappos' idea." (Yes, that section of the Manual of Patent Examining Procedure really exists! And it is only *halfway through* that multi-thousand-page codex of federal regulations, the brainchild of the U.S. Patent and Trademark Office. Which is, in turn, only one of many offices within the United States Department of Commerce. As a practicing patent attorney, I can assure you that that Sec. 2133.03(a)(II)(A)(4) of the

MPEP is quite safe from Middle America! It is sheltered from Middle America not only by the natural obscurity which attends its specificity to patent law, but also by the matryoshka principle: layer upon layer of nested, unelected bureaucracies.[60])

And unlike Congress, federal agencies provide no public records detailing the intra-agency debates which generated their regulations.[xix] (So even if citizens *did* elect agency Commissioners—which they don't—they would never know whom to target in elections.)

And even if agencies *did* publish records detailing intra-agency, regulatory-generative debates, there is no way for Middle Americans to remove sitting Commissioners because they don't come up for reelection. They were never elected in the first place.

And Middle Americans cannot very well remove sitting agency staff by petitioning their *elected* officials, either. There are many reasons for this. First of all, both the elected official who appointed the Commissioner in question (e.g., the president), as well as his successor (e.g., a president since then), can only remove independent agency Commissioners *for cause* (viz., the Commissioner became incapacitated or did something illegal. And promulgating agency regulations—however contrary to the Constitution!—is not considered "illegal"). Moreover, the elected official who appointed the Commissioner in question is unlikely to care that Middle Americans wish to have the Commissioner removed. After all, the elected official appointed the commissioner because he knew the Commissioner's track record and had a good idea of what sorts of policies the Commissioner would implement. If political fallout results from selection of a Commissioner, the elected official has plausible deniability: "When I appointed Chairman Genachowski I had no idea he would do that. But he did. It is not my fault; the Chairman did that on his own initiative." Finally, independent agency commissioners' terms do not generally match the length of the presidency. They are longer than Presidential terms, and staggered. So it is highly unlikely that Middle Americans select presidents based on which independent agency commissioners' terms are ending. Probably they should, but they don't.

This is not government of, by, and for the People. It is quite the opposite. It is an end-run around representative government. Once socialist programs are swept under the Incrementalist rug of federal agencies, there is little Middle Americans can do to end them. Such a state of affairs is irreconcilable with liberty under local government. It is the definition of

---

[xix] U.S. CONST. art. I § 5 requires both the House and the Senate to "keep a Journal of its Proceedings, and from time to time publish the same, . . . and the Yeas and Nays of the Members of either House on any question shall, at the Desire of one fifth of those Present, be entered on the Journal." But of course independent administrative agencies are unmentioned in the Constitution. So they are *not* bound to publish a journal of *their* proceedings.

domination by distant, unresponsive, monolithic government. Just like Parliament and its Board of Customs Commissioners.

Just as Incrementalism planned it.

And so the Fourth Head, dictating everything from Internet connectivity to how many of your tax dollars are spent on marine shrimp marathons, is free to carry on the work of Incrementalism without oversight by Middle Americans. The work of Incrementalism continues incessantly, behind hundreds of thousands of closed doors, in practically unmarked federal office buildings, by nameless clerks and election-proof Commissioners, year-in and year-out. Unrelenting. Even during Winter Solstice Recess.

And squirrel hunting is avoided for another year.

* * *

Now, there are plenty of people who want net neutrality. And there are plenty of people who would prefer Sub-Saharan Africans wash their penises after sex. Those are perfectly reasonable positions to take, and there are surely people reading this book for whom such questions are of manifest importance. But that is not the issue.

The issue is simply whether government ought to be able to *force all Americans* to obtain their Internet connectivity from a "net neutral," bandwidth-congested network; and *spend all American tax-payers' money* to investigate whether Africans can be taught to wash their penises; *without Americans' consent.* The question is one of liberty versus coercion—of self-government versus monolithic government—of representative republicanism versus unfettered bureaucracy: Should the federal government be able to make such decisions free from citizen oversight and the threat of electoral recall? Without being subject to restraints imposed by a constitutional separation of powers? From within the electoral safety of multiply-nested bureaucracies?[61] Or should the federal government be limited to making such decisions with the (1) explicit and (2) regular, periodic consent of (3) a majority of Americans?[xx]

The Constitution is clear: The federal government must only be able to make law,[xxi] and spend money,[xxii] and create money,[xxiii] and go into debt,[xxiv]

[xx] By explicit and regular, *periodic* consent we mean *elections.* No one is suggesting that we convene a national vote on each and every single decision made by the federal government, as would be required by a system of pure democracy.

[xxi] "All legislative Powers herein granted shall be vested in a Congress of the United States, which shall consist of a Senate and a House of Representatives." U.S. CONST. art. I § 1.

[xxii] "The Congress shall have Power To . . . provide for the . . . general Welfare of the United States." U.S. CONST. art. 1, § 8, cl. 1.

[xxiii] "The Congress shall have Power . . . To coin Money, [and] regulate the Value thereof." U.S. CONST. art. 1, § 8, cls. 1 & 5.

[xxiv] "The Congress shall have Power . . . To borrow Money on the credit of the United States." U.S. CONST. art. 1, § 8, cls. 1 & 2.

with the explicit and regular, periodic consent of a majority of Americans.[xxv] That was the agreement between the independent States and their free citizens. And the nascent federal government bought its very existence by agreeing to abide forever under those restrictions.

Middle Americans concur: The federal government must only be able to make law, and spend money, and create money, and auction debt, with the explicit and regular, periodic consent of a majority of Americans. Anything less fails to represent the will of the People. Anything less runs the serious hazard of becoming *ir*-representative government. Such arrangements cannot stand. And never have free Americans and their independent States amended the Constitution to permit electorally unsupervised federal overreach.

But socialists and their Incrementalist allies cannot agree to abide by the terms of constitutional government. Socialists recognize that independence from the will of the middle class is the foundation stone upon which all socialist societies are built. And socialism's Incrementalist allies are useful idiots: they have some *special* purpose which government must fix at all costs. Neither group has any use for a Constitution: They both have non-majoritarian intentions. They both seek federal domination of local affairs.

And they both wish to see monolithic advances *last.*

And so, to insulate government from the will of Middle Americans; to expropriate and to redistribute private wealth and innovations; to combine legislative, executive, and judicial powers within a single body; to create a government sufficiently powerful to carry out their monolithic plans—they foist upon us the Fourth Head.

[xxv] Congress (the Senate and House) are subject to regular, periodic elections—every two years. U.S. CONST. art. I §§ 2, 3, 4; amend. XVII.

Further Notes to Chapter 3

[1] African Development Foundation, established in 1980 by Congressional Act.
[2] Corporation for Public Broadcasting, established in 1967 by Congressional Act.
[3] National Transportation Safety Board, established in 1967, but made *independent* only later in 1975 by way of Congressional Act.
[4] NRLB.
[5] EPA.
[6] U.S. Sentencing Commission, established by Act of Congress in 1984.
[7] This description summarizes diverse accounts of the Pullman Strike. Today, socialists remain very proud of this part of their history, and explicitly socialist accounts of the Pullman Strike are quite revealing. *See, e.g.*, Jon Allen, *Capital Versus Labor: The Pullman Strike Showdown*, Political Affairs (Sept. 28, 2007) ("The Pullman strike set the stage for the passage of protective labor laws and for successful strike action in the future. Without the Pullman strike, legislation we take for granted like the eight-hour workday, minimum wage and workplace safety standards might not exist."). http://www.politicalaffairs.net/capital-versus-labor-the-pullman-strike-showdown/.
[8] ADOLPH EDWARDS, THE ROOSEVELT PANIC OF 1907, 66-69 (Antirock Publishing Co. 1907).
[9] IRS, *Railroad Industry Overview Series – Government Regulatory Requirements* (Oct. 2007). http://www.irs.gov/businesses/article/0,,id=175295,00.html.
[10] *Ibid.*
[11] *See, e.g.*, ICF International in cooperation with the Federal Railroad Administration, *Comparative Evaluation of Rail and Truck Fuel Efficiency on Competitive Corridors*, U.S. Dept. of Transportation 4 (Nov. 19, 2009). http://www.fra.dot.gov/Downloads/Comparative_Evaluation_Rail_Truck_Fuel_Efficiency.pdf.
[12] Rocky Mountain Institute, *Rail Versus Trucking: Who's the Greenest Freight Carrier?*, TREEHUGGER (May 20, 2009). Well, they grossly exaggerate the efficiency of truck transport (at 130 ton-miles per gallon "average," they cherry pick the most efficient of truck transport fuel efficiencies. *See* ICF International in cooperation with the Federal Railroad Administration, *Comparative Evaluation of Rail and Truck Fuel Efficiency on Competitive Corridors*, U.S. Dept. of Transportation 4 (Nov. 19, 2009)). But they still admit it.
[13] Make no mistake: Redistribution was the chief justification for creating federal administrative agencies from the very beginning. This much is admitted by Incrementalists themselves. And in this regard, Incrementalists often portray federal agencies' endless regulations very carefully (under their linguistic campaign) as a *new and better "freedom"* (!). An excellent example of such reasoning can be found in Incrementalist Professor John A. Vieg's masterful treatise on the rise of administrative agencies in America:

> It required, therefore, a long and slow development, through decades blotted with innumerable instances of helpless poverty and social injustice, to raise political thinking above the standard of *freedom from regulation* of any kind to a higher standard. This higher standard of the present age is *freedom under regulation* designed *to safeguard the general welfare*. Until the new development was well under way [sic], public administration had only halting and tentative relationships with the national economy. Today governmental activities in countless ways [!] sustain our economic life.

John A. Vieg, *The Growth of Public Administration*, as printed in JAMES W. FESLER ET AL., ELEMENTS OF PUBLIC ADMINISTRATION 13-14 (Fritz Morstein Marx [!] ed., Prentice-Hall, Inc. 1946) (emphasis added). Yes, you read that right—*"freedom under regulation"* (!). Meaning regulation takes priority, while freedom must duke it out with all other subsidiary American virtues in the backseat.

Prof. Vieg rightly emphasizes that "[i]t required . . . a long and slow development" to achieve a redistributionist standard in America. After all, proactive redistribution supervised by irrepresentative, unelected administrative agencies was *not* what our Predecessors envisioned when ratifying the Constitution. Our Predecessors had gone to war with England to stamp out mercantilist redistribution and irrepresentative, unelected administrative agencies. And that is why the Constitution establishes the Legislature as the most powerful federal body, and why it minimizes Executive power.

Incrementalists recognize these facts as well. As Prof. Vieg conspicuously notes:

> Until the first gains, during World War I, of the movement for state [meaning national] administrative reorganization, perhaps the best way to describe the impact of the British example on state [meaning national] government would have been in terms of "reverse English." American experience with royal colonial administration had been such that, when the people themselves came into control after 1776, they reversed the model of the powerful chief executive. In organizing their new state governments they vested preponderant power in the legislative assembly. . . . [I]t took the nation approximately a century to overcome its fears and suspicions of centralized authority, even under popular and legislative control. The movement for administrative integration under a strengthened executive which has been the key to much of the progress [!] made in state government [meaning *national* government] during the past generation is a relatively recent development.

Ibid. at 10.

14 In the formulation of two prominent Incrementalists, the Internet's

> overriding logic—and the starting point for all policy discussions—must be as an institution operated on public interest values, *at bare minimum as a public utility*. . . .
>
> In sum, the Internet, left prey to capitalism—to having the hunt for profits dictate its development—has veered off in a direction that downplays and undermines, rather than exploits and accentuates, the most revolutionary and democratic [!] aspects of its technology. . . .
>
> Communication is more than an ordinary market. Indeed, it is properly not a market at all. It is more like air or water—*a form of public wealth, a commons.*

John Bellamy Foster & Robert W. McChesney, *The Internet's Unholy Marriage to Capitalism*, MONTHLY REVIEW: AN INDEPENDENT SOCIALIST MAGAZINE, vol. 62 issue 10 (March 2011) (emphasis added).

15 Robert W. McChesney, former editor and current director of Monthly Review (an independent socialist periodical) and co-founder of Free Press (an organization which has served as the point of the spear for "network neutrality"), *The U.S. Media Reform Movement: Going Forward*, MONTHLY REVIEW: AN INDEPENDENT SOCIALIST MAGAZINE, vol. 60 issue 4 (Sept., 2008). Mr. McChesney continues:

> [I]f the media system was inhospitable to democracy and social justice and we were serious about democracy and social justice, we had to change the media system. . . .
>
> The FCC has also agreed to hold public hearings in 2008 on the future of the Internet, due to activist pressure. In 2008, too, Representative Edward Markey (D-Mass.) and Chip Pickering (R-Miss.) co-sponsored *the Internet Freedom Act, legislation that not only calls for Network Neutrality* but requires the FCC to hold a minimum of eight major public "broadband summits" across the nation on the future of the Internet. *This is all revolutionary,* the democratization of media policymaking, and it may be the one great contribution of the movement to activists working in other areas of public life. . . .
>
> *No one thinks any longer that media reform is an issue to solve "after the revolution." Everyone understands that without media reform, there will be no revolution. . . .*
>
> This is our moment in the sun, our golden opportunity, and as political economists of the media we must seize it.

Ibid. (emphasis added). This idea that socialism must reorganize *all* systems of private communications into public, state-owned ones is really very old. Socialists have been trying to do this for centuries. *See, e.g.*, AUGUST BEBEL, SOCIETY OF THE FUTURE, Book 1, *Basic Laws of Socialist Society*, chap. 8, *Abolition of Trade, Reorganisation of Communications* (Progress Publishers, 1971) (1879) ("The telegraph and telephone systems, railways, postal service, river and marine fleets, trams, lorries and cars, airships and other flying apparatus—and whatever kinds of contrivances and vehicles there may be which make up society's communications—now become *social property*.") (emphasis original). http://www.marxists.org/archive/bebel/1879/society-future/ch01.htm.

[16] Perhaps Incrementalists within the federal government were also tired of ISPs making them wait longer for bandwidth-intensive, peer-to-peer, child pornography downloads? "[T]here is a general sense of disbelief when child pornography is found on a [federal] government system, and those outside of the [Office of The Inspectors General of the United States] are typically unaware of the extent to which it occurs." Council of Inspectors General on Integrity and Efficiency, THE JOURNAL OF PUBLIC INQUIRY, 11 (Spring/Summer 2010). Indeed! Hundreds—if not *thousands*—of Department of Defense employees were actively downloading child pornography in 2006. Bryan Bender, *Pentagon Lagged on Pursuing Porn Cases*, BOSTON.COM (Jan. 5, 2011). http://articles.boston.com/2011-01-05/news/29335792_1_child-pornography-investigation-pentagon. And yes—downloading child pornography was then, and remains now, a crime.

[17] 47 U.S.C. §§ 154 (a) and 154 (c).

[18] *In re Formal Complaint of Free Press & Pub. Knowledge*, 23 F.C.C.R. 13,028 (2008).

[19] In particular, they demanded un-delayed BitTorrent uploads and downloads. Again we are left to wonder why. *See, e.g.*, n. 16.

[20] 47 U.S.C. § 151 *et seq.*

[21] Under 47 U.S.C. § 154(i)—which must also be based upon express delegation of regulator authority (*Comcast Corp. v. FCC*, 600 F.3d 642, 652 *et seq.* (D.C. Cir. 2010)).

[22] *Comcast Corp. v. FCC*, 600 F.3d 642 (D.C. Cir. 2010).

[23] FCC FAQ, *Universal Service*, (Feb. 16, 2012) (emphasis added), http://www.fcc.gov/encyclopedia/universal-service.

[24] Barack H. Obama, *Statement by the President on Today's FCC Vote on Net Neutrality*, The White House (Dec. 21, 2010). http://www.whitehouse.gov/the-press-office/2010/12/21/statement-president-today-s-fcc-vote-net-neutrality.

[25] *In re Preserving the Open Internet Broadband Industry Practices*, GN Dkt. 09-191, WC Dkt. 07-52, FCC Dkt. 10-201 (Dec. 23, 2010).

[26] *Ibid.*

[27] *Ibid.* at ¶ 78.

[28] *Ibid.* at ¶ 63.

[29] *Ibid.* at p. 39 n. 204.

[30] *Just 21% Want FCC to Regulate Internet, Most Fear Regulation Would Promote Political Agenda*, RASMUSSEN REPORTS (Dec. 28, 2010).

[31] *Ibid.*

[32] Declan McCullagh, *Obama To Hand Commerce Dept. Authority Over Cybersecurity ID*, CNET (Jan. 7, 2011); Declan McCullagh, *Obama Moves Forward with Internet ID Plan*, CNET (April 15, 2011).

[33] Mark Hosenball, *Homeland Security Watches Twitter, Social Media*, REUTERS (Jan. 11, 2012).

[34] Brendan Sasso, *FCC Eyes Tax on Internet Service*, THE HILL (Aug. 26, 2012).

[35] *Ibid.*

[36] FCC Commission Document, *FCC Reforms, Modernizes Lifeline Program for Low-Income Americans* (Jan. 31, 2012), http://www.fcc.gov/document/fcc-reforms-modernizes-lifeline-program-low-income-americans. File on copy with author.

[37] *See supra* n. 8 and accompanying text.

[38] The Federal Reserve Act of 1913, Pub. L. 43, 63d Congress, H.R. 7837, § 1 (1913). http://www.llsdc.org/attachments/files/105/FRA-LH-PL63-43.pdf.

[39] *Ibid.*

[40] Bradley Keoun and Craig Torres, *Foreign Banks Tapped Fed's Secret Lifeline Most at Crisis Peak*, BLOOMBERG (April 1, 2011); Phil Kuntz & Bob Ivry, *Fed's Once-Secret Data Compiled by Bloomberg Released to Public*, BLOOMBERG (Dec. 22, 2011).

[41] Bradley Keoun and Craig Torres, *Foreign Banks Tapped Fed's Secret Lifeline Most at Crisis Peak*, BLOOMBERG (April 1, 2011); Phil Kuntz & Bob Ivry, *Fed's Once-Secret Data Compiled by Bloomberg Released to Public*, BLOOMBERG (Dec. 22, 2011).
[42] The White House Council on Environmental Quality, *Progress Report of the Interagency Climate Change Adaptation Task Force: Recommended Actions in Support of a National Climate Change Adaptation Strategy*, 71 (Oct. 5, 2010).
[43] *Ibid.*
[44] Mathew Cole, New Al Qaeda Video: American Muslims Should Buy Guns, Start Shooting People, ABCNEWS (June 3, 2011). http://abcnews.go.com/Blotter/al-qaeda-video-buy-automatic-weapons-start-shooting/story?id=13704264.
[45] Project No. 3U01MH066701, *Community-Based HIV VCT: South Africa* (2009). http://projectreporter.nih.gov/project_info_description.cfm?aid=7814411&icde=5021426.
[46] Well, not quite a million—$823,200.00 to be exact. Project No. 3U01MH066701, *Community-Based HIV VCT: South Africa* (2009). For NIMH details on this project, go to the NIMH project information page: http://projectreporter.nih.gov/project_info_details.cfm?aid=7814411&icde=5021426.
[47] *Ibid.*
[48] Tom Coburn, *The National Science Foundation: Under the Microscope*, (April 2011); Stephen Dinan, *Tax Dollars Fund Shrimp on Treadmills, Jell-O Wrestling in Antarctica*, THE WASHINGTON TIMES (May 26, 2011).
[49] Pub. L. 85-568, 72 Stat. 426 (1958).
[50] Charles Bolden, *Talk to Al Jazeera*, Interview with Imran Garda (June 30, 2010). http://english.aljazeera.net/programmes/talktojazeera/2010/07/201071122234471970.html.
[51] *See, e.g.*, U.S. Dept. of Justice, *A Review of ATF's Operation Fast and Furious and Related Matters*, OFFICE OF THE INSPECTOR GENERAL, OVERSIGHT AND REVIEW DIVISION 103 *et. seq.* (Sep., 2012).
[52] *See, e.g., Ibid.* at 103; 133-34.
[53] One of those guns was apparently used to murder Customs and Border Protection Agent Brian Terry on December 14, 2010—which is how Operation Fast and Furious came to light in the first place. *Ibid.* at 103 (Sep., 2012).
[54] *See, e.g., Ibid.*
[55] Social Security Administration, *Request for Quotation*, OFFICE OF ACQUISITION AND GRANTS (Aug. 7, 2012), copy on file with author. At least as of September 20, 2012, the SSA's *Request for Quotation* can still be found on the Federal Business Opportunities website, *Request for Quote for Ammunition*, Solicitation No. SSA-RFQ-12-1851, https://www.fbo.gov/index?s=opportunity&mode=form&id=6c39a2a9f00a10187a1432388a3301e5&tab=core&_cview=0&fb_source=message.
[56] Social Security Administration, *Request for Quotation*, OFFICE OF ACQUISITION AND GRANTS (Aug. 7, 2012), copy on file with author. *See Ibid.*
[57] Office of External Relations, *Social Security's OIG Responds to Concerns Over Ammunition Procurement*, OFFICE OF THE INSPECTOR GENERAL (Aug. 16, 2012).
[58] "From fiscal year 2002 through fiscal year 2011, Federal agencies published about 38,000 final rules in the *Federal Register*." Office of Management and Budget, *2012 Draft Report to Congress on the Benefits and Costs of Federal Regulations*, OFFICE OF INFORMATION AND REGULATORY AFFAIRS 10 (2012). *See also* Office of Management and Budget, *2011 Report to Congress on the Benefits and Costs of Federal Regulations*, OFFICE OF INFORMATION AND REGULATORY AFFAIRS 12 (2011).
[59] Penny Starr, *Under Obama, 11,327 Pages of Federal Regulations Added*, CNS NEWS (Sep. 10, 2012).
[60] To be perfectly fair, the U.S. Patent and Trademark Office (USPTO) is not an *independent* agency; as Under Secretary of Commerce for Intellectual Property and Director of the USPTO, Chairman Kappos serves at the pleasure of the President. But as we have seen, for all other intents and purposes such traditional, executive agencies function in the same manner as their formally independent counterparts.
[61] Incremental socialists answer "Yes!" to all of the foregoing questions. For example, AFL-CIO President Richard Trumka demands total independence from Middle Americans as follows: "We call on leaders from both sides of the aisle to defend the independence of the National

Labor Relations Board. Political interference with any independent agency sets a dangerous precedent that should not be tolerated." Richard Trumka, *Labor Praises "Modest" Improvements in Union Regulations: Statement by AFL-CIO President Richard Trumka on NLRB Election Standards*, POLITICAL AFFAIRS (June 21, 2011)

4

Muzzling Middle America

History shows that guns don't kill people, language does.

—Thomas McGowan[i]

"Speak when you're spoken to!" the Queen sharply interrupted her.

"But if everybody obeyed that rule," said Alice, who was always ready for a little argument, "and if you only spoke when you were spoken to, and the other person always waited for *you* to begin, you see nobody would ever say anything, so that—"

"Ridiculous!" cried the Queen. "Why, don't you see, child—" here she broke off with a frown, and after thinking for a minute, suddenly changed the subject of the conversation.

—Lewis Carroll[ii]

WHY SUBMIT TO THE PAINSTAKING demands of rebranding? Why the meticulous linguistic campaign? Why hide on the Democrat Bus? Why the assiduous effort to create a new, unconstitutional, unelected, fourth branch of government? Why the diligence in shipping decisions "of, by, and for the People" over to the new, unelected, Fourth Head?

In short: *Why Incrementalism?*

There are myriad political considerations. Many of these we have already investigated, and most have to do with irksome Middle Americans. Which is to say, with so many Middle Americans—and their consistent rejection of

[i] Thomas McGowan, *The Dangers of Violent Political Language*, THE COMMERCIAL APPEAL (Jan. 14, 2011).

[ii] LEWIS CARROLL, ALICE'S ADVENTURES IN WONDERLAND *AND* THROUGH THE LOOKING-GLASS AND WHAT ALICE FOUND THERE 220 (Hugh Haughton ed., Penguin Classics 1998) (1872) (this particular passage is taken from *Through the Looking-Glass*).

socialism—socialists' options are limited. (The horror of squirrel hunting weighs heavily in the balance.)

But socialists content themselves with the gradual gains of Incrementalism for another reason as well.

Socialists know a secret: Many of Incrementalism's modifications are a one way street. Socialists know that once a nation drives down certain political lanes it can *never* come back—at least, *not legally*; not through elective means. Socialists know that citizens' expectations soon accommodate new federal regulations, new group "rights," new redistributions, increasing federal power, and consequent reductions in liberty. Citizens conform quite rapidly to such changes. Indeed they must—or they are fined and jailed. Hence today's Incrementalist modifications become tomorrow's *custom*.

And therefore also tomorrow's *culture*. This holds true where Incrementalist modifications represent seemingly small deviations from yesterday's practice, appear limited in scope, or adjust only certain circumscribed portions of American life. At the same time, large deviations from former liberties—when indulged in for even a brief period—set the stage for even greater, future governmental abuses. In either case, as citizens' expectations conform to Incrementalist programs, those programs embed themselves in American culture—and become essentially repeal-proof. Like Imperial Rome's wheat dole. (Sure, Rome reformed the wheat dole multiple times in various ways—but the wheat dole could never be abandoned no matter how dire the Empire's financial situation. It had become an appendage of Roman *culture*.)

The cultural permanence of Incrementalist social programs is well-attested but seldom considered outside socialist circles. Take Social Security for example: the largest Ponzi scheme created by man, a tremendous source of entitlement fraud, well-known to be bankrupt, and less than seventy-six years old (as of 2011). Not only is Social Security *itself* bankrupt, but the unfunded and "guaranteed" obligations it creates upon federal finance have largely bankrupt the entire nation. To the tune of $21.4 *trillion* dollars.[1] Such a sum boggles the mind; one requires scientific notation and astrophysical comparisons to get a handle on a number of such scale. For the unlettered such a sum is entirely incomprehensible. Divided into fathomable chunks, this unfunded social security liability comes out to roughly $183,400.00 per American household. (Median annual income per household was $49,445.00 in 2010.[2] And it has decreased since then.) That is how much *your household* owes for one, single government program: Social Security.

But you won't find a candidate for political office running on a platform to *repeal* Social Security! (Or Medicare either, for that matter—which is even younger, at 46 years of age, yet represents *another* $24.8 trillion in unfunded obligations, for a *further* $212,500.00 debt per American household.) The boldest of politicians suggest *reform* of some sort—but never repeal! And the reforms politicians suggest are generally further *expansions* of Social Security (or Medicare)—or else completely new obligations to fill boundary cases or loopholes which old programs overlooked.

Why do politicians favor reform over repeal of bankrupt social programs? For a very simple political reason: Politicians know too many constituents possess settled expectations of participating in that group "right" when they turn sixty-five (or is it sixty-seven now?). After all, tax-paying constituents have contributed to the Social Security "fund" for their entire lives—and they expect to receive a payout. (If only a Social Security *fund* really existed! We wouldn't be on the hook for $21.4 trillion!) In other words, constituents are *accustomed* to Social Security. Social Security has become a fixture of American *culture*. And as a fixture of American culture, the socialist pension becomes permanent. (A fact in which socialists take great pride.[3])

In the not-too-distant future people will feel the same about Obamacare. ("How did anyone afford health insurance before the government forced insurers to ignore preexisting conditions?") And someday soon people will feel accustomed to Dodd-Frank financial regulatory "reform," too. ("How did people dare invest back when federal regulators didn't identify and shutter risky firms?")

The cultural permanence of federal *agencies* and *regulations* work in much the same way. Can you imagine a candidate for political office proposing the privatization of all functions of the FAA (the Federal Aviation Administration, a tentacle of the Fourth Head governing all aviation-related activities in the United States)? Never mind the conflict of interest created when airlines and pilots become functional customers of the FAA. Never mind that FAA bosses take time out during mandatory staff meetings to urge FAA employees to hop on the Democrat Bus in the coming election.[4] Never mind that air traffic controllers regularly sleep on the job.[5] And watch movies, play video games, and gamble online.[6] Just make a single FAA officer resign; he can take the fall for systemic negligence![7]

You won't hear calls for privatization of airline regulation even after aviation catastrophes. People just feel safer if an all-knowing, all-powerful federal bureau regulates air safety. They feel so because they have become accustomed to federal administrative agency regulation. Once exposed to seemingly inveterate governmental presence, a population simply cannot imagine living without it. It becomes a fixture of culture. And once a component of culture, federal regulation is rendered quite permanent.

Yes, Incrementalism provides far more than mere *political solutions* to socialism's difficulties in America. Incrementalist modifications become American custom. And once American custom, such modifications soon become American *culture*.

And culture has advantages.

Advantages of Cultural Transformation

Culture goes practically unnoticed precisely because of its thoroughgoing pervasiveness. Like the fish that swims deep and fails to realize he is wet, the great majority of people are fully submerged in contemporary culture—and thus oblivious to its very existence.

Much like gravity. We know that water tends to run downhill; from high to low. This tendency is rarely "noticed." It is simply *assumed.* And it is never questioned. We only rarely ask *why* water runs downhill—and we almost never model the origin of that phenomenon with accuracy (in non-scalar form: $\mathbf{F}_g = -Gm_1m_2\ \hat{\mathbf{r}}_{12}/|r_2 - r_1|^2$). Gravity is so deeply embedded in daily life that it is easier to simply accept all resulting phenomena as heuristic (among other things, that water runs downhill) than to interrogate their actual cause (gravity). Because water *does* run downhill. It just does.

Because culture is so deeply embedded in daily life, it is—like gravity—*practically invisible.* Because it is so pervasive, culture is also—like gravity—*rarely examined.* And because it is assumed, culture remains—like gravity—*virtually unquestioned.* These attributes make culture an exceptionally attractive tool for advancing Incrementalist objectives.

An example may be illustrative. Every one knows that (1) breast cancer is the most common type of cancer, and (2) breast cancer kills more people annually than any other. No one asks why; it just *is.* And so professional athletes wear pink socks, or pink gloves, or pink-highlighted uniforms. And ubiquitous pink ribbons decorate cars, windows, and lapels. To raise awareness! And federal research dollars are naturally spent disproportionately on solving the riddle of breast cancer.

There is only one problem: Beast cancer is *not* the most common type of cancer. And breast cancer does *not* kill more people than any other type.[iii] And most people are unaware of these truths, and inordinately distressed by the risk of breast cancer—*because they are submerged in a culture which overemphasizes the female bosom.* The cultural *cause* for our overemphasis on breast cancer remains practically invisible. It is rarely examined. And it is almost never interrogated.

Likewise, everyone knows that diversity is a glorious and astonishing virtue—the diadem in the crown of the human soul. No one seems to know why, and no one seems to be asking why—it just *is.* Of course, what everyone fails to recognize is that diversity is a pet value of that culture in which we live; while diversity has been praised to the skies for a few decades, it is not self-evident truth. It is merely a passing fashion in contemporary American culture—

[iii] National Cancer Institute, *SEER Cancer Statistics Review 1975-2007*, (2007). http://seer.cancer.gov/csr/1975_2007/results_merged/topic_race_ethnicity.pdf.

something akin to eighteenth century Americans' fondness for powdered wigs. And so the origins of our emphasis on diversity go safely unnoticed.

But the Incrementalist advantages of transforming culture are not limited to culture's general invisibility, or to its concomitant abstention from popular examination and interrogation. Culture offers further benefits: Many people fail to recognize their own, personal independence from the culture in which they swim. That is, people regularly fail to make a distinction between contemporary culture and their own personal views, individual values, inner goals, and private beliefs. Socialism knows this well.[iv] Indeed, to this end socialism explicitly intends to *direct culture*—and thereby to simultaneously determine all views, all values, all goals, and all beliefs. To complete the socialist revolution.[8] To reify the hive mentality. Indeed, directing culture is a fundamental platform of socialism—one which socialists refer to as The Party's "vital and proud history of *cultural work*."[9] Or, in more candid moments, simply as The Party's "*cultural programming*."[10]

And there are still further Incrementalist advantages to cultural transformations. People tend naturally to focus on their own, frenetic, day-to-day lives. They are limited to one lifetime, after all! And so people's attention is focused narrowly on the here and the now; tasks requiring a few minutes, hours, or occasionally weeks to perform. Tasks requiring multiple lifetimes to unfold are therefore rarely noticed. Meanwhile, culture is a ponderous beast and changes slowly over time. Revolutions in culture can take many lifetimes to complete. Indeed, in order to perceive revolutionary changes in culture (and the great gains of Incrementalism!), one must be willing to step back from the immediacy of the present and take an historical perspective. This requires research, or at least regular reading—tasks which many find unamusing. As a result, most people—even those few who *do* consistently recognize the existence and import of culture, and who *do* constantly remain aware of their personal independence from it—nevertheless generally *fail to recognize the direction and speed of cultural drift.* And so long as cultural *drift* goes largely unnoticed by a frantic, present-living public, the grand and remarkable work of Incrementalist cultural *guidance* goes unnoticed as well.

Even in that rarified air where cultural drift *is* recognized, there remain yet further Incrementalist advantages to cultural transformations. Cultural transformations appear to be *spontaneous* outgrowths of the times—and therefore ostensibly (1) *undirected* and also (2) *representative of majority will.* Who

---

[iv] To be precise, orthodox socialists deny that individual persons have any views, values, goals, or beliefs *aside from those which are thrust upon them by the culture in which they live.* This concept has been referred to by socialists as "political consciousness," which is one facet of socialism's overarching hive mentality. *See* TEA WITH SOCIALISTS, Book I (The Hive Mentality), chap. 2, *The Hive Mentality.*

would fight against the spontaneous expression of majority will? Zeitgeist is democracy at its finest, is it not? Not even a vote is required! And so, even cultural drift which *is recognized* nonetheless avoids public scrutiny. (But are all cultural transformations necessarily spontaneous, undirected, and representative of majority will? These are threshold inquiries of the first order!)

Incrementalist cultural reorganizations have one final advantage: Culture has unimaginable inertia. So even when a majority recognize some aspect of culture, identify it as unsavory, and agree to extirpate it, it may well not be eradicated for generations. Slavery provides a nice American example, but there are so many others. The point is that Incrementalist gains in the cultural arena are far more lasting than, say, independent agencies' funding of sick shrimp marathons. And there is reason to doubt whether some Incrementalist cultural transformations can ever be rolled back—unless, as was the case with slavery, a substantial proportion of Americans decide they are prepared to die to change it. (That level of conviction has proven rare in recent American history—so Incrementalist gains of the cultural variety appear quite safe!)

Practically invisible, in both essence and trajectory, unquestioned when perceived, immeasurable in inertia, and ostensibly a free expression of majority will, Culture is a mighty weapon.

One which Incrementalism intends to wield.[11]

Silencing Subjects

Chieftains, monarchs, maliks, caliphs, khans, huángdìs, shoguns, sultans, shahs, tsars, emperors, warlords, and caesars—in a word, rulers of all types—have always sought to eliminate opposition to their own authority. And from the earliest times rulers perceived the most dangerous threat to their power lay in the simplest and most natural of means: *independent thinking among their own subjects.*

Ideas with the humblest of beginnings, sprouting from the mind of one or a few subjects, could spread across the land and take root in an entire population. Ideas could grow quickly. In little time they could overhang the rule of the status quo. When mature, ideas could fall violently upon the status quo—destroying rulers, empires, and modes of governing alike. (The idea of replacing dynastic monarchs with elective government, for example, put a good number of rulers out of a job . . . .)

As a consequence, rulers have always preferred their subjects think *uniformly.* To be precise, rulers have always preferred that their subjects uniformly support the ruler's ongoing dominion.

But no matter what rulers did to promote uniform thinking, those dratted little subjects had their own individual opinions, their own private assumptions, their own peculiar ways of thinking. With independence of thought, subjects sometimes stumbled upon very dangerous ideas. Sometimes one or two subjects suggested that life might be better under a *different ruler*. Or under a *different method* of rule. Or simply under *less rule* by the same ruler and same method. At other times one or two subjects challenged *the assumptions* on which the ruler's authority had been maintained. Or the *legitimacy* of the ruler's authority under those assumptions. Or the most reliable *supporters* of contemporary rule. Or the *expectations* of their fellow subjects for government.

Rulers would have loved to nip such ideas in the bud—at their source, in the individual mind, as they put forth the first tender shoots. But individual thoughts were, so long as they remained within the originative mind, both tasteless and odorless. They were invisible and mute. And one couldn't feel them, either. So rulers were unable to detect ideas at their root. And even if rulers could have detected ideas at the moment they first sprouted, mind control did not appear feasible: Those outrageous little apostates just went right on thinking independently no matter how rulers tried to make them conform. Even when wizards, witches, shamans, soothsayers, sorcerers, genies, magicians, medicinemen, enchanters, and priests were consulted and well paid for their services—those cursed subjects kept on thinking for themselves.

But early on, rulers hit upon a partial solution to the dangerous independence of subjects' thought: Rulers would simply *silence* any dangerous ideas which made themselves audible! After all, before ideas could grow to dangerous proportions, they had to be *communicated* to other persons. Subjects didn't possess a collective consciousness; they thought discretely, individual by individual. Individuals only rarely hit upon identical ideas, and when this did happen it never occurred simultaneously. So to make anything big happen, ideas had to be communicated from one individual to the next until a number of subjects could cooperatively act on the new idea. Yes—it was through dialog that dangerous ideas spread and festered! And so, rulers have always attempted to control what was spoken.

In primitive times, rulers seized subjects who offended through speech and simply cut out their tongues. With the low rate of literacy endemic to the age, that buried (former) speakers' ideas for good! And it provided a lasting, living reminder to all who were tempted to speak out against the ruler's authority (or theories upon which it was based) in the future.

As civilization matured, rulers had to appear more reasonable. So they seized those who spoke out against their rule (or the theories on which it was based) and had them drawn, hung, disemboweled, and quartered. The quarters could then be paraded dramatically through the largest villages, and hung over the gates and bridges of principal cities, as an admonition to all who were similarly inclined to speak their mind. This method had a profound effect on witnesses to the speaker's punishment—but unfortunately in this case, the admonition to silence deteriorated along with the speaker's quartered remains.

In America, our Predecessors decided that such practices should be confined to the barbarous past. They had only recently dealt with Parliament's heavy-handed restrictions on speech—which, truth be told, still prescribed drawing and quartering. Our Predecessors made the old British practice of drawing and quartering unconstitutional.[v] And they forever freed political speech from all federal restraints.[vi] This effort to free political speech was central to our Predecessors' new plan for representative government: (1) From now on, it was to be *the People* who made the decisions; (2) Only through open and public debate could a majority solution, representing the will of the People, be determined; and (3) Good decisions could be identified only through a frank contest of ideas where winning ideas were recognized, and mistaken views displaced. For all these reasons, (4) Citizens' individual right to share their political opinions—*no matter how offensive to the sensitivities of others*—was constitutionally preserved in spite of the cost to federal authority.[12]

In modern times *outside* America, however, monolithic rulers remained free from Constitutional restraints on their power over speech. Outside America, ruling policy remained much as it had been before: *silence all opposition!* Due to Western squeamishness about torturous punishments, public relations suffered when rulers used the old treatments for politically dangerous speech. So rulers further refined their methods. They simply locked away forever or, alternatively, quietly put to death those who dared to speak against their rule (or the theories upon which it was based). And in the twentieth century, this latter procedure was perfected on an industrial scale. It was carried out with Taylorized vigor even within those nations where industrialization had not been achieved in other respects! Indeed, the new procedure for silencing opposition throve especially among economically primitive, pre-industrial, socialist nations such as Russia, China, Cambodia, Cuba, and North Korea. In the twentieth century, dissenting subjects living there disappeared *by the tens of millions.*

The quiet, twentieth-century method of silencing subjects proved quite effective at rooting out the most dangerous of speakers. (And it still goes on today in the twenty-first century.) But unfortunately, because the twentieth-century method was carried out in relative secrecy—in prison isolators and "special" camps—it provided the remaining subjects with less than an ideal reminder to keep quiet. So more and more subjects had to be rounded up and silenced. As a result, the twentieth-century method of silencing subjects was quite taxing on socialist workforces. (That is, socialist workforces simply disappeared.) And, as a result, it became quite taxing on socialist economy. (Even pre-industrial socialist economies collapsed.)

---

[v] U.S. CONST. amend. VIII.

[vi] U.S. CONST. amend. I.

Until, that is, socialist rulers rediscovered the economic potential of slave labor—and erected hard labor camps across the tundra for political prisoners.

Two birds with one stone!

Silencing Americans

Once socialist rulers hit upon hard labor camps, the twentieth-century method of silencing subjects became a great success.

American socialism requires monolithic government too, of course. And monolithic government demands silence. But unlike other socialist countries, the disappearance of discontented speakers might be noticed here in America. It was the usual problem: those darned Middle Americans and their precious Constitution. So in this difficult field—the field of silencing *American* subjects—Incrementalism settled upon an incremental yet effective, *nonpolitical* solution. It settled upon a *cultural* solution.

Incrementalist overseers in America determined to simply exaggerate a virtue which Middle Americans already admired: *politeness*. That is, the proactive eschewal of offense to others through speech or action—and especially through speech.

Alternatively referred to as public civility or courteousness, politeness had always been viewed as a subsidiary virtue: It had value so long as it did not trample other, more important virtues like justice, candor, sincerity, honesty, truthfulness, courage, integrity, responsibility, prudence, reason, logic, philomathy, wisdom, and autonomy—which were always in danger of being trampled by politeness. (Indeed, politeness often turns up as a socially-acceptable disguise for injustice, guile, duplicity, deceit, cowardice, irresponsibility, carelessness, vacuity, ignorance, naïveté, and servility.) Or virtues like charity, chastity, humility, salubrity, modesty, and piety—which occasionally found themselves in opposition to politeness. And you certainly wouldn't name politeness to your top 100 virtues list (unless as a perilous, socially-comfortable, and habitual rival to loftier virtues).

But Incrementalist overseers would! In fact, Incrementalists magnified politeness until it swallowed up all other virtues. And politeness became a pet virtue of our age.

Once lifted to such heights, politeness had an extraordinary effect: Any remark that might possibly be construed as offensive *to someone*—whether that someone was present or not—became absolutely off-limits. The *un*offended began to take it upon themselves—as surrogates for the hypothetical, non-present person who *might* take offense—*to be offended by proxy.*

And then politeness hit its Incrementalist stride: Any remark that could possibly be interpreted as questioning the plan of tacit socialist revolution; or the political, ethical, cultural, or intellectual foundations upon which it rests; whether directly or indirectly; whether spoken publicly or privately; became utterly taboo. Because *someone* might take offense if they heard such things. Namely, *a supposed beneficiary of group "rights" proposed by the unspoken revolution.*[vii] (And if no supposed beneficiary of group "rights" who *might* be offended were present, then someone who wasn't offended at all would nobly leap into the breach—and be *offended in their place.*) The conversation was over—and speech dangerous to Incrementalism triumphantly suppressed.

Over time, the cult of politeness grew into a cultural institution. In order to assist American subjects in remembering and applying the principle of *Politeness Über Alles*, Incrementalists translated their politeness campaign into opaque yet catchy Sloganese, like the following:

"Spread the word

"To end the word."[viii]

Once politeness had been cast in dazzling gold; once the idol was erected, and subjects had been taught how to perform obeisance to it, how to prostrate themselves before it, how to make offerings of pretended offense; once Incrementalists proclaimed "Behold your god, which brought you up out of the land of England!"—politeness received a new and terrifying name worthy of its divinity, creative power, and ineffable influence: "POLITICAL CORRECTNESS." (And this was a perfectly appropriate appellation, given that—politically speaking—there *was* only one correct view. *The rulers' view.* And that view entailed adoration of Incrementalist plans . . . and due reverence for socialism's supposed beneficiaries.)

With the other virtues safely subdued, Incrementalist overseers then *taught the subjects to police themselves* where political correctness was concerned. Incrementalists instructed subjects that for lesser offenses, speaking out against the silent revolution or its beneficiaries should be punishable by

---

[vii] Who are the supposed beneficiaries of modern socialism? As we have seen, they are no longer merely "workers," as classical socialists insisted. Under Incrementalism, the expected beneficiaries of socialism are extended to include also "women, indigenous peoples, black people, young people, children, pensioners [i.e., the elderly], people of diverse sexual orientations [i.e., the LGBT community], people with disabilities, and others." Marta Harnecker, *Latin America & Twenty-First Century Socialism: Inventing to Avoid Mistakes*, MONTHLY REVIEW: AN INDEPENDENT SOCIALIST MAGAZINE, vol. 62 issue 3 (July-August, 2010).

Marta is not alone in identifying the foregoing supposed beneficiaries of socialism. Sam Webb, for example, identifies the following beneficiaries: "the working class . . . coupled [to] communities of the nationally and racially oppressed, women, . . . youth[,] . . . seniors, family farmers [i.e., farming subsidy recipients], professional[s] and intellectuals, gays and lesbians, etc. . . ." Sam Webb, *Reflections on Socialism*, 14 (Communist Party USA, June 4, 2005).

[viii] *See* www.r-word.org, noting with approval that, "On October 5, 2010, U.S. President Barack Obama officially signed bill S. 2781 into federal law. Rosa's Law, which takes its name and inspiration for 9-year-old Rosa Marcellino, removes the terms 'mental retardation' and 'mentally retarded' from federal health, education and labor policy and replaces them with people first language 'individual with an intellectual disability' and 'intellectual disability.'"

Wonderful: Now we can abandon another perfectly legitimate, medical term to the scrapheap of playground taunts. Along with moron, imbecile, idiot, feeble-minded, and all other medical terminology related to subnormal cognition.

ostracism. In exemplary cases, punishment would also entail pecuniary fines. And for more egregious, public violations, the forfeiture of one's career should be required.

Teaching the subjects to police themselves was a fun game! Why, you could take a world renowned surgeon, like Dr. Lazar Greenfield—President of the American College of Surgeons, eponymous inventor of the Greenfield Filter (which by preventing pulmonary emboli during surgery has saved many thousands of lives), author of more than 350 scientific articles published in peer reviewed journals, professor emeritus of surgery at the University of Michigan, and Editor of Surgery News—and *make him resign* for writing an editorial citing a scientific, peer-reviewed study[13] documenting the psychological benefits to women of vaginal exposure to the (recently-discovered) anti-depressive properties of semen.[14]

You see, scientific veracity is not the issue.[15] The mere fact of semen's antidepressant effects could be construed as *sexist*. Its mention might possibly offend female surgeons.[16] (To be sure, there are more male surgeons than female surgeons—and Dr. Greenfield is a *male* surgeon.) Or women in general.[17] (A group prominently positioned as supposed beneficiaries of group "rights."[18]) And lesbians in particular.[19] (Another group positioned as supposed beneficiaries of group "rights,"[20] and one whose access to the benefits of semen is necessarily limited.)

No matter that Dr. Greenfield had had "an exemplary career . . . as a longtime mentor and advocate of women in surgery." No matter that, as Dr. Mary Hawn noted post editorial, "he went out of his way to recruit women on the trainee and faculty level." No matter that fellow professor of surgery at the University of Michigan, Dr. Diane Simeone, observed after his resignation, "he has always been a role model for supporting women in surgery."[21] And no matter that he apologized profusely for his offending speech.

What outrages did Dr. Greenfield commit? What atrocities did he utter? Let the impartial reader judge: The offending editorial is reproduced in full in the endnotes below.[22]

The result of the Greenfield campaign was exemplary: "Many surgeons chose not to comment on [Dr. Greenfield's resignation], for fear of professional repercussions."[23] Why, that was precisely the effect Incrementalism hoped for! *Silence* among the subjects! *Fear* to speak one's mind! All based on the threat of imminent, culturally-enforced reprisals!

Teaching the subjects to police themselves was fun in other contexts, too—especially among thick-skinned audiences, at fora enjoying traditional privileges to speak freely. Like on the basketball court, for example. Everyone knows that National Basketball Association players habitually scream any profanity that comes to mind at other players, at fans, and at referees alike. Trash-talking is part of the game of basketball, and possesses a long and storied pedigree. Trash-talking is how you get into an opponent's head, how you silence opposing fans, and how you influence referees. It is a talent shared by and celebrated in the greatest basketball players of all time. Jordan. Bird. Johnson. Barkley. Payton.

Mothers, family members with lifetime disabilities, IQs, and any four-letter words you please are fair game on the hardwood.

But don't blaspheme a group singled out for special privileges under socialism! (Or rather, don't get caught blaspheming *on camera*, by vigilant lip-readers.) Do that and you will be publicly fined and nationally humiliated. It was in this spirit that Kobe Bryant was recently fined $100,000.00 for disputing a referee's call by referring to the referee as a "faggot."[ix] As summarized by NBA Commissioner and resident Incrementalist David Stern,

> Kobe Bryant's comment during last night's game was *offensive and inexcusable*. . . . Such a distasteful term should never be tolerated. . . . Kobe and everyone associated with the NBA know that insensitive or derogatory comments are not acceptable and *have no place in our* game or *society*.[24]

What Commissioner Stern actually meant to say was that any term at all, no matter how derogatory, insensitive, or offensive, is absolutely condoned by the NBA—unless the root of that word is "fag." (And players: Don't respond to a drunk, incessantly abusive, and harassing *fan* with a term using that root, either—or you will receive the Kobe treatment.[25])

Don't misunderstand: I am no fan of Kobe Bryant. He epitomizes conceit. He is also a whiner, a complainer, and an overrated basketball player. But this is not the point. The point is that political correctness has the power to shame, fine, and silence even the brashest of megalomaniacal sports celebrities. This is no small feat. And if political correctness overwhelms even sports megastars—who are forced to approach the interview microphone with tail between legs, to apologize at length, and to admit that the punishment they received for such speech was just[26]—then how much influence does political correctness have over the rest of us?

As observed by Incrementalist President and CEO of the Phoenix Suns Rick Welts after another fag-fining-incident, "It's another teachable moment. It should generate more intelligent dialogue."[27] What Mr. Welts actually meant to say was that it's another opportunity to teach the subjects *not* to speak. That it should generate more intelligent *silence*. And when handled in this way by the NBA, it certainly does that.

And don't forget to check your headset occasionally! If the microphone gets stuck in the "broadcast" position, even romantic preferences you express "privately" may result in termination of your employment. Like the twelve-

---

[ix] Yes, members of the LGBT community constitute yet further beneficiaries of socialism, according to Incrementalists themselves. *See supra* n. vii.

year Southwest pilot with a squeaky-clean record who recently confided in a co-pilot that, while he would like to party with airline staff, differences in age, weight, and sexual orientation made it difficult to find common ground.

Why, here was another "teachable moment"! (Yes, Incrementalism intends to instruct subjects on the dangers of speech in *private* conversations, too.) The Southwest pilot's romantic preference for women of similar age and weight was yet another example of homophobia, sexism, ageism, and insensitivity among the subjects! It was yet another assault on supposed beneficiaries of socialism![28] Fortunately, an administrative agency (the ever-vigilant Federal Aviation Administration) was quick to pitch in by identifying the offending speech and sending an audio recording of it to Southwest Airlines "for action"—i.e., so Southwest could handle this dire air-safety emergency itself.[29] The FAA also courageously (and publicly) resolved that "the FAA expects a higher level of professionalism from flight crews." And the CEO of Southwest was quick to add, "I am personally deeply disappointed that one of our employees *would think*—much less say—such things."[30] Only one solution was appropriate in such a case: suspension of employment.

But for Incrementalists, the most teachable moments of all do not concern scientific veracity, trash-talking during athletic contests, or ostensibly private locker-room talk. The most teachable moments of all concern political speech itself. This is why we subjects are admonished—particularly when Incrementalists are preparing for, or recovering from, a drubbing at the polls—that political discourse is frightfully dangerous and frequently leads *to murder*.[31] (Or, in Sloganese, "HATE SPEECH = MURDER."[32]) This is why we subjects are instructed that political rhetoric must never employ certain metaphors or analogies, which might be misunderstood by the masses (or by lone sociopaths) and thereby prompt *murder*.[33] This is why we are told that there is "a problem with current political discourse." That "the type of violent rhetoric that is now common on Fox News and talk radio creates a climate of fear, suspicion, and paranoia that could lead to another Oklahoma City."[34] That political speech must never be provocative or offensive. That political speech must be careful and circumscribed.

And when it comes to political speech touching socialist programs or their intended beneficiaries, phrases like "entitlement society" and "poor work ethic" are imputed by Incrementalists to be *racist euphemisms*—allegedly used by speakers to "deny any responsibility for the racial content of [their] message."[35] And so are historical, cultural, and legal phrases such as "Founding Fathers," "Constitution," and "old-fashioned American values."[36] (Wouldn't want to remind the sheeple of their legal independence or liberty-loving past.)

But why stop there? According to the Chief Diversity Officer of the U.S. State Department (a revered position within the Fourth Head!), phrases like "holding down the fort" are racist, too.[37] Likewise the phrase "rule of thumb" is sexist.[38] According to Chris Matthews, referencing the city of "Chicago" is racist.[39] And according to principals at public secondary schools, even the phrase "peanut butter sandwich" is racist.[x]

Yes, Incrementalists openly lament the traditional American freedom of political speech, which "in many other developed countries [is] not allowed."[40]

The Politics of "Politeness"

That "peanut butter sandwich" is considered racist is no exaggeration. This "politeness" business is deadly serious. And particularly when it comes to politics.

So even if you are the senior *political* analyst, on a cable *news* program, during *political debate*, don't use a potty-word to negatively characterize how you thought a sitting President acted! Even when directly asked for your opinion. And don't expect the seven-second-broadcast-delay-with-censorship-option to save your career, either. Even if you ask beforehand whether it is safe to say something that will *need* censoring. And even if you are told "Well we have it, we can use it, right Alex? Yeah, sure . . . . Alex, hit the button. I'm behind you, if you fall down I'm gonna catch you. So go ahead"—say what you feel: Alex and the rest of the techies are ready to bleep it out.[41] When you let fly with offensive political analysis your news anchor peers will visibly recoil, in hopes that the stain of your insensitive speech will not touch them. They will wring their hands in terror. They will smirk blankly and lick nervous lips, like a child trying to distance herself from the four-letter word a playmate just let slip in front of daddy.

Don't waste your time sincerely apologizing.

In response, the Presidential Mouthpiece will make a statement: "The comment that was made was inappropriate. It would be inappropriate to say that about any president of either party. And on behalf of the White House, I expressed that sentiment to executives at the network."[42] You will be "suspended indefinitely" by the cable news network.[43] Because such comments are "completely inappropriate and unacceptable."[44] Because the First Amendment rights to freedom "of speech" and "of the press" no longer matter: they have been overrun by the cultural imperative of political correctness.

And if you are the host of a *politically* themed, nationally syndicated talk radio program, *beware.*

When a thirty-something law student testifies before congress[45] that women at Georgetown University Law Center need student insurance to

---

[x] How could the phrase "peanut butter sandwich" be construed as a racist? Verenice Gutierrez, principal at Harvey Scott (K-8) in Northeast Portland, explains the racism inherent in that phrase as follows: "What about Somali or Hispanic students, who might not eat sandwiches?" *See, e.g.*, Jennifer Anderson, *Schools Beat the Drum for Equity*, PORTLAND TRIBUNE (Sep. 5, 2012).

provide $3,000.00 worth of contraception during three years of legal studies, don't state the obvious. Don't suggest that the costs of sexual gratification lie with the pleasured. Don't note that Ms. Sandra Fluke is a practiced provocateur.[46] Don't point out that Georgetown is a private Jesuit institution—and therefore fundamentally opposed to contraception in all its forms.[xi] Don't illustrate that, even if contraception really *did* cost $1,000.00/year in D.C., that's a drop in the bucket compared to a Georgetown legal education (which Georgetown Law's Financial Aid Office estimates will cost $73,500.00 over the nine-month 2012-2013 academic year[47]—a rate which, when annualized like health insurance,[xii] comes to $98,000.00 per annum).

And especially don't calculate how many sexual encounters $3,000.00 of birth control would cover over a three-year legal education. (For example: As of March 13, 2012, two packages having 36 units each of Trojan® ENZ® lubricated condoms can be bought on Amazon for $18.08. Which comes to 25.1¢/unit. Which, at Ms. Fluke's recommendation of $1,000.00 of birth control/year, yields *3982 encounters per year*. Which is *76 encounters per week*, every week of the year. Which is more than *10 encounters per day*—every day of the year, for three years straight. Which is a lot of playtime for someone who claims to be a fulltime law student.)

And don't suggest condoms are a shortsighted contraceptive solution. Don't note that an unlimited amount of playtime can be had for roughly $9 per month. (Which is the cost of the pill at Target pharmacies in the D.C. area.[48] Which comes to $108 per year. For a grand total of $324 over a three-year tenure at law school. Not $3,000.00.)

Don't note that enterprising law students can get the pill *for free*. Don't allude to the unlimited playtime which can be achieved by visiting any of a number of federally-funded Planned Parenthood clinics near Georgetown's law school campus.[49] (As everyone knows, Planned Parenthood specializes in providing "free" contraception as a "public service." And Planned Parenthood's Presidential Clinic stands within 1.6 miles of the Law Center![xiii] That is within easy walking distance—even for Ms. Fluke and her "underprivileged" law student friends.)

And whatever happens, for heaven's sake don't kid around! Don't state that Sandra Fluke has determined *others* must pay for her and her law

---

[xi] POPE PAULUS VI, HUMANAE VITAE 14, 17 (Encyclical Letter on the Regulation of Birth, July 25, 1968).

[xii] Georgetown's student health insurance plans cover students not only while studying, but also while away from school during summer break.

[xiii] The campus of Georgetown University's Law Center is located at 600 New Jersey Ave., NW, Washington, DC, 20001. At 1108 16th Street NW, Washington, DC, 20036, Planned Parenthood's Downtown Center stands nobly facing (and in extraordinarily close proximity to!) the front door of the White House. So Planned Parenthood's Downtown Center is just a quick jaunt from the Gewirz Student Center: WNW up Massachusetts Ave., West through Mount Vernon Square, West down K Street, then North on 16th Street. 1.6 miles.

school sisters' to have sex! In a whole week of discussing the Sandra Fluke affair, don't give voice to what your listeners are thinking! Don't observe that Ms. Fluke desires government provide *all* her contraceptive desires! Don't unscramble Ms. Fluke's argument for your audience: Don't say she "wants to be paid to have sex."[xiv]

And heaven forbid, man—don't complete that metaphor!

Do not let the words "slut" or "prostitute" pass your lips![xv]

Do so and your words will be construed to slur *all women*. (A group specially privileged as beneficiaries of socialist group "rights.")[50]

Do so and you will pay.[xvi]

Yes, you may be an independent talk-radio host who has built your program from the ground up. You may have more regular listeners than any radio program in history. You may consider yourself the Cicero of our time.

But you have *advertisers*.

Incrementalists know this. They know that companies advertise during your daily radio program. They know this is how you and syndicators get paid. And they know that the people who manage such companies—just like everyone else in modern America—are *terrified of being associated with the impolite*.[xvii]

Besides, free speech is not corporate managers' concern; managers are paid to guard the bottom line. So when Incrementalist agitators working for

---

[xiv] Rush Limbaugh, *The Rush Limbaugh Show*, PREMIER NETWORKS (Feb. 29, 2012).

[xv] *Ibid.*

[xvi] How will you be made to pay? Well, in the same manner as other blasphemers against Politeness have been made to pay. Economically, stigmatically, professionally, and in any other way that can be devised. In the words of Incrementalist celebrity attorney Gloria Allred, "Hitting him economically is one price that he has to pay. He needs to be accountable in every way possible." Min Jung Lee, *Gloria Allred Seeks Rush Limbaugh Prosecution*, POLITICO (March 9, 2012).

[xvii] Media Matter's economic terrorism campaign is surprisingly explicit:

> "The liberal Media Matters for America is using a past campaign against Glenn Beck as a template. . . .
>
> While a law student, Carusone was active in a campaign to reach [Glenn] Beck's advertisers that began after the commentator said in July 2009 that President Barack Obama had 'a deep-seated hatred for white people.' Eventually, more than 400 advertisers said they didn't want to be part of Beck's show and, for Fox, the ad revenue was nowhere near what would be expected for a TV show as popular as Beck's. . . .
>
> "*The idea with Limbaugh is similar: take advertisers away so rates go down, Carusone said.* Couple that with the need to keep track of ever-changing lists of who will advertise with Limbaugh and who won't, and *Media Matters hopes that station managers, market by market, may someday conclude that it's just not worth the trouble* [to carry Limbaugh's program]."

David Bauder, *Radio Campaign Next Step Against Rush Limbaugh*, THE WASHINGTON TIMES (March 22, 2012).

Media Matters organize online petitions threatening to boycott your advertisers,[51] managers of your threatened advertisers will immediately leap to the ground—and prostrate themselves before the shrine of Politeness! Oh, how they will grovel! They will prove their heartfelt sincerity; they will weep and gnash their teeth! They will lament the day they signed that advertising contract! They do not wish to be associated with the unpardonable sin against Political Correctness—they will flee! They will self-flagellate! They will promise contrition! They will shrive themselves immediately at the nearest (public) confessional![52]

Yes—your advertisers will boycott your radio program as surely as leftist agitators threaten them. Within a couple weeks Incrementalist news outlets will glibly report that fifty companies have dropped all marketing on your program.[53] (And Media Matters will proudly list them by name.[54])

This is not all.

Incrementalist celebrity attorneys like Gloria Allred will personally request the Palm Beach County state prosecutor exercise his prosecutorial discretion—and *sue you* for completing the metaphor![55] Such attorneys will lament that Sandra Fluke "was simply exercising her free speech and her right to testify before congress on a very important issue to millions of American women,"—namely government-subsidized birth control—and you "vilified her. [You] defamed her and engaged in unwarranted, tasteless and exceptionally damaging attacks on her."[56] In other words, while Sandra Fluke has a right to free speech, *you* have only a right to silence. Because while Sandra Fluke's speech supports the socialist cause, yours questions it.

Socialist agitators calling themselves "The Women of the 99 Percent" will make illegal robocalls nationwide in an attempt to shame you into silence. They do so to combat the "war on women" your joke purportedly "launched."[57] These automated calls will carefully explain that *you* insult, *you* degrade, and *you* verbally abuse women.[58] (And by virtue of their fastidious genericism, said robocalls will imply that you insult, degrade, and verbally abuse *all* women.)

Incrementalist media personalities will gloat over your advertising snafu, too. They will stifle grins. They will shake their righteous heads, and wag their holy fingers. They will anathematize you. They will blink anxiously and nod in knowing agreement, reverently confirming one another's denunciations.

Occasionally the pious mask will fall—they will chuckle and they will sneer: Then they will do their best to pile on. They will try their damnedest to build advertiser-flight momentum. Speaking of stations which carry your show, they will prophesy: "They are losing money every day they put Rush Limbaugh on the Radio, period!"[59] They will cross their fingers and pray for the impossible: "Imagine Rush losing WABC New York, WLS Chicago, and major stations in Detroit, Dallas, Washington—that would be a death-blow to his show on the scope [sic] we know it now!"[60]

Jealous media personalities will present the Fluke affair as yet another "teachable moment." For anyone else who is professionally engaged in political speech—and by extension, all the rest of us who are not: "It's not just Limbaugh getting a big lesson in the consequences of hate speech. . . . [I]t's a wakeup call to every radio talker in America about what's ahead in the landscape and what's acceptable. Racism and sexism are not acceptable."[61] (Racism? To be sure, Incrementalists are famous for alleging "racism" where none can be found. But when a white man jokes about a white woman's repute, the charge of "racism" strains even Incrementalist conventions for journalistic integrity.)

The media chorus will drone ever on and on:

This is "sexism!"[62]

This is "misogyny!"[63]

This is "hate speech!"[64]

Because in Incrementalist America, speech is far from free.

Even for a modern Cicero.

Haranguing the Troops

Teaching subjects to police themselves in matters of political correctness has worked very well for Incrementalism.

But where the dangers of *political* speech are concerned, Incrementalists within the federal government still prefer to lead from the front. Thus we find Senator Jay Rockefeller (Democrat, West Virginia) warning cable news CEOs as follows during a Cable and Broadcast Subcommittee hearing:

> So let me caution our witnesses today. If you fail to fix this situation—all three parts of it—we're going to fix it for you. . . . [W]e will seek to do more than referee your corporate money disputes. Because more than just retransmission consent ails our markets. We need new catalysts for quality news. And entertainment programming.
>
> I hunger for quality news. I'm tired of the right and the left. There's a little bug inside of me which wants to get the FCC to say to Fox and to, and to MSNBC: "Out. Off. End. Goodbye."
>
> *It would be a big favor to political discourse; our ability to do our work here in Congress, and to the American people, to be able to* talk with each other and *have some faith in their government* and more importantly, in their future.[65]

Yes, you read that right. Senator Rockefeller is threatening to shut down news programming that is not to his liking. (With a little help from a most brilliant and necessary administrative agency within the new and unelected fourth branch of government—the FCC.) So long as Congress languishes with the lowest approval rating in the history of our Republic, Congressional Incrementalists would prefer news programming display them in a better light. The threat is direct and explicit: You cable executives are formally warned. Fix the problems we accuse you of, or else we will fix them for you. We require "quality news." By "quality news" we mean news that helps American people trust us. You know—sort of congressional propaganda, for lack of a better term. If you don't provide this sort of news we may shut down FOX and MSNBC, and by so doing threaten any other news programming that is critical of our monolithic work.

Oh, yes—and eliminating choices in news programming will "be a big favor to political discourse" as well!

How exactly the elimination of freedom of the press and freedom of speech would favor political discourse is unclear, unless by "political discourse" Senator Rockefeller means "political censorship." It is a bit of a stretch from "discourse" to "censorship," but under a strict regimen of political correctness all things are possible.

There is only one difficulty with Senator Rockefeller's proposed censorship: There is that troublesome First Amendment, always poised to spoil Incrementalists' enlightened programs for citizen benefit. You know, the one part of the Constitution they let you study in school? The part they suggested meant you could frequent girlie clubs; engage in sexual aberrations of your choosing; and publish, transport, sell, and view any erotica you wish—and the government could never deprive you of that right? Well, along with Incrementalism's new, sexualized freedom of speech, the First Amendment also guarantees that "Congress shall make no law . . . abridging the freedom . . . of the press."[xviii] If Congress has no power to make a law so much as *abridging* the freedom of the press, then of course a subsidiary organ of the federal government (like the FCC) has no power to *censor* news outlets it finds distasteful, either.

It is incredible that Senator Rockefeller—one of only 100 persons among hundreds of millions of citizens elected to the highest elective office below the presidency—could have forgotten the First Amendment. But he did. He forgot it. Because in modern American *culture*, political correctness is more important than free political speech. And for the same reason, the cable CEOs forgot the First Amendment, too. None of them called Senator Rockefeller on it. And it matters little if the FCC starts shuttering recalcitrant news outlets *today*; the threat of censorship has been expressed by a U.S. Senator and Chairman of a powerful and intrusive Senate Committee; the threat is endured by those in media, government, and at home; the liberty of the First Amendment is further soiled, minimized, and forgotten. Incrementalism is happy to wait for increased support for Senator Rockefeller's plan—and an appropriate "crisis" to put the plan into actual effect.

[xviii] U.S. CONST. amend. I.

Don't expect to get off the hook because you are a private citizen, as opposed to a cable news CEO or a talk radio host. Oh, no! Say you are a Coptic Christian refugee from the Muslim pogroms of modern-day Egypt. Don't speak your mind: Don't make a low-budget, fourteen-minute video clip presenting a negative opinion of Islam. And don't publish any part of that "movie" on the internet. When the Middle East blows up in the Administration's face, the full weight of the federal government will be leveled against you—yes you, homemade movie maker! As though that shoestring flick you produced, which sat quietly on the Internet for months, caused Muslims to spontaneously storm U.S. embassies across the Middle East on the anniversary of 9/11.[66] As though your stupid kitsch forced Middle-Easterners to kill a U.S. Ambassador and other staff at the consulate in Benghazi, Libya. The Administration won't condemn the fatal *actions* taken by the mob which killed the Ambassador; they will blame you and your discourteous *speech*![67] (Even though the President of Libya assures us your film had "nothing to do with this [U.S. consulate] attack."[68])

And the federal government won't stop there. It knows a fatwa will issue, *Salmon-Rushdie-style*.[xix] It knows a Pakistani price will be put on your head.[xx] So don't waste too much of your time creating false identities or holing up in hiding. Because the federal government will fetch you *after midnight*—to question you about your "probation."[69] It will parade you before the cameras.[70] It will reveal your identity to the entire world.[71] Yes, it will expose you—so murderous Muslim madmen can finish you *à la Theo Van Gogh*.[xxi] It stoops to conquer.

The federal government cannot very well cut out your tongue. But it wishes to forever excise your speech. So it will bully YouTube: It will request that your puerile video be removed.[72] Because like rulers of every age, it cannot tolerate speech which impedes its rule. The President himself will address the United Nations General Assembly, and will pledge that "The future must not belong to those who slander the prophet of Islam."[73] That means *you*—the maker of the fourteen minute YouTube video. The future must not belong to *you*.

Because you have spoken out of turn.

And today, just as gangster rap albums come with parental advisories

---

[xix] Salmon Rushdie is the prize-winning author whose novel THE SATANIC VERSES (1988) merited a fatwa courtesy of Ayatollah Ruhollah Khomeini, Supreme Leader of Iran, in 1989.

[xx] As of September, 2012, the going rate for fundamentalist Muslim assassinations appears to be $100,000. As Pakistani Government Minister Ghulam Ahmad Bilour recently offered, "I will pay whoever kills the makers of this video [i.e., *Innocence of Muslims*] $100,000. If someone else makes other similar blasphemous material in the future, I will also pay his killers $100,000." *Anti-Islam Film: Pakistan Minister Offers Bounty*, BBC NEWS (Sep. 22, 2012).

[xxi] The Dutch director and filmmaker who was shot, stabbed, and (mostly) decapitated *in broad daylight* for producing the ten-minute film "*Submission*," criticizing Islam's treatment of women, with Ayaan Hirsi Ali. His assassin was Mohammed Bouyeri.

warning of explicit lyrics, so our founding legal documents *come with prominent parental disclaimers.* Like the following warning which was attached to the Constitution, the Declaration of Independence, and the Federalist Papers:

> This book is a product of its time and does not reflect the same values as it would if it were written today. *Parents might wish to discuss with their children how views on race, gender, sexuality, ethnicity, and interpersonal relations have changed since this book was written before allowing them to read this* classic work.[74]

With political correctness in full flower, even *ancient* political speech—and especially that which might disturb the foundations of American socialism!—is impugned. Formerly free political speech—indeed, the legal basis for what remains of free speech—is today retroactively recategorized as "hate speech."

Mindless Efficacy

Eventually, after decades of "teachable moments," after thorough instruction, subjects themselves became experts in policing both public and private violations of political correctness. After innumerable persons were publicly shamed, publicly fined, publicly suspended, and publicly terminated for expressing views which could be construed as questioning the aims of socialist revolution, the premises on which it was based, or its supposed beneficiaries, the threat of ostracism was realized. After political discourse was equated with murder, after Senators threatened to shutter news outlets for unflattering reports on Congress, after founding political documents were printed with parental advisories, Americans were fully enculturated. Political correctness seized American culture, and the refrain was uniform and deafening:

"That's hate speech!"

"You're a racist!"

"You're a sexist!"

"Homophobe!"

"Xenophobe!"

"Chauvinist!"

"Misogynist!"

"Bigot!"

Of course, the most effective teachable moments of all never made the nightly news. They were conducted in private: shamings and ostracisms conducted amongst fellow students, coworkers, neighbors, family members, or friends. You can likely recall a painful occasion or two when you were revealed as the cultural outsider due to an unfortunate slip of the tongue—and the quick rebuke that followed under the authority of political correctness. Even if you can't remember specific occasions, they have surely occurred. And they have likely left lasting impressions on your psyche. Perhaps you can even recall an occasion or two upon which you, yourself had the opportunity to exhibit adroit cultural awareness, to reveal yourself as the most intellectually fashionable member of your peer group, to endear yourself to courteous people everywhere—and you singlehandedly crushed an associate's casual observation with an appeal to political correctness.

Submerged in a culture of political correctness, Americans now fear saying what they think for fear of being labeled what they aren't. Americans debate less. They leave debate to the rulers. To the experts. To the professors. To the media. To the elites. To professional political correctness advocates.

In our culture of political correctness, certain lines of questioning are abandoned altogether. Does dedicating 55.7% of federal government expenditures to social welfare programs actually assist the poor? What percentage of those incarcerated in U.S. prisons are illegal aliens serving time for crimes unrelated to immigration status? Does affirmative action really help black people? Is affirmative action just? What is the long term effect of the burgeoning U.S. debt? Has homo sapiens really altered world climate? Which government programs are responsible for U.S. debt? Are men and women innately different? What role does Islam play in worldwide terrorism? What role does Islam play in worldwide war-making? Why does the federal government assume it is the final authority on State issues? Can abortion have negative psychological effects on mothers? Does keeping openly homosexual soldiers in combat units improve battle readiness? Does inserting women into combat teams and submarines improve battle readiness? What is the effect of homosexual parenting on children?

Socialism's answer to such uncomfortable questions is simple: "Racist!" "Bigot!" "Chauvinist!" No matter how critical the issue, such lines of questioning no longer develop into arguments. The debate is over before it begins, and speakers bold enough to touch such sensitive questions are left hoping no one in a position to terminate their employment will hear about it. *Free speech*—the Constitutional right of the individual to question, to remark, to say things which may be found by someone, somewhere, to be offensive—has been abandoned for a new cultural premise: that such communication is *hate speech*. That it might be found offensive somewhere within the hive. Or at least by the hive's overseers.

And why is the culture of political correctness so compelling?

Political correctness is ruthlessly effective because it plays upon innate psycho-social needs. Humans are, after all, social animals. As such they wish to be accepted by other humans—and even by "society at large," whom they will never actually meet. From early childhood on, humans wish to fit in. They seek a peer group In elementary school they reveal such innate desires by wearing matching outfits to a birthday party. In middle school they exhibit such wishes by clawing their way into the most popular of cliques. In college they affirm them by doing whatever is required during Spring Break festivities.

Most people outgrow those particular, youthful, *expressions* of the desire for social acceptance. But the desire itself nevertheless persists throughout life. And for most people it remains very strong. *Expressions* of the desire to fit in simply become increasingly subtle, as they are cloaked by ever more experienced inhibitions. (That is, adults want to fit in, too. Few adults wish to be thought of as immature by their adult peers. So they stop matching outfits with friends.)

But adults still make a great many choices based on anticipated peer approval: what clothes to wear (skinny jeans or boot-cut low-riders?), what interests to have (reality TV or music lessons?), what publications to read (New York Times or the classics?), what entertainments to experience (shopping or nature?), what neighborhoods in which to live (uptown or south of the tracks?), what faith to practice (one into which they were born, or one in which they believe?), and especially *what views to hold* (hive-conscious or independent?).

Yes, most adults are still looking to peers for validation—just like they were in middle school. So once Incrementalism made certain political inquiries culturally taboo, only a moron or a misanthrope would open his mouth in opposition to the Incrementalist plan. Or in discord with the supposed beneficiaries of Incrementalist group "rights." To do otherwise might well result in self-banished hermitage.

As a result, almost no one is willing to buck political correctness.

Political correctness is also compelling because it crowns the vilest of argumentation techniques. Political correctness' logic is simple: *institutionalize the ad hominem attack!* Instead of refuting an argument, just attack the person making it. We all remember the *ad hominem* attack from the grade school playground, where it was the great Ender of All Arguments:

"If you swallow that piece of gum, it will stay in your stomach for *seven years*!"

"Come on, that doesn't make any sense. You mean it swims against the current in there, while everything else falls out?"

"Well . . . . I mean . . . . Well, my dad's bigger than your dad!" (!?!) (Hysterical laughter from peers.)

"I don't think so, but—what's that got to do with gum in my stomach?"

"Four-eyes!" (!?!) (More hysterical laughter.)

Argument over.

The *ad hominem* attack is not really an argument, of course. It is instead a way of avoiding argument on the topic at hand. It is an attempt to win a debate without debating; it is an attempt to mock one's opponent into submission. For these reasons the *ad hominem* attack has traditionally been rejected as a cheap shot, a non sequitur of argumentation, and as generally having no bearing on the point at issue. We dropped any credence we had given *ad hominem* attacks en masse when we graduated from elementary school.

But Incrementalism resurrected the *ad hominem* attack, and made it Champion of Incrementalism! The *ad hominem* attack does, after all, possess remarkable advantages: (1) As we have seen, one need not refute another's argument at all—one need only mock a supposed attribute of the other *person.* As a result, (2) one need not even *understand* the other's argument! And (3) one need not possess a superior alternative to the other's argument, either. Implementing the *ad hominem* attack thus requires neither intelligence, nor wisdom, nor facts—nor even truth.

Which is to say, political correctness arms troglodytes and halfwits with a debate-ending trump. Political correctness can be implemented by the least competent members of the hive to instantaneously derail the purest and most undeniable of arguments. For this reason political correctness is absurdly effective. For this reason it has become the de facto Guardian of socialist policy and theory.

Political correctness is also effective because it establishes a positive feedback loop. (And by "positive" we refer to continuously building with repetition; we do not mean "beneficial.") This is because cultural taboos grow in direct proportion to their perceived taboo-ness. So as citizens become sensitized to a particular politically-incorrect taboo, citizens feel free to discuss that subject in fewer and fewer circles. The new taboo becomes something that can only be spoken of with trusted friends. The fewer people with whom one dares discuss the taboo, the more powerful the taboo becomes. So the political taboo can be discussed safely in even fewer circumstances, and only with one's closest confidants. Which further strengthens the taboo. Which further shrinks the number of people with whom one dares discuss it. And so on.

When few remain who dare discuss the taboo—much less debate it publicly!—that political inquiry becomes anathema. One more front in the Incrementalist war is silenced. The hive mentality is reified. And Incrementalism can proceed apace.

And now we have come to the most important paragraph of this chapter. Humans are verbal creatures. While gifted with extraordinary powers of abstract reasoning, humans can access those powers of abstract thought *only through language.* That is, you can explore all sorts of hypothetical situations, actions, reactions, and phenomena; you can relive past events; you can contemplate the future; you can travel through space and time; all in the privacy of your own mind. But you cannot do so without human language.[xxii]

[xxii] It is true that one can perform astonishingly complex calculations in one's head without language. For example, one can (with experience) quickly and accurately predict the trajectory of a frisbee, so as to place one's hands in exactly the right place at exactly the right time so as to catch it. But such a calculation, while complex (one would not wish to solve for the position of the frisbee at a future time on paper!), does not represent *abstract* thought. A dog can perform this calculation just as accurately, and just as quickly. What we are talking about with respect to abstract thought is, for example, the subject matter of this book. You cannot explore such

As a result—precisely because we are verbal creatures—*political correctness endangers not only speech, language, communication, and debate, but also threatens human thought itself.* For having suppressed our *expression* of certain questions, notions, and ideas over a lifetime, we put ourselves in danger of suppressing even those very questions, notions, and *ideas themselves.*

At this point on our tour of Cultural Incrementalism we are forced to pause and to marvel at the remarkable achievements of political correctness. In a few short generations, political correctness singlehandedly attained what past rulers sought after for millennia yet failed to achieve. Political correctness manages rulers' ultimate aim: It reaches within the mind of the individual subject, and extinguishes ideas before they have a chance to develop. Before they can spread to others. Before they can interrupt ruling plans. Political correctness achieves this even without collaboration from hordes of wizards, witches, shamans, soothsayers, sorcerers, genies, magicians, medicinemen, enchanters, and priests. Political correctness needed merely harness *culture*, and then it let subjects themselves do the rest.

We must also take time out of our tour of Cultural Incrementalism to note how theoretically pristine the concept of political correctness is. Remember the hive mentality?[xxiii] It is the foundation stone upon which socialist thought and policy are built. But rather than serving merely as socialism's ontological foundation, as a descriptive premise or theoretical basis, *socialism intends to reify the hive mentality.* That is, socialism aims not merely at constructing socialist policy according to the premises of the hive mentality, but also at actually *enforcing hive groupthink.* Socialism wants unswerving dedication by the worker caste to those goals which Incrementalist overseers set. Socialism doesn't want members of the worker caste to *question* socialism's plan. If possible, socialism doesn't want workers to even *think outside* the plan. Political correctness is the cultural rule by which Incrementalism intends to take the (erroneous) premises of the hive mentality, and make them fact.

* * *

It took time for political correctness to take hold upon Middle Americans. After all, it was the antithesis of the most cherished of all individual rights: free speech. But deployed gradually, as a cultural norm, it was practically invisible. It was not as though socialists had passed some new law limiting speech, against which Middle Americans could rebel. No—political correctness snuck up on Middle Americans over a period of decades, largely

---

subjects if you are a dog. Moreover, you cannot explore such subjects even if you are human—unless you allow yourself *language.*

xxiii TEA WITH SOCIALISTS, Book I (The Hive Mentality), chap. 2, *The Hive Mentality.*

unnoticed, under cover of politeness—and embedded itself in the fabric of daily life. Its punishments were swift and sure. And they were meted out by society-at-large, not by government. So there was no tangible antagonist which one could overthrow.

Most everyone worshipped before the hypnotizing shrine of political correctness—employers, neighbors, peers, extended family, employees, workplace rivals, acknowledged freinemies. Even one's own children. No one could be sure who might be offended, or who might pretend offense. Nor could anyone be certain who might later be revealed as a politeness informant—and report what one said to still *others*, who might themselves claim offense by proxy. It became dangerous to open one's mouth. The safest path was self-censorship. Eventually, no one dared tell his fellow serfs in public or in private, "The Emperor hath no clothes!"

So Americans scuttled the political right to open one's mouth, as embodied in the Constitution. In its place, Americans embraced the cultural imperative to never say anything which could be construed to offend.

America went silent.

And stopped thinking.

Further Notes to Chapter 4

[1] Dennis Cauchon, *U.S. Funding for Future Promises Lags by Trillions*, USA TODAY (June 7, 2011); Dennis Cauchon, *Government's Mountain of Debt*, USA TODAY (June 7, 2011).
[2] U.S. Census Bureau, Table H-8, *Median Household Income by State: 1984 to 2010* (2011). A link to the data can be found at: http://www.census.gov/hhes/www/income/data/statemedian/index.html.
[3] "[D]espite talk of privatization, eliminating [Social Security] altogether is off the table. The political and societal changes of the '60s couldn't be rolled back either: Nixon expanded the Great Society and even launched the Environmental Protection Agency." Simon Rosenberg and Peter Leyden, *The 50-Year Strategy—Beyond '08: Can Progressives Play for Keeps?*, MOTHER JONES 67 (Nov., Dec. 2007).
[4] This is, of course, a federal crime under the Hatch Act, formally An Act to Prevent Pernicious Political Activities (1939). *See, e.g.*, Manuel Valdes, *Group: FAA Bosses Urged Workers to Vote Democrat*, REAL CLEAR POLITICS (Sep. 5, 2012).
[5] *See, e.g.*, Randolph E. Schmid, *Sleeping Air Traffic Controllers Highlight Challenges of Odd Work Schedules*, THE HUFFINGTON POST (April 16, 2011); Dan Levy, *Air Traffic Controllers Asleep on the Job*, NEWS 13 (WNYT.com) (April 24, 2011) http://wnyt.com/article/stories/s2079596.shtml.
[6] Alan Levin, *Midnight Was Movie Hour, Nap Time in New York Air Tower*, BLOOMBERG (May 11, 2012).
[7] Namely Hank Krakowski, former COO of the FAA's Air Traffic Organization. Fran Golden, *FAA Official Resigns Over Sleeping Air Traffic Controllers*, AOL TRAVEL (April 14, 2011).
[8] Socialists' intent to direct culture—and thereby socialist revolution—is detailed throughout socialist literature. *See, e.g.*, John Pietaro, *Power of the Written Word: Communist Cultural Workers, 1919-1939*, POLITICAL AFFAIRS (Sept. 2, 2009).

But the socialist intent to direct culture—and revolution—was advanced with more erudition by the Frankfurt School, and especially by Max Horkheimer and Theodore W. Adorno. *See, e.g.*, Max Horkheimer, *Traditional and Critical Theory* (1937) (trans. Michael J. O'Connell). Here Horkheimer explored the necessity of using the social "sciences," not to *describe* society, but instead to *rearrange* it—and to thereby accomplish socialist revolution. "To strive for a state of affairs in which there will be no exploitation or oppression, in which an all-embracing subject, namely self-aware mankind, exists, and in which it is possible to speak of a unified theoretical creation and a thinking that transcends individuals—to strive for all this is not yet to bring it to pass. The transmission of the critical theory in its strictest possible form is, of course, a condition of its historical success. But the transmission will not take place via solidly established practice and fixed ways of acting but via concern for social transformation. . . . [C]ritical theory has no specific influence on its side, except concern for the abolition of social injustice. . . . Its own nature, therefore, turns it towards a changing of history and the establishment of justice among men." *Ibid.* at 241-43.

The Frankfurt School's goal of *changing* culture instead of merely describing it in positivist terms is an ancient socialist ideal: "Philosophers have hitherto only interpreted the world in various ways; the point is to change it." KARL MARX, THESES ON FEUERBACH (Thesis XI) (1845) (taken from Karl Marx, Marx/Engels Selected Works, Vol. 1 (W. Lough trans., Progress Publishers 1969)).
[9] "While the Party, during its history, has largely focused on wide issues . . . it quickly came to establish a vital and proud history of *cultural work*, probably rooted in the dissident arts of Reed and Fraina. . . . This influence was but one of several reasons that the [Party] realized the prominence of literary arts in their *cultural programming*. The proletarian novel, the radical drama, revolutionary poetry and the progressive screenplay all came of age in the hands of Communist Party authors—or at least those that were close fellow travelers [*i.e.*, Incrementalists].") John Pietaro, *Power of the Written Word: Communist Cultural Workers, 1919-1939*, POLITICAL AFFAIRS (Sept. 2, 2009) (speaking exclusively of American socialism) (emphasis added).
[10] *See, e.g.*, John Pietaro, *A Brief Study of the Art and Culture of the Socialist Party USA*, EMERGENCY LABOR NETWORK, which references "cultural programming" five times in a brief article

praising socialist efforts to direct culture in the United States. http://www.laborfightback.org/cultural_brief_study.htm. *See also* n. 9, *supra.*
[11] *See supra* n. 8, n. 9, and n. 10 and accompanying text; *see infra* the rest of the chapter.
[12] *See supra*, n. vi.
[13] The study he cited: Gordon G. Gallup, Jr., Rebecca L. Burch, & Steven M. Platek, *Does Semen Have Antidepressant Properties?*, 31 ARCHIVES OF SEXUAL BEHAVIOR No. 3, 289-93 (2002).
[14] Gardiner Harris, *Head of Surgeons Group Resigns Over Article Viewed as Offensive to Women*, THE NEW YORK TIMES (April 17, 2011); Pauline W. Chen, M.D., *Sexism Charges Divide Surgeons' Group*, THE NEW YORK TIMES (April 15, 2011).
[15] *See, e.g.*, Steven Platek, Rebecca Burch, & Gordon Gallup Jr.'s (i.e., the offending semen researchers') joint response to Dr. Greenfield's semen fiasco (as published in Michael Smerconish, *Lazar Greenfield's 'Semengate' Stuns Scientific Community*, THE HUFFINGTON POST (April 25, 2011). http://www.huffingtonpost.com/michael-smerconish/semengate-stuns-scientifi_b_853164.html).
[16] Pauline W. Chen, M.D., *Sexism Charges Divide Surgeons' Group*, THE NEW YORK TIMES (April 15, 2011).
[17] *Ibid.*
[18] *See supra* n. vii.
[19] Pauline W. Chen, M.D., *Sexism Charges Divide Surgeons' Group*, THE NEW YORK TIMES (April 15, 2011).
[20] *See supra* n. vii.
[21] Pauline W. Chen, M.D., *Sexism Charges Divide Surgeons' Group*, THE NEW YORK TIMES (April 15, 2011).
[22] As republished at http://retractionwatch.wordpress.com/2011/04/06/forget-chocolate-on-valentines-day-try-semen-says-surgery-news-editor-retraction-resignation-follow/:

"One of the legends of St. Valentine says that he was a priest arrested by Roman Emperor Claudius II for secretly performing marriages. Claudius wanted to enlarge his army and believed that married men did not make good soldiers, rather like Halsted's feelings about surgical residents. But Valentine's Day is about love, and if you remember a romantic gut feeling when you met your significant other, it might have a physiological basis.

"It has long been known that *Drosophila* raised on starch media are more likely to mate with other starch-raised flies, whereas those fed maltose have similar preferences. In a study published online in the November issue of the Proceedings of the National Academy of Sciences, investigators explored the mechanism for this preference by treating flies with antibiotics to sterilize the gut and saw the preferences disappear (Proc. Nad. Acad. Sci. U.S.A. 2010 Nov. 1).

"In cultures of untreated flies, the bacterium L. *plantarum* was more common in those on starch, and sure enough, when L. *plantarum* was returned to the sterile groups, the mating preference returned. The best explanation for this is revealed in the significant differences in their sex pheromones. These experiments also support the hologenome theory of evolution wherein the unit of natural selection is the "holobiont," or combination of organism and its microorganisms, that determines mating preferences.

"Mating gets more interesting when you have an organism that can choose between sexual and asexual reproduction, like the rotifer. Biologists say that it's more advantageous for a rotifer to remain asexual and pass 100% of its genetic information to the next generation. But if the environment changes, rotifers must adapt quickly in order to survive and reproduce with new gene combinations that have an advantage over existing genotypes. So in this new situation, the stressed rotifers, all of which are female, begin sending messages to each other to produce males for the switch to sexual reproduction (Nature 2010 Oct. 13). You can draw your own inference about males not being needed until there's trouble in the environment.

"As far as humans are concerned, you may think you know all about sexual signals, but you'd be surprised by new findings. It's been known since the 1990s that heterosexual women living together synchronize their menstrual cycles because of pheromones, but when a study of lesbians showed that they do not synchronize, the researchers suspected that semen played a role. In fact, they found ingredients in semen that include mood enhancers like estrone, cortisol, prolactin, oxytocin, and serotonin; a sleep enhancer, melatonin; and of course, sperm, which makes up only 1%-5%. Delivering these compounds into the richly vascularized vagina also turns out to have major salutary effects for the recipient. Female college students having unprotected sex were significantly less depressed than were those whose partners used condoms (Arch. Sex. Behav. 2002; 31:289-93). Their better moods were not just a feature of promiscuity, because women using condoms were just as depressed as those practicing total abstinence. The benefits of semen contact also were seen in fewer suicide attempts and better performance on cognition tests.

"So there's a deeper bond between men and women than St. Valentine would have suspected, and now we know there's a better gift for that day than chocolates."

[23] Pauline W. Chen, M.D., *Sexism Charges Divide Surgeons' Group*, THE NEW YORK TIMES (April 15, 2011).

[24] *Bryant Cops a Big Fine for Gay Slur*, CHINA DAILY (April 15, 2011) (emphasis added).

[25] *E.g.*, Joakim Noah was fined $50,000.00 for the same slur in May, 2011. Herb Gould, *Bulls Joakim Noah: $50,000 Fine for Gay Slur is Fair*, CHICAGO SUN TIMES (May 25, 2011).

[26] Speaking of his $50,000.00 fine for responding to a drunken fan with an anti-gay slur, Joakim Noah stated: "I think it's fair. I made a mistake, learn [sic] from it and move on [sic]." He stated further that he would "learn from his mistakes." *Joakim Noah fined $50K*, ESPN CHICAGO (May 24, 2011). Kobe Bryant made similar statements of contrition after being fined $100,000.00 for disputing a referee's call with an anti-gay slur. *See, e.g.*, Mark Pasetsky, *Kobe Bryant Apologizes for Gay Slur After Twitter Explodes*, FORBES (April 13, 2011).

[27] *Joakim Noah fined $50K*, ESPN CHICAGO (May 24, 2011).

[28] Yes, beneficiaries of socialism include not only workers, women, racial minorities, and homosexuals, but also seniors. *See supra* n. vii.

[29] *See, e.g.*, The CNN Wire Staff, *Pilot Disciplined for In-Flight Rant*, ABC 7 NEWS (June 22, 2011).

[30] Scott Gordon, *Pilot Behind Rant is from North Texas*, NBC DFW (June 24, 2011) (emphasis added).

[31] *See, e.g.*, official statements by the CPUSA and the National Organization for Women, respectively, *Regarding the Tragic Shootings on Jan. 8, 2011*, POLITICAL AFFAIRS (Jan. 9, 2011); Richard Trumka, *Promote Peace in Our Politics*, POLITICAL AFFAIRS (Jan. 11, 2011); David Brock, *Violent Rhetoric Can Lead to Tragedies Like Arizona Shooting*, U.S. NEWS & WORLD REPORT (Jan. 14, 2011); *see also* n. i and accompanying text.

[32] *See, e.g.*, Chris McGreal, *Arizona Shooting: 'Does She Have Any Enemies?' 'Yeah. The Whole Tea Party'*, GUARDIAN UK (Jan. 9, 2011).

[33] Thomas McGowan, *The Dangers of Violent Political Language*, THE COMMERCIAL APPEAL (Jan. 14, 2011) ("Saturday's shocking act of violence in Tucson, Ariz., [sic] in which a gunman outside a supermarket shot six people to death and wounded 14 others, including U.S. Rep. Gabrielle Giffords, suggests just how dangerous [American political discourse] is. . . . It is irresponsible to assume that sociopaths would be able to appreciate the difference between symbol and behavior when violence and politics are commonly associated, as they now are. This is a problem all Americans should be concerned about, regardless of their political identity. . . . It is true that cultural and political leaders do not control the various ways in which their words may be taken, but this does not absolve them of responsibility regarding what they say. On the contrary, it is precisely *because* one cannot control the interpretation of what one says or writes, that one must speak and write with care and acumen.").

[34] David Brock, *Violent Rhetoric Can Lead to Tragedies Like Arizona Shooting*, U.S. NEWS & WORLD REPORT (Jan. 14, 2011).

[35] Juan Williams, *Racial Code Words Obscure Real Issues*, THE HILL (Jan. 30, 2012) ("Race is always a trigger in politics, but now a third of the nation are people of color—and their numbers are growing. With those minorities solidly in the Democratic camp and behind the first black president, the scene is set for a bonanza of racial politics. The language of GOP racial politics is heavy on euphemisms that allow the speaker to deny any responsibility for the racial content of his message. . . . [listing phrases]").

[36] *Ibid.*

[37] John M. Robinson, Office of Civil Rights, *Wait, What Did You Just Say?*, 569 STATE MAGAZINE 8 (July-Aug., 2012).

[38] *Ibid.*

[39] *Chris Matthews: Saying "Chicago" is Racist*, REAL CLEAR POLITICS (Aug. 30, 2012). And according to Chris Matthew's MSNBC colleague Lawrence O'Donnell, getting booed while making a speech to the NAACP is also racist (!). Lawrence O'Donnell, *The Last Word With Lawrence O'Donnell*, MSNBC (July 11, 2012); *see also* Toby Harnden, *Mitt Romney 'Deliberately Got Booed by the NAACP to Appeal to White Racists'*, MAIL ONLINE (July 12, 2012).
[40] Leo Sigh, *Sarah Palin's Political Career Over After Gabrielle Giffords' Shooting and 'Cross Hairs' Comments?*, LEO SIGH (Jan. 8, 2011) ("Unfortunately, in modern America, hate speech and hate rhetoric has gained a foothold in the media and has become somewhat 'acceptable.' Unlike in many other developed countries, where this type of speech is not protected under 'free speech' and thus not allowed, in America it is.").
[41] *See* the actual pre-statement negotiation at, *e.g.*, http://www.youtube.com/watch?v=Z2-HjBI_1ag.
[42] White House Press Secretary Jay Carney's comments to reporters. *See, e.g.*, David Gardner and Fiona Roberts, *White House's Anger at MSNBC After Top Political Analyst Called Obama a 'D***' During Live TV Debate on Plan to Tax The Rich*, MAIL ONLINE (July 1, 2011); Greg Braxton, *White House Blasts MSNBC for Mark Halperin's 'Inappropriate' Obama Remark*, LOS ANGELES TIMES (June 30, 2011).
[43] Chris Ariens, *Mark Halperin Suspended Indefinitely From MSNBC*, TVNEWSER (June 30, 2011); for the highly entertaining, actual exchange which led to Mark Halperin's indefinite suspension—including the on-air, pre-statement negotiation regarding seven-second delays and live censorship which precipitated it, and the betrayal which resulted—*see, e.g.*, http://www.youtube.com/watch?v=Z2-HjBI_1ag.
[44] Chris Ariens, *Mark Halperin Suspended Indefinitely From MSNBC*, TVNEWSER (June 30, 2011).
[45] House Democratic Steering and Policy Committee, (Feb. 23, 2012).
[46] Who later takes center stage at the Democratic National Convention. *See, e.g.*, *DNC 2012: Sandra Fluke's Speech at the Democratic National Convention (Full Text)*, THE WASHINGTON POST (Sep. 5, 2012).
[47] Georgetown Law Financial Aid Office, *2012-2013 Academic Year Budget*, GEORGETOWN UNIVERSITY LAW CENTER (March 15, 2012) (copy on file with author).
[48] *See, e.g.*, John McCormack, *Georgetown Students Go Broke to Buy Birth Control? Target Sells Pills for $9 Per Month*, THE WEEKLY STANDARD (Feb. 28, 2012) ("Birth control pills can be purchased for as low as $9 per month at a pharmacy near Georgetown's campus. According to an employee at the pharmacy in Washington, D.C.'s Target store, the pharmacy sells birth control pills—the generic versions of Ortho Tri-Cyclen and Ortho-Cyclen—for $9 per month. 'That's the price without insurance,' the Target employee said. Nine dollars is less than the price of two beers at a Georgetown bar.").
[49] For example, Planned Parenthood's Downtown Center located at 1108 16th Street NW, Washington, DC, 20036; Planned Parenthood's Northeast Egypt Center located at 3937A Minnesota Ave. NE, Washington, DC 20019; Planned Parenthood's Silver Spring Center located at 1400 Spring Street #450, Silver Spring, MD 20910; Planned Parenthood's Falls Church Center located at 303 S. Maple Avenue, Suite 300, Falls Church, VA 22046; etc. As of March 2012, according to Planned Parenthood's health center tracker (copy on file with author).
[50] *See supra* n. vii.
[51] *See supra*, n. xvii.
[52] David Friend (CEO of Carbonite, an advertiser which pulled its advertising from the Rush Limbaugh Show on March 3, 2012) made a contrite confession which is illustrative of this trend:

> "Over the past two days we have received a tremendous amount of feedback on Rush Limbaugh's recent comments. I too am offended and very concerned about his comments. . . .
>
> "No one with daughters the age of Sandra Fluke, and I have two, could possibly abide the insult and abuse heaped upon this courageous and well-intentioned young lady. [Are Mr. Friend's daughters also seeking government-sponsored contraception? Because if not, it is difficult to see how Mr. Limbaugh's insult is relevant to them.] Mr. Limbaugh, with his highly personal attacks on Miss Fluke, overstepped any

> reasonable bounds of decency. Even though Mr. Limbaugh has now issued an apology, we have nonetheless decided to withdraw our advertising from his show. We hope that our action, along with the other advertisers who have already withdrawn their ads, will ultimately contribute to a more civilized public discourse."

David Friend, *A Message from Carbonite CEO, [sic] David Friend Regarding Ads on Limbaugh*, CARBONITE HOME BLOG (March 3, 2012).

[53] Feminist Newswire, *Update: Number of Companies Pulling Ads from Limbaugh Show Up to 50*, MS. MAGAZINE (March 9, 2012).

[54] *The Rush From Limbaugh: 60 Advertisers Abandon Limbaugh's Show*, MEDIA MATTERS FOR AMERICA (March 19, 2012).

[55] Min Jung Lee, *Gloria Allred Seeks Rush Limbaugh Prosecution*, POLITICO (March 9, 2012).

[56] *Ibid.*

[57] Toby Harnden, *Illegal Robocalls Accuse Republicans Over Rush Limbaugh and "Slut" Slur*, MAIL ONLINE (March 9, 2012).

[58] More fully, the Women of the 99 Percent's robocalls generically allege that "Republican spokesman Rush Limbaugh insults, degrades, and verbally assaults women." *Ibid.*

[59] Eric Boehlert, Senior Fellow at Media Matters, speaking on THE ED SHOW, *Rushing Away*, MSNBC (March 12, 2012).

[60] Holland Cook, Talk Radio Consultant, speaking on THE ED SHOW, *Rushing Away*, MSNBC (March 12, 2012).

[61] Ed Schultz, THE ED SHOW, *Rushing Away*, MSNBC (March 12, 2012).

[62] "It's misogyny, it's sexism, it's rampant all over talk radio!" Eric Boehlert, Senior Fellow at Media Matters, speaking on THE ED SHOW, *Rushing Away*, MSNBC (March 12, 2012).

[63] *Ibid.*

[64] Ed Schultz, THE ED SHOW, *Rushing Away*, MSNBC (March 12, 2012).

[65] Senator Jay Rockefeller, Chairman of the U.S. Senate Committee on Commerce, Science, & Transportation, addressing Mr. Britt, Chairman, President and CEO of Time Warner Cable; Mr. Carey, Deputy Chairman, President, and COO of News Corporation; Mr. Rutledge, COO of Cablevision Systems Corp.; Mr. Uva, President and CEO of Univision Communications, Inc.; and Mr. Segars, CEO of Ovation, at the *Television Viewers, Retransmission Consent, and the Public Interest Hearing* (Nov. 18, 2010). Note that the U.S. Senate Committee on Commerce, Science, & Transportation website does not provide the more interesting points of Senator Rockefeller's "Majority Statement." Apparently the Senate Committee likes to censor the more incendiary parts of their own content as well. To hear those more interesting parts of the Senators remarks, you must resort to an actual recording of the hearing. *See, e.g.*, http://www.youtube.com/watch?v=QUZDPVo3ACE.

[66] According to Susan Rice, U.S. Ambassador to the United Nations, "There's no question, as we've seen in the past with things like *The Satanic Verses*, with the cartoon of the Prophet Muhammad, there have been such things that have sparked outrage and anger and this has been the proximate cause of what we've seen. . . . What happened in Benghazi was in fact initially a spontaneous reaction to what had just transpired hours before in Cairo, almost a copycat of the demonstrations against our facility in Cairo, prompted by the video." NBC News Staff, *Ambassador Rice: Benghazi Attack Began Spontaneously*, NBC NEWS (Sep. 16, 2012).

[67] "We also need to understand that this is a fairly volatile situation and it is in response not to United States policy, not to obviously the administration, not to the American people. It is in response to a video, a film that we have judged to be reprehensible and disgusting." Press Secretary Jay Carney, *Press Briefing by Press Secretary Jay Carney*, THE WHITE HOUSE, OFFICE OF THE PRESS SECRETARY (Sep. 14, 2012).

[68] As the Libyan President noted, the low-budget *Innocence of Muslims* had been available for many months before the attack: "Reaction should have been, if it was genuine, should have been six months earlier. So it was postponed until the 11th of September. They chose this date, 11th of September to carry a certain message." NBC News Staff, *Libyan President to NBC: Anti-Islam Film Had 'Nothing To Do With' U.S. Consulate Attack*, NBC NEWS (Sep. 26, 2012).

[69] *See, e.g.*, *Federal Probation Officers Interview Man At Center of Anti-Islamic Movie*, CBS LOS ANGELES (Sep. 15, 2012); Daily Mail Reporter, *The Man Who Set the Middle East Ablaze Hides His*

Face in Shame: Californian Filmmaker Behind Mohammed Movie Interviewed by Police, MAIL ONLINE (Sep. 15, 2012).

[70] *See, e.g.*, Daily Mail Reporter, *The Man Who Set the Middle East Ablaze Hides His Face in Shame: Californian Filmmaker Behind Mohammed Movie Interviewed by Police*, MAIL ONLINE (Sep. 15, 2012).

[71] Associated Press, *US Identifies Anti-Muslim Filmmaker Blamed for Attacks*, CBS DC (Sep. 13, 2012).

[72] Greg Risling, *Judge: Anti-Muslim Clip Can Stay on YouTube*, SALON (Sep. 21, 2012) ("The White House has asked YouTube to take [*Innocence of Muslims*] down and the company has refused, saying it doesn't violate its content standards."); Andrew Miga, *Innocence of Muslims Film: YouTube Owner Google Won't Take Down Anti-Muslim Video, But Restricts Access in Some Countries*, The Huffington Post (Sep. 16, 2012) ("Google is refusing a White House request to take down an anti-Muslim clip on YouTube, but is restricting access to it in certain countries."); Dawn C. Chmielewski, *'Innocence of Muslims': Administration Asks YouTube to Review Video*, LOS ANGELES TIMES (Sep. 13, 2012).

[73] Barack Obama, *Remarks by the President to the UN General Assembly*, THE WHITE HOUSE, OFFICE OF THE PRESS SECRETARY (Sep. 25, 2012).

[74] FOUNDATIONS OF FREEDOM: COMMON SENSE, THE DECLARATION OF INDEPENDENCE, THE ARTICLES OF CONFEDERATION, THE FEDERALIST PAPERS, THE U.S. CONSTITUTION, title page (Wilder Publications 2008), ISBN 10:1-60459-270-2; ISBN 13:978-1-60459-270-2 (emphasis added).

5

Diluting Middle America

Immigrants are the best hope for the labor movement.

—Eliseo Medina[i]

Immigrants bring to our country their cultures, labor power, and their traditions of struggle. . . . Their spirit is militant and anti-capitalist.

—Sam Webb[ii]

The dignified spectacle of millions of working-class immigrants marching through our cities' streets shows what the potential is for the immigrant giant that is now awakening. Those who march for immigrants' rights today, will march tomorrow for labor rights for all, for a raise in the minimum wage, for a national health care system, for quality schools and all the other things that all workers want.

—Emile Schepers[iii]

AH, CULTURE!

What a tool.

For those cunning enough to wield it, culture is a ruler's best friend: It works so very well to silence those little subjects!

And because *socialism* intends to rule, culture is also socialism's best friend: It works so very well to silence those suspicious, overly-inquisitive, loudmouthed, Middle American subjects.

Yet socialism continues to have difficulties with Middle America.

---

[i] Eliseo Medina, Secretary Treasurer of SEIU (Service Employees International Union), as quoted in John Wojcik, *Unions Link Arms With Advocates for Immigrant Workers*, PEOPLE'S WORLD (May 11, 2011).
[ii] Sam Webb, *A Party of Socialism in the 21st Century: What It Looks Like, What It Says, and What It Does*, POLITICAL AFFAIRS (Feb. 3, 2011).
[iii] Emile Schepers, *The Struggle for Immigrants* [sic] *Rights Today*, POLITICAL AFFAIRS MAGAZINE (April 19, 2006).

Despite their newfound silence, Middle Americans still tend to cleave to Middle American traditions of liberty, self-reliance, and independence from government. True, Middle Americans are far more manageable when silent—yet they remain reluctant to swallow the socialist plan. Even when it is cut into bite-size pieces for comfortable mastication, and even when it is gently spooned in with Incrementalist care.

And those incorrigible Middle Americans are terribly numerous.

Perhaps culture could again be of assistance?

Of Kings, Mice, and Cheese

There once lived a King who ruled a realm famed for its production of delectable cheeses.[1]

The realm was at peace. The cheese export business was good. The cheesemakers were happy and prosperous. The subjects were happy and prosperous. The King was happy and prosperous. Even the dairy cows were happy and carefree.

There was only one problem.

The mice were *also* happy and prosperous. The kingdom's mice noted the fragrant scent of cheese wafting through the night air, and followed it to its source. The mice consumed any cheese they could find. And in that realm, there was a *lot* of cheese to find. Consequently, the realm's mice experienced a population explosion.

Soon mice were everywhere.

Mice filled subjects' homes. They swam through cheesemakers' milk-curdling vats. They lived in cheesemakers' cheese-ripening vaults. They nested in used cheese cloths. They scurried about the streets. They made themselves at home in the marketplace and aboard merchants' cheese-export vessels. They were in every room of the King's palace. Anywhere cheese could be found, mice could be found.

The King summoned his wise men and asked them what could be done to remedy the kingdom's mouse problem. The wise men replied that the mouse problem presented a most formidable conundrum, requiring time to formulate a prudent response. The King granted his wise men all the time they should require.

The King's wise men poured over their scrolls, codices, and illuminated manuscripts. They busied themselves among their flasks, fires, crucibles, beakers, and observatories. They surveyed the flight patterns of birds. They consulted astrological tables. They unpacked their astrolabes, and with fastidious precision they measured and re-measured the planets' relative positions—to be certain of the accuracy of their predictions. They studied the realm's ecosystem. They numbered every native plant and animal, from the least to the greatest. And they determined the relationship of each living thing in the realm to all others.

Finally, when the wise men's calculations were complete, they delivered a most excellent reply to the king. The wise men were unanimous in their response:

Import cats!

The King followed his wise men's counsel.

In no time at all, and just as the King's wise men had promised, the cats consumed or chased off all the mice in the realm.

There was only one problem.

Now there were too many cats. Like the mice before them, cats were everywhere and always underfoot. They invaded subjects' homes. They lived under cheesemakers' milk-curdling vats. They napped in cheesemakers' cheese-ripening vaults. They slurped cream from cheesemakers' milk basins. They wandered the streets. They got stuck in trees. They crowded the marketplace and merchants' ships. They inundated the King's palace. They shredded the King's magnificent drapes! They caterwauled and hissed and fought all the night long. The cats very much liked living within the realm. But neither the King, nor his subjects, nor his wise men could sleep.

Everyone was forced to admit that the cat problem was a greater inconvenience than the mouse problem which it redressed.

Again the King convened a special council, and again he entreated his wise men: What might be done to solve the cat problem? The wise men went away as before, and performed abstruse and inscrutable calculations. When the wise men returned, they delivered a brilliant, unanimous, and discerning reply:

Import dogs!

In no time at all, and just as the King's wise men predicted, the dogs displaced all the cats. The dogs very much enjoyed living within the realm.

There was only one problem.

Now there were too many dogs.

The dog problem was more severe than even the cat problem which preceded it.

Again the King summoned his wise men. After rigorous consultations amongst themselves, the wise men unanimously suggested a bold and admirable plan: Import lions (!) to destroy or chase off the dogs. The King did so. And the dogs disappeared.

The lions liked living within the realm very well indeed.

But the realm developed a grave lion problem.

The King recalled his wise men. After austere and lengthy deliberations, the wise men delivered a keen and enlightened answer: Import elephants (!!!) to chase off the lions. The King did so. And the lions disappeared.

The elephants liked living within the realm very well.

And the realm soon had a terrific elephant problem.

It was mutually agreed that the elephant problem was more distressing by far than any of the realm's previous pest predicaments. The elephants trampled people as well as lions. They bellowed and trumpeted. They knocked buildings over (sometimes by accident, and sometimes on purpose). They terrified the cows, which stopped producing milk. They stripped bark and leaves off every tree. They munched every plant and shrub. They soon ate up everything in the land (including the cheese). Cheese production throughout the realm ground to a halt.

In desperation and tears, the King again besought his wise men: How can the elephant problem be resolved?

Again, the wise men solemnly retreated to their scrolls, their instruments, their calculations, and their secret councils. Again, when they returned, the wise men's recommendation was unanimous:

Import *mice*.

The King did so.

The mice chased off all the elephants—who were absolutely terrified of mice.

Slowly, life within the realm returned to normal. Plants re-grew their leaves. Cows were consoled, and began again to lactate. Cheesemakers returned to work. Fine cheeses were again produced. Cheese merchants made sales. Prosperity returned to the realm. The subjects were happy. The King was happy.

In the end, the King learned to share his cheese with an overabundance of mice.

(And the subjects were left to forever wonder if the King's wise men were really so wise after all.)

Of course the King, his mice, and their cheese are mere fable. But similar experiments have been attempted in real life—by real wise men—upon many occasions.

For example, Australians had a terrible time farming sugar cane due to a native pest called the cane beetle (*dermolepida albohirtum*). Adult beetles munched sugar cane leaves. And their larvae munched sugar cane roots. Which all made for poor sugar cane harvests in Australia.

So the Australian Government consulted its wise men at the Bureau of Sugar Experiment Stations, and asked them what could be done about the cane beetles. Wise men at The Bureau took their time; they consulted their books. They attended international environmental, zoological, and agricultural symposia. They meticulously evaluated the Australian ecosystem. They numbered every native plant and animal—and feral and foreign species as well—from the smallest to the largest. They mapped the relationships of every living Australian thing to all others. They combed over decades of sugar cane and cane beetle data. They deliberated amongst themselves for years.

In the end, wise men at The Bureau were unanimous in their response. They made a most thoughtful and ingenious reply:

Import giant cane toads!

Now that sounded like a good idea! To be sure, cane toads are *giant.* They can weigh as much as five pounds, and they can measure more than a foot in length from snout to vent (and nearly two feet from snout to toes). To grow like that, cane toads must gobble *a lot* of food! Indeed, cane toads' appetite is scientifically documented to be positively *insatiable.* Surely giant cane toads would dispose of Australia's cane beetles in short order.

So in 1935, the Australian Government did as The Bureau's wise men suggested. They introduced cane toads to Australia, in faithful expectation that cane toads would promptly finish off those pesky cane beetles.

But cane toads ("giant neotropical toads," *bufo marinus*) are unlike other toads. They consume *inanimate* as well as moving foods. And they aren't picky, either. So the cane toads ate other amphibians, and marsupials, and rodents, and lizards, and birds, and arthropods of every description. They also ate plants, and cat food, and dog food, and . . . people's trash. After consuming such a varied diet with legendary vigor, cane toads didn't have much of an appetite. So they ate a few cane beetles. But not very many. Almost none, in fact.

And just as the King's imported cats, dogs, lions, and elephants learned to enjoy living within the realm, so the imported cane toads learned to make themselves quite at home in Australia.

Cane toads can live more than fifteen years in the wild, and they are famously prolific. They begin reproducing at one year of age, and they lay sixty foot long clutches of eggs—10,000 to 40,000 eggs in a single load. Besides, cane toad eggs, tadpoles, and adults are highly poisonous—so it is not as though Australian predators are going to eat a lot of cane toads. (At least, not successfully.) Indeed, on the contrary, cane toads appear to be exterminating native Australian carnivore populations which lack resistance to cane toad bufotoxins.

Today cane toads rule North Eastern Australia, where they constitute a plague of biblical proportions. They are nomadic. They adapt to most any tropical or subtropical environment possessing a little water. Their mating croaks deafen the gloaming hours. With renowned ardor, they amplex with anything that moves.[iv] They infest Australians' homes. They congregate under every nighttime light. (To catch moths. But not cane beetles.) On roadways they are crushed by the millions, raising an abominable stench. They have spawned a unique Queensland drug culture of toad-lickers (*bufotoxins* have hallucinatory properties at doses insufficient to stop the heart). They outcompete (and also tirelessly consume!) native Australian amphibians. They

[iv] The *male* toads amplex with anything that moves, of course.

kill the ignorant, native Australian snakes, kookaburras, and monitor lizards which try to eat them. They spoil native Australian ecosystems.

But cane toads have never so much as dented the cane beetle population they were sent to destroy.

Like the King's subjects, Australian citizens today are left to wonder if The Bureau's wise men were so very wise.

Similar enterprises have been attempted the world over to solve one pest problem or another. In retrospect, such enterprises are generally regarded—like the Kings' elephants and Australia's cane toads—as having been unwise and terribly destructive. And like Australia's cane toads, such projects are generally found *not* to be reversible. (Yet remarkably, that insightful coterie of Australian wise men—The Bureau of Sugar Experiment Stations—persists to this very day!)

Perhaps the most memorable North American example of ecological invasion concerns the white man's replacement of the red. When exploration first exposed North America's abundant natural resources to European, African, and Asian settlers, those resources were free to be developed by whoever was willing and able. In such an environment, he who possessed superior technology, independence, and work ethic outcompeted his peers. In a relatively short period of time, and across an entire continent, foreign settlers displaced Native North Americans. Indeed, over the space of a few short centuries, foreign settlers became the new American "natives." And this was especially true in those lands which would later become the United States of America.

Incrementalists may not have heard of the King, his mice, and their cheese. Incrementalists may not be aware of Australia's experiment with cane toads. But socialists of all stripes are well aware of the Native American narrative. Indeed, the injustice of that encounter between Native Americans and our Predecessors frames the foundational mythos of socialism.

Incrementalists have long cogitated upon the lessons of the Native American narrative. They have long explored the demographic imperative contained therein. And after long deliberation, Incrementalists have come to a striking conclusion:

Perhaps the tables might be turned on that invasive breed of foreign transplants living in North America. Yes—now that meddlesome Middle Americans are the North American natives, perhaps a new invasion might be devised to displace *them.*

American Cane Beetles

Incrementalists' striking conclusion—that just so surely as Native Americans were replaced by Middle Americans, Middle Americans might in turn be replaced by a new migration—derives not only from socialism's antagonistic relationship with Middle America. No, Incrementalists' conclusion proceeds also from historical observation.

You see, socialism has always had explosive revolutionary success in countries possessing a large underclass: Russian serfs, German urban laborers, Chinese rice-farmers, Cuban hospitality service providers, Cambodian peasants.

This makes good sense, because socialist revolution requires substantial public support for proactive redistributive injustice, for group "rights," and for the difference principle.[v] One can't very well expect members of a nation's *middle* class to knowingly and uniformly favor policies confiscating their own toil and redistributing the proceeds to others! But one may find support for such policies among members of a nation's *underclass*, whose interests naturally favor redistribution—i.e., redistribution from others (who are economically "better off") to themselves. And if a nation's underclass is sufficiently large, it may even provide that critical mass necessary to effect socialist revolution.

So it is that *socialism always seeks a substantial underclass.*

Unfortunately for domestic socialists, American society differs markedly from those found in twentieth century Russia, Germany, China, Cuba, and Cambodia. Indeed, *America has never exhibited a plentiful lower class.* The hallmark of America's social structure has always been a numerous and politically puissant *middle* class—one which we have termed "Middle America."

Socialists in America found themselves in a bind: Without a numerous underclass, socialists could not drum up meaningful public support for socialist policy. Worse yet, Middle Americans comprised by far the largest socio-economic class—and Middle Americans actively opposed socialist policy. Worst of all, the Middle American dream subsisted in liberty, independence, and the concomitant opportunity to ascend the economic and political ladder. So socialists couldn't very well engineer a society in which Middle Americans *sought* enslavement, dependency, or relegation to membership in an underclass, either.

In other words, socialists view Middle Americans in the same way the king viewed his cheese-spoiling mice. Socialists consider Middle Americans in the same way the Australian Government considered its sugarcane-spoiling cane beetles. For socialists, Middle Americans are an obstacle to the ideal society. For socialists, Middle Americans are pests which need eradicating.

---

[v] Socialists have long recognized this fact. And so we find Engels in the 19th Century noting that: "In France, whose soil has for more than a hundred years absorbed revolution upon revolution . . . and where the conditions for an insurrectional *coup de main* are far more favorable than in Germany—even in France socialists increasingly understand that no lasting victory is possible for them, without first winning over the great majority of the people. . . . The long work of propaganda and parliamentary activity are also recognized here as the first task of The Party." Freidrich Engels, *Introduction* to the 1895 Edition of KARL MARX, THE CLASS STRUGGLES IN FRANCE 1848 TO 1850, (Berlin, 1895). http://www.marxists.org/archive/marx/works/1895/03/06.htm. And we find the Chairman of the CPUSA quoting Engels' observation with approval today. Sam Webb, *A Party of Socialism in the 21st Century: What It Looks Like, What It Says, and What It Does*, POLITICAL AFFAIRS (Feb. 3, 2011).

So Socialism consulted its wise men: What could be done about America's native pests—that is, about Middle Americans? Incrementalism had produced the finest welfare services in the world—but those cursed Middle Americans spoiled the harvest of dependency! Even when muzzled by political correctness, even while dominated by the irrepresentative government of the Fourth Head, Middle Americans continued to maintain—in their private lives—as much liberty and independence as they could muster. Middle Americans resisted socialist progress at every turn. What could be done?

This was a profound inquiry.

Socialism's wise men took their time formulating a response.

First, socialist wise men noted that through a gradual and successful operation of Incrementalism, the American ecosystem had been altered. In the *New* America—the one premised on New (Socialist) Deal programs of taking from one citizen and giving to others—the nature and distribution of American resources had shifted. No longer were American resources freely available to whoever wished to develop them through personal industry, individual initiative, thrift, and sacrifice. Instead, American resources (or their proceeds) were now largely expropriated by monolithic government at every stage of their liberation and development. And those same American resources (or their proceeds) were now redistributed largely by monolithic government to favored groups. Such redistribution was styled "social welfare," "social subsidies," "entitlements." And redistribution was safely directed by election-proof agencies and Incrementalist politicians, who determined upon whom such group "rights" would be conferred.

Second, Socialism's wise men noted that Middle Americans were not particularly competitive when it came to obtaining the *new*, government-distributed American resources.

But others were.

Socialism's wise men were aware of other tribes of *potential* subjects. These other tribes lived outside of the United States. And once imported, they were highly competitive at laying hold on the new, government-administered American resources! Indeed, these other tribes *demanded* government-administered American resources. These other tribes were unfortunate—poor, undereducated, and superstitious. They hailed from countries in which political and economic independence were either illegal or practically impossible. In Cold War parlance they were delicately referred to as inhabitants of the "Third World." And they were precisely what socialism needed in America: A large underclass to first legitimize, and later ratify, the socialist revolution.

Yes, this would work! Imported from near or far, Third-World transplants would outcompete Middle Americans for the new, government-distributed resources any day of the week! Just as surely as desirable, invasive species had been imported and had eradicated undesirable, native fauna in other environments and at other times, Third-World immigrants could be imported to eradicate troublesome Middle Americans. Third-World immigrants were better adapted to the New American ecosystem. Third-world immigrants were prolific.

And as an added bonus, Third-World transplants brought with them Third-World *culture*—a dependent, fatalistic, political and economic sensibility. Bearing such a cultural burden, Third-World immigrants could be counted upon to evangelize the benefits of socialized (federalized) health care. And socialized (federalized) mortgage relief. And socialized (federalized) food subsidies. And the prodigious federal debt necessary to finance such programs. And highly progressive, graduated income taxes. Third-World immigrants would preach the necessity and even beauty of all federalized social programs. Over time, Third-World immigration could be counted upon to influence Middle American culture as well.

Socialism's wise men returned from their deliberations. They delivered an inspired and unanimous response:

Import a Third-World underclass!

An International Aside

While the answer to socialism's difficulties in America was simple enough, the logistics of actually importing a Third-World underclass were no small task. Such a massive project would require significant time and effort. One couldn't import tens of millions of Third-Worlders in a day! An enterprise of such scale would not have its intended effect in a year, or even over a decade. But over time its influence would become incalculable. And for results like that, Incrementalism was willing to wait.

Which is to say that the underclass-import-strategy is, in every sense of the word, an *Incrementalist* solution. Socialist wise men pulled it from the Incrementalist quiver—right alongside independent administrative agencies and political correctness. (Squirrel hunting could again be avoided!)

To be fair, the underclass-import-strategy is not exclusively an *American* innovation.[2] Our American wise men drew heavily on a broader, classical, internationalist socialist tradition in formulating their plan for eradicating the American cane beetl—I mean, the American middle class. So in order to understand domestic socialists' motivations for implementing an underclass-import-strategy, one must take a broader view.

You see, socialism has always preferred a single, unified, world government.[3] Indeed, the very idea of a self-contained socialism—i.e., socialism subsisting independently within given national borders—is a fairly recent, twentieth-century innovation.[4] (There is still some debate regarding to whom this innovation is properly attributed; but the honor belongs either to Stalin [and his "Socialism in One Country" of late 1924] or Hitler [and his exposition of "National Socialism," as elaborated at length in Mein Kampf—which, though not published until 1925, had been written starting at least by the beginning of 1924, and possibly as early as the end of 1923].) In any case, only under a unified, planetary administration would the rise of monolithic government be complete: Devoid of potential contributors free from socialist expropriation; lacking potential recipients independent from government distribution; and bereft of members in either group free to make choices contrary to the dictates of socialist policy.[vi]

Socialists with classical, internationalist inclinations typically couch this desire for planetary government in terms of class-struggle. For example, they regularly describe national borders as a sort of capitalist licensing gimmick to depress laborers' wages.[5] However it may be described, planetary government is nothing more than a natural and necessary consequence of socialist ontology. We must remember that socialist thought is premised on the hive mentality—an alternative universe where free will does not exist. As we have already seen, in a universe devoid of free will, morality necessarily reduces to material outcome—and as Professor Rawls has shown us, the only just material outcome is an egalitarian one.[vii] Within this determinist universe, where domestic redistributive justice is good, international redistributive justice is *better*.

But talk of planetary government comes off sounding a little scary. Especially to Middle Americans.

So, under a cloak of Incrementalist care, socialists usually reference their ultimate aim of global government by means of a soothing corollary. Truly international government, in which all territories are managed identically by a single administration, is synonymous with a single-nation planet. Or, expressed in another way, a *lack of nations and borders*.

[vi] As Lenin said, "the final victory of Socialism, in the sense of full guarantee against the restoration of bourgeois relations, is possible only on an international scale". (As quoted by Stalin in a letter to Ivanov, Feb. 12, 1938. STALIN, COLLECTED WORKS, Vol. 14 (Red Star Press Ltd., 1978), http://www.marxists.org/reference/ archive/stalin/works/1938/01/18.htm.) Many socialists still feel that way today. *See, e.g.*, John Holloway, *Can We Change the World Without Taking Power?: A World Social Forum Debate*, 106 INTERNATIONAL SOCIALISM (April 5, 2005) ("A radical change in the organisation [sic] of society, that is, revolution, is more urgent than ever. And this revolution can only be world revolution if it is to be effective.").

As we saw in Book I, while a free society can very happily coexist with pockets of voluntary socialism, socialist systems are extremely threatened by pockets of voluntary capitalism. This is because socialism is premised on monolithic government: any comparison to free systems present a serious risk of mutiny among socialist subjects. For this reason—in global as well as national contexts—socialism races to extinguish every capitalist pocket it can find.

[vii] *See* TEA WITH SOCIALISTS, Book I (The Hive Mentality), chaps. 2 *The Hive Mentality* and 4 *The Non-Commutativity of Rights*.

Such a system implies free and unimpeded emigration from every region, anywhere in the world—and, importantly, unimpeded immigration into any other region, anywhere in the world. That doesn't sound so scary. In fact, it sounds kinda fun! So socialists emphasize this euphemistic accessory to world government: Open borders. Free immigration. Or whatever the euphemism of the day.

In this sense open borders are a policy *goal* which *International* socialism has yet to fully achieve.

Yet the open borders principle also has special import for American Incrementalism. Open borders are the specific means by which American Incrementalists hope to supplant those savage, anti-social pests—Middle Americans. The principle of open borders also possesses a long and storied tradition among American socialists.[6] And as we shall see, open borders are a primary salient in the *cultural* front of the Incrementalist war.

In this latter sense, "open borders" are a contemporary *tactic* of *American* socialism.

And now we can comfortably return to the subject of Socialism's wise men and their most excellent solution for eradicating Middle Americans.

American Cane Toads

Any underclass-import-strategy would, of course, first of all require revisions to American immigration law.

Because in the past, legal American immigration had always created the vast majority of its new citizens out of First-World foreigners.[7] And legal American immigration had placed exceptional candidates—those who were objectively educated, specially skilled, tangibly motivated, and therefore expected to positively and immediately contribute to American economy or culture—at the front of the immigration line.[viii]

On the other hand, American immigration law had made foreigners who were "likely at any time to become public charges" (i.e., likely to become welfare recipients) "ineligible to receive visas and . . . excluded from admission into the United States."[8]

In hopes of encouraging real assimilation into American society, American immigration policy had further required immigrants to learn English prior to naturalization.[9]

[viii] *E.g.*, The McCarren-Walter Immigration and Nationality Act of 1952, § 203 (H.R. 13342; Pub.L. 414; 182 Stat. 66) (preference for half of all quota visas given to those aliens "whose services are . . . needed urgently in the United States because of the *high education, technical training, specialized experience, or exceptional ability of such immigrants and to be substantially beneficial prospectively to the national economy, cultural interests, or welfare of the United States*," and family members accompanying them) (emphasis added).

And in an effort to preserve American liberty, American immigration policy had absolutely excluded immigration by foreigners suspected of monolithic-leaning political associations—particularly radical socialist ones.[10]

American immigration law had thus traditionally served to enhance and enlarge Middle America, and therefore also tended to thwart socialism.

Incrementalist wise men would change all that.

Instead of creating the vast majority of its new citizens from educated, independent, freedom-loving, First-World foreigners who would naturally become Middle Americans, Incrementalists' underclass-import-policy would *limit* the number of *First*-World immigrants. Simultaneously, Incrementalists' underclass-import-policy would explosively increase the number of *Third*-World immigrants accepted annually.

As Incrementalist wise men well knew, Third-World immigrants were far less likely to have had opportunities for education—and were consequently less likely to make immediate and positive contributions to American economy upon arrival. Instead, Third-World immigrants were more likely to become dependent on social welfare programs—thus providing American socialists with a long sought-after underclass who would validate the "need" for socialist redistribution. (The wise men were certainly right about Third-World immigrants' appetite for welfare: Among households headed by an immigrant having less than a high school diploma, a full 80% make use of U.S welfare programs.[11] And even after living for twenty years here in the U.S., 53% of immigrant households of *all* levels of education still make use of U.S. welfare programs.[12])

Third-World immigrants were also less likely to assimilate Middle American culture than First-World immigrants. Which would tend to prevent Third-World immigrants from becoming Middle Americans themselves. And—happy day!—Third-World immigrants often brought experience with and sympathies for socialist government. Which would prepare American culture for Incremental revolution.

This is not rhetorical exaggeration. As emphasized by one wise man planning the Incrementalist ascension of socialism in 2011, "Immigrants bring to our country their cultures, labor power, and their traditions of struggle. . . . *Their spirit is militant and anti-capitalist.*"[13]

The idea that immigrants tend to be "militant and anti-capitalist" is nothing new. This tendency has been noted—and also cultivated—by American socialists for over a century. Why, Daniel DeLeon himself was an immigrant![ix] As early as 1886, fliers promoting socialist (specifically

---

[ix] Daniel DeLeon, 1852-1914, Marxist theorist, leader of the Socialist Labor Party of America from 1890 to 1914, and eponymous inventor of De Leonism (a Syndicalist-Marxist brand of socialism), was born in Curaçao, educated in Germany and the Netherlands, and immigrated to

Anarchist) rallies in Chicago—the very fliers which fomented the Haymarket Affair, and led from thence to May Day celebrations forevermore—were printed with full-length German translations. And no surprise there: five of the eight socialist (Anarchist) ringleaders tried for murder in the wake of the Haymarket Affair were German immigrants.[14] (A sixth was an American citizen, but of very recent German immigrant stock, and educated as a boy in Germany.[15]) As Lulu Martinez reminded fellow socialists at a 2011 Haymarket Affair memorial,

> The Haymarket martyrs were primarily immigrants . . . . These are the tasks of undocumented youth today. . . . I ask you to stand beside immigrants, undocumented immigrants, and undocumented youth because we cannot continue moving [socialism] forward without the support of our communities and the leaders in other movements.[16]

In any event, by limiting First-World immigration and greatly increasing Third-World immigration, Incrementalist immigration policy had the potential—*over time*—to establish an American underclass. Third-World immigration held the possibility of diluting Middle America numerically and then, as a result, politically. Indeed, Third-World immigrants had the potential to supplant the majority, liberty-loving American middle class with a new, socialist-leaning underclass. Through an endless supply of Third-World immigration, a numerous and politically powerful underclass could finally be established in America. A Third-World underclass would naturally favor redistributive policies. Over time, such an underclass could transform American culture. And through the silent operation of culture, such an underclass would transform American traditions and political norms into an environment more favorable to socialism.

Limiting First-World immigration and greatly increasing Third-World immigration held an inchoate promise to lower the standard of living in America. The independence of the average American citizen would decline in direct proportion to the growth of the underclass.

The new, Third-World, American underclass would outcompete Middle America to the new, government-redistributed resources. The new American underclass would evangelize. Its very existence would prove the necessity of socialism. Given sufficient time, it would pave the way for socialism in America.

And through the operation of demographic imperative, Middle American resistance to socialism could be extinguished.

Incrementalism's Third-World underclass-import-strategy does possess a certain elegance. It kills three birds with one, quiet stone: It not only (1) provides an underclass which ostensibly *needs* socialist intervention in order to

---

the U.S. in 1872 or thereafter. And it only took him eighteen short years to become head of the Socialist Labor Party of America!

become productive members of American society; but (2) the underclass it imports tends to bring with it socialist conceptions of moral government, group rights, and government's prerogative to rule supreme over the individual; and (3) in a politically open country like America, the underclass can be counted on to make its voice heard—so the socialist ideology it brings can influence *other* Americans as well. Especially those other Americans whose business depends on appealing to the (increasingly immigrant) public—like politicians, members and owners of the media, owners and officers of corporations which sell products to the public, and plenty of academic types as well.

Congressional Wise Men

Incrementalist Immigration policy made its first appearance with the Hart-Celler Immigration and Nationality Act of 1965,[17] under which Third-World immigration explosively expanded. Under the new immigration law, First-World quota immigration continued at its previous rate—while for the very first time a separate, larger, Third-World immigration quota was added.[18]

The Immigration Act of 1965 also codified nepotism as the new and primary basis upon which immigrants would be admitted into the U.S, as *immediate relatives of U.S. citizens would henceforward be admitted in unlimited numbers.*[19] In one brief paragraph all numerical restraints on American immigration were forever abandoned and replaced with *limitless chain migration.*[x] And in the same breath, American immigration's traditional emphasis on *merit* (i.e., "high education, technical training, specialized experience, or exceptional ability of such immigrants and to be substantially beneficial prospectively to the national economy"[20]) was forever dropped for *nepotistic considerations.*[21]

Presidents and congresspersons publicly discussed the Hart-Celler Immigration and Nationality Act of 1965 prior to its enactment. They uniformly denied it would result in a great increase in immigration (!).[xi,xii] In

---

[x] Chain migration proceeds thus:

One woman immigrates to America.

She is later naturalized as a U S. citizen.

Then her parents, spouse, and children automatically qualify as legal immigrants—no matter how many hundreds of thousands of quota immigrants are admitted in that year.

Then her parents, spouse, and children are naturalized as U.S. citizens.

Then the parents, spouses, and children of her parents, spouse, and children automatically qualify as legal immigrants, too—again, without reference to numerical immigration limitations.

Then they are naturalized as citizens. . . .

This cycle is repeated indefinitely, without reference to any numerical limitations on immigration which would otherwise apply. Hence the label "limitless chain migration."

[xi] *E.g.*, during Senatorial debate over the bill (S.500) which would become Hart-Celler,

Senator Frank E. Moss (D-UT) assured us: "I emphasize that this bill would not attempt to make any drastic changes in our overall immigration numbers."

Senator William Proxmire (D-WI): "S.500 . . . . would not substantially increase the total number of immigrants to be admitted to the United States."

saying so, either they were stupid or they were devious. Most probably they were devious: Everyone else expected an explosion in immigration. Even the Fourth Head understood the consequences of Hart-Celler perfectly, and prepared for an immigration eruption. Make no mistake: Even correspondents at federally-subsidized media conglomerates recognize that,

> In 1965, the political elite on Capitol Hill may not have predicted a mass increase in immigration.
>
> But Marian Smith, the historian for Customs and Immigration Services, showed me a small agency booklet from 1966 that certainly did. *It explains how each provision in the new law would lead to a rapid increase in applications and a big jump in workload—more and more so as word trickled out to those newly eligible to come.* Smith says a lifetime of immigration backlogs had built up among America's foreign-born minorities. These immigrants would petition for relatives to come to the United States, and those relatives in turn would petition for other family members.[22]

Yes, unlimited chain-migration was well understood at the signing of Hart-Celler. And so, quite predictably, "The annual intake of legal immigrants *doubled* between 1965 and 1970."[23]

By passing a single law—one "not popular with the public"[24]—Incrementalists forever altered America. As noted by one left-leaning commentator, "it was the Immigration Act of 1965 that changed the face of America. That act changed who would enter America, reorienting our new

---

Senator Daniel K. Inouye (D-HI): "While the national origins rule will be eliminated in establishing quotas for foreign countries, this does not mean that the bill would permit a floodtide of new immigrants into this country. As a matter of fact, the total number of potential immigrants would not be changed very much."

Senator Hugh Scott (R-PA): "I do not think it [S.500] amounts to a serious increase in the number of persons admitted."

Senator Edward ("Ted") Kennedy (D-MA): "First, our cities will not be flooded with a million immigrants annually. Under the proposed bill, the present level of immigration remains substantially the same. . . . Secondly, the ethnic mix of this country will not be upset. . . . Contrary to the charges in some quarters, S.500 will not inundate America with immigrants from any one country or area, or the most populated and economically deprived nations of Africa and Asia."

Hearings Before the Subcommittee on Immigration and Naturalization, Committee of the Judiciary, United States Senate, First Session, on S.500 to Amend the Immigration and Naturalization Act, and for Other Purposes, 89th Cong., Part 1 (Feb.-March 1965), Part 2 (March-Aug. 1965), CONGRESSIONAL INFORMATION SERVICE, INC.) ((Part 2, book 3, p. 856); (Part 2, book 3, p. 857); (Part 2, book 3, p. 853); (Part 1, book 1, p. 136); (Part 1, book 1, pp. 1-3).

[xii] During House debate, remarks on H.R. 2580 were similar:

As Representative Spark Matsunaga (D-HI) reassured us: "It would change the basis for allotting immigrant visas but it does not provide for an overwhelming increase in immigration as some people seem to fear. . . . Actual immigration, counting nonquota and quota immigrants, would be increased around 50,000 or roughly 17 percent over current average annual immigration of around 300,000. This is certainly not a throwing open of the floodgates."

Hearing Before Subcommittee No. 1, Committee of the Judiciary, House of Representatives, on H.R. 2580 'To Amend the Immigration and Naturalization Act and For Other Purposes,' 89th Cong., book 1, p. 200 (March-June 1965) CONGRESSIONAL INFORMATION SERVICE, INC.).

immigrant pool from Europe, as it had been for over 300 years, to Latin America and Asia. And America changed."[25] Other leftist commentators go further, asserting that the Immigration and Nationality Act of 1965—and the resulting influx of Third-World immigrants—made President Obama's 2008 electoral victory possible.[26]

But Incrementalist immigration policy had only just begun with the Hart-Celler Immigration and Nationality Act of 1965. There was so much more to be done!

So in 1976, Incrementalism's preference for nepotism over merit was extended to *First*-World quota immigration, too.[27] (So much for merit.) In addition, First-World quota immigration was limited for the first time by a fixed ceiling of 20,000 per country.

In 1978 the previously separate and independent quotas for First- and Third-World immigrants were combined into a single, worldwide quota of 290,000: no further guarantees would be made to preserve First-World immigration.[28]

In 1990 the roof was blown off quota immigration generally: thenceforth, roughly 700,000 quota immigrants would be admitted annually.[29] The Immigration Act of 1990 additionally waived English speaking requirements for naturalization.[30] And in a transparently monolithic move, it also *dropped the former exclusion of immigrants suspected of monolithic-leaning political associations.*[31]

The Immigration Act of 1990 also added an entirely new class of immigrant: the so-called "Diversity Immigrant".[32] The Diversity Immigrant further distanced American immigration policy from its roots in selective admission of objectively educated, motivated, freedom-lovers who would naturally fit into the American scheme of liberty.

How does the law define "Diversity Immigrant"? A Diversity Immigrant is a foreigner hailing from a country "underrepresented" in the U.S. population (i.e., from the Third-World).[33] For the first time, the Immigration Act of 1990 granted 55,000 visas annually to Diversity Immigrants *under a blind lottery system.*[34] That way, the federal government could admit the undereducated and the unmotivated without taking any responsibility for doing so. By employing a visa lottery in those countries where most everybody was a member of an uneducated underclass, Incrementalists ensured that (1) the vast majority of "Diversity Immigrants" would be members of the underclass, and (2) government need never take the blame for selecting and admitting an underclass which would surely burden the American welfare state. After all, the federal government had not *specifically* selected undereducated members of an underclass: it simply opened an impartial lottery, and the results were the results!

And in the 2000s, Incrementalists found they could achieve Middle American dilution far more quickly by leaning on federal administrative agencies. Yes—the Fourth Head approves immigrant visas, too! Visa applications are inspected, appraised, and approved by USCIS (U.S. Citizenship and Immigration Services—a sub-agency nested safely, according to the matryoshka principle, within DHS). It is a simple procedure: Incrementalists at the top like Alejandro Mayorkas (Director of USCIS, an immigrant himself, whose mantra regarding comprehensive amnesty is "get to yes") put "immense pressure" on USCIS visa agents to quickly approve dubious visa applications.[35] Even when this requires "overlooking concerns about fraud, eligibility or security."[36]

How are USCIS visa agents pressured by Mr. Mayorkas and his friends? Why, those who refuse to approve fishy visa applications are *demoted or transferred* to less desirable offices.[37] By this simple means—just gently turning the screws!—we now have an astonishing 86% annual visa approval rate.[38] That's 86% of 3.9 *million* visa applications annually.[39] We know about the USCIS pressure cooker due to an official report issued by OIG[40] (the Office of the Inspector General, a group of administrative agencies in charge of auditing *other* government agencies and investigating accusations of illegality. But this particular report by the Inspector General contains information deemed too sensitive to reveal to Middle Americans, who might be terribly upset to know just how the Fourth Head approves immigrant visas. And so, unlike most reports issued by the Inspector General, this one has *not* been released to the public.[41]).

Over the years socialists have refined the science of Incrementalist immigration. Socialists have discovered that, while immigrants in general may be militant and anti-capitalist, immigrants from certain regions are more militant and more anti-capitalist than others. In particular, socialists admire the Latin American component of immigration—because Latin America provides paradigmatic examples of Incrementalist success. In a few decades time, Incrementalism has delivered multiple Latin American countries into socialist hands.[42] As socialists are proud to point out, the majority of Latin American countries are now governed by socialists.[43] Indeed, as socialists themselves are wont to note, *Latin America is both the geographic origin and intellectual birthplace of Incrementalism itself.*[44] Accordingly, socialists expressly recommend the Latin American experience as instructive regarding Incrementalist undertakings in America today—*as the guide to a quiet, gradual, parallel socialist revolution here*:

> In recent years, radical social transformations have occurred in relatively peaceful (peaceful is not passive) circumstances in Latin America. There an active, organized, and overwhelming majority of the working people led by left coalitions (in which communists are a part) and its allies have democratically won political positions in state structures and then utilized them to isolate elites, dislodge neoliberal governments, and clear the ground for democratic, social, socialist transformations.

> A party of socialism in the 21st [sic] century should study this experience closely. Broadly speaking, the transition to socialism in the U.S., I suspect, will follow a similar path, differences notwithstanding.[45]

Moreover, of all immigrants from every corner of the globe, Latin Americans exhibit the very highest rates of welfare utilization.[46] For example, 75% of Mexican, 75% of Guatemalan, 82% of Dominican Republic, and 70% of Ecuadorian immigrant households with children make use of U.S. welfare programs.[47] (For comparison, 7% of British immigrant households with children make use of U.S. welfare programs.[48])

And so it is that socialists rhapsodize the Latin American component of immigration. As socialists see it, the Hispanic immigrant is one tolerant of monolithic government, experienced in Incrementalist struggles, expectant of group-oriented privileges, and sympathetic to socialist political norms. As socialists see it, the Hispanic immigrant is exceptionally suggestible when it comes to socialist causes.[49] And Hispanics have already proven that, here in America, they can *deliver elections*.[50] As socialists eagerly note, the influence of the Hispanic vote is already overwhelming[51]—and it will grow rapidly (i.e., *geometrically*) in the years to come.[52]

Now *that* is the sort of immigrant socialists specially wish to import!

Further Notes to Chapter 5

[1] The following is adapted from NANCY GURNEY & ERIC GURNEY, THE KING, THE MICE AND THE CHEESE (Random House 1965).

[2] Indeed, in the words of United Nations Migration Chief Peter Sutherland, Europe "should be doing its best to undermine" its traditional "homogeneity" through Third-World immigration. Brian Wheeler, *EU Should 'Undermine National Homogeneity' Says UN Migration Chief*, BBC NEWS (June 21, 2012). Meanwhile, socialists like President Cristina Fernández de Kirchner of Argentina are pushing to have foreigners vote in Argentinian elections. *See, e.g.*, Michael Warren, *Argentina Wants Foreigners, 16-Year-Olds to Vote*, THE ASSOCIATED PRESS (Aug. 20, 2012).

[3] *See, e.g.*, Karl Marx & Friedrich Engels, *Manifesto of the Communist Party*, (Feb., 1848) ("Workers of all countries, unite!"); August Bebel, *Socialism and Internationalism*, vol. 9 SOCIAL DEMOCRAT no. 8, 491-93 (Aug. 15, 1905) ("The aim of all international action should be a *world-parliament*, in which should sit representatives of all civilised [sic] nations, and which should regulate all international relations, making them more and more close.") (emphasis added); John McLean, *Candidature Address for General Election*, November 1922, http://www.marxists.org/archive/maclean/index.htm ("When all empires are broken up and the workers by political control start to make land and wealth-producing property common property, when of the wealth produced all get sufficient to give them life abundantly with leisure and pleasure and education added thereunto, *then all the independent workers' republics will come together into one great League or Parliament of Communist Peoples*, as a stage towards the time in the future when inter-marriage will wipe out all national differences and *the world will become one.*") (emphasis added); H. G. Wells, THE NEW WORLD ORDER 67-68 (The Mayflower Press, Plymouth England 1940) ("We can ask, 'What is to be done to end the world chaos?' and also 'How can we offer the common young man a reasonable and stimulating prospect of a full life?' These two questions are the obverse and reverse of one question. What answers one answers the other. The answer to both is that *we have to collectivise* [sic] *the world as one system* with practically everyone playing a reasonably satisfying part in it.") (emphasis added).

[4] As opposed to classical socialism, which has always emphasized the necessity of simultaneous, worldwide revolution. *See, e.g.*, Frederick Engels, *The Principles of Communism*, Nos. 19 and 22 (1847):

> 19. Will it be possible for this revolution to take place in one country alone? No. By creating the world market, big industry has already brought all the peoples of the Earth, and especially the civilized peoples, into such close relation with one another that none is independent of what happens to the others. Further, it has co-ordinated [sic] the social development of the civilized countries to such an extent that, in all of them, bourgeoisie and proletariat have become the decisive classes, and the struggle between them the great struggle of the day. It follows that the communist revolution will not merely be a national phenomenon but must take place simultaneously in all civilized countries—that is to say, at least in England, America, France, and Germany. . . . It is a universal revolution and will, accordingly, have a universal range. . . .
>
> 22. What will be the attitude of communism to existing nationalities? The nationalities of the peoples associating themselves in accordance with the principle of community [i.e., communism] will be compelled to mingle with each other as a result of this association and thereby to dissolve themselves, just as the various estate and class distinctions must disappear through the abolition of their basis, private property.

As published in KARL MARX & FREDERICK ENGELS, SELECTED WORKS, Vol. 1, 81-97 (Progress Publishers, 1969), http://www.marxists.org/archive/marx/works/1847/11/prin-com.htm).

[5] Jane Hardy, *Migrants and the Economic Crisis*, SOCIALIST REVIEW (Feb. 2010) ("[T]he reality of capitalism is that it relies on exploiting low-cost foreign labour [sic] and it is in its interests to keep these workers in a vulnerable position."); Richard Trumka, *Remarks by AFL-CIO President Richard L. Trumka at the City Club of Cleveland, Cleveland Ohio*, AFL-CIO MEDIA CENTER SPEECH

(June 18, 2010) ("[A]t the heart of the failure of our immigration policy is an unpleasant fact, one that you almost never hear talked about openly: Too many U.S. employers actually like the current state of the immigration system—a system where immigrants are both plentiful and undocumented—afraid and available Too many employers like a system where our borders are closed and open at the same time—*closed enough to turn immigrants into second-class citizens, open enough to ensure an endless supply of socially and legally powerless cheap labor.*") (emphasis added); Joelle Fishman, Rosalío Muñoz, & Emile Schepers, *Immigration: Myths vs. Facts*, PEOPLE'S WORLD (Jan. 18, 2008) ("Big business interests want cheap labor but do not want low-paid workers to have rights. So they whip up scare campaigns against immigrant workers. Their aim is to keep them quiet and underpaid, and the workers divided.").

[6] A tradition starting at least as early as the agitation of Humberto ("Bert") Corona. *See, e.g.*, David Bacon, *El Valiente Chicano*, DAVID BACON AT INSTITUTE FOR GLOBAL COMMUNICATIONS (Jan. 19, 2001). http://dbacon.igc.org/Portrait/07Corona.htm.

[7] *See, e.g.*, the Johnson-Reed Immigration Act of 1924, §11 (H.R. 7995; Pub.L. 68-139; 43 Stat. 153) (limiting immigration almost exclusively to first-world immigrants); the McCarren-Walter Immigration and Nationality Act of 1952, § 201 (H.R. 13342; Pub.L. 414; 182 Stat. 66) (maintaining nearly all former preferences for First-World immigration).

[8] The McCarren-Walter Immigration and Nationality Act of 1952, § 211(e)(15) (H.R. 13342; Pub.L. 414; 182 Stat. 66).

[9] Naturalization Act of 1906, § 8 (H.R. 3592, June 29, 1906) ("No alien shall hereafter be naturalized or admitted as a citizen of the United States who can not [sic] speak the English language: Provided, That this requirement shall not apply to aliens who are physically unable to comply therewith, if they are otherwise qualified to become citizens of the United States.").

[10] The McCarren-Walter Immigration and Nationality Act of 1952, § 212(a)(3)(D)(i) (H.R. 13342; Pub.L. 414; 182 Stat. 66) ("Any immigrant who is or has been a member of or affiliated with the Communist or any other totalitarian party (or subdivision or affiliate thereof), domestic or foreign, is inadmissible.").

[11] Steven A. Camarota, *Welfare Use by Immigrant Households with Children: A Look at Cash, Medicaid, Housing, and Food Programs*, CENTER FOR IMMIGRATION STUDIES 10, Table 3 (April 2011).

[12] *Ibid.* at 8, Table 2.

[13] Sam Webb, *A Party of Socialism in the 21st Century: What It Looks Like, What It Says, and What It Does*, POLITICAL AFFAIRS (Feb. 3, 2011).

[14] August V. T. Spies, George Engel, Adolph Fischer, Michael Schwab, and Louis Lingg.

[15] Oscar Neebe.

[16] Lulu Martinez, *The Labor and Immigrant Movement*, speech in commemoration of International Workers' Day 2011, Forest Park, IL (May 1, 2011). *See, e.g.*, http://www.iyjl.org/?p=2175. The Haymarket "martyrs" are not alone; parallel examples of socialists cultivating "militant and anti-capitalist" tendencies abound.

For example, another major branch of socialism in America (specifically Syndicalist) was comprised largely of Finnish immigrants. The major Syndicalist party, the Industrial Workers of the World, even published multiple Finnish-language labor magazines. This was no small task (ever tried to learn Finnish?). *Tie Vapauteen* (1919-1937) was a monthly publication, but *Industrialisti* (1914-1975) was a daily newspaper—and the only daily publication the IWW ever published. All published right here in the U.S.A.—in Finnish. And the IWW's leadership was also largely comprised of immigrants—though not especially of Finnish ones (Swedish, Irish, Italian, etc.).

[17] Pub.L. 89-236.

[18] Hart-Celler Immigration and Nationality Act of 1965, § 201(a) (Pub.L. 89-236) (amending § 201 of the Immigration Act of 1952) (third-world quota immigration expanded from almost zero to 170,000 annually—*instantaneously eclipsing first-world quota immigration* [which remained unchanged] *for the first time*).

[19] Hart-Celler Immigration and Nationality Act of 1965, § 201(b) (Pub.L. 89-236) (amending § 201 of the Immigration Act of 1952) ("The immediate relatives specified in this subsection who are otherwise qualified for admission as immigrants shall be admitted as such, without regard to the numerical limitations in this Act.").

[20] The McCarren-Walter Immigration and Nationality Act of 1952, § 203 (H.R. 13342; Pub.L. 414; 182 Stat. 66).
[21] The Hart-Celler Immigration and Nationality Act of 1965 emphasized nepotism over merit in a number of ways. As we have seen, numerical restraints were dropped altogether for "immediate relatives" of U.S. citizens—while merit immigration remained capped. Nepotism was also emphasized over merit based on the declining percentage of quota visas reserved for those exhibiting objective education and economic independence criteria (from 50% to 10%). And nepotism was emphasized over merit by switching relative *positions of preference* on the quota visa schedule (merit was demoted from first position to third position, and placed *behind "family reunification criteria"*). *Cf.* the McCarren-Walter Immigration and Nationality Act of 1952, § 203 (H.R. 13342; Pub.L. 414; 182 Stat. 66); Hart-Celler Immigration and Nationality Act of 1965, § 203 (Pub.L. 89-236) (amending § 203 of the Immigration Act of 1952).
[22] *See, e.g.*, Jennifer Ludden, *1965 Immigration Law Changed Face of America*, NPR (May 9, 2006) (emphasis added).
[23] DAVID FRUM, HOW WE GOT HERE: THE 70'S, THE DECADE THAT BROUGHT YOU MODERN LIFE 269 (Basic Books 2000) (emphasis added).
[24] Jennifer Ludden, *1965 Immigration Law Changed Face of America*, NPR (May 9, 2006).
[25] Simon Rosenberg, *On Obama, Race and* [sic] *the End of the Southern Strategy*, NDN (Jan. 4, 2008). http://ndn.org/blog/2008/01/obama-race-and-end-southern-strategy.
[26] Peter S. Canellos, *Obama's Victory Took Root in Kennedy-Inspired Immigration Act*, 19 THE SOCIAL CONTRACT 1 (Fall 2008).
[27] Immigration and Nationality Act Amendments of 1976 (H.R. 14535; Pub.L. 94-571; 90 Stat. 2703).
[28] Immigration and Nationality Act Amendments of 1978 (92 Stat. 1046).
[29] Immigration Act of 1990, § 101 (amending § 201 of the Immigration Act of 1952) (Pub.L. 101-649; 104 Stat. 4978).
[30] Immigration Act of 1990, § 403 (Waiver of English Language Requirement for Naturalization) (Pub.L. 101-649; 104 Stat. 4978).
[31] Immigration Act of 1990, § 601(a)(3)(A) (amending § 212(a)(3)(A) of the Immigration Act of 1952) (Pub.L. 101-649; 104 Stat. 4978); *cf.* The McCarren-Walter Immigration and Nationality Act of 1952, § 212(a)(3)(D)(i) (H.R. 13342; Pub.L. 414; 182 Stat. 66).
[32] Immigration Act of 1990, § 131 (further amending § 203 of the Immigration Act of 1952) (Pub.L. 101-649; 104 Stat. 4978).
[33] *See* Immigration Act of 1990, § 131 (further amending § 203 of the Immigration Act of 1952) (Pub.L. 101-649; 104 Stat. 4978).
[34] *See* Immigration Act of 1990, §§ 101(e); 131 (further amending § 203 of the Immigration Act of 1952) (Pub.L. 101-649; 104 Stat. 4978).
[35] Sarah Ryley, *Rubber Stamp: Probe Reveals Feds Pressuring Agents to Rush Immigrant Visas—Even If Fraud Is Feared*, THE DAILY (Jan. 3, 2012).
[36] *Ibid.*
[37] *Ibid.*
[38] *Ibid.*
[39] For the most recent available period, measured from October 2008 through October 2009. *Ibid.*
[40] *Ibid.*
[41] *See ibid.*
[42] "While the results are uneven, the [political trends in Latin America] have been to the left, in a radicalizing direction with socialist orientations in terms of real policies in many countries. . . . As the U.S. ruling class looks at Latin America today, it faces growing militancy and the fresh face of a socialist movement it declared dead when the Soviet Union was dismembered in the early 1990s." Norman Markowitz, *Socialism and Latin America Today*, POLITICAL AFFAIRS (March 23, 2007). *See also* Jean Boulang, *Latin America Heads for Socialism*, POLITICAL AFFAIRS (Nov. 28, 2007).
[43] Some socialists state this proposition generally: "left-wing leaders . . . govern most of the Latin American countries." Marta Harnecker, *Latin America & Twenty-First Century Socialism:*

Inventing to Avoid Mistakes, MONTHLY REVIEW: AN INDEPENDENT SOCIALIST MAGAZINE, vol. 62 issue 3 (July-August, 2010).

Others are more specific:

> Chavez, Morales, Lula, Kirchner, Bachelet, Ortega, left and center-left governments and movements, continuing in the 21st century the rich progressive and revolutionary traditions of Latin American people, a tradition and a path that stems from the understanding of workers, peasants and intellectuals that looking to the market for salvation is an exercise in futility and a surrender of their freedom and future. . . . The advance of socialism in Latin America is in the interest of the North American working class.

Norman Markowitz, *Socialism and Latin America Today*, POLITICAL AFFAIRS (March 23, 2007).

[44] In a detailed, two-part series detailing the origins of Incrementalism (and praising its efficacy), socialist theorist Marta Harnecker informs us, "*The first to assimilate these ideas and visions were the Central American politico-military movements.*" Marta Harnecker, *Latin America & Twenty-First Century Socialism: Inventing to Avoid Mistakes*, MONTHLY REVIEW: AN INDEPENDENT SOCIALIST MAGAZINE, vol. 62, issue 3 (July-August, 2010) (emphasis added). This is highly-recommended reading.

[45] Sam Webb, *A Party of Socialism in the 21st Century: What It Looks Like, What It Says, and What It Does*, POLITICAL AFFAIRS (Feb. 3, 2011). *See also* Alfonso Gonzales, *Beyond the Consensus: Oppositional* Migrante *Politics in the Obama Era*, NORTH AMERICAN CONGRESS ON LATIN AMERICA REPORT ON THE AMERICAS 15, 19 (Nov.-Dec. 2010) ("Although organizing in a different context, Latino social movement organizations in the United States have much to learn from the experience of their Latin American counterparts. For oppositional Latino organizations to be effective, they will have to build unity within and forge alliances with other racial and ethnic groups that share the same class interest and develop a 10- to 20-year protracted strategy.").

[46] The average rate of welfare use in Hispanic immigrant households was a whopping 71% in 2009. Steven A. Camarota, *Welfare Use by Immigrant Households with Children: A Look at Cash, Medicaid, Housing, and Food Programs*, CENTER FOR IMMIGRATION STUDIES 7, Table 1 (April 2011). *See also ibid.* at 13, Table 4.

[47] *Ibid.* at 13, Table 4.

[48] *Ibid.*

[49] *See, e.g.* Combined Sources, *Latino Organizations Support Workers and Collective Bargaining*, POLITICAL AFFAIRS (March 7, 2011).

[50] Simon Rosenberg & Peter Leyden, *The 50-Year Strategy—Beyond '08: Can Progressives Play for Keeps?*, MOTHER JONES 66 (Nov. 2007) ("Add to this reliable Democratic base the heavily Hispanic states of Arizona, New Mexico, Colorado, Nevada, and Florida (whose Hispanic population, incidentally, is no longer majority Cuban or majority Republican), all of which went for the Democratic presidential candidate in at least one of the last four elections and are now much more Democratic because of the epic shift in the Hispanic vote.").

[51] Simon Rosenberg & Peter Leyden, *The 50-Year Strategy—Beyond '08: Can Progressives Play for Keeps?*, MOTHER JONES 65 (Nov. 2007) ("In the border states, Hispanics already make up 30 to 45 percent of the population—and between 10 and 30 percent of the voters—but their influence extends throughout the country.").

[52] Simon Rosenberg & Peter Leyden, *The 50-Year Strategy—Beyond '08: Can Progressives Play for Keeps?*, MOTHER JONES 65 (Nov. 2007) ("At 15 percent of the population, Hispanics are now the nation's largest minority group and the fastest growing part of the electorate. By 2050, one in four Americans will be of Hispanic origin.").

6

¡Sí Se Puede!

¡Hoy marchamos, mañana votamos!

—Illegal Immigration Slogan[i]

The roots of modern xenophobia arguably lie not simply in the monstrous nature of modern nation states with their unrelenting nationalist and racist propaganda from politicians and the media, but also in the competitive dynamic central to the process of capitalist accumulation.

—Christian Hogsbjerg[ii]

COMPREHENSIVE ALTERATIONS TO AMERICAN immigration law produced fantastic rewards for quiet socialism. A revolutionary underclass was rapidly taking shape.

Yet the pace of legal immigration left something to be desired.

No doubt a numerous American underclass was assembling. Yet Incrementalists calculated this process could be accelerated without gravely alarming Middle America. Due to the strongly socialist nature of Latin America's underclass, a consequentially robust preference for Hispanic immigrants, and the fortuitous geographic proximity of Latin America to the U.S., a further opportunity presented itself: *Incrementalists' underclass-import-strategy could more quickly be realized simply by turning a willfully blind eye on the southern border!* As the full weight of Latin immigration pushed the flood gates

[i] "Today we march, tomorrow we vote!" A favorite slogan among Hispanic May Day marchers, and used with special relish during the AFL-CIO-organized immigration marches of 2006. *See, e.g.*, Terrie Albano, *United We March—Sí Se Puede!*, PEOPLE'S WORLD (May 5, 2006).

[ii] Christian Hogsbjerg, *X is for Xenophobia*, SOCIALIST REVIEW (June, 2009).

open, Incrementalists within the federal government would demurely look the other way. Instead of proactively importing immigrants, federal Incrementalists would just allow a few hundred thousand cane toads to hop across the border under their own power every year.

To implement this tactic federal immigration law need not even be revisited; it would merely be *unenforced.* Ignored. Underfunded. And occasionally accused of irregularities. It would be easy; it would be cheap; and it would reshape American culture in record time.

Because Latino aliens so desperately wish to "share" their own cultures with their American hosts![iii]

Crooked Utensil

Incrementalism opened the *illegal* immigration prong of its underclass-import-strategy by simply *legalizing* illegal immigrants with the Simpson-Mazzoli Amnesty of 1986.[1] This was an unusual leap for Incrementalism, to rise up one day and provide such a bold and comprehensive amnesty. But it appeared quite effective: In one fell swoop, it added three million Third-Worlders to the burgeoning American underclass. And far more importantly, it forever set a precedent of periodic immigration amnesties—thereby encouraging future generations of aliens to ford the Rio Grande in expectation of similar treatment.

But the amnesty of 1986 was a mere feint; a misdirection. Incrementalism accomplished its illegal immigration objectives far more gently. The real process of Incrementalism's illegal immigration strategy was different: It chronically underfunded CBP (the U.S. Customs and Border Protection agency), thereby making hiring adequate border patrol personnel impossible[2]—and consequently turning the Arizona desert into a narcotic and human trafficking highway.[iv] It prosecuted and sentenced (for 11 years!) Hispanic border control agents who (1) attempted to apprehend, then (2)

[iii] As Jose Mangandi, a Salvadoran illegal alien on the "No Papers, No Fear" bus tour recently explained: "We have customs, we have cultures. We want to share this with this country . . . ." Miranda Leitsinger, *'No Papers, No Fear': Undocumented Immigrants Declare Themselves on Bus Tour,* NBC NEWS (Aug. 17, 2012).

Yes, socialists are very excited about "the cultural and historical traditions that immigrants from Mexico bring with them when they come to the United States." They are excited specifically because Mexican cultural and historical traditions strongly favor socialist revolution. David Bacon, *Equality and Rights for Immigrants—The Key to Organizing Unions*, MONTHLY REVIEW: AN INDEPENDENT SOCIALIST MAGAZINE, vol. 62, issue 5 (Oct. 2010).

[iv] Indeed, the federal government's response to the growing danger of drug and human traffickers in Arizona deserts has been to have the Bureau of Land Management post warning signs: "Danger —Public Warning Travel not recommended —Active Drug and Human Smuggling Area —Visitors may encounter armed criminals and smuggling vehicles traveling at high rates —Stay away from cash, clothing, backpacks and abandoned vehicles —If you see suspicious activity, do not confront!" *E.g.*, Joel Waldman, *Feds' Latest Answer to Desert Smuggler Violence: Warning Signs*, KGUN9, TUCSON (June 16, 2010).

pursued, and finally (3) fired upon a repeat drug smuggler and illegal alien in the act of transporting 800 pounds of narcotics into the U.S.[3]—thereby teaching all border control agents to stand down and never perform their duty in the future. (On the other hand, federal Incrementalists paid for that repeat drug smuggler's buttock repair surgery, and bequeathed complete transactional immunity upon him, in exchange for his testimony against the border patrol agents who attempted to apprehend him.[4] These actions were well-executed in high-Incrementalist fashion—by a *Republican* Administration. And they continue today under a Democrat one.[5])

And really—why man the border at all? In 2011 the federal government decided to build, for the very first time, an *unmanned* port of entry on the Mexican border. Simply present your documents to the kiosk's camera and receive your clearance—from a customs officer located 100 miles or more away![6] This way foreigners can cross our southern border unmolested by Border Control. (The federal government bills this new arrangement as a "*security upgrade*"—because the alternative of wading the Rio Grand unobserved, and not checking in at all, is so easy for foreigners.[7] In any case, you can be sure unmanned ports of Mexican entry will multiply in the wake of this precedent.)

Incrementalism continued its illegal immigration strategy by directing the DOJ (Department of Justice, an administrative agency representing the federal interest in legal matters) to proactively file lawsuits against any county or municipal government brave enough to pass wildly popular local legislation *in support of federal immigration law*—for example, local laws discouraging employers from hiring illegal aliens, or discouraging real estate owners from renting properties to illegal aliens.[8]

And this is to say nothing of the Incrementalist response to *States* and *State institutions* which attempt to support federal immigration law.

For example, Arizona House Bill (HB) 2162[9] requires those applying for federal welfare benefits to submit documentation indicating that their presence in the U.S. is lawful. Documentation such as an Arizona drivers license, a non-operating identification license, a birth certificate, a domestic passport, a foreign passport with U.S. visa, a refugee travel document, a tribal certificate of Indian blood, or any number of other documents suffice.[10] Arizona HB 2162 similarly requires documentation of lawful presence for those applying for State and local welfare benefits.[11] And it requires State law enforcement personnel to make "a reasonable attempt . . . when practicable, to determine the immigration status" of a person during lawful stops, detentions, or arrests "where reasonable suspicion exists that the person is an alien who is unlawfully present in the United States."[12] In other words, Arizona HB 2162 makes State resources available to assist the federal government in enforcing its own, *federal* immigration laws—a duty which the federal government has shown Arizonans for decades it will not fulfill when left to its own devices.

Arizona's HB 2162 embodies ideas fantastically popular not only among Arizonans, but among Middle Americans nationwide. Nationally, 71% support "requiring State and local police to determine the status of a person if there is 'reasonable suspicion' that they are illegal immigrants," while only 22% oppose.[13] And again, 71% support "arresting people who are unable to provide documentation to prove they are in the U.S. legally," while only 23% oppose.[14]

But in response to this uncommonly popular Arizona law, and in further pursuit of its illegal immigration strategy, Incrementalists directed the DOJ to *sue the State of Arizona*. (Yes, you really can sue a State! An unusual procedure, but you can do it.) The DOJ filed suit in federal court, of course—and managed to obtain an injunction enjoining enforcement of much of Arizona HB 2162.

Incrementalists at the DOJ also rejected South Carolina's voter fraud law in 2011[15] and Texas' voter fraud law in 2012.[16] These State laws simply required voters to present a photo I.D. at the polls. The idea was to prevent people from casting ballots for persons other than themselves, multiple times, during an election.[v] If one values democracy it seems like a reasonable idea; after all, each fraudulent vote cancels out a legitimate one.

But Incrementalists at the DOJ would not have it: According to Attorney General Eric Holder, State laws requiring photo identification to vote are "poll taxes" (!).[17] And according to Assistant Attorney General Thomas Perez, "tens of thousands" of "minorities" might be prevented from voting under the South Carolina law because they don't have the "right" photo I.D.[18] (Now, which "*minorities*" does Assistant Attorney General Perez mean would be prevented from voting under the South Carolina law? Surely not racial or ethnic minorities *in general*, though that is the way he phrased the issue. Let's be real: It is not as though South Carolina refuses to issue drivers licenses to African Americans. [Though South Carolina did do that sort of thing in the past—under *Democrat* administrations]. Moreover, South Carolina "issues free State photo identification cards" which qualify the holder to vote.[19] So Assistant Attorney General Perez must be understood to mean that the South Carolina law would prevent *illegal alien minorities in particular* from voting. And if that is what the South Carolina law does, why should we be suspicious? Isn't that what we all want? To prevent fraudulent U.S. elections?)

Incrementalists at the DOJ similarly demanded Florida discontinue its purge of illegal alien voter registrations in 2012[20]—even though Florida had discovered 180,000 illegal alien voters registered to vote within the State![21] (And

---

[v] Admittedly, asking for a photo I.D. is not going to dispose of voter fraud entirely. If we are to believe the New York Post, with $260 and an hour's time one can score a convincing counterfeit green card, social security card, and a State drivers license (!). Candice M. Giove, *One Hour and $260 Can Get You Phony Green Card, Soc. Security and License*, THE NEW YORK POST (Feb. 26, 2012).

we are left to wonder—if these Incrementalists at the DOJ care so desperately about democracy, then why do they insist upon fraudulent elections?)

Incrementalists at the DOJ also filed lawsuits against *specific community colleges* which requested foreigners to verify their legal working status by presenting a green card[22]—thereby discouraging *all* employers, State or otherwise, from verifying potential employees' legal status. (But isn't that the whole purpose behind federally-issued U.S. Permanent Residence cards? To verify that foreigners have legal status to work here? And didn't the Simpson-Mazzoli Immigration Reform and Control Act of 1986 criminally penalize employers who failed to verify the immigration status of employees?[23])

Incrementalism also furthers the illegal immigration prong of its underclass-import-strategy through an histrionic unwillingness to revisit the Fourteenth Amendment's citizenship-by-birth provision[vi] in light of changing circumstances—*i.e.*, the contemporary phenomenon of "birth tourism" and the resulting "anchor babies." Let us remember: It is only because Southern Democrats refused to recognize blacks' citizenship after the Civil War that this provision of the Fourteenth Amendment was added in the first instance. And getting Democrats to recognize blacks' citizenship no longer appears to be a problem. In any case, refusal to revisit the citizenship-by-birth provision of the Fourteenth Amendment strongly incentivizes increasing numbers of pregnant foreigners to cross the border *just to deliver the baby here* (world-class obstetrics on the public account, no less!)—so that the resulting child will automatically qualify as a U.S. citizen. And combined with Incrementalism's new, nepotistic standards for *legal* immigration, the resulting child-citizen's parents and siblings qualify as unlimited-class immediate relative immigrants. The child thus prevents removal of her (illegal) parents—and unlimited, Incrementalist chain migration proceeds from a new, seven-pound grappling iron.

In fact, to service insatiable international demand for free U.S. citizenship under the Fourteenth Amendment, an entire birth tourism industry has sprung up.[vii]

Yes, Incrementalism's illegal immigration strategy has proven wonderfully successful. Even high-profile Americans—like the President of the United States—maintain notorious illegal immigrant relatives domestically. These illegal immigrant relatives are unemployed. They live in government-financed housing. They collect publicly-funded disability checks. Of course, they never paid into such welfare programs as actual U.S. citizens do; but no

---

[vi] U.S. CONST. amend. XIV, § 1.

[vii] For example, the Turkish owned Marmara Manhattan hotel offers an all-inclusive birth tourism package: a month-long stay at the hotel, complete with airport transfer, baby cradle, and gift set for the mother. Parul Rohatgi, *Hotel Targets Expectant Mothers with 'Birth Tourism' Packages*, SPRINGWISE.COM (May 27, 2010). http://www.springwise.com/tourism_travel/marmara/.

matter—they remain on government assistance, and at the front of the line. Though subject to an explicit deportation order, executed by a judge in a formal immigration proceeding many years ago, they nevertheless remain. They illegally contribute money to their nephew's presidential campaigns. They are personally invited to attend, and personally do attend, the coronation—I mean, inauguration—of their presidential nephew.

And still they have the chutzpah to say, "I did not take any advantage of the system. The system took advantage of me!"[24]

(?)

They are not shy about such behavior. On the contrary, they exude brazen self-assurance. Their belligerence and self-righteous demand for ongoing American assistance cannot be satisfactorily described. It must actually be *viewed* to be appreciated. They (literally) wag their fingers at us, (literally) turn up their noses, (literally) shake their heads, (literally) flash the wild whites of their eyes, and they demand: "If I come as an immigrant, you have the obligation to make me a citizen!"[viii] In other words, they must be granted citizenship *because they are here.* (One must pause here and consider—what does such an argument mean? It could only mean that the very concepts of citizenship, borders, and national sovereignty are no longer valid. Which is precisely what classical socialism aims to accomplish. Such immigrants truly are, as socialist wise men prophesied, both "militant and anticapitalist."[25])

Who are "they"? Well, among others, "they" are Zeituni Onyango—the illegal alien Aunt of our current President. She lives in Boston. She likes living there very well. And she does not wish to return to Kenya.

Of her own accord she tells us frankly, "I owe them [i.e., Americans] nothing!"[26]

The First Aunt provides the paradigmatic example of Incrementalism's power to import a revolutionary underclass. Let us be perfectly clear: The illegal alien aunt of a sitting president sets quite a benchmark, one way or the other. She will provide an imposing example of the current condition of U.S. immigration law whether you choose to engage her or not. Deport her and you say to all illegal aliens already living here, and to all foreigners contemplating illegal immigration in the future, "The federal government will enforce

---

[viii] Zeituni Onyango, illegal alien and aunt of the President of the United States, in an interview with Jonathan Elias for WBZ-TV, CBS BOSTON (*Obama's Aunt: Silence Broken*, Sept. 21, 2010). Curiously, Ms. Onyango claims that she has gone through such a "hell of a lot" of difficulties here in the U.S. that, for her, the American Dream has become an American Nightmare. Which compels the question: If it is so bad here, why not get the hell out of America and go back to Kenya?

Unfortunately, WBZ-TV, CBS BOSTON appears to have removed the video interview from its website. It can still be seen elsewhere; *e.g.*: http://www.youtube.com/watch?v=QHoAuk76fT8&feature= feedwll&list=WL.]

its immigration laws—no matter who you are, and no matter to whom you are related." Do nothing, let her remain here living off the public dole, and you say to all illegal aliens and to all foreigners contemplating illegal immigration, "The federal government will *not* enforce its immigration laws—no matter who you are, and no matter to whom you are related. Come on over: Free food, disability awards, and housing available!"

Incrementalism was not satisfied with the latter route—with celebrating open-borders by doing *nothing* with respect to the President's illegal alien Aunt. No, Incrementalism went out of its way *to specifically prevent the apprehension and deportation of the President's illegal aunt even prior to her nephew's presidential election!* Senator Obama was a mere presidential candidate at that time. And Incrementalists in the federal government were perfectly aware of his aunt's presence. They were perfectly aware of her illegal alien status, and the order of deportation which had issued against her in a court of law. But they did not wish to disturb her; and they especially did not wish to disrupt her nephew's run at the White House. Instead, they did everything within their power to proactively *prevent* her apprehension and deportation. Because apprehending Senator Obama's illegal aunt would focus public attention on the fact of her illegal presence—and that, heaven forbid, might upset election results. Worse yet, it would direct public scrutiny to the delicate subject of Incrementalist immigration.

It was tricky business. Incrementalists could not very well shut down illegal immigration apprehension programs in Boston alone during the election, or it would be obvious what they were doing—singling out Senator Obama's illegal aunt for special protection. And so, just to be sure Senator Obama's illegal aunt remained unmolested, Incrementalists *shut down all illegal immigration apprehension programs nationwide.*[27] To ensure that one high-profile alien remained illegally within the U.S., no illegal aliens at all would be apprehended or deported around election time. (Again, these operations were executed in high-Incrementalist fashion—by a Republican Administration.)

In accomplishing such a feat under the very noses of Middle Americans, during election season when Middle Americans were on high alert, Incrementalists proved just how mature their illegal immigration operation had grown. If celebrity aliens were possible, what immigration ruse could not be achieved?

Enter the Fourth Head

The *effect* of the 1986 amnesty was fantastic. It alone was cause for celebration.

But the potential *cost* of such congressional amnesties is high. Amnesty by congressional Act requires, of course, a public vote by federal politicians. And amnesty is not a popular idea with Middle Americans. Middle

Americans have seen the results of amnesty (i.e., further illegal immigration since the Simpson-Mazzoli Amnesty of 1986), and they do not want another. Middle Americans overwhelmingly prefer that the border remain secure. Meaning securely *shut.* And there are still sufficient Middle Americans to vote in large numbers during elections.

So when proud Incrementalists like Representative Louis Vicente Gutiérrez (D Ill., member Congressional Progressive [Socialist] Caucus) submitted a new multi-million man amnesty bill in 2001, they had serious difficulties securing the necessary congressional votes. No matter what artifice they used to pass it.

It didn't matter if they limited the amnesty to specially beloved groups—like those who had attended high school, or who wished to attend college, or had a family member in the military, or wished to serve in the armed services themselves, or had "primary responsibility" for other family members' care (and who, of course, hadn't been convicted of a serious felony). It didn't matter if they conferred inspiring names upon the new amnesty bill, like "The American Dream Act," or, alternately, the "DREAM Act."[ix] It didn't matter how many times they proposed new amnesty bills in the House or in the Senate. (And they tried desperately to do so, again and again, *in each and every congress over an entire decade.*[28]) It didn't matter that they tacked the new amnesty onto National Defense Appropriations Bills (in a clever effort to make opponents swallow amnesty or take credit for defunding embattled American soldiers overseas).[29] Congresspersons would not vote for another amnesty.

It didn't matter that the new amnesty was translated into masterfully-rhymed Sloganese; or that crowds of illegal immigrants thronged the President and serenaded him with chants of "EDUCATION, NOT DEPORTATION!"[30] It didn't matter that President Obama boldly declared to those who thronged him, "Some [illegal immigrants] were brought here as young children and discovered the truth only as adults. They put their futures on the line in hopes they will spur the rest of us to live up to our most cherished values."[31] (And how exactly did such illegal immigrants, ignorant until so recently of their immigration status, "put their futures on the line" in hopes of reforming "the rest of us" citizens? If we are to believe the President's premise, it seems they had little to do with the

---

[ix] I.e., the "Development, Relief and Education for Alien Minors Act." By private sector standards, such an acronym comes off a little stilted; a little forced. But by congressional legislative standards, this is high poetry. Unfortunately, Rep. Gutiérrez was unable to compose this transportive and memorable acronym on his own, so he was unable to introduce his amnesty bill (H.R. 1918, 107th Congress) under that title in 2001. But other Incrementalists quickly saw the importance of Rep. Gutiérrez's new amnesty bill, and amongst pro-immigration Progressive Caucus membership, they managed to concoct it. They are so proud of this accomplishment that they have stuck with the title "DREAM Act" ever since.

decision to immigrate—they came here as luggage.) It didn't even matter that progressive Democrats controlled filibuster-proof supermajorities in both houses of Congress, and also held the Presidency. Career politicians knew if they voted for another amnesty, their careers would be over in the next election. Just as surely as Incrementalists could never pass congressional "net neutrality" bills against the will of the People, so Incrementalists failed to pass a second amnesty bill.

But electoral difficulties had not impeded "net neutrality" for long! As the reader will remember, Incrementalists had simply shipped "net neutrality" to a more trustworthy and electorally independent branch of the federal government (the FCC), where the threat of future elections could not subdue agency Commissioners. Might not the new and tremendously unpopular amnesty *also* be transferred to an electorally secure branch of the federal government? Might not the new and profoundly unpopular amnesty *also* be transferred to the Fourth Head?

Why yes, yes indeed it might! In a country where practically all government decisions are made by unelected members of one agency or another, immigration enforcement—and lack of same—is similarly dictated by unelected bureaucrats safeguarded within federal agencies. Administrative agencies had already been successfully employed to prosecute and jail loyal border control agents. Administrative agencies had already victoriously filed suit against municipalities passing local laws supporting federal immigration law. Administrative agencies had also profitably filed suit against States promoting federal immigration law; and against State institutions verifying the immigration status of potential employees in compliance with federal immigration law.[x] And best of all, those administrative agencies in charge of rounding up and deporting illegal immigrants, visa-breakers, and outright deportation-order-absconders had proven during the last Presidential election they could be counted upon to sit on their hands when ordered to do so.

All that Incrementalists required of federal agencies now was non-enforcement of federal immigration law on a somewhat *grander scale.*

Certainly this was the formal suggestion made by American socialists. And so, in 2008 and 2009, American socialist publications began to issue appeals for an administrative agency solution to the DREAM Act debacle. For example:

---

[x] Federal requirements and penalties were established as an integral part of the Simpson-Mazzoli Immigration Reform and Control Act of 1986, § 101 (Pub.L. 99-603). *See, e.g.*, 8 U.S.C. §§ 1324(a)(1) and 1324 (b)(1) (2011) (requiring employers to verify the immigration status of employees); 8 U.S.C. § 1324(f) (2011) (imposing criminal and pecuniary penalties for failing to verify employees' immigration status). But apparently, the federal government no longer wishes to enforce these provisions of the amnesty. It wants the amnesty, yes, but not the immigration enforcement which purchased it.

We need to keep pushing the following demands:

> * Comprehensive immigration reform that includes legalization for the undocumented [i.e., amnesty] and adjustments in visa programs to reflect the reality of continued immigration of workers and farmers from Mexico and other poor countries [i.e., visas for all].
>
> * *While immigration reform is worked on, a moratorium on enforcement actions by Homeland Security*, except those which target criminals, drug dealers and real terrorists who threaten our people's security [i.e., amnesty by the Fourth Head].[32]

Rumors circulated of federal agencies' internal evaluations of just such administrative amnesty schemes. Yes, the Fourth Head was looking into the very possibility socialists suggested: Imposing a new amnesty via agency lawmaking—as opposed to constitutional, representative legislation by Congress,[xi] which had proven impossible. A leaked memorandum of strategy and policy written by staffers at the USCIS (United States Citizenship and Immigration Services—a sub-agency nested safely, according to the matryoshka principle, within the Department of Homeland Security) confirmed those rumors in 2009.

The USCIS memo argued that administrative agencies retain broad "discretion" in executing the laws. The USCIS memo argued that agency "discretion" was so broad it could be used to "reduce the threat of removal [i.e., deportation] for certain individuals present in the United States without authorization [i.e., illegal aliens]."[33] In other words, administrative agencies could unilaterally arrange an amnesty by precisely those means socialist theorists were suggesting: by a "*moratorium on enforcement actions by Homeland Security.*"

The USCIS memorandum specifically recommended a new amnesty could be accomplished by means of "issuing new [administrative agency] guidance and regulations, exercising discretion . . . , [and] deferred action."[34] The new amnesty could also be furthered by "work[ing] more aggressively with the Department of Commerce."[35] In plain English, the USCIS memo advocated a new amnesty by (1) publishing a few agency regulations in the Federal Register, (2) pursuing an arbitrary, case-by-case deportation policy as directed by agency whim, (3) proactively refusing to execute immigration law, and (4) aggressively colluding with other federal agencies against the will of the People. Best of all, as the USCIS memorandum pointed out, such an amnesty could all be achieved "*In the absence of Comprehensive Immigration Reform.*"[36] In other words, Congress was unnecessary; there was no need to consult citizens! And there need be no risk of losing Incrementalist seats in Congress. If Americans disliked administrative amnesty there was little they could do about it.

[xi] "All legislative powers herein granted shall be vested in a Congress of the United States, which shall consist of a Senate and House of Representatives." U. S. Const. art. 1, § 1.

The USCIS memo provides a blueprint for monolithic government. Of *non*-representation of citizens' will. Of intentional circumvention of electorally accountable lawmaking. Of national, top-down control. Of arbitrary and boundless discretion.[xii] Of stealth. Of collusion between non-elected, administrative agencies against the People's will. These are the fruits of the Fourth Head.

Middle Americans understood this perfectly, and they did not appreciate USCIS' machinations. But when questioned about the amnesty memo, Incrementalists at the USCIS demurred:

We cannot comment on the memo!

The memo does not represent an "official action or policy" of the Department!

The memo is not *really* intended to outline procedures for pushing amnesty through unelected federal agencies!

The memo represents a mere "exchange of ideas;" it is a mere thought exercise; the product of one brainstorming session among thousands; no more than that![37]

Here at the USCIS we would *never* consider forcing amnesty via agency rule-making! No, no! "*We continue to maintain that comprehensive bipartisan legislation*, coupled with smart, effective enforcement, *is the only solution* to our nation's immigration challenges."[38]

Administrative Amnesty

After the memo kerfuffle, administrative agencies flew in radio silence. For two years.

But the Fourth Head's intent to deliver the DREAM Act by agency fiat was never shaken. Behind closed doors, administrative agencies continued to plan the DREAM amnesty. Agencies continued to organize. Agencies continued to coordinate. Agencies awaited an opportune moment to strike.

While agencies bode their time, socialists outside government continued to press their previous suggestions for an immediate amnesty via the Fourth Head. Socialists of the Syndicalist variety, like Richard Trumka (President of the AFL-CIO), challenged the federal government as follows:

> While President Obama's commitment to comprehensive immigration reform is vitally important, so much more can and should be done now

---

[xii] Oh, how monolithic government loves *discretion*. The USCIS memo utilizes the term many times—even within the first few pages: "This would permit individuals for whom relief may become available in the future to live and work in the U.S. without fear of removal. A corollary to this exercise of agency *discretion* is for USCIS to issue Notices to Appear (NTAs) strategically, rather than across the board." U.S. Citizenship and Immigration Services Memorandum, *Administrative Alternatives to Comprehensive Immigration Reform*, 2 (undated; leaked in Aug., 2010), authored by Denise A. Vanison et al., and sent to Alejandro N. Mayorkas, Director of USCIS (emphasis added). http://www2.nationalreview.com/memo_UCIS_072910.html.

> to help ensure a solid foundation for tomorrow's new Americans ["tomorrow's new Americans"—what a poetic euphemism! Of course, what it means is *today's illegal aliens*]. The president [sic] can announce a policy of allowing DREAM Act-eligible young people to stay in America until Congress passes comprehensive immigration legislation . . . .
>
> And the President can implement a humane and common-sense new *prosecutorial discretion policy* in keeping with ICE's existing enforcement priorities.[39]

In other words, in contravention of federal immigration law, *deport only illegal aliens who do not qualify for amnesty under the miscarried DREAM Act.* In other words, in contravention of federal immigration law, *deport only illegal immigrants who have* also *committed violent felonies.*

In the face of such bold taunts, administrative agencies could not wait for Winter Solstice Break to spring the DREAM amnesty (the way they had with the Internet Solstice Grab). Yet agency officials were nevertheless careful not to make the amnesty announcement while Congress was in session, or while the President was in town. Unveiling a policy so unpopular as amnesty-by-agency-fiat required a natural and profound silence in Washington. Congressional dissent could not be allowed; and presidential interviews might prove uncomfortable.

So the Fourth Head quietly released two *internal* memoranda summarizing the Dream Amnesty on June 17, 2011.[40] But it waited until August—when Congress was safely on Summer Recess, and President Obama was unavailable for comment (on a long vacation out of Washington)[41]—to *publicly* announce that the long-awaited amnesty had arrived. It was delivered by the only government body sufficiently distanced from the will of the People to birth such a monstrosity—the Fourth Head.

To whom would the new, administrative agency amnesty apply? Why, to all those who attended high school, or wished to attend college, or had a family member in the military, or wished to serve in the armed services themselves, or had "primary responsibility" for other family members' care (and hadn't been convicted of a serious felony)—against such persons deportation proceedings would be dropped.[42] In other words, the new amnesty applied identically to those groups who *would have* benefited under the DREAM Act, had the DREAM Act ever passed both Houses of Congress and been signed into law by the President!

And really, the administrative amnesty was better than even the DREAM Act: In order to qualify for this amnesty, *no proof of high school attendance, or family military service, or primary responsibility for other family members' care, or anything else would be required.* No indeed! DHS ordered ICE officers to just *ask* the aliens if they attended high school, or had a family member in the service, or wished to join the armed forces themselves, or had "primary responsibility" for other family members' care. If the aliens nodded in agreement or mumbled in the affirmative—if they *said* they did—that was the end of the inquiry.[xiii] Catch and release. And if ICE agents should do otherwise—if they should become more inquisitive—they would be fired.[xiv]

And the new, administrative amnesty would apply to *more* than those aliens covered under the DREAM Act. The new, administrative amnesty would also apply to those who organized unions,[43] and to those who "complain to authorities about employment discrimination or housing conditions."[44] (I.e., foreign Incrementalists are especially welcome!) And, under an excellent new legal principle called "victim-based immigration relief,"[45] it would also apply to alleged "victims of domestic abuse."[46] And alleged "witnesses involved in pending criminal investigations or prosecutions," too.[47]

The new amnesty was immediately welcomed by Incrementalists as an administrative implementation of the congressional DREAM Act. And as such the new amnesty was applauded:

> The decision would, through administrative action, help many intended beneficiaries of legislation that has been stalled in Congress for a decade. The sponsor of the legislation, Senator Richard J. Durbin of Illinois, the No. 2 Senate Democrat . . . said he believed the new policy would stop the deportation of most people who would qualify for relief under his bill, known as the Dream Act (formally the Development, Relief and Education for Alien Minors Act).[48]

And what methods would administrative agencies use to effect this new amnesty? Why, they would issue new agency guidance and regulations. They would exercise discretion. They would defer action. They would collude more aggressively with other administrative agencies to achieve amnesty. In other words, amnesty would be executed by precisely those methods proposed in the USCIS's abortive memorandum[49]—precisely those methods which

---

[xiii] "Prosecutorial discretion for DREAMers is solely based on the individual's claims. Our orders are, if an alien says they went to high school, then let them go. If they say they have a G.E.D., then let them go. Officers have been told that *there is no burden for the alien to prove anything.* Even with the greatly relaxed new policies, the alien is not even required to prove that they meet any of the new criteria. . . . At this point we don't understand why DHS even has criteria at all, as there is no requirement or burden to prove anything on the part of the alien. We believe that significant numbers of people who are not DREAMers are taking advantage of this practice to avoid arrest." Chris Crane, President of the National Immigration and Customs Enforcement Council (representing 7,200 ICE agents), speaking at Senator Jeff Sessions Press Conference (July 26, 2012). http://www.youtube.com/watch?v=Xb2_3R6oHSQ.

[xiv] "The Administration's new policies do not provide officers with new options or increased flexibility, but instead order officers not to enforce laws, and not to take enforcement actions against specific groups—with officers under threat of losing their jobs if they do so." Chris Crane, President of the National Immigration and Customs Enforcement Council (representing 7,200 ICE agents), speaking at Senator Jeff Sessions Press Conference (July 26, 2012). http://www.youtube.com/watch?v=w2fTxn6QYy8&feature =relmfu.

USCIS expressly denied it wished to implement. ("Comprehensive bipartisan legislation, coupled with smart, effective enforcement, is the only solution to our nation's immigration challenges!")

In making the Fourth Head's amnesty announcement, Janet Napolitano (head of the Department of Homeland Security) stated transparently that DHS would attempt to formulate "guidance on how to provide for appropriate *discretionary consideration*" for "compelling cases" where aliens had already been ordered deported but—in the Agency's view—should nevertheless remain.[50] (At other times, agency personnel employed the euphemism "*prosecutorial discretion.*")

Yes, Secretary Napolitano really used the word "discretion." Because that is what monolithic government requires: So very much discretion that "deport illegal aliens" means "do *not* deport illegal aliens." So very much discretion that law itself no longer has meaning.[xv]

In an hilarious feint, Incrementalists like Harry Reid actually argued that the new policy would *conserve* strained resources—i.e., it would *cost less*—so that DHS could "focus on serious felons, gang members, and individuals who are a national security threat."[51] Even though the administrative amnesty's stated purpose is *to re-review 300,000+ deportation case files* for persons already apprehended, persons in deportation proceedings, and (later) persons already slated for deportation—*in a new effort to prevent deportation!* But surely that case-by-case review will require considerable resources? And surely that will leave fewer resources to investigate, track, and apprehend "serious felons, gang members, and individuals who are a national security threat"?

And in a characteristically monolithic impingement on American culture, Janet Napolitano's new, administrative amnesty will define "family" broadly so as to include unmarried gay partners.[52] So much for the federal government's congressionally-legislated marriage and family laws, like the Defense of Marriage Act of 1996—which proscriptively defines marriage as

---

[xv] In a surprisingly revealing passage, the DREAM Amnesty Memorandum actually defines the lawlessness of monolithic government's purported discretion. After detailing 19 separate factors justifying prosecutorial discretion (i.e., the non-enforcement of immigration law), ICE Director John Morton commands:

> "*This list is not exhaustive and no one factor is determinative.* ICE officers, agents, and attorneys should *always consider prosecutorial discretion on a case-by-case basis.* The decisions should be based on the totality of the circumstances, with the goal of conforming to ICE's enforcement priorities."

Which is to say, immigration law no longer exists; we do as we like. Memorandum from John Morton, Director of U.S. Immigration and Customs Enforcement, *To All Field Office Directors, All Special Agents in Charge, All Chief Counsel*, Policy Number 10075.1, FEA Number 306-112-0026 (June 17, 2011) (emphasis added), http://www.ice.gov/doclib/secure-communities/pdf/prosecutorial-discretion-memo.pdf.

between one man and one woman for the purposes of all administrative agency regulations:

> *In determining the meaning* of any Act of Congress, or *of any ruling, regulation, or interpretation of the various administrative bureaus and agencies of the United States*, the word "marriage" means only a legal union between one man and one woman as husband and wife, and the word "spouse" refers only to a person of the opposite sex who is a husband or a wife.[53]

And so much for State marriage and family law as well. With the printing of a single agency rule in the Federal Register, representation of the People's will—at both federal and State levels—is instantaneously obliterated.

Family Reunion

The First Aunt had provided such a brazen and memorable test-case for Incrementalist illegal immigration policy. By very publicly allowing her to remain here; on the public dole; despite the formal order of deportation against her; by suspending apprehension and deportation proceedings across the country to ensure her stay through the election; Incrementalism had graven its illegal immigration policy in granite. Incrementalism had effectively bellowed to all illegal aliens and to all foreigners everywhere, "The federal government *will not enforce its immigration laws*—no matter who you are, and no matter to whom you are related!"

That was just the sort of celebrity test-case Incrementalists needed again, to legitimize the Fourth Head's newly-minted, anti-electoral, administrative-agency DREAM Act.

Unfortunately, the First Aunt was no longer available to spearhead illegal immigration drives. In the end, she had secured a waiver of deportation—with a little help from prominent immigration attorneys Margaret Wong and Scott Bratton, who successfully argued that Auntie Zeituni deserved special treatment (asylum) *because she was the President's Aunt.* Because the First Aunt, don't you know, might possibly be subjected to political reprisals upon return to Kenya—by Kenyans with political grievances against her nephew, President Obama. (Now who would those Kenyans be? And who paid for such pricey legal representation? Surely Auntie Zeituni, as a "disabled" invalid living in public housing, could not afford such representation?) In other words, the First Aunt was now (and still is!) a *legal* resident of the United States. As a legal resident she spent her time writing memoirs, like TEARS OF ABUSE (2012), detailing her mistreatment here in America (!) and elsewhere.[54] Consequently, she was no longer available to demonstrate the inviolability of the Fourth Head's new, administrative amnesty.

What to do?

Fortunately for American socialism, the President's family is prolific on the Kenyan side. Genealogies are a little confusing on that branch of the family tree, what with the polyamorous nature of Kenyan marriage customs. But the President had taken a field trip to Kenya in 1988 to sort all that out.[xvi] And he wrote about his genealogical discoveries at length in his memoir, *Dreams from My Father*. While in Kenya, the President learned from estranged relatives that certain other Kenyan relatives had disappeared while "temporarily" in America. In particular the President learned of a shadowy figure—an "Uncle Omar"—who had moved to America, "to the West . . . in Boston."[55] Uncle Omar had "promise[d] to return after completing school." He had promised to "send for the family once [he got] settled."[56] He had left for America decades and decades ago, but had never been heard from since. Sadly, he was—like many other African émigrés—"lost."[57]

Fortunately for the President and his Kenyan relatives, and fortunately for Incrementalists and illegal immigrants within the U.S., as well as for all foreigners everywhere who have ever considered illegally immigrating—the President's prodigal Uncle *has today been found!* And conveniently, the First Uncle was "found" only *ten days* after the Fourth Head announced its new agency amnesty. So the new, administrative amnesty could be validated immediately!

On August 24, 2011, the President's Uncle Omar—formally Onyango Obama—was tipping back a few cold ones at the Chicken Bone Saloon in Framingham, Massachusetts. Uncle Onyango left inebriated and, after running a stop-sign and making a sharp left turn across traffic, nearly struck a police car. He was pulled over by Officer Val Krishtal of the Framingham Police Department. Uncle Onyango's eyes were "red and glassy."[58] His speech was slurred.

Yet the First Uncle would not allow officer Krishtal to talk. He kept interrupting, and challenging officer Krishtal's assessment of his inebriation. When officer Krishtal explained that a collision had narrowly been avoided, the First Uncle insisted such a characterization was inaccurate—because the First Uncle had not personally heard the officer's "tires screeching."[59] When asked how much he had had to drink, the First Uncle insisted he had had *nothing* to drink. Not one beer.

Later he admitted that he had had one beer.

Later yet he admitted he might have had two.

But when officer Krishtal tried to administer a sobriety test, the First Uncle continued talking over officer Krishtal's instructions. The First Uncle tried to start the test "approximately seven times without being told to do so." He "could barely keep himself from falling."[60] After failing three field sobriety tests, he was arrested, cuffed, and escorted to the police station.

[xvi] Actually, despite the President's efforts to sort out his Kenyan family tree, he was only partially successful. No one is really sure who the father of the President's brother Bernard is. It's complicated. BARACK H. OBAMA, DREAMS FROM MY FATHER: A STORY OF RACE AND INHERITANCE 335 (Crown Publishers 2004) (1995).

When a breathalyzer was finally employed at the station, the First Uncle's blood alcohol level was almost twice the legal limit (specifically, 0.14% blood alcohol.[61] And at Onyango's body weight, that is about six drinks. Not two). Uncle Onyango was charged with driving under the influence of alcohol, failure to yield at an intersection, and negligent operation of a motor vehicle.[62] He was mercifully ordered released on his own recognizance by a municipal judge.[63]

While in jail, Onyango Obama was offered the traditional telephone call to arrange payment of bail. Incredibly, the First Uncle *decided to arrange bail by calling the White House*.[64] After all, the First Uncle's most Presidential Nephew lived there! The President had previously made special arrangements for the First Uncle's sister, Zeituni.[xvii] It seemed like a good bet the President could afford to post Onyango's bail, too.

But as it turned out, the First Uncle could not be released on bail as originally ordered. An outstanding warrant for the First Uncle's arrest had been in effect for two decades. You see, the First Uncle immigrated to the U.S. on a student visa in 1963. But shortly after his arrival, he dropped out of school.[65] It took the federal government twenty-five years to realize that Uncle Onyango was not attending his classes, and therefore was in violation of his student visa. But eventually the federal government figured out Uncle Onyango was playing hooky. And so, in 1989—twenty-six years after he arrived—the federal government ordered Uncle Onyango to leave the country.[66]

Uncle Onyango appealed that decision, but lost his appeal in 1992. His deportation order was made final at that time.[67] But like so many others—like his sister the First Aunt, for example—Uncle Onyango did not comply with his court-ordered deportation. He simply absconded. No one could find him, so no one could deport him. A warrant was issued and placed on file—and when he was finally located decades later, the First Uncle's warrant was discovered. So the First Uncle was then held by the U.S. Bureau of Immigration and Customs Enforcement (ICE) on an immigration detainer.[68]

Yes, the First Uncle is *also* an illegal immigrant. He was formally exiled two decades before his arrest in 2011. But he has, nevertheless, lived quite comfortably in the U.S. for half a century. Somehow or other, he obtained and has used *a valid social security number since 1992* (i.e., nineteen years before his 2011 arrest), according to Massachusetts Registry of Motor Vehicles spokesman Michael Verseckes.[69] Somehow or other, he obtained and has used a valid Massachusetts drivers license since 1992 as well (again, for nineteen years

[xvii] Yes, Zeituni Onyango (the First Auntie) and Onyango Obama (the First Uncle) really are brother and sister. This was confirmed by Michael Rogers, spokesman for Zeituni and Onyango's immigration attorney Margaret Wong. *See, e.g.*, Denise Lavoie, *Obama Uncle Held in US by Immigration Officials*, NEW HAVEN REGISTER (Aug. 29, 2011) (© Associated Press 2011).

before his 2011 arrest).[70] He lived well, like any citizen. He drove a white Mitsubishi SUV. He liked living outside Boston very much indeed.

And he did not wish to return to Kenya.

The spokesman for immigration attorney Margaret Wong—who represents both Auntie Zeituni and Uncle Onyango—stated he "wouldn't know how" Uncle Onyango got that valid social security number.[71] Or that valid driver's license. And in fact nobody in government seems terribly concerned about how the First Uncle obtained a valid social security number or a driver's license as an illegal immigrant subject to a specific and final order of deportation.

Instead, everyone in government is concerned with how best to apply the new, administrative amnesty to Uncle Onyango. Fortunately, the First Uncle had wished to attend school. That is why he came to the Land of Opportunity in the first place, after all! And he had never been convicted of felonious assault, rape, homicide, or other crimes of gravity. So under the Fourth Head's new DREAM amnesty, the First Uncle qualifies!

In summary, the greater part of the First Uncle's life has been spent in America. After decades living as a deportation-order absconder, he was finally apprehended and positively identified. But on September 8, 2011—*just two weeks after his arrest and detainment*—the First Uncle was *released*.[72]

Spokesmen for ICE refuse to say whether or not the First Uncle posted bail. Or who posted bail for him. Spokesmen for ICE claim the agency cannot comment on individual cases due to "privacy laws."[73] And Janet Napolitano agrees.[74] (But of course no privacy laws prevent publication of illegal aliens' case files! ICE simply has a general policy of *magisterial discretion*—including an aristocratic reticence in matters of straightforward public accountability. You see, when pursuing a "case-by-case" implementation of immigration law, refusing to discuss individual cases renders ICE unaccountable for *all* decisions it makes. And that establishes yet another layer of insulation between ICE's autonomous decisions and the contrary will of prying Middle Americans. Besides, ICE does not wish to answer uncomfortable questions about one of its star aliens.)

And so, as quickly as he had after the final order of deportation was entered against him in 1992, Uncle Onyango again disappeared.

The First Uncle has not returned to work.[75] So citizens are left to wonder precisely how he is covering his bills. (Perhaps the First Aunt has advised him how best to qualify for disability as an illegal alien? Perhaps the First Aunt has advised her brother how to secure public housing?)

For Middle Americans, the Ballad of Onyango Obama has been an exercise in frustration from beginning to end. But Administrative Agencies got their celebrity test-case.

And the results are in:

The Fourth Head's amnesty is a grand success!

Journalists called the First Uncle's sister, First Auntie Zeituni, to interview her over the telephone about her brother's recent arrest. Like the First Uncle, she promptly referred them to her most Presidential Nephew: "Why don't you go to 1600 Pennsylvania Ave. [sic] in Washington, D.C., and ask your president? Not me."

Then she hung up.[76]

It was a fitting conclusion to the Presidential Family Reunion.

1-855-ILLEGAL

The Presidential Family Reunion finally came to an end.

But the Fourth Head's new, administrative amnesty was just warming up! After successfully preventing deportation of yet another fugitive celebrity alien, after curtailing deportations by one-third in mere months,[77] the Fourth Head was prepared to execute even broader illegal immigration outreach.

So ICE opened a 24/7, toll-free hotline for detained illegal aliens—to provide them with assistance in *resisting* deportation (!).[78] (In case any presidential relations should need this assistance in the future, the hotline's number is 1-855-448-6903.[79]) And not to worry, immigration fugitives: The hotline provides translation services in multiple languages every day of the week—Saturdays, Sundays, and Holidays, too![80]

And to further hinder deportation of illegal aliens, ICE also amended its immigration detainer forms.[81] The new immigration detainer forms include a notice of alien rights, mercifully translated for the convenience of the detained, into Spanish (surprise, surprise), Chinese, Vietnamese, Portuguese, and French.[82] The new detainer form emphasizes that State and local law enforcement may detain an individual for only 48 hours—*and urges detained aliens to request State or local law enforcement release them if ICE has not taken custody within that time frame.*[83] Of course for its own part, ICE no longer wishes to take custody of illegal aliens; so the new form is just a long way of insisting on a policy of catch and release.

The new immigration detainer form also makes ICE detainment "operative *only upon the individual's conviction of the offense for which he or she was arrested.*"[84] (Just try that the next time you get pulled over for rolling a stop sign [local offense] and the officer finds a baggie of crack rocks in your pocket [federal offense]. After having the traffic ticket dismissed, just tell the court: "But Your Honor, I haven't been *convicted* of the antecedent offense! I haven't been *convicted* of rolling the stop sign—so you have to dismiss the federal crack possession charge, too! After all, the officer never would have found the crack unless he had stopped me for rolling the stop sign—and I haven't been convicted of that!" Just see how far that gets you.)

Meanwhile ICE's sister agency, USCIS, has also proposed new immigration regulations. Instead of initiating removal proceedings against illegal aliens, USCIS will now be granting them "provisional unlawful presence waivers."[85] Such waivers will be awarded to any alien who is already (illegally) here, and who has one immediate relative who is a U.S. citizen.[86] USCIS will then abstain from serving Notices to Appear and initiating removal proceedings against any and all aliens possessing "provisional unlawful presence waivers."[87] Yes, you understood perfectly well: *The Fourth Head is now granting illegal aliens tangible licenses which entitle them to amnesty.*

ICE's current operations under the new, administrative DREAM amnesty obscure the agency's purpose. So let us be clear: Enforcement of immigration law is the purpose for which ICE was created. The agency's very name indicates its design as a federal bureau of "U.S. *I*mmigration and *C*ustoms *Enforcement*."[88] When ICE came into existence, it assumed control of INS's (Immigration and Naturalization Service's) detention and deportation assets. And ICE maintains an entire division called ERO, whose responsibility is "Enforcement and *Removal* Operations."[89] I.e., *enforcement* of immigration law, and *removal* of violators.

ICE's original purpose—enforcement of immigration law and removal of immigration fugitives—was supported by Americans when ICE was created in 2002. And ICE's original purposes are still supported by citizens today.

But like so many other alphabet agencies before it, ICE aspires to a higher purpose than that to which it was originally assigned. Instead of *enforcing* immigration law, ICE has decided to proactively *prevent enforcement* of immigration law. ICE has decided to work for amnesty. ICE has chosen to work for the aliens.

Illegal immigration is one federal "service" almost no citizens wish to fund. Yet nested safely within the Fourth Head, such operations of an irrepresentative, monolithic government are very well financed—by citizens' own tax dollars. And those operations are quite well-hid. (Who would think to look for illegal immigration services, advocacy, and incentives within the bureau of "U.S. Immigration and Customs *Enforcement*"?)

So Incrementalism marches ever on and on . . . .

Impacts of Incrementalist Immigration

How successful has Incrementalism's underclass-import-strategy been?

Well, it is difficult to be numerically precise when considering the *illegal* component of Incrementalist immigration. We shall save the particulars for later.

But to briefly put illegal immigration into perspective here, according to non-partisan research it appears that *one in thirteen children born in the United States is now born to an illegal alien parent.*[90]

Those results aren't too shabby.

Yet illegal immigration represents, as we have seen, only one prong of Incrementalist immigration strategy. Taken as a whole, Incrementalist modifications to American immigration—from explicit legislation (*legal* immigration policy) to the proactive non-enforcement of what little federal immigration law remains (*illegal* immigration policy)—have resulted in a colossal influx of Third-World immigrants. Just how many? It appears that today, *more than one in seven American adults is an immigrant.*[91]

Now those are impressive results!

Better yet, due to immigrants' superior fertility rates, *immigrants are the parents of 23% of all U.S. children aged 17 and younger.*[92] Which bodes very well for Incrementalists in future elections! And best of all, *56% of U.S. population growth over the past decade (2000 to 2010) is due to Hispanic population growth alone.*[93]

One cannot overlook the cultural significance of such demographic scale. And socialists certainly don't.[94]

Perhaps the best people to ask about the success of Incrementalism's underclass-import-strategy are socialists themselves. How successful has Incrementalist immigration been? As noted with approval by Simon Rosenberg,

> When I was born in 1963 the country was almost 89 percent white, 10.5 percent African-American and less than 1 percent other. . . .
>
> Today [January 2008] America is 66 percent white and 33 percent 'minority'. . . . America is going through the most profound demographic transformation in its long history. If current trends continue, *America will be majority minority in my lifetime or soon thereafter. In a single lifetime we will have gone from a country made up largely of white Europeans to one that looks much more like the rest of the world. . . .*
>
> *What should leave us all optimistic is that only 15 percent of the country is truly alarmed about the new wave of immigrants arriving in America.* Consistently about 60 percent of the country says we need to leave all the undocumenteds [sic] here, indicating a pragmatic acceptance of the changes happening around our people and their families.[95]

Which is to say, the cane toads are ascendant! They will supplant Middle Americans within our lifetime! And almost no one is alarmed! Oh, happy day—to live in such auspicious times! The wise men's underclass-import-stratagem could not have worked better!

Incrementalist wise men's delivery is always somewhat oblique within public fora. (Obliquity is, after all, the soul of Incrementalism.) As a result it can be difficult to parse Incrementalist wise men's public statements. Yet despite Incrementalists' obliquity, the cane toads themselves perfectly understand their role in Incrementalists' underclass-import-strategy. Like their Incrementalist masters, they, too envision a Mexican *Anschluß*. And unlike their Incrementalist masters, cane toads' delivery can be quite direct. Professor José Angel Gutiérrez illustrates:

> Our numbers now are such that we are critical mass [sic] throughout the nation. Depending on what State you're in, we're on the verge of already being a majority minority. . . .
>
> It is not our fault that whites don't make babies, and blacks are not growing in sufficient numbers, and there's [sic] no other groups with such a goal to put their homeland back together again. We do. Those numbers will make it possible.[96]

True, the cane toad population is reaching critical mass. And true, it is not cane toads' fault that cane beetles—whether white or black (or yellow)—are no longer reproducing. Professor José Angel Gutiérrez continues with exemplary cane toad candor:

> This is *our* homeland. We cannot, we will not, and we must not be made illegal in our homeland. We are not immigrants that came from another country to another country; we are migrants, free to travel the length and breadth of the Americas because we belong here.
>
> We are millions. We just have to survive. We have an aging white America. They are not making babies. They are dying. It's a matter of time. The explosion is in our population.[97]

Which is to say, cane toads are outbreeding native cane beetles! Cane beetle populations are dwindling! *It is only a matter of time.* Cane toads know it. And as Augustin Cebada explains, cane toads would like to speed up that replacement process:

> [W]e are the majority here, and we are not going to be pushed around. . . . We're here . . . . to show white, Anglo-Saxon, Protestant L.A., the few of you who remain, that we are the majority, and we claim this land as ours, it's always been ours, and we're still here, and, uh, none of this talk about deporting. If anybody's going to be deported it's going to be you. . . .
>
> Go back to Boston! Go back to the Plymouth Rock, Pilgrims! Get out! We are the future. You're old and tired. Go on. We have beaten you; leave like beaten rats.
>
> You old white people, it is your duty to die. Even their own ethicists say that they should die; that they have a duty to die. They're taking up too much space, too much air. . . .
>
> The vast majority of our people are under the age of fifteen years old. Right now we're already controlling those elections, whether it's through violence or nonviolence. Through love of having children we are gonna take over.[98]

Now there is straightforward clarity: Go back to Plymouth Rock, Pilgrims! Get out! You old white people, it is your duty to die! (And same for you old black people! And you old yellow ones, too!) Cane toads claim this land. They anticipate replacing Middle Americans altogether. They plan on doing so very soon. So let's get it over with, Middle Americans—exile yourselves. Or hurry up and die. (Of course, not all immigrants speak this way. But some do. [99] And who is encouraging them? Certainly not we cane beetles! In any event, these cane toads know of what they speak. They fully comprehend the demographic imperative.)

The magnificent success of Incrementalists' underclass-import-strategy is reflected even in contemporary political campaigns: "¡Sí se puede!" is utilized as the theme, featured slogan, and rallying anthem of campaign speeches by immigrant-oriented, winning presidential candidates.[100] Of course, they regularly translate "¡Sí se puede!" into English, for more palatable consumption among the remaining cane beetles ("Yes we can!"). They use the slogan in 2008, and they trot it out again in 2012.[101] They openly admit the slogan's socialist origins.[102] Surely the repetitive use of such a well-known slogan, with such a lengthy historical record, with such weighty socialist and immigrant overtones, can be no oversight. Surely it was planned? Surely it was intended to resonate with immigrants? And especially with the bilingual? After all, it was used a dozen times, within a span of 100 seconds, within a single primary concession speech.[103] (And that is not counting the audience's twenty-eight, speech-interruptive incantations of that phrase over the same period.[104])

And this is not all. In contemporary politics, illegal aliens openly address party delegates at the Democratic National Convention. They give their real names. They tell their own stories. They do so without fear of exile. They know the new, administrative amnesty will deliver them. They proudly mount the podium—and personally invite us to join them on the Democrat Bus.[105]

Yes, a veritable underclass is here.

Incrementalist immigration has already created an underclass-oriented generation, dubbed the "millennial generation," consisting of (according to socialists) "the boomer babies and young immigrants born from 1978 to 1996."[106] As noted by socialist thinkers, this millennial generation "holds a wide range of progressive values," including "deep concern for today's income inequalities and social stratification,"[107] and "believ[ing] in government again. (Sixty-three percent think government should do more to solve the nation's problems.)"[108] Now that is encouraging for Incremental socialism!

Indeed, "a comprehensive review of available data from a range of polls and surveys in recent years shows just how fortuitous this generation is for progressives. Millennials are emerging as an enormous asset for progressives going forward—as enormous as the sheer size of this, the largest American generation ever."[109] And what sort of asset is this millennial generation? "This generation is poised to become the core of a 21st century progressive coalition."[110]

Which is to say, the cane toads have successfully altered America's political ecosystem. The wise-men's underclass is here, and it's ready for socialist intervention.

Not only is this millennial generation "poised" to become the core of a 21st century progressive coalition, socialists intend to ensure it becomes precisely that: "Today these new demographic realities are creating an opening for progressives to craft the next great electoral strategy . . . bringing together enough progressive and progressive-leaning voters throughout the rest of the country to forge a real 21st century majority."[111] A majority so strong, socialists predict it will free progressives "from the need to win significant victories in the nation's most conservative places," thereby "allow[ing] progressives to be progressive, to avoid some of the brutal ideological battles that can cripple a movement, and most important, to take risks and think big."[112]

In other words, Incrementalists will get their socialist revolution.

All this talk of millennial generations, of majority-minority, of explosive immigrant population growth, obscures the culturo-political significance of these events. Class ratios represent a zero-sum game in any society: Proportional growth in one group necessitates an equal and offsetting shrinkage among others.[xvii] So the question is, while the immigrant underclass has grown exponentially in America, which class (or classes) has (or have) correspondingly shrunk? Let us phrase the inquiry in Incrementalist terms: *Do decades of explosive Third-World immigration, does majority-minority, does the millennial generation, mean the end of the American middle class?* More precisely: Since the Hart-Celler Immigration and Nationality Act inaugurated Incrementalist immigration policy in 1965, has the American middle class declined significantly in relative terms?

Indeed it has! The data "clearly show a steady decline in the proportion of families living in middle-class neighborhoods from 1970-2010 . . . . In 1970, 65 percent of families lived in 'middle-income' neighborhoods . . . . by

---

[xviii] This holds true of any orthogonal partition of a population: the sum of relative percentages must of course add up to 100%!

For example, assume in one year 52% of the population in a given society is female. (This would of course imply that 100% (total population) - 52% (female) = 48% are male.)

Now say the female group grows from 52% to 54% of the population in that society. No matter how the overall population in that society has grown or shrunk over the same period of time, there must be an equal and offsetting decrease in the proportion of males in that society—that is, *the percentages of females and males must still add up to 100%*. So after proportional growth in the female population, we have 100% (total) - 54% (female) = 46% (male).

2007, only 44 percent of families lived in such neighborhoods."[113] In 1970 Middle Americans still comprised an overwhelming majority; during a few decades of Incrementalist immigration, Middle America has declined by a third in relative terms. Since shortly after Incrementalist immigration got underway, the middle class has been disappearing.

Which is to say, the wise men's calculations were correct! An American underclass *could indeed be imported.* That imported underclass is outbreeding Middle Americans. It is outcompeting Middle Americans for the new, Government-issued American resources. *As a result, we will be rid of that dreaded pest, the Middle American.* And the harvest of dependency will be secure forevermore!

Incrementalism's wise men viewed their creation.

And saw that *it was* good.

Cane Beetle Submission

Why did Middle Americans sit idly by while being systematically supplanted by a Third-World underclass?

Why did Middle Americans not rise up when immigration law was changed in 1965? Or in 1976? Or 1978? Or 1990?

Why did Middle Americans not rise up when illegal immigrants were made *de jure* citizens in 1986? Or *de facto* citizens in 2011?

There are at least two reasons. First, aside from the startling amnesty of 1986, the changes made to American immigration policy were delicate, gradual affairs. They built logically one upon another, and each step was a very short distance from the last. They went practically unnoticed. (I.e., no single step gave occasion for squirrel hunting.) Moreover they were billed as measures for reuniting families, and they were passed with assurances of more vigorous enforcement of immigration law in the future—propositions which were, in isolation, perfectly agreeable to Middle Americans.

But all of the foregoing can be said more simply: Socialist's underclass-import-strategy was executed in superb Incrementalist style.

Second, Incrementalism brought its Champion—Political Correctness—to fight its immigration battles. There were so many "teachable moments" in the immigration arena! With Political Correctness waiting in the wings, always ready to assist socialism at a moment's notice, one couldn't make even a three-sentence argument about immigration without being shouted down:

"Well, I don't blame foreigners for sneaking across the border in an attempt to improve their family's condition. I am sure I would do the same thing if I were in their situation. *But I would expect immigration officers to be looking for me, just like they do in any other country—and I would expect them to deport me if ever they found me out.*"

Before arriving at the punch line, you would be cut off:

"Racist!"

"Bigot!"

"Xenophobe!"

Argument over.

Few dared speak a word about the problem of illegal immigration—much less the problem of modern American *legal* immigration. Actually, let's be careful—let's not call it a "problem"! That would be impolitic! No, that would be xenophobic! And as most immigrants are no longer Caucasian, it would be racist, too! Hate speech, even!

Under the foregoing conditions the subject of American immigration became, like actual cane toads, quite poisonous—a subject which few dared handle.

So the sensitive issue of socialist immigration was tabled.

And eventually, few thought much about it.

America had *simply changed.*

No one could put their finger on the reason.

It was a cultural shift, really.

Undirected from above.

Perfectly democratic.

Truly spontaneous.

Mere Zeitgeist.

Who could argue with that?

Further Notes to Chapter 6

[1] Simpson-Mazzoli Immigration Reform and Control Act of 1986, § 201 (Pub.L. 99-603; 100 Stat. 3359) (granting amnesty to illegal aliens who had been in-country since Jan. 1, 1982).
[2] Mimi Hall, *Despite New Technology, Border Patrol Overwhelmed*, USA TODAY (Feb. 22, 2005). Some readers will remember that the Obama Administration sent 1,200 National Guard troops to the U.S.-Mexico border in June 2010 "in an effort to bolster the U.S. Border Patrol and try to prevent the growing drug violence in Mexico from spilling into the U.S." But in early 2012, this subsidiary Border Patrol will be cut in half. Or more. Stephen Dinan, *Obama to Slash National Guard Force on U.S.-Mexico Border*, THE WASHINGTON TIMES (Dec. 12, 2011).
[3] *See, e.g.*, Two Border Patrol Agents Face 20 Years in Prison: Officers Prosecuted—Wounded Drug Trafficker Given Full Immunity In Exchange for Testimony, WORLDNETDAILY (Aug. 7, 2006); *Border Patrol Agents Sentenced to Prison: 11-12 Years for Shooting Drug-Smuggling Suspect in Buttocks as He Fled Across Frontier*, WORLDNETDAILY (Oct. 20, 2006).
[4] *Ibid.*
[5] Stephen Dinan, *DOJ Dismisses Leniency Request for Border Patrol Agent*, THE WASHINGTON TIMES (Feb. 22, 2012); Perry Chiaramonte, *Border Patrol Union Blasts Homeland Security Instructions to 'Run Away' and 'Hide' from Gunmen*, FOX NEWS (June 29, 2012).
[6] Christopher Sherman, *U.S. Proposes Unmanned Border Crossing with Mexico*, THE DETROIT NEWS (Dec. 11, 2011).
[7] *Ibid.*
[8] *E.g.*, Farmers Branch, a Texan city north of Dallas, passed municipal ordinances fining landlords for knowingly renting properties to illegal immigrants. The measure passed by popular referendum on May 12, 2007 by a vote of 68% to 32% (Can you imagine a landslide of this scale? What would it mean if the popular vote in a presidential election were skewed to this degree?). Incrementalist forces could not wait—they immediately filed a lawsuits against Farmers Branch, accusing its ordinance of unconstitutionality under the doctrine of preemption—a ludicrous theory, but under the watchful eye of an Incrementalist arbiter, it worked. For the time being. As of this writing, the case is in appeal in the 5th Circuit.
[9] Enacted in 2010 as a modification of Arizona SB 1070, the Support Our Law Enforcement and Safe Neighborhoods Act.
[10] Arizona HB 2162 § 1 (amending §1-501(A)). Of course, this provision applies only to those federal welfare benefits "that require[] participants to be citizens of the United States, legal residents of the United States or otherwise lawfully present in the United States," and which are "administered by this state [Arizona] or a political subdivision of this state." *Ibid.*
[11] Arizona HB 2162 § 2 (amending §1-502(A)).
[12] Arizona HB 2162 § 3 (amending Arizona Revised Statutes §11-1051(B)). HB 2162 also adds penalties for concealing, harboring, or shielding aliens from detection, as well as for encouraging or inducing an alien to reside in Arizona, and for transporting or moving illegal aliens in furtherance of their illegal presence. Which is to say HB 2162 penalizes *the coyotes*. The *human traffickers*. Arizona HB 2162 § 6 (amending Arizona Revised Statutes §13-2929(A)(2), (A)(3), and (A)(1), respectively).
[13] Angus Reid Public Opinion Poll, *Americans Voice Support for New Arizona Immigration Legislation*, 5 (April 28, 2010). *See http://www.angus-reid.com/polls/38836/americans_support_arizona_immigration_bill/* for link to complete .pdf of poll results. *See also* Stephen Dinan, *Majority Backs Arizona on Immigration Crackdown Law—Poll: Voters Want Similar Immigration Laws for Their States*, THE WASHINGTON TIMES (July 10, 2012).
[14]*Ibid.*
[15] Benjamin Myers, *Justice Dept. Rejects South Carolina Voter ID Law, Calling it Discriminatory*, THE WASHINGTON POST (Dec. 21, 2011).
[16] Sari Horowitz, *Justice Department Bars Texas Voter ID Law*, THE WASHINGTON POST (Mar. 12, 2012); Pete Yost, *Justice Dept Opposes Texas Voter ID Law*, THE ASSOCIATED PRESS (Mar. 12, 2012).

[17] Attorney General Eric Holder, speaking to the NAACP in Houston, July 10, 2012. Ramit Plushnick-Masti & Pete Yost, *Eric Holder: Voter ID Laws Are 'Poll Taxes'*, THE HUFFINGTON POST (July 10, 2012).
[18] Benjamin Myers, *Justice Dept. Rejects South Carolina Voter ID Law, Calling it Discriminatory*, THE WASHINGTON POST (Dec. 21, 2011); *see also* Meg Kinnard, *SC Voter ID Law Rejected by Justice Department*, MY WAY (Dec. 23, 2011).
[19] Meg Kinnard, *SC Voter ID Law Rejected by Justice Department*, MY WAY (Dec. 23, 2011).
[20] Marc Caputo, *Feds to Florida: Halt Non-Citizen Voter Purge*, THE MIAMI HERALD (Mar. 31, 2012).
[21] Dara Kam, *Florida Non-Citizen Voter List Will Be Vetted Against Homeland Security Database*, The Palm Beach Post (May 17, 2012); *cf.* Janell Ross, *Voter Purge, Minority Voting Rights Flashpoints of New Showdown in Florida*, THE HUFFINGTON POST (May 27, 2012).
[22] *See* Jerry Markon, *U.S. Files New Suit on Ariz. Immigration Issue*, THE WASHINGTON POST (Aug. 31, 2010).
[23] *See, e.g.*, 8 U.S.C. §§ 1324(a)(1) and 1324 (b)(1) (2011) (requiring employers to verify the immigration status of employees); 8 U.S.C. § 1324(f) (2011) (imposing criminal and pecuniary penalties for failing to verify employees' immigration status).
[24] Zeituni Onyango, illegal alien and aunt of the President of the United States, in an interview with Jonathan Elias for WBZ-TV, CBS BOSTON (*Obama's Aunt: Silence Broken*, Sept. 21, 2010).
[25] Sam Webb, *A Party of Socialism in the 21st Century: What It Looks Like, What It Says, and What It Does*, POLITICAL AFFAIRS (Feb. 3, 2011).
[26] Zeituni Onyango, illegal alien and aunt of the President of the United States, in an interview with Jonathan Elias for WBZ-TV, CBS BOSTON (*Obama's Aunt: Silence Broken*, Sept. 21, 2010). http://www.youtube.com/watch?v=9xeCsGrnudc&feature=related.
[27] Michelle Malkin, *Dubya and Zuni—The Rest of the Story on Obama's Illegal-Alien Aunt*, NATIONAL REVIEW ONLINE (Nov. 12, 2008) ("An Immigration and Customs Enforcement source familiar with Western field offices told me: 'The ICE fugitive-operations group throughout the United States was told to stand down until after the election from arresting or transporting anyone out of the United States. This was done to avoid any mistakes of deporting or arresting anyone who could have a connection to the election, i.e., anyone from Kenya who could be a relative.'").
[28] *See, e.g.*, in the 107th Congress (2001) both H.R. 1918 and S. 1291; for the 108th Congress (2003) H.R. 1684 and also S. 1545; in the 109th Congress (2005) both H.R. 5131 and S. 2075; and in the 110th Congress (2007) H.R. 1275 and also S. 774; in the 111th Congress (2009) both S. 3992 and S. 3827; etc.
[29] National Defense Authorization Act for FY 2011.
[30] Erica Werner, *Obama Pledges Help for Illegal Immigrant Grads*, MY WAY NEWS (April 29, 2011) (© 2011 Associated Press).
[31] *Ibid.*
[32] Emile Schepers, *Undocumented Immigrants and Health Care*, POLITICAL AFFAIRS MAGAZINE (Sept. 14, 2009) (emphasis added); *see also* David Bacon, *Change Immigrants and Labor Can Believe In*, THE NATION (Nov. 26, 2008) ("In its first 100 days, a new administration could take simple steps to . . . stop ICE from seeking serious federal criminal charges, with incarceration in privately run prisons, when a worker lacks papers or has a bad Social Security numbers [sic]."); Alice Gordon, *APN Chat with US Rep. Gutierrez (D-Il) on Immigration Reform*, THE ATLANTA PROGRESSIVE NEWS (March 2, 2009) ("There is a need to have . . . a moratorium on the deportations, until Congress is able to act. . . . We need to reprioritize and to deport [only] those who sell drugs, those who smuggle, and those who have come to the United States to be terrorists and do us harm.").
[33] U.S. Citizenship and Immigration Services Memorandum, *Administrative Alternatives to Comprehensive Immigration Reform*, 1 (undated; leaked in Aug., 2010), authored by Denise A. Vanison et al., and sent to Alejandro N. Mayorkas, Director of USCIS. http://www2.nationalreview.com/memo_UCIS_072910.html.
[34] *Ibid.*
[35] *Ibid.*
[36] *Ibid.*

[37] In relation to all of the above, *see* the USCIS' Formal Response when its amnesty memo was leaked. A copy of the USCIS' formal response is preserved on many immigration attorney's websites and blogs; *see, e.g.*, Michelle Gee, *Leaked Immigration Memo Shows Practical Solutions as well as High Hopes*, SILICON VALLEY IMMIGRATION LAWYER BLOG (July 30, 2010), http://www.siliconvalleyimmigrationlawyer.com/2010/07/leaked-immigration-memo-shows.html; Jacob Sapochnick, *How Does USCIS See a Possible Immigration Reform?—Read the Internal Memo!*, VISA LAWYER BLOG (Aug. 2, 2010), http://www.visalawyerblog.com/2010/08/hoe_does_uscis_see_a_possible.html.

[38] USCIS' Formal Response (*see supra* n. 37 and accompanying text) (emphasis added).

[39] Richard Trumka, *Workers Must Unite for Better Immigration Policy*, THE HILL (April 28, 2011) (emphasis added).

[40] Memorandum from John Morton, Director of U.S. Immigration and Customs Enforcement, *To All Field Office Directors, All Special Agents in Charge, All Chief Counsel*, Policy Number 10075.1, FEA Number 306-112-0026 (June 17, 2011), http://www.ice.gov/doclib/secure-communities/pdf/prosecutorial-discretion-memo.pdf; Memorandum from John Morton, Director of U.S. Immigration and Customs Enforcement, *To All Field Office Directors, All Special Agents in Charge, All Chief Counsel*, Policy Number 10076.1, FEA Number 306-112-002b (June 17, 2011), http://www.ice.gov/doclib/secure-communities/pdf/domestic-violence.pdf.

[41] Stephen Dinan, *Obama to Deport Illegals by 'Priority': Case-By-Case Plan Will Curb Numbers*, THE WASHINGTON TIMES (August 18, 2011).

[42] Memorandum from John Morton, Director of U.S. Immigration and Customs Enforcement, *To All Field Office Directors, All Special Agents in Charge, All Chief Counsel*, Policy Number 10075.1, FEA Number 306-112-0026 (June 17, 2011), http://www.ice.gov/doclib/secure-communities/pdf/prosecutorial-discretion-memo.pdf; *see also* Stephen Dinan, *Obama to Deport Illegals by 'Priority': Case-By-Case Plan Will Curb Numbers*, THE WASHINGTON TIMES (August 18, 2011); Robert Pear, *Fewer Youths to be Deported in New Policy*, THE NEW YORK TIMES (August 18, 2011).

[43] Memorandum from John Morton, Director of U.S. Immigration and Customs Enforcement, *To All Field Office Directors, All Special Agents in Charge, All Chief Counsel*, Policy Number 10076.1, FEA Number 306-112-002b, p. 2 (June 17, 2011), http://www.ice.gov/doclib/secure-communities/pdf/domestic-violence.pdf.

[44] *Ibid.*

[45] *Ibid.* at 3.

[46] *Ibid.* at 2.

[47] *Ibid.*

[48] Robert Pear, *Fewer Youths to be Deported in New Policy*, THE NEW YORK TIMES (August 18, 2011).

[49] U.S. Citizenship and Immigration Services Memorandum, *Administrative Alternatives to Comprehensive Immigration Reform*, 1-2 (undated, leaked in Aug., 2010), authored by Denise A. Vanison et al., and sent to Alejandro N. Mayorkas, Director of USCIS. http://www2.nationalreview.com/memo_UCIS_072910.html.

[50] Stephen Dinan, *Obama to Deport Illegals by 'Priority': Case-By-Case Plan Will Curb Numbers*, THE WASHINGTON TIMES (August 18, 2011).

[51] Robert Pear, *Fewer Youths to be Deported in New Policy*, THE NEW YORK TIMES (August 18, 2011).

[52] *Ibid.*

[53] 1 U.S.C. § 7 (2011) (emphasis added).

[54] Howie Carr, *Don't Cry for Auntie Zeituni*, THE BOSTON HERALD (May 11, 2012); Caroline May, *Obama's 'Auntie Zeituni' Pens Memoir: 'Tears of Abuse'*, THE DAILY CALLER (May 11, 2012).

[55] BARACK H. OBAMA, DREAMS FROM MY FATHER: A STORY OF RACE AND INHERITANCE 307 (Crown Publishers 2004) (1995).

[56] *Ibid.*

[57] *Ibid.*

[58] Billy Baker & Glen Johnson, *Obama Kin Arrested on DUI Charge*, THE BOSTON GLOBE (Aug. 30, 2011).

[59] *Ibid.*

[60] *Ibid.*
[61] *Ibid.*
[62] *Ibid.*
[63] *Ibid.*
[64] Billy Baker & Glen Johnson, *Obama Kin Arrested on DUI Charge*, THE BOSTON GLOBE (Aug. 30, 2011); Kerry Picket, *Obama's Illegal Uncle Arrested; 'Uncle Omar' Almost Hits Cop Car, Tries to Call White House*, THE WASHINGTON TIMES (Aug. 28, 2011).
[65] Maria Sacchetti, *Obama's Uncle Quietly Released from Jail*, THE BOSTON GLOBE (Sept. 9, 2011).
[66] *Ibid.*
[67] *Ibid.*
[68] Kerry Picket, *Obama's Illegal Uncle Arrested; 'Uncle Omar' Almost Hits Cop Car, Tries to Call White House*, THE WASHINGTON TIMES (Aug. 28, 2011).
[69] Dave Wedge and Laurel Sweet, *President Obama's Uncle Had Social Security ID*, THE BOSTON HERALD (Aug. 30, 2011).
[70] *Ibid.*
[71] *Ibid.*
[72] Maria Sacchetti, *Obama's Uncle Quietly Released from Jail*, THE BOSTON GLOBE (Sept. 9, 2011).
[73] *Ibid.*
[74] Stephen Dinan, *House Chairman: Obama's Uncle Got 'Backdoor Amnesty'*, THE WASHINGTON TIMES (Sept. 9, 2011).
[75] Maria Sacchetti, *Obama's Uncle Quietly Released from Jail*, THE BOSTON GLOBE (Sept. 9, 2011).
[76] Dave Wedge and Laurel Sweet, *President Obama's Uncle Had Social Security ID*, THE BOSTON HERALD (Aug. 30, 2011).
[77] Paloma Esquivel, *Number of Deportation Cases Drops By Nearly a Third, Report Says*, THE LOS ANGELES TIMES (February 24, 2012).
[78] U.S. Immigration and Customs Enforcement, *ICE Establishes Hotline for Detained Individuals, Issues New Detainer Form*, ICE NEWS RELEASES (Dec. 29, 2011). *See also* MacKenzie Weinger, *ICE Launches Hotline For Busted Immigrants*, POLITICO (Dec. 29, 2011).
[79] U.S. Immigration and Customs Enforcement, *ICE Establishes Hotline for Detained Individuals, Issues New Detainer Form*, ICE NEWS RELEASES (Dec. 29, 2011).
[80] *Ibid.* ("Translation Services will be available in several languages from 7 a.m. until midnight (Eastern) seven days a week."). And while ICE establishes a toll-free hotline to assist illegal immigrants, Secretaries of the Departments of Education (Arne Duncan) and Labor (Hilda Solis) conduct official meetings with illegal immigrants at Department of Education headquarters. Meetings to discuss what they, as administrative agency chiefs, are doing to assist illegal immigrants land college educations and high-paying jobs. Such meetings are proudly proclaimed from the Dept. of Education's official blog. Claire Jellinek, *Secretaries Duncan and Solis Meet with DREAMers*, HOMEROOM (official blog of the U.S. Dept. of Educ.) (Dec. 21, 2011). The Secretaries' heartfelt concern can be readily discerned in furrowed brows and quizzical looks, pictured prominently in the Dept. of Labor's official newsletter, as the Secretaries meet with illegal aliens. *Working to Make DREAM a Reality* (slideshow), DOL NEWS BRIEF, (Dec. 15, 2011). These photos are priceless, and not to be missed.
[81] U.S. Immigration and Customs Enforcement, *ICE Establishes Hotline for Detained Individuals, Issues New Detainer Form*, ICE NEWS RELEASES (Dec. 29, 2011). *See also* MacKenzie Weinger, *ICE Launches Hotline For Busted Immigrants*, POLITICO (Dec. 29, 2011).
[82] U.S. Immigration and Customs Enforcement, *ICE Establishes Hotline for Detained Individuals, Issues New Detainer Form*, ICE NEWS RELEASES (Dec. 29, 2011).
[83] *Ibid.*
[84] *Ibid.*
[85] *Provisional Unlawful Presence Waivers of Inadmissibility for Certain Immediate Relatives*, 77 Fed. Reg. 19,902 (April 2, 2012) (to be codified at 8 C.F.R. 103; 212).
[86] *Ibid.*
[87] "USCIS does not envision issuing Notices to Appear (NTA) to initiate removal proceedings against aliens whose provisional waiver applications have been approved." *Ibid.*
[88] *See, e.g.*, http://www ice.gov/.
[89] *See, e.g.*, http://www ice.gov/ under the "Enforcement & Removal" tab.

[90] Jeffrey S. Passel et al., *Unauthorized Immigrants and Their U.S.-Born Children*, PEW HISPANIC CENTER REPORT 1 (Aug. 11, 2010) (340,000 babies born to illegal immigrant parents out of 4.3 million babies born in the U.S. = 7.9%. One of thirteen = only 7.7%.).
[91] To be more precise, it appears that 15.7% of the U.S. adult population is immigrant. Jeffrey S. Passel et al., *Unauthorized Immigrants and Their U.S.-Born Children*, PEW HISPANIC CENTER REPORT 3 (Aug. 11, 2010). And most of those 15.7% are from the Third-World.
[92] *Ibid.*
[93] Jeffrey S. Passel et al., *Census 2010: 50 Million Latinos—Hispanics Account for More Than Half of Nation's Growth in Past Decade*, PEW HISPANIC CENTER REPORT 1 (March 24, 2011).
[94] *See, e.g.*, Sam Webb, *A Party of Socialism in the 21st Century: What It Looks Like, What It Says, and What It Does*, POLITICAL AFFAIRS (Feb. 3, 2011); Simon Rosenberg & Peter Leyden, *The 50-Year Strategy—Beyond '08: Can Progressives Play for Keeps?*, MOTHER JONES 64-65 (Nov. 2007).
[95] Simon Rosenberg, *On Obama, Race and* [sic] *the End of the Southern Strategy*, NDN (Jan. 4, 2008) (emphasis added). http://ndn.org/blog/2008/01/obama-race-and-end-southern-strategy.
[96] Interview with Professor José Angel Gutiérrez, (Aug. 8, 1999), http://www.insearchofaztlan.com/gutierrez.html. The interview was conducted by Jesús Salvador Treviño, Patrisia Gonzales, and/or Roberto Rodriguez during the production of the film *In Search of Aztlan* (directed by Jesús Salvador Treviño, written by Espíritu de Tonantzin, executive producer Gabriel Carmona, 2003).
[97] José Angel Gutiérrez, professor of political science at the University of Texas, Arlington, and a former leader of La Raza Unida, speaking at a Latino conference held at the University of California, Riverside (Jan. 14, 1995).
[98] Augustin Cebada, of the Movimiento Estudiantil Chicano de Aztlan, speech at a Fourth of July celebration (!) at the Wilshire Federal Building in Westwood, California (July 4, 1996).
[99] And so do some cane beetles, who have incoherently taken up the cause of Mexican illegal immigration, and speak in precisely the same manner about it as the cane toads who wish to sweep them off the face of North America. *See, e.g.*, Benny Johnson, *Farrakhan Laments: 'Sad That Mexico Lost California, Arizona, Colorado, New Mexico' Through American 'Trickery'; Soon Whites 'Will Be The Minority' in the Country They 'Took'*, THE BLAZE (May 29, 2012).
[100] *E.g.*, Barack Obama's campaign speech to the Culinary Workers Union Local 226 (Las Vegas, Jan. 11, 2008). *See* video of this speech at, *e.g.*, http://www.metacafe.com/watch/1039161/latino_hispanic_workers_unions_barack_obama_si_se_puede/; http://www.dailymotion.com/video/x41zo5_latino-hispanic-workers-unions-bara_news.
[101] Reid J. Epstein, *Obama Widens Latino Voting Gap*, POLITICO (June 22, 2012).
[102] When presenting the Medal of Freedom to socialist immigration activist Dolores Huerta, the co-founder of the United Farm Workers of America, President Obama remarked: "Dolores was very gracious when I told her I had stolen her slogan, 'Si, se puede.' Yes we can." Editorial, *United Farm Workers' Huerta Receives Medal of Freedom*, PEOPLE'S WORLD (May 31, 2012).
[103] Transcripts of this New Hampshire primary concession speech record the phrase "Yes we can!" only ten times (*see, e.g.*, Obama Campaign, *Barack Obama's Speech in New Hampshire*, NORTHWEST PROGRESSIVE INSTITUTE OFFICIAL BLOG (Jan. 8, 2008)). However, in the heat of the moment, the presidential candidate got carried away—and repeated "Yes we can!" a dozen times in just 100 seconds (*see* coverage of the speech's actual delivery, *e.g.*, http://www.youtube.com/watch?v=Fe751kMBwms).
[104] Obama Campaign, *Barack Obama's Concession Speech after New Hampshire Primary*, (Jan. 8, 2008) http://www.youtube.com/watch?v=Fe751kMBwms.
[105] Stephen Dinan, *Young Face Put on Illegal Migration at DNC: Noncitizen Takes Convention Stage*, THE WASHINGTON TIMES (Sep. 5, 2012); Andrew O'Reilly, *Democratic Convention: DREAMer Benita Veliz Takes Center Stage*, FOX NEWS LATINO (Sep. 5, 2012).
[106] Simon Rosenberg & Peter Leyden, *The 50-Year Strategy—Beyond '08: Can Progressives Play for Keeps?*, MOTHER JONES 64-65 (Nov. 2007).
[107] Peter Leyden, Ruy Teixeira, & Eric Greenberg, *The Progressive Politics of the Millennial Generation*, NEW POLITICS INSTITUTE (June 20, 2007).
[108] Simon Rosenberg & Peter Leyden, *The 50-Year Strategy—Beyond '08: Can Progressives Play for Keeps?*, MOTHER JONES 65 (Nov. 2007).

[109] Peter Leyden, Ruy Teixeira, & Eric Greenberg, *The Progressive Politics of the Millennial Generation*, NEW POLITICS INSTITUTE (June 20, 2007).
[110] Simon Rosenberg & Peter Leyden, *The 50-Year Strategy—Beyond '08: Can Progressives Play for Keeps?*, MOTHER JONES 65 (Nov. 2007).
[111] *Ibid.* at 66.
[112] *Ibid.*
[113] SEAN F. REARDON & KENDRA BISCHOFF, GROWTH IN THE RESIDENTIAL SEGREGATION OF FAMILIES BY INCOME, 1970-2009 11(Advisory Board of the US2010 Project, Nov. 2011). *See also Ibid.* Fig. 1 at 12.

7

Entertainment Submission

The public has long since cast off its cares; the People who once upon a time handed down military command, high civil office, legions and all else, now restrains itself and longs eagerly for just two things: bread and circuses!

—Juvenal[i]

Literature and art which sing the praises of socialism are necessary.

—Kim Il-sung[ii]

WHO CAN FORGET THE MAYANS?

Across the Yucatán and throughout the Chiapas Highlands, they erected mountainous stone pyramids. They laid vast stone plazas. They built sprawling stone palaces. And exquisite stone temples. And nifty stone observatories. True, they never progressed beyond stone tools or corbelled arches, yet Mayans remain the unrivaled architects of ancient America.

The Mayans measured time and seasons with calendars of unparalleled accuracy and scope. (Their long-count calendar tallied time according to *b'ak'tun*, a period of 144,000 days.) They were skilled astronomers who delighted especially in tracking Venus. Their understanding of mathematics was similarly impressive: They independently developed mathematical notation for the number zero (which is no mean feat).

---

[i] DECIMUS IUNIUS IUVENALIS, THE SATIRES, Book IV, satire x, referring to Romans' free grain dole (later baked bread dole) and lavish, public entertainments (chariot races, theatrical spectacles, and gladiatorial games).

[ii] KIM IL-SUNG, DUTIES OF LITERATURE AND ARTS IN OUR REVOLUTION 123 (Foreign Languages Publishing House, Pyongyang 1972).

The Mayans also exhibited sophistication in the visual arts. They made animal hair brushes for use in detailed and expressive paintings. They developed striking pigments, like *azul Maya*, for use in enormous murals. They developed ingenious stone-working techniques to engrave marvelously intricate monoliths. They had an affinity for extravagant headdresses. They developed a complex logosyllabic writing system. They employed professional artisans and scribes. And they combined all these artistic faculties in the medium of colossal stelae, commemorating the marvelous conquests of their rulers.

The Mayans did not limit themselves to gnawing on manioc tubers in the forest. Heavens, no! They raised corn. And beans. And squash. And tomatoes. And chili peppers. And papaya. And chayote. They utilized terracing. They cultivated cacao trees—and sipped the resulting chocolate beverages! By Mesoamerican standards Mayans were skilled agronomists. Indeed, agricultural efficiency allowed Mayans to live in large cities spanning multiple square miles at tremendous residential densities—tens of thousands to a single city.

Yes, Mayan civilization must be credited with tremendous achievements. But the Mayans' greatest achievement of all was in the realm of *entertainment*. Indeed we may say that when Mayans put their stamp on the Mesoamerican ballgame, they developed the most compelling entertainment of all time.[iii]

Under Mayan direction, the Mesoamerican ballgame was transformed into a spectacle not to be missed. And Mayans never missed it. When it was time to play ball, Mayans descended from their pyramids and temples. They poured out of palaces and grass huts. They emptied from observatories and plazas. Ruler and artisans, priests and paupers, drummers and captives alike. They all crowded around the rim of the ball court, to witness the most irresistible entertainment ever devised.

Mayan ball courts, too, were fashioned of stone. Shaped roughly like a capital "I," ball courts formed a deep alley roughly four times longer than wide, with steeply sloping or even vertical walls. Some ball courts (like "The Great" at Chichén Itzá) were as large as a football field. Others were rather quaint, roughly the size of a racquetball court. Regardless of size, interior ball court surfaces were finished in stucco and finely polished. A pair of hoops, also made of stone, was attached to the walls—high above the contestants below, one on each side, at the alley's midpoint.

Within that stone alley rested the hopes and fears of all Mayans. There the gods were imitated. There the rituals were fulfilled. There the creation

[iii] It is true that the Mayans did not *invent* the Mesoamerican ballgame; it had been played for centuries. (While there remains some debate about which particular Mesoamerican group invented the famous ballgame, 3,500 year old ball courts have been unearthed.) But as a form of entertainment, the Mayans took the ballgame to a whole new level.

allegory played out. There the astronomical bodies were restored to their proper alignments and kept on schedule. There the gods were satiated. There lay the portal to *Xibalba*: the underworld itself.[iv]

Drums began to throb. The ball court erupted with cheers. Contestants paraded into the ball court below: Strapping Mayans, in full ceremonial regalia—jade, jaguar pelts, quetzal plumes, unwieldy headdresses and all. To the shouts of frenzied onlookers, contestants removed their ceremonial costumes and donned the spartan habit of a ballplayer: leathern, wood, and wicker girdles, to armor hips against the heavy, punishing, solid rubber ball. Knee pads, gloves, and forearm guards to protect limbs from the stone-and-stucco ball court. Otherwise contestants' glistening bodies were unadorned—and magnificently naked.

Contestants were divided into two opposing teams.

And then the game began.

The Mesoamerican ballgame was a hardscrabble blend of soccer (the ball could never be touched with the hands), racquetball (the ball stayed in play off the walls of the ball court), volleyball (the ball was to remain in play—i.e., in the air—between the two teams, and points were awarded when the ball bounced too often without a successful return), and basketball (the game ended when the ball passed through one of the stone hoops).

Contestants ran, and leapt, and dove, and slid, and spun—in desperate contortions to keep the ball in play. And, if possible, to launch it through one of the stone hoops high above. Primarily the hips (with protective girdle!) were used to strike the ball. And this provided high entertainment: Just a slight miscalculation on the part of a contestant might result in serious injury or death. Yes, it was a game of inches: If that heavy, hurtling, solid rubber ball were to strike abdomen or groin instead of armored pelvis . . . .

[iv] In Mayan tradition, ballgame contestants are quite literally *summoned* by the gods of the underworld (a frightful proposition, to be sure). According to the Mayan Scriptures:

> "[A]ll they did was throw dice and play ball, every day. They would play each other in pairs, the four of them together. When they gathered in the ball court *for entertainment* . . . .
>
> "Since it was on the road to Xibalba that they played, they were heard by One Death and Seven Death, the lords of Xibalba: 'What's happening on the face of the earth? They're just stomping and shouting. They should be summoned to come play ball here. We'll defeat them, since we simply get no deference from them. They show no respect, nor do they have any shame.
>
> "'You're going, you Military Keepers of the Mat, to summon [the ball players]. You'll tell them, when you arrive: . . . "Would that they might come to play ball with us here. Then we could have some excitement with them . . . . [T]hey should bring their playthings, their yokes and arm guards should come, along with their rubber ball."'"

POPOL VUH 91, 93 (Dennis Tedlock trans., Simon & Schuster rev. ed. 1996) (1558) (emphasis added). *See also ibid.* at 112-113 (describing the similar summons of Hunahpu and Xbalanque to *Xibalba*.)

Due to scoring intricacies—and the difficulty of directing a hefty, solid rubber ball through a stone hoop high above with the flick of one's hips—the ballgame *could last for days without pause.* At night torches were held aloft to light the ball court until dawn. And the drums thundered. And cheers rang through the ball court. And the contestants fought on. At dawn the torches were extinguished, and the game continued apace. The drums rumbled. The spectators roared. The stone court reverberated with the shrieks of contestants and the bellows of the entertained.

And still the contestants played on.

What a game!

Sometimes exquisite contrivances were indulged: To encourage spectator fervor, the ruler himself would play! In such cases, it was customary to select his opponents from among prisoners of war. That way the outcome was certain. That way the ruler—who was well-fed, well-exercised, and unintimidated—could showcase his ineffable power![v] (And who was going to miss a few captives? The gods didn't seem to mind whose blood was spilt, so long as it was regularly offered.)

Whoever the contestants were, anticipation was amplified with every hip thrust. With each passing minute, tension within the ball court mounted. Every hour that passed, anxiety grew.

Why all the buildup?

Well, the stakes could not have been higher. The contestants, for their part, were fully motivated. Winners received the red-carpet treatment. They became instant celebrities. They were cheered and danced for days. They were hoisted on the shoulders of the most fanatical sports fans ever to grace the earth. They recouped wagers plus winnings. They received trophies of quetzal plumes or finely woven textiles. They were made intimates of the royal court. They wore special insignia around town marking them as champions. Their exploits were sung at the hearthside. They were hailed as gods.

As for the losers—well, the losers never saw the red carpet.

Actually, let us be frank: Among many other cultural innovations, Mayans also coined the phrase "The agony of defeat." It may be cliché exaggeration these days, but the Mayans meant it quite sincerely. By entering the ball court, contestants had wagered life itself on the outcome of the game.[vi] For the sake

---

[v] This was a brilliant innovation, which simultaneously increased the popularity of both ruler and game. Just imagine this principle of entertainment transferred to our own time: If the president should agree to don helmet and shoulder pads, and play in the Super Bowl, it would be must-see TV.

[vi] Mayan ballers likely wagered things other than their lives as well; perhaps spectators did the same. Among the Aztecs—who played Rome to Post Classic Mayans' Greece—people wagered all things on ballgame outcomes. This included their moveable property (jewels, slaves, quetzal feathers, battle gear, mistresses), real property (homes, fields, granaries), pulque source (maguey

of the innocent and the squeamish, let's just say the losers lost their heads.[vii] With a little help from a percussion-flaked stone blade.

Yes, ballgame losers made their descent to *Xibalba* before spectators' very eyes! While winners might be celebrated for days, it was losers who always featured most prominently at Mayan afterparties. It was losers who provided the high point of Mayan entertainment. Losers' departure for *Xibalba* yielded the apex of Mayan pageantry, so often recreated in bas relief.

Finally, losers' crania took their place among scores of others upon the awe-inspiring skull-rack.

The game was over.

---

plants), personal liberty, lives—and even their own children. DIEGO DURÁN, BOOK OF THE GODS AND RITES AND THE ANCIENT CALENDAR 315-19 (Fernando Horcasitas trans., Doris Heyden ed., University of Oklahoma Press 1971) (1579).

[vii] Occasionally you will hear that it was not the ballgame losers, but the *winners* who lost their heads. Do not be fooled. Such claims are attempts to make human sacrifice *among the Mayans* appear somehow more noble, more tasteful, more desirable, more civilized—and more pure. But such claims are not based on the historical record.

A quick look at the panels the Great Ball Court at Chichén Itzá are sufficient to resolve this matter. Take portion D of the east central panel, for instance: Only the beheaded ball player is kneeling in submission. The ball player who holds his head is triumphant, standing, still holding the stone knife—holding the severed head by the hair, and disrespectfully low to the ground. *See, e.g.*, LINDA SCHELE & MARY ELLEN MILLER, THE BLOOD OF KINGS: DYNASTY AND RITUAL IN MAYA ART 244 Fig. VI.3 (George Braziller, 1986).

Or take the Mayan Scriptures at their word: To vanquished ball players, the Lord(s) of Xibalba state(s):

> "'Very well. This very day, your day is finished, you will die, you will disappear, and we shall break you off. Here you will hide your faces: you are to be sacrificed!' said One Death and Seven Death.
>
> "And then they were sacrificed and buried. They were buried at the Place of Ball Game Sacrifice, as it is called. The head of One Hunahpu was cut off; only his body was buried with his younger brother."

POPOL VUH 97 (Dennis Tedlock trans., Simon & Schuster rev. ed. 1996) (1558) (When dealing with gods and heroes in the Mayan pantheon, the question "Singular or plural?" is not a simple matter. A certain divine dualism imparts doppelgangers to all important characters. Hence One Death and Seven Death, who are never apart from each other, speak as one. Are they one? Are they two? No, they are simultaneously both one and two.).

Moreover, sacrifice was not—as Mayan revisionists would have us believe—a consensual practice. This is clear from the fact that sacrificial victims were none too excited about their glorification as offerings. Again the Mayan Scriptures illustrate:

> "They underwent heart sacrifice there, and the heart sacrifice was performed on the two lords only for the purpose of destroying them.
>
> "As soon as they had killed the one lord without bringing him back to life, the other lord had been meek and tearful before the dancers. He didn't consent, he didn't accept it:
>
> "'Take pity on me!' he said when he realized."

Ibid. at 138. Sounds like fun.

It was a hassle, to be sure. You couldn't win the ballgame every time! (Not unless you were the ruler, anyway.) Yet ballgame entertainments remained a defining aspect of Mayan culture for centuries. And such entertainment provided certain benefits: The celestial bodies remained in their proper orbits. The sun chose not to remain in *Xibalba*, but arose punctually the next day. The seasons came and went on schedule. Plagues and pestilence were minimized. The rains watered the crops. The harvest was good. The gods were appeased.

Mayan entertainment had other benefits, too.

The ballgame had a positively hypnotic effect on the entertained. It distracted multitudes of commoners—for multiple days and nights at a stretch!—from the fact that they would be back at the limestone quarry again tomorrow, splitting multi-ton blocks with Neolithic tools for the "public" benefit. It distracted from the fact that they would be laying stones for the new pyramid the week after that. And the new palace, as soon as the pyramid was complete. It distracted from the fact that they would be raising new stelae commemorating the ruler's exploits next year. It distracted from the fact that they cultivated cacao orchards, and dried cacao beans, and ground them into chocolate drinks they would never be permitted to enjoy.

It distracted commoners from the caste system, too—which provided stupendous privileges for some at the expense of many others. It distracted from the fact that everything was the ruler's and his priests'. It distracted from the fact that it was the ruler's priests who were doing most of the sacrificing. It distracted from a social order which prohibited commoners from ever becoming either ruler or priest. It distracted from the fact that, since commoners lived outside the acropolis proper, they might well be swept up in a neighboring city-state's raid—and therefore become captive contestants in a neighboring city-state's ballgame sacrifice. In a word, the ballgame distracted from the ruler and his priests' hegemony over society in name of the "public" good.

Yes, the enthralling ballgames distracted from all else. They distracted from life itself.

> Miserable Mayans!
> You achieved so very much.
> But you relinquished your stupendous potential—
> *You lived and died for entertainment.*

High-Tech Yucatán

The numerical dilution of Middle America was a tremendous addition to Incrementalism's culture of silence. Middle Americans were far more manageable when silent—and now there would be *so many fewer of them!* Let them carry on their primitive traditions of independence in silence; over time Middle Americans could simply be bred out of existence.

But there was a further dilution for Incrementalist culture to accomplish. And this watering-down would not be numerical. It would be *spiritual.*

(We must be perfectly clear what we mean by spiritual. We do not mean "religious." We do not mean the ritual perfection or regularity with which one recites the Credo, the Sh'ma Yisrael, or the Sura Al-Fatiha. By "spiritual" we connote that innate human yearning to discover one's proper place in the universe—and the tranquil stoicism and profound grounding which results from its contemplation.)

And in Incrementalists' spiritual dilution strategy, *entertainment* would prove pivotal.

As technology advances and the psychological profiling of audiences progresses, easy entertainment becomes inexpensive, ubiquitous, and curiously habit-forming.

Televisions are ready for duty in living rooms, bedrooms, kitchens, bathrooms—even in your vehicle! The electronic media experience becomes increasingly immersive: high definition, projection, plasma, LCD, LED-LCD, and 3-D. Pair such a picture with high fidelity, multichannel surround audio powered by dedicated (monoblock) power amplifiers and active (preamp) crossover filtering and you have something special. You have *Gesamptkunstwerk* worthy of Wagnerian praise.

Not only does the modern electronic experience *feel* increasingly real, but the *content is also real.* Reality programming of every imaginable description; sporting competitions in real time; documentaries about real persons, objects, and events; real-time shopping; current affairs; celebrity news; do-it-yourself specials. All real, real, *real!* For $50 a month you can have thousands of television programs piped into your home; and with DVR (or Roku) you can watch and re-watch them at your leisure.

A computer or two also inhabits the modern home. Internet connectivity and speeds increase annually. Email inboxes, group and solo gaming, online news, blogs, and YouTube are open for business at any hour of the day or night. Instantaneous consumption and a new, digital dimension are added to electronic entertainment.

And with computerized entertainment comes social networking. Now *that* is entertainment!

It is so very entertaining to play Director of Public Relations on Facebook, Twitter, Instagram, or one's own blog. It starts innocently enough: When choosing photographs to upload to your Facebook profile, you don't select the *worst* ones. Friends—both old and new—are going to see this. So you select the most flattering photos. You manage exposure. And before you know it, you have created a cyber-persona as perfect—and as deceitful—as those crafted by celebrities.

Many people prefer the flexibility social networking gives them: The virtual anonymity when roaming old acquaintances' profiles; The instant gratification when sharing an accomplishment for all to see; The power of posting comments one would never dare utter in public; The satisfaction which comes from knowing hundreds of persons curious to know how you "turned out" have access to only your flawless cyber-persona. Such control would be terribly costly and impossibly inconvenient to maintain in *real* life. (Just ask a real celebrity how much she spends annually on public relations.) But in cyberspace, control is cheap and feasible. Which can make online socializing more enticing than real-life socializing.[viii] (Indeed, many of the younger generation have begun to *prefer cyber life to real life.*[1] And those who have an even dimmer view of reality—children and adults alike—now suffer delusions of grandeur in which *they believe themselves to be unwilling stars of reality shows about their own lives.*[2])

While trifling inanities are the primary currency of social network communications ("Goin' to the grocery store with Amy!"), Facebook, Twitter, and blogs nevertheless require constant vigilance if one is to maintain one's cyber-social standing. It is, after all, in the frequency of status updates and the alacrity of replies that one's cyber-status inheres.

Fortunately, cellular networks are now so fast that computer-based entertainments are also available on your mobile device. With high-speed cell networks, electronic entertainment becomes ubiquitous! And so it is that many audit social networking sites day and night; as soon as they arise in the morning; immediately before they retire to bed; at work and at leisure; during exercise and repose; at business meetings and over lunch.

Reader!

Look about you!

Look around at the ballpark. You will see people who are not fully "there," though physically in attendance. They are updating Twitter feeds, or texting friends, or following *other games'* scores, or scrutinizing Facebook accounts, or talking on their smartphones. While doing so they are missing real life. They are missing the experience of the game itself. They are missing conversation with a friend, a date, a son. They slight precious memories.

[viii] Indeed, surveys show that "39% of Americans spend more time socializing online than they do with friends in the real world. But sadly, nearly one third (31 percent) also admit to sometimes getting lonely, and 35 percent would like to increase their circle of friends." My question is, *which circle of friends?* The online ones? Or the real ones? In either case, it's sad. *Americans Spend More Time Socializing Online Than in Real World*, TECH JOURNAL (April 26, 2012); Adelina Moisan, *Social Media Influence: Almost 40% of Americans Prefer Online Socializing to Real Communication*, MARKETING ALL INCLUSIVE (April 26, 2012).

Look about your favorite restaurant. You will observe couples eating together, yes—yet some are present in body only. One is conducting business, or replying to work emails, or checking stock prices, or examining news headlines, or updating calendars, or arranging lunch meetings, or buying airline tickets, for most of dinner—while a partner languishes, looking on in silence at a plate of vegetables.

Try taking a walk with your nineteen-year-old sister. She will spend much of the time plugged in—texting friends. Yes, she will do it discreetly. She will multitask. She will try not to fumble her conversation with you—to stop texting and ask "What?" She will evince delight in the weather and amusement at your remarks. But she cannot be fully present. Because her thumbs are working overtime. Because her reality is elsewhere—in cyberspace.

Look around the mall. Or on the freeway. Or at the park. Or in the theater. Or at church. Or at home. You will find that many people are focused not on the activities at hand, but instead on their mobile device, their laptop, or their television.

Now look in the mirror.

Probably you have felt it too, dear Reader—a hankering to check your email while spending time with loved ones. A compulsion to update your Twitter feed or your Facebook status when a real friend needs your support. An inclination to text a friend while conversing with a present family member. An enchanting tug to continue gaming through the dark hours despite tomorrow's exam. A slight twinge of nostalgia when turning off your favorite sitcom for the night—as though the characters were actual acquaintances about whom you care; as though storylines were real events in which you participated; as though the set were some familiar place you, yourself have spent much time.

The intellect knows it is not so—yet you *feel* it in your very bones. Electronic entertainment has become real for you. Through the marvels of a plastic brain, electronic forgeries have become *life*.

It is difficult to admit. But for modern electronic entertainments we miss the most important moments of our own lives. Yes: while we mesmerize ourselves with one electronic distraction or another, *real life* trickles through our open fingers like water. It slips down the drain never to be scooped back up, no matter how desperately we grasp after it. We shall never regain that precious time with friends and loved-ones at the ballpark. Or the restaurant. Or on that walk. Or anywhere else for that matter.

The years, the seasons, the days fly ever faster. Soon we, too, shall make our descent into *Xibalba*.

And still we refuse to unplug.

Like aboriginals in the Yucatán, we relinquish our lives for entertainment. Not so quickly, perhaps—not at the business-end of an obsidian knife. But just as surely we forsake our lives for a quick "*hurrah*!"

Fellow Traveler, we pass this way only once.

We act our role upon the stage of life a single time.

What will we take from our adventure here? When we lay quietly on our deathbed—not long hence, dear Reader!—what will we smile to remember? Will it give us pleasure to remember solitary hours spent brilliantly managing social media accounts? Making clever status updates? The alacrity with which we updated a Twitter feed? Will we swell with satisfaction to remember the times we stayed awake a little longer, the times we accomplished much, by re-watching and deleting whole portfolios of old, TiVoed programming? When we burned life playing video games through the night—alone? Will we smile back upon how deftly we multitasked—on how many texts we generated while "spending time" with loved-ones? How we ignored a lover to stay better plugged in? How we dismissed a child to complete a favorite program?

We will not.

We will not remember reclusive "entertainments." We shall instead remember the *real* moments. The times spent together. Quiet talk over sunset. Lifting the spirits of a careworn friend. Breathing in the perfume of a wife's sweet hair. Holding a child's pudgy hand on a neighborhood walk. Guileless conversation with a sibling. Discontinuing solo recreation to accommodate a partner's affection. Reconnecting with a parent after a period of estrangement. Introducing a toddler to some new plant or animal, and sharing their unrivalled wonder.

It is about the relationships. Soon enough we shall all wish we had spent more of our time in these little moments.

The little moments *with others*.

The little moments of *real* life.[ix]

[ix] If you doubt this, spend some time at a rest home. Or in the terminal ward of a hospital. See what people there wish to discuss; what moments they wish to relive; what they still wish to do; which memories they value; what advice they have. It will not involve getting the most out of your iPad.

Spiritual Lobotomy

To be sure, the most perilous danger of modern electronic entertainment is the loss of life itself.

But like the ancient Mayan ballgame, electronic entertainments harbor secondary costs as well. While these expenses are necessarily paid by the entertained, they have the tendency to redound to rulers' benefit.

The first of these secondary entertainment costs is cognitive: In order to be entertained, one must *suspend disbelief*. For example, you can't very well enjoy a movie (or a video game) in a skeptical, rational mindset. If you are yelling "*Unrealistic!*" at the screen every twenty seconds you soon find yourself fatigued, uninterested, un-invested in the characters and the plot (or the gameplay), and dreadfully un-entertained. To derive benefit from entertainment one must temporarily suspend disbelief, give the story, acting, and special effects the benefit of the doubt, and *believe*. If only for a short time. When starting a movie (or loading a video game) you recognize that this suspension of disbelief is only temporary. And you realize it is required for your viewing pleasure. You do it without hesitation. This is a given.

But to enjoy entertainment one must suspend not only *dis*belief in an imperfect entertainment medium. One must also suspend *belief itself*. That is, one must suspend *belief in real life*. For example, you can't very well be entertained while worrying about next week's rent. You must partition consciousness and, so long as you are entertained, you must shut out the real. You must temporarily shelf the nagging concern about rising health care premia. You must temporarily disregard that abominable project you will be starting at work Monday morning. You must ignore the state of the economy. You must wink at the expanse of your student loans. You must forget about the taxes you will pay in a few months time; and you must especially forget how they will be spent. You must put aside the falling value of your home. You must exclude all apprehensions that an administrative agency may fondle you before your flight two weeks from now. You must defer recognition that federally-directed inflation is consuming your savings. You must neglect the fact that while sovereign debt threatens to wreck world economy, Congress is again debating how best to *raise* the U.S. debt ceiling (!).

Indeed, it is this very suspension of belief in reality that gives entertainment its appeal. And probably also its value to the human organism. In any case, so long as we are entertained we put real life behind us.

And what if we are *most often entertained*—throughout the day, moving from radio alarm clock, to car radio, to mobile device, to work computer, to car radio, to workout iPod, to plasma big-screen, to evening internet surf, to bed? In such a case disposable time has been consumed by entertainment. By unreality. The rest of our time and thoughts are devoted to real life, to be sure—but these are the parts of real life we *must immediately* think about: the quotidian chores of work, raising a family, paying the bills, feeding the dog, etc. Balanced on a razor's edge between necessity and entertainment, many of the most important questions of life—*inward and forward-looking ones*—are rarely considered.

Flashes of insight tend not to come when we are engaged in everyday toil. Nor do we usually experience epiphanies while being actively entertained. The most momentous realizations are usually made during quiet moments. Often in solitude. On a park bench or in a pew. In bed, shortly before going to sleep or shortly after waking up. When we *think our own thoughts*. Not the thoughts of necessity. And not the thoughts contrived by entertainment. When we reach out—and in—and we *feel*. When we are sufficiently quiet to *hear our own answers*.

And so we must ponder: When will we cast our eyes up at the stars? When will we give audience to the nighttime melody of crickets, frogs, and owls? When will we pause to feel a cold winter breeze whistling through our hair? When will we watch squirrels chase each other round the bole of an ancient oak? When will we smell the damp earth after a spring rain, the heavy perfume of summer flowers, or the crisp air of autumn mornings? When will we be still enough to hear the purr of dragonfly wings? When will we distinguish every color of the rainbow above a dawn horizon? When will we experience the exhilaration and clarity of thought that come only when we push our hearts near the limit on a long run?

Our ears are deafened;
Our noses plugged;
Our eyes blinded;
To inner vision.

If we are forever entertained, when will quiet, introspective moments come? As we rush hysterically from one entertainment to the next, blinding ourselves to quiet insights, benumbing spiritual antennae, and sidestepping life itself, Incrementalism proceeds apace—*unnoticed and unmolested.* Like spectators at the Mayan ball court, we forget that yet another pyramid must be built "for the public benefit" next week. Once reinvigorated and refreshed, nauseated by yet another entertainment binge, we rededicate ourselves to finishing that "public" pyramid. We stand down. We surrender imagination. We kneel before a plasma screen, and willingly receive our spiritual lobotomy.

And that is precisely how Incrementalism wishes to keep it.

Incremental Luddites

We have said many things. Let us clarify:

None of the foregoing is intended to suggest that entertainment is unimportant. On the contrary, entertainment is an *immutable requirement for the human organism.*[x]

And no one is advocating for TV police. Instead, people must be free to choose how much of their own time and money they will invest in entertaining themselves. Indeed, they should use their televisions, computers, and mobile devices to whatever degree they like—even when it means choosing dissipation over life.[3]

Nor does the foregoing imply that contemporary technologies which make electronic entertainment available should be rejected. We are fortunate indeed to live at a time and in a place where technological marvels are so powerful and so cheap! (Why, for the price of a meal one can purchase a number of digital musical recordings. All that is required to reproduce lifelike music are a decent pair of headphones and a portable music player. Close your eyes and you are at the symphony. That every citizen can experience the wonder of music at such a bargain is positively miraculous. Previous generations would rightly have called it magical.)

Nor do we argue that socialists themselves pioneered the technology that now enthralls us. On the contrary, socialists are devoted Luddites! They fear technological progress because each advance in efficiency "puts someone out of a job." Like their Luddite forebears, socialists race from one innovation to the next—impeaching, outlawing, dismantling, and burning any technical progress they can find. As a result, both socialists and the economies they manage make poor inventors. (As the Luddite in Chief reminded us on the 2012 campaign trail, ATMs have put bank tellers out of a job (!).[4] The dratted Internet has put travel agents out of a job (!).[5] And those damned computers have put phone operators out of a job (!).[6] But surely he doesn't propose discarding ATMs? And the Internet? And computers?)

Consequently, socialist economies the world over are notorious for technological backwardness. (Would you purchase a car designed in Myanmar? Or Vietnam? Or Cuba? Do they even design vehicles in such places? No, they do not. Indeed, for fifty years after the socialist revolution, until September 2011, *Cuba made it illegal for citizens to purchase or own modern, post-1959 automobiles.*[7] No matter where they were designed and by whom they

[x] Still, it is wise to remember that like every human necessity—food, drink, sunlight, sex—*even entertainment becomes a vice when consumed to excess.*

were manufactured. Only guys sitting atop the monolithic pyramid were allowed such a technological "privilege."[8])

Yes, socialists despise technology. But they are conflicted: In America, Incrementalism is the method by which socialism has most successfully been advanced. Incrementalism is premised upon using any means *presently available* to advance socialist revolution—and technological enslavement fits the bill. And so, with a wink and a nod to the more erudite socialists among its ranks, Incrementalism embraces technology *in the present.* (But once the revolution is complete and socialist economy sets in, don't expect next-generation, big-screen TVs to be available!)

The point is simply that the low cost of modern entertainment, combined with the high quality and availability of technology, is a boon to Incrementalism today in much the same way that the ballgame was a boon to Mayan rulers, or chariot races were a boon to the Roman Emperor: So long as Americans are enjoying faux reality via electronic entertainment, real-life Incrementalism is freed to proceed unimpeded. The Mayan king did not invent the Mesoamerican ballgame; the Roman Emperor did not invent chariot races. But each took full advantage of such entertainments to distract citizens from contemporary political reality. And Incrementalists do the same today.

The citizen who is fully entertained has little knowledge of how his country is changing. He has little time for such considerations. Indeed, he has little time for life itself. And he has no time at all for individual insight.

And how different are we? We will do most anything so long as we can spend three hours a day entertaining ourselves into a stupor. This is a bargain Incrementalism is happy to make: While citizens are immersed in transportive entertainments, they are necessarily unconcerned with the state of the Republic. Incrementalism advances unhindered by Middle Americans who would be up in arms—if only they spent a *little* less time entertained. If only they had a *tad* more time for real life. If only they took a *bit* more time for introspection . . . .

The Content of "Real Life"

Yes, socialists make sterile inventors.

But they are prolific propagandists!

Which is to say, while planned economies won't produce a faster computer or the next high-definition TV, socialists nevertheless create a disproportionate amount of the *content* which will play on them.

What sort of entertainment content do socialists create? A library could be filled with this subject alone. We will limit our discussion of content to one familiar facet of entertainment: film.

As with other arts, international socialists have thoroughly analyzed the motion picture medium—and they have concluded that the propagandistic potential of film is second to none. For example, in socialist strong-man Kim

Jong Il's masterful treatise *On the Art of the Cinema*, we learn that "The cinema is now one of the main objects on which efforts should be concentrated in order to conduct the revolution in art and literature. . . . *[I]t is a powerful ideological weapon for the revolution and construction*."[9]

Indeed!

And should socialists find that their own films fail to live up to the lofty cinematic standards about which they so eloquently theorize, socialists simply *kidnap capitalist directors from foreign countries and force* them *to direct socialist films instead* (!).[xi] (Which goes to show how very highly socialists regard the medium of film. For socialists, the content and execution of film is a matter of *national security and international espionage*.)

Domestically, too, socialists hold the motion picture medium in high regard. The cinematic arts have historically harbored a disproportionate number of socialist writers, directors, producers, and actors in America. Yes—since silent films and Charlie Chaplin. And socialists' disproportionate representation in Hollywood endures today.

For example, A-list actors (like Jack Nicholson, Sean Penn, Leonardo DiCaprio, and others) perform self-imposed pilgrimages to South American socialist dictators. Some join socialist dictators' reelection campaigns—they share the stage; they wave to the crowds.[10] Others return to the States with glowing reports: "Fidel Castro is a genius! We spoke about everything. . . . Cuba is simply a paradise!"[11] After (very quickly) returning from socialist paradise, A-list actors write sycophantish travelogues aimed at conveying foreign, socialist perspectives on American elections.[xii] They grant interviews on the subject, too: "I went to Caracas first time [sic] in 2006. Um. . . I. . . sort of spurned [sic!] on by, um, Pat Robertson's, uh, encouragement of the assassination of President Chavez of Venezuela."[12]

[xi] In 1978—only five years after publishing his treatise ON THE ART OF THE CINEMA—Kim Jong-il had South Korean director Shin Sang-ok and his actress wife Choi Eun-hee kidnapped and imprisoned in North Korea. Once safely imprisoned in North Korea, Shin Sang-ok was forced to direct seven films (in which Kim Jong-il acted as executive producer, editor, and censor!). Eight years after his kidnapping, Shin Sang-ok and his wife Choi Eun-hee escaped to the U.S. Embassy while in Vienna for a film festival. *See* John Gorenfeld, *The Producer From Hell*, THE GUARDIAN (April 3, 2003).

Shin Sang-ok's story is not so extraordinary by socialist cinema standards. Directorial kidnapping and slavery has been known to socialist regimes for generations. Kurt Gerron provides another fine example; he was captured by National Socialists during WWII and persuaded—as a Jew—to direct a propamentary about how delicately and kindly Socialist Germany was treating the Jewish people. But security was not so careless in socialist Germany as it was in socialist North Korean—and Mr. Gerron's end was tragic.

[xii] For a revelation in how little one can say with so many words, *see, e.g.*, Sean Penn, *Mountain of Snakes*, Parts I and II, THE HUFFINGTON POST (Nov. 30, 2008), http://www.huffingtonpost.com/sean-penn/mountain-of-snakes_b_146765.html; *see also* Sean Penn, *Conversations with Chavez and Castro*, THE NATION (Dec. 15, 2008).

In Hollywood, mindless ditherings of this sort pass as political genius. And there is plenty more where that came from. One need not prod to get these thespian Einsteins talking:

> He [Chavez] is clearly *not* a dictator by *any* international standard. . . . The elections are some of the, uh, most transparent and incredible elections in the world today. There's also mythology related to his oppression of the press. . . .
>
> I had a hunch, and a little bit of information beyond what I felt was generally reported in the United States, to trust that the demonization of these people [i.e., Chavez and Castro] was a myth. President Chavez was very gracious and spent time with all of us; then we travelled to Cuba.[13]

Incrementalist actors are not alone in their adulation of socialism. A-list *directors* and *executive producers* (like Steven Spielberg, Francis Ford Coppola, Robert Redford, Oliver Stone, Pedro Almodovar, etc.) also perform self-imposed pilgrimages to worship at the feet of socialist dictators.[14] They create stirring biopics, and even "documentaries," concerning socialist dictators and their noble hatchet men, past and present.[xiii] Those directors and executive producers who fail to make socialist pilgrimages do penance *by also creating* moving, multipart biopics about socialist dictators and their loyal butchers.[xiv]

Of course, simply featuring a socialist actor, a socialist director, or even a socialist producer does not make for a socialist movie per se. Not in the didactic sense, anyway. To create truly socialist movies, a socialist *writer* is required. It is only a socialist writer who can create socialist *content*. It is only a socialist writer who can give us historical fictions like *There Will Be Blood*, or *Gangs of New York*, or *Wall Street*.

From such enthralling entertainments we, willing spectators, imbibe history according to socialist revision. In *Gangs of New York* (2002, nominated for ten Academy Awards) we learn how America was founded on the principle of xenophobia—and how native cane beetles are bad, and foreign cane toads good.[xv] In *There Will Be Blood* (2007, based on socialist

---

xiii For an introduction into the socialist biopic genre, try Robert Redford's *The Motorcycle Diaries* (2004, recipient of Cannes and Academy awards). For an introduction into the socialist propamentary genre, try Oliver Stone's *South of the Border* (2009), *Looking for Fidel* (2004), and *Comandante* (2003).

xiv Steven Soderbergh's *Che* (2008, Cannes Film Festival award for Best Actor) provides a nice example.

xv The extent of socialist lies in *Gangs of New York* deserves a chapter unto itself. We can only take the time here to point out the following: The film's wicked cane beetle antagonist, Bowery Boy gangster William "The Butcher" Cutting (based on the historical William Poole, a butcher by trade, and also a member of the Bowery Boys), was no murderer. And he was especially no murderer of cane toads. On the contrary, Bill "The Butcher" *was murdered by cane toads.*

Why was Bill murdered by cane toads?

Well, a Goliath among cane toads (Irish-born John Morrissey, of Tammany Hall fame), a renowned heavyweight boxer, challenged Bill to a fight. Goliath offered a bet of twenty-to-one odds (!) that he would whip Bill, and still Bill would not take the fight. You see, Bill was a

extraordinaire Upton Sinclair's novel *Oil!*, nominated for eight Academy Awards, and winner of two) we learn how America was built upon the greed of murderous, misanthropic capitalists and the lies of cowardly, Christian charlatans.

In *Wall Street* (1987, Academy Award winner) we learn that capitalists—especially bankers, traders, and speculators, but also businessmen in general—are unscrupulous hucksters *as a rule.* (In counterpoise, a sympathetic protagonist chokes back heart-felt tears while teaching us that a union boss is "the only honest man I know."[15]) But this is not all: In *Wall Street* we have perhaps the finest socialist caricature of capitalism ever created. As villain Gordon Gekko so famously informs us,

> The point is, ladies and gentlemen, that greed—for lack of a better word—is *good.* Greed is *right.* Greed *works.* Greed clarifies, cuts through, and captures the essence of the evolutionary spirit. Greed in all of its forms—greed for life, for money, for love, knowledge—has marked the upward surge of mankind, and greed—you mark my words!—will not only save Teldar Paper, but that other malfunctioning corporation called the USA. Thank you very much.[16]

A single installment of homiletic content was not enough. And so, in 2010, Oliver Stone bequeathed us *Wall Street: Money Never Sleeps*—the same stereotyped narrative, but updated to pin the financial meltdown of 2008 exclusively on greedy capitalists. And herein lies the strength of part deux: while retelling the financial collapse of 2008 in vivid detail, mortgage derivatives and all—*it never once mentions the Community Reinvestment Act!*

---

middleweight. Like any rational boxer, Bill did not wish to fight well outside his weight class. Bill offered to fight Goliath any at any time, so long as Goliath would meet Bill in the same weight class. But Goliath had no intention of cutting weight (and meeting Bill on equal footing!).

After considerable public provocations, Bill eventually agreed to fight Goliath anyway. (I.e., Bill did not make a practice of fighting scrawny man-children like Leonardo DiCaprio. Instead he fought men far larger than himself.) The match was set for the following morning at 7:00 am, Amos Street wharf.

Despite an extreme disadvantage in size, Bill convincingly won the rough-and-tumble at the Amos Street wharf. Indeed, Bill whipped Goliath so handily he was laid up for weeks.

And now we come to Bill's murder: Goliath and the rest of the cane toads were terribly chagrined at the outcome of this highly-publicized bare-knuckle match. A match they themselves had insisted upon. Unable to prevail upon Bill with their fists, and in order to save face, the cane toads conspired to have Bill *eliminated.* ("We can't let some natural-born American whip our champion!") So once Goliath had fully recovered from his beating—seven months after the match—Goliath and his cane toad minions found Bill in a bar. They spat in his face. And then they shot him dead. *See, e.g., A Prize Fight Between John Morrissey and William Poole*, THE NEW YORK DAILY TIMES, vol. 3, no. 0892, p. 4 (July 28, 1854); *Terrible Shooting Affray in Broadway*, THE NEW YORK DAILY TIMES, vol. 4, no. 1074, p. 1 (Feb. 26, 1855).

A socialist writer could never bring himself to admit such a history. It just wouldn't fit the socialist narrative about cane beetles—who are always pictured as rabidly xenophobic exploiters. Which is why the *Gangs of New York* script writer invented quite a different American "history" in its place.

Instead, it presents the 2008 housing debacle as the inescapable outgrowth of capitalism.[17]

So long as a plot supplies romance and accommodates socialist dogma, socialist writers rehash it over and over again, across disparate landscapes and genres, and for divergent audiences. The banality of such clichéd socialist storylines is difficult to endure, but in Hollywood they abound. And in this regard it is tough to beat the one about armies of cruel, ignorant, white, Westerners who—*for capitalist avarice alone!*—steal the land and destroy the environment of noble savages who live peacefully, communally, in beautiful harmony with nature, bereft of property, capitalist guile, and the abhorrent profit motive. The audience is led by a sympathetic protagonist (always a member of the ignorant capitalist horde) on an astonishing journey of personal growth and self-discovery among the natives. The protagonist's stirring personal journey inevitably includes charming cross-cultural misunderstandings; humorous linguistic hurdles; budding friendships; touching reconciliation with former rivals; communal debates regarding Western capitalists' encroachment; recognition of group fellowship, cooperation, and identity—and finally a realization that whereas the savages live a fair, spiritual, and equitable life, the Western system is rapacious, exploitive, greedy, and empty.

In due course—*be still, my heart!*—our bumbling Westerner falls passionately in love with a comely and enticingly exotic member of the tribe (preferably a chieftain's daughter). His affections are requited. And finally, in a sincere display of solidarity with his newfound family, our protagonist risks life and limb to reject Western society, culture, and economy: He joins the savages, and with them does mortal battle against encroaching capitalists! Through the protagonist's eyes we come to see the serenity and perfection of the aboriginal's socialistic mode of life—and the depravity of our own.

Oh, it's grand art. (And so believable, too: In clashes between capitalist civilization and Neolithic aboriginals there are so many examples of capitalists running away to join the Injuns!) Yes, this plot is tried and true. And when films recapitulate this most socialist narrative, they are practically guaranteed an Oscar. It is the key to eternal favorites like *Dances With Wolves* (1990, multiple Academy Award Winner for Best Picture; Best Director; Best Adapted Screenplay; Best Film Editing; Best Sound; Best Original Score [got to give it to them there]; and Best Cinematography [and there, too]); *Pocahontas* (1995, multiple Academy Award Winner for Best Original Movie Score; Best Original Song); *Avatar* (2009, multiple Academy Award Winner for Art Direction; Cinematography; and Visual Effects).

Come on now, you say—*Avatar* was no socialist manifesto! It was just a fun, 3-D, Christmas action flick!

As lazy consumers seeking a fun, holiday distraction we may not be well-attuned to socialist content. But socialists are. Which is why socialist leaders like native son Evo Morales (leader of the Bolivian cocaine growers' union, chairman of the Movement for Socialism party, and President of Bolivia) immediately recognized the socialist content of *Avatar*. And it is also why Evo praised it: Because "it makes a perfect model for the struggle against capitalism,"[18] and represents a "profound show of resistance to capitalism."[19] (Evo will be thrilled to learn that writer-producer-director James Cameron is working up three sequels to *Avatar*. Yes, three sequels—*Avatars* II, III, IV.[20])

How do socialist-themed films garner so many Academy Awards? Well, only Hollywood producers, directors, writers, and actors get to vote on which films deserve an award.[21] And when it comes time to vote, Hollywood's disproportionate enthusiasm for socialism yields equally disproportionate support for socialist-themed films.

Popular "documentaries" pitch socialist content, too. In this field it is difficult to outstrip the prolific Michael Moore, who graces us with another Gonzo-journalism hit piece every few years. Moore alone has given us *Capitalism: A Love Story* (2009, a *Money Never Sleeps* redux in propamentary form), *Sicko* (2007, recommending the Cuban health care system as superior to that of the U.S.; nominated for an Academy Award), *Bowling for Columbine* (2002, attacking Americans' right to bear arms; Academy Award winner for Best Documentary Feature), *Roger And Me* (1989, an early attempt at anti-capitalist propaganda in the vehicle manufacturing industry; 100% fresh rating on Rotten Tomatoes[22]), and many other titles.

But this field is not tilled exclusively by Michael Moore. Others plant socialist propamentaries, too. They make films like *The Island President* (2012, global warming scare piece; 98% fresh rating at Rotten Tomatoes[23]), *We Were Here* (2011, recounting the HIV/AIDS outbreak, and instructing what medical care, social services, and community support a "just" society must offer citizens; 100% fresh rating on Rotten Tomatoes[24]) *Phil Ochs: There But For Fortune* (2011, praising socialist propagandist and protest singer Phil Ochs;[25] 100% fresh rating at Rotten Tomatoes[26]); *Gasland* (2010, fossil fuel scare piece; 97% fresh rating at Rotten Tomatoes[27]), *Inside Job* (2010, yet another redux of *Money Never Sleeps* in propamentary form; 98% fresh rating on Rotten Tomatoes[28]), *An Inconvenient Truth* (2006, global warming scare piece; winner of two Academy Awards for Best Documentary Feature and Best Original Song), *Howard Zinn—You Can't Be Neutral on a Moving Train* (2004, lauding a preeminent socialist agitator, academic, and author Howard Zinn; 97% fresh rating on Rotten Tomatoes[29]), *Enron: The Smartest Guys in the Room* (2004, positing Enron's corruption as both outgrowth and microcosm of capitalism; 97% fresh rating at Rotten Tomatoes[30]), *The Corporation* (2003, attack on capitalism concluding that corporations are psychopathic entities; 91% fresh rating on Rotten Tomatoes[31]).

And how do socialist-themed documentaries amass such critical acclaim? Well, it turns out that film critics, too, harbor a disproportionate number of socialists among their ranks.[32] So when it comes time to rate films, they, too disproportionately praise those exhibiting socialist content.

Now, films promoting liberal philosophy make far less than those exhibiting conservative perspectives.[33] So Hollywood's zeal for socialist content cannot be ascribed to profit alone. And films fixated on ideology are anything but "art for art's sake." Indeed, the concept of *l'art pour l'art* is anathema to socialists.[xvi] Which is to say that we are not talking about *art*, so much as we are talking about *instruction*. And in particular we are talking about socialist ideological instruction. As Dear Leader Kim Jong Il so eloquently put it in his magnum opus ON THE ART OF THE CINEMA, "*In each case the value of the* [cinematic] *work is assessed on the basis of its content.* No matter how great an event and how wide the scope of life depicted in a work, it will not be a masterpiece unless its content is profound and rich. On the contrary, a work with profound and rich ideological content is fully entitled to be called a masterpiece even if its dimensions are small. . . . [*T*]*he content, and not the form, makes a work a masterpiece.*[34]

And so it is no surprise that, come election time, the professional panderers of socialist content line up to write, produce, brand, and narrate Incrementalists' campaign messages. For example, immediately after the Tea Movement's electoral triumph in November, 2010, Nancy Pelosi hired Steven Spielberg as a rebranding consultant for Democratic members of the House of Representatives.[35] (The Spielberg pick was a wise one. He is a proven hand at propaganda: "a power player in Democratic politics for years," Spielberg had previously "work[ed] on everything from President Bill Clinton's millennial celebrations to the 2008 Democratic National Convention."[36]) And for the November 2012 election, President Obama's reelection campaign released *The Road We've Traveled* (2012): An Obama reelect advertisement narrated by Tom Hanks and directed by Philip Davis Guggenheim. Yes, Guggenheim was the trusty director of *An Inconvenient Truth*.

[xvi] KIM JONG IL, ON THE ART OF THE CINEMA, 25; 54 (Foreign Languages Publishing House, Pyongyang 1989) (1973) (emphasis added):

> Since the artistic quality is defined by the clarity and emotional force with which a given ideological content is represented, the significance of the ideological content itself must first be absolutely clear. *If a writer regards technique as everything and ignores substantial ideological content, he will tend to follow the path of art for its own sake. . . .*
>
> [A] masterpiece ought to concern itself with the indispensable theme of the basic problems of the revolutionary cause of the working class. This principle concerns the content of literary works, not their form. It is one reason why *the content, and not the form, makes a work a masterpiece.*

See also Ibid. at 50-57.

And so it is no surprise that, when redistributive programs like Obamacare are found to be horrifically unpopular, federal tax monies are spent to weave Obamacare into the plots of popular prime-time television shows. For example, our tax dollars are spent pushing Modern Family and Grey's Anatomy use Obamacare as a plot device.[37] And pushing Spanish-language soap operas to use Obamacare as a plot device.[38] And "pitch[ing] a reality television show about 'the trials and tribulations of families living without medical coverage.'"[39] But don't think small, Mr. Federalized-Health-Insurance-Bureaucracy-man! And he doesn't: "I'd like to see ten of the major TV shows, or telenovelas, have people talking about 'that health insurance thing.'"[40] After all, "There are good storylines here."[41] Because for socialists, art is not about technique. It is about *content.* And by content socialists mean *political ideology.*

None of the foregoing is meant to imply that socialist filmmakers should be prevented from creating socialist content. Or even from bald-faced socialist propaganda. On the contrary, socialist filmmakers must be allowed to go on producing socialist content! Free persons prefer not to muzzle their adversaries, but to triumph over them in an open contest of ideas.[xvii] This can only occur where ideas—even the most destructive ones—can be freely expressed by all. (And until the socialist revolution is complete, socialists will have an unfettered Constitutional right to produce films promoting whatever political message they please!)

The point is simply that modern entertainment is perfectly saturated with socialist content. It is saturated to such an extent that the whole of American history and current events blend together into a single Incrementalist whole. The American experience now looms before the average consumer of entertainment like a Diego Rivera mural. We follow its contours along the walls: Pristine native cultures living in glorious prosperity, sublime peace, and admirable harmony with the environment. White men arriving, complete with sardonic grins. Torturing native nobles and leveling whole ecosystems—*for profit alone.* Factories fill to the brim with slaving workers. Sneering owners, bankers, clergymen, and generals plot in secret backroom meetings. Moneyed interests oppress and exploit peasants and laborers alike. High society frolics merrily on profits stolen from workers' labors. Capitalists of every stripe race money bags to the bank. Oh, righteous workers! Oh, depraved owners! Laborers organize, strike, and do battle with fascist overlords; valorous revolutionaries arm for the coming conflict!

[xvii] This preference for an open contest of ideas has been prominent among Western thinkers for centuries. Milton articulated it best: "[T]hough all the winds of doctrine were let loose to play on the earth, so Truth be in the field, we do injuriously, by licensing and prohibiting, to misdoubt her strength. Let her and Falsehood grapple; who ever knew Truth put to the worse, in a free and open encounter?" JOHN MILTON, AREOPAGITICA: FOR THE LIBERTY OF UNLICENSED PRINTING TO THE PARLIAMENT OF ENGLAND (1644).

Standing above the fray like Moses—biblical beard, imperious brow, determined expression and all—a colossal figure painted in hierarchical perspective grips a poster like tables of stone: "TODA LA HISTORIA DE LA SOCIEDAD HUMANA HASTA EL DIA ES UNA HISTORIA DE LUCHA DE CLASES." Signed, "Carlos Marx." And He Himself points the way to the Promised Land: just there—high on the horizon, not far away!—a shining city on a hill. Clean, orderly, and modern. The unbounded promise of socialist utopia![xviii]

Only the introspective step back from the mural, fold their arms, and consider—can I agree with the *content* of such entertainment?

With its *message*?

With its *ethic*?

Its *worldview*?

Its "*moral*"?

The Content of "News"

Propaganda has always fascinated socialists.

For generations, they have thoughtfully scrutinized propaganda for any advantages it might provide to the socialist cause. And the verdict is in: For socialists, "the correct use of propaganda is a true art."[xix]

Not just any art. Propaganda is *special.* Propaganda is a "frightful" means to the only worthwhile end (i.e., socialist revolution). And fortunately for socialists, it is an art which "has remained practically unknown to the bourgeois parties."[xx] In other words, capitalists make poor propagandists—so the field is wide open to enterprising socialists.

Of the many socialist studies on the utility of propaganda, it is hard to beat Hitler's. It may well be that Hitler borrowed a bit from Le Bon. But within a single personality Hitler combined both artist's eye and despot's rule. And Hitler's study of propaganda was far more than speculative abstraction: He put his theory of propaganda to demonstrable and devastating effect.

Hitler's conclusions on the "true art" of "correctly using propaganda" are quite enlightening. They may be summarized in six points as follows:

[xviii] No, this is no caricature. This is an unadorned description of Diego Rivera's Palacio Nacional de Mexico murals. Mr. Marx stands atop the central portion of *Class Struggle* (Nov. 20, 1935), the left panel of the monumental stairway triptych.

[xix] ADOLF HITLER, MEIN KAMPF 176 (Ralph Manheim trans., Houghton Mifflin Co. 1999) (1925). Furthermore, "propaganda is no more than a weapon, though a frightful one in the hand of an expert." *Ibid.* at 179.

[xx] On the other hand, "I saw that the Socialist-Marxist organizations mastered and applied this instrument with astounding skill." ADOLF HITLER, MEIN KAMPF 176 (Ralph Manheim trans., Houghton Mifflin Co. 1999) (1925).

(1) Propaganda must be addressed *exclusively to the less-educated.*[xxi]

(2) Propaganda must *excite the emotions*—not the intellect.[xxii]

(3) Propaganda must *be one-sided.*[xxiii]

[xxi] ADOLF HITLER, MEIN KAMPF 179-80 (Ralph Manheim trans., Houghton Mifflin Co. 1999) (1925):

> "The second really decisive question was this: To whom should propaganda be addressed? To the scientifically trained intelligentsia or to the less educated masses?
>
> "It must be addressed always and exclusively to the masses. . . .
>
> "The function of propaganda does not lie in the scientific training of the individual, but in calling the masses' attention to certain facts, processes, necessities, etc., whose significance is thus for the first time placed within their field of vision.
>
> "The whole art consists in doing this so skillfully that everyone will be convinced that the fact is real, the process necessary, the necessity correct, etc. . . .
>
> "All propaganda must be popular and its intellectual level must be adjusted to the most limited intelligence among those it is addressed to. Consequently, the greater the mass it is intended to reach, the lower its purely intellectual level will have to be."

[xxii] ADOLF HITLER, MEIN KAMPF 180; 183 (Ralph Manheim trans., Houghton Mifflin Co. 1999) (1925):

> "[I]t's effect for the most part must be aimed at the emotions and only to a very limited degree at the so-called intellect. . . .
>
> "The more modest its intellectual ballast, the more exclusively it takes into consideration the emotions of the masses, the more effective it will be. . . .
>
> "The art of propaganda lies in understanding the emotional ideas of the great masses and finding, through a psychologically correct form, the way to the attention and thence to the heart of the broad masses. . . .
>
> "The people in their overwhelming majority are so feminine by nature and attitude that sober reasoning determines their thoughts and actions far less than emotion and feeling."

[xxiii] ADOLF HITLER, MEIN KAMPF 180-84 (Ralph Manheim trans., Houghton Mifflin Co. 1999) (1925):

> "It is a mistake to make propaganda many-sided, like scientific instruction, for instance. . . .
>
> "As soon as you sacrifice this slogan and try to be many-sided, the effect will piddle away, for the crowd can neither digest nor retain the material offered. In this way the result is weakened and in the end entirely cancelled out. . . .
>
> "What our authorities least of all understood was the very first axiom of all propagandist activity: to wit, the basically subjective and one-sided attitude it must take toward every question it deals with. . . .
>
> "What, for example, would we say about a poster that was supposed to advertise a new soap and that described other soaps as 'good'? . . . .
>
> "And this sentiment is not complicated, but very simple and all of a piece. It does not have multiple shadings; it has a positive and a negative; love or hate, right or wrong, truth or lie, never half this way and half that way, never partially, or that kind of thing. . . .
>
> "[T]he rabid, impudent bias and persistence with which this lie was expressed took into account the emotional, always extreme, attitude of the great masses and for this reason was believed."

(4) Propaganda must *be limited to a very few points.*[xxiv]
(5) Propaganda must *be repeated unflinchingly.*[xxv] And finally,
(6) Propaganda must *never* make an objective study of the *truth.*[xxvi]

Mainstream newsmakers' conformation with Hitler's principles of propaganda was on display during coverage of the Trayvon Martin shooting. Why, some mainstream news outlets even went to the trouble of prejudicially editing the tape of George Zimmerman's 911 call—*so as to more*

[xxiv] ADOLF HITLER, MEIN KAMPF 180-81; 185 (Ralph Manheim trans., Houghton Mifflin Co. 1999) (1925):

> "[A]ll effective propaganda must be limited to a very few points and must harp on these in slogans until the last member of the public understands what you want him to understand by your slogan. . . .
>
> "Thus we see that propaganda must follow a simple line . . . .
>
> "[O]nly after the simplest ideas are repeated thousands of times will the masses finally remember them.
>
> "When there is a change, it must not alter the content of what the propaganda is driving at, but in the end must always say the same thing. For instance, a slogan must be presented from different angles, but the end of all remarks must always and immutably be the slogan itself. Only in this way can the propaganda have a unified and complete effect."

[xxv] ADOLF HITLER, MEIN KAMPF 184-85 (Ralph Manheim trans., Houghton Mifflin Co. 1999) (1925):

> "But the most brilliant propagandist technique will yield no success unless one fundamental principle is born in mind constantly and with unflagging attention. It must confine itself to a few points and repeat them over and over. Here, as so often in this world, persistence is the first and most important requirement for success. . . .
>
> "But the masses are slow-moving, and they always require a certain time before they are ready even to notice a thing, and only after the simplest ideas are repeated thousands of times will the masses finally remember them. . . .
>
> "[S]teady, consistent emphasis, allows our final success to mature. And then, to our amazement, we shall see what tremendous results such perseverance leads to—to results that are almost beyond our understanding."

[xxvi] ADOLF HITLER, MEIN KAMPF 182-83 (Ralph Manheim trans., Houghton Mifflin Co. 1999) (1925):

> "The function of propaganda is, for example, not to weigh and ponder the rights of different people, but exclusively to emphasize the one right which it has set out to argue for. Its task is not to make an objective study of the truth, in so far as it favors the enemy, and then set it before the masses with academic fairness; its task is to serve our own right, always and unflinchingly. . . .
>
> "The broad mass of a nation does not consist of diplomats, or even professors of political law, or even individuals capable of forming a rational opinion; it consists of plain mortals, wavering and inclined to doubt and uncertainty. As soon as our own propaganda admits so much as a glimmer of right on the other side, the foundation for doubt in our own right has been laid. The masses are then in no position to distinguish where foreign injustice ends and our own begins. In such a case they become uncertain and suspicious, especially if the enemy refrains from going in for the same nonsense, but unloads every bit of blame on his adversary."

convincingly present their storyline of racist murder. So as to more effectively present an emotional, one-sided, limited, repetitive, subjective narrative for the less-educated.

Yes, NBC broadcast a recording of Zimmerman's pre-homicide 911 call in which he was quoted (well, *abridged*) to unilaterally offer that, "This guy looks like he's up to no good. *He looks black.*"[42]

Of course, such a statement could be construed to imply Zimmerman thought the "guy looked like he was up to no good" *because* "he was black." Such a construction would make Zimmerman racist. But NBC's misleading parody of Zimmerman's 911 call is not how it went down. The call actually went like this:

> **Zimmerman:** "This guy looks like he's up to no good. Or he's on drugs or something. It's raining and he's just walking around, looking about."
>
> **911 Dispatcher:** "OK, and this guy—is he black, white, or Hispanic?"
>
> **Zimmerman:** "He looks black."

So Zimmerman never mentioned Trayvon Martin's race until the 911 dispatcher demanded a racial identification. Meaning racist motivations cannot be inferred from Zimmerman's 911 call.[xxvii]

And really—how could the content of mainstream "news" be anything *but* propaganda? The mainstream news industry—like the mainstream film industry—is saturated with Incremental socialists. There is quite a lot of crosspollination between Hollywood and the Press. And this is how we get Incrementalist movie producer Harvey Weinstein [*Sicko* (2007), *Fahrenheit 9/11* (2004), *Gangs of New York* (2002)] guest-hosting CNN's *Piers Morgan Tonight*—and discussing with Bill Clinton how the movie *High Noon* (1952, Academy Award winner for Best Actor, Best Film Editing, Best Musical Score, and Best Song) was fantastic *because it was "an anti-McCarthy" movie created by a "very political producer and activist named Stanley Kramer," and because it presented a veiled allegory of McCarthyist blacklisting of socialist writers.*[43] They call this

---

[xxvii] But never fear: NBC conducted a thorough and unbiased review of their misleading 911 editing process. (*Inside Politics: NBC News to Probe Misleading Edit of Zimmerman 911 Tape*, THE WASHINGTON TIMES (April 2, 2012).) They discovered that this simple and accidental "mistake" was caused by a "seasoned" producer. (Christopher Francescani and Peter Lauria, *NBC News George Zimmerman Probe Finds "Seasoned" Producer Made Editing Error*, THE HUFFINGTON POST (April 6, 2012).) Somehow this little mistake slipped past a script editor, senior producer oversight, and both legal and journalistic standards department reviews. *Ibid.* NBC is "shocked" this mistake ever occurred. *Ibid.* Because NBC is so very concerned with producing unbiased journalism. (Yet NBC will not release the names of employees involved, and they will not fire them (*ibid.*)—NBC wishes them to stay on and continue "reporting"!) Besides, NBC "Executives have vowed to take rigorous steps to formalize editorial safeguards in the news division following the incident." *Ibid.* NBC is serious about this 911 editing snafu: "*rigorous steps to formalize editorial safeguards.*" So there is really no chance that any biased broadcasts will slip out of NBC in the future!

"news." (Afterwards Weinstein retreated to one of his many mansions to host another lavish, $35,800-per head fundraiser for the Incrementalist in Chief.[44])

Yes, mainline news anchors, writers, and producers express the "news" through a rosy, socialist filter.[45] Why, nearly ninety percent of persons working in the news media send political contributions to a single establishment party—the Democrat Bus.[46] News outlets set the national political agenda by publishing stories favorable to socialist positions, burying those that aren't, and carefully excising those portions of reported stories which might be unfavorable to the socialist cause.[47] The Chairman of the Associated Press gushes publicly about the President.[48] When an Incrementalist president briefly visits U.S. soldiers in Afghanistan, mainline news hosts compare him to Henry V.[49] Mainline news producers actively court known zealots[50] for "stories" with the intent to change election outcomes.[51] Mainline news producers strategize with campaign directors (!).[52] Mainline executive producers hold stories back until just before elections[53]—to achieve maximum electoral impact. And mainline news outlets rabidly defend the veracity of forgery-based stories. They keep it up even when such stories' underlying documentary "evidence," reportedly produced by a typewriter in the 1970s, is discredited for anachronistic superscripts and proportional spacing common to modern word processing software like Microsoft Word.[54]

Yes, the "news" is quite biased. It is intended to be so, and in making it so mainstream newsmakers follow a proud socialist tradition. After all, as Marx taught us the point is not to describe the world; "*the point is to change it.*"[55] Mainstream newsmakers specialize in prevarication, equivocation, and misleading omission because they know what Hitler knew: They know that propaganda is a "frightful weapon" in the hands of "an expert." They know that propaganda "remains practically unknown to the bourgeois parties." They know that media demigods influence gullible citizens' politics. *They know that propaganda alters the outcome of elections.*[xxviii]

Happily for socialists, exposure to mainstream news *causally* affects citizens' political behavior. This fact can be, and has been, scientifically tested to exclude confirmation bias and selection effects.[xxix] Even a short, ten-week

---

[xxviii] That media exposure influences political behavior cannot be disputed. Biased news influences consumers in more than one way. First, *slanted* news influences voters' choice. Stefano DellaVigna & Ethan Kaplan, *The Fox News Effect: Media Bias and Voting*, vol. 122 no. 3 QUARTERLY JOURNAL OF ECONOMICS 1187 (2007). But this is not all: Media sources also influence voters *by choosing what to cover and what not to cover.* Lisa M. George and Joel Waldfogel, *The New York Times and the Market for Local Newspapers*, vol. 96 no. 1 AMERICAN ECONOMIC REVIEW 435 (2006).

[xxix] "Our investigation of the effect of newspapers on political attitudes, behavior, and subject knowledge of news events found that *even a short exposure to a daily newspaper influences voting behavior* as well as some public opinions." Alan Gerber, Dean Karlan, & Daniel Bergan, *Does the Media Matter? A Field Experiment Measuring the Effect of Newspapers on Voting Behavior and Political Opinions*, YALE ECONOMIC APPLICATIONS AND POLICY DISCUSSION PAPER NO. 12, 18 (April 18, 2007) (emphasis added) http://aida.econ.yale.edu/karlan/papers/newspapers.pdf; *see also* Alan

exposure to the Washington Post yields an astonishing 11% swing in support for Democratic gubernatorial candidates among voters, and a 7% increase in support among the public as a whole.[56] And while making gubernatorial elections, ten weeks' exposure to the Post nevertheless *completely fails to "improve[] the subject's ability to answer factual questions about the recent news.'*[57] (Now those are impressive results—good enough to make Herr Hitler smile!)

The causal effect of mainstream "news" on voters' political behavior remains safely hidden from most. Yet the Left-leaning slant of mainstream journalism is something of an open secret.[58] It is apparent to the casual observer.[xxx] It is recognizable because mainstream newsmakers' game is so simple: *Those who bat for socialism play under a different set of rules than those who do not.* Those who bat for socialism get extra swings. And extra outs. And extra innings. And tighter strike zones. In mainstream news, those who bat for socialism always play with home field advantage. Because in the mainstream news, those who bat for socialism always receive the benefit of the doubt.

So when Ed Schultz slurred a conservative author as "right-wing slut,"[59] that didn't justify comment on the evening news. It's alright; *he's on our team.* And when Bill Maher called Sarah Palin a "twat" and a "cunt" (sorry, mom—his words not mine), you never heard about those incidents on the evening news.[60] It's not newsworthy; *he bats for us.* (Which is clearly evidenced by Maher's personal donation of a million dollars to President Obama's 2012 reelection Super PAC.[61]) After all, Political Correctness hews only one direction—nearer to socialism with every stroke.

But if, say, Rush Limbaugh should point out that Sandra Fluke is an agitator who wishes to make the government provide her with contraception—i.e., to "pay her to have sex"—then Katy, bar the door! Calling Sandra Fluke a slut is "misogyny!"[62] It's "sexism!"[63] It's "hate speech!"[64] By saying it of one woman, he says it of all![65] Why, this is the spearhead of a "Republican war on women!"[66] That lunatic shock-jock must be taken off the air! Boycott his advertisers![67] Sue him for slandering a woman's repute![68] Yes, you've surely heard of Limbaugh's slur. Because Limbaugh *plays for the wrong team.* The *bad* team. The *non*-socialists. So the rules are different here; what constitutes "appropriate" speech is different for Limbaugh than for Schultz or Maher.

Gerber, Dean Karlan, & Daniel Bergan, *Does the Media Matter? A Field Experiment Measuring the Effect of Newspapers on Voting Behavior and Political Opinions*, vol. 1 no. 2 AMERICAN ECONOMIC JOURNAL: APPLIED ECONOMICS 35, 36 (2009).

[xxx] A large plurality of Americans, 47%, perceive a liberal bias in mainstream news. A tiny minority of Americans, 13%, perceive a conservative bias in mainstream news. *Majority in U.S. Continues to Distrust the Media, Perceive Bias*, GALLUP POLLS (Sept. 22, 2011) (poll on file with author). Those 13% in the latter group are hard-core socialists.

This Incrementalist double standard is present in mainstream "news" every day of every year. But it becomes more conspicuous around election time.

Take Candidate Obama in the 2012 election. Because he bats for the correct team, he is free to express Christian piety. He may state with candor that he lives a devout Christian life. He may publicly reference daily prayer and scripture study:

> [I]n my moments of prayer, I'm reminded that faith and values play an enormous role in motivating us to solve some of our most urgent problems. . . .
>
> I wake up each morning and I say a brief prayer, and I spend a little time in scripture and devotion. . . .
>
> But I don't stop there. I'd be remiss if I stopped there; if my values were limited to personal moments of prayer or private conversations with pastors or friends. So instead, I must try—imperfectly, but I must try—to make sure those values motivate me as one leader of this great nation. . . .
>
> I have fallen on my knees with great regularity since that moment—asking God for guidance not just in my personal life and my Christian walk, but in the life of this nation and in the values that hold us together and keep us strong. I know that He will guide us. He always has, and He always will. And I pray his richest blessings on each of you in the days ahead.[69]

This sounds so *Christian.* Some might even say *Fundamentalist.* Why, the President himself deigns to bless *us*—as though he were a priest, a holy man, or the pastor of our own particular flock.

But an Incrementalist President (and candidate!) can do far more than express personal devotion. An Incrementalist President may openly assert that *his Christian faith compels policy decisions.* Yes, indeed! He may declare quite matter-of-factly that he pushes monolithic, redistributive programs like (1) Dodd-Frank financial "reform," (2) Obamacare, and (3) federalized mortgage relief because "I believe in God's command to 'love thy neighbor as thyself.'"[70,xxxi,xxxii] He may state that an increasingly redistributive tax code

---

[xxxi] But wait a moment—what is meant by the Bible's command to "love thy neighbor as thyself"? Is this a rule of material redistribution? In its original context, it does not appear to be:

15 Ye shall do no unrighteousness in judgment: thou shalt not respect the person of the poor, nor honour the person of the mighty: *but* in righteousness shalt thou judge thy neighbour.
16 Thou shalt not go up and down as a talebearer among thy people: neither shalt thou stand against the blood of thy neighbour: I am the Lord.
17 Thou shalt not hate thy brother in thine heart: thou shalt in any wise rebuke thy neighbour, and not suffer sin upon him.
18 Thou shalt not avenge, nor bear any grudge against the children of thy people, but thou shalt love thy neighbour as thyself: I *am* the Lord.

Leviticus 19:15-18; *cf.* Matthew 22:35-40; Mark 12:28-34; Luke 10:25-37 (King James).

"coincides with Jesus' teaching that 'for unto whom much is given, much shall be required.'"[71,xxxiii,xxxiv,xxxv] After all, "We can all benefit from turning to

---

[xxxii] There is also the difficulty of hypocrisy. Let's say, for the purpose of argument, that President Obama's reading of the biblical injunction to "love thy neighbor as thyself" is correct. Let's say it really *is* a rule of material redistribution. Does he follow it?

Well, he is a millionaire and the president of the United States of America. His youngest brother lives in a one-room shack in a Kenyan shantytown on one dollar a month. He has known this brother, George Hussein Onyango Obama, for twenty-some odd years. (Indeed, Pres. Obama speaks of their interaction at length in his memoir, DREAMS FROM MY FATHER.) But he does not reach out a helping hand to his brother; he does not materially redistribute. Andrew Malone, *Obama's Slumdog Brother*, MAIL ONLINE (Aug. 10, 2012); Nick Pisa, *Barack Obama's 'Half-Brother Discovered in Kenya, Living on a Dollar a Month'*, MAIL ONLINE (Aug. 20, 2008).

Perhaps he never heard the one about "Am I my brother's keeper?"

[xxxiii] But wait a minute—is the principal that "for unto whomsoever much is given, of him shall be much required" a matter of *redistributive injustice*? Again, in context, it does not appear to be. It appears instead to stand for the principle that *punishment should be proportionate to a malefactor's knowledge of the law.*

> 47 And that servant, which knew his lord's will, and prepared not *himself*, neither did according to his will, shall be beaten with many *stripes*.
> 48 But he that knew not, and did commit things worthy of stripes, shall be beaten with few *stripes*. For unto whomsoever much is given, of him shall be much required: and to whom men have committed much, of him they will ask the more.

Luke 12:47-48 (King James).

[xxxiv] But wait—I thought Jesus' answer to the young rich man was *personal*: didn't he say, "If *thou* wilt be perfect, go and sell that *thou* hast, and give to the poor, and *thou* shalt have treasure in heaven: and come and follow me"? (Matt. 19:21. (King James) (emphasis added); *cf.* Mark 10:21 (King James).) I thought Jesus taught righteousness was the exclusive domain of the *individual?* (*See, e.g.*, The Parable of Lazarus and Dives, Luke 16:19-31 (King James).) I certainly don't remember him saying that *personal misdeeds* were absolved through compliance with *compulsory government action?*

But no: With a philosophical foundation firmly rooted in the hive mentality, socialists cannot comprehend an individual morality like that taught by Jesus. As we have seen in Book I, the "ethics" of socialism are necessarily (1) *communitarian* and (2) the exclusive province of *material result.* They are therefore also the exclusive province of *monolithic government. See, e.g.*, Barack H. Obama, *Address at National Prayer Breakfast*, Washington, D.C., (Feb. 2, 2012), as transcribed in *National Prayer Breakfast: President Obama's Speech Transcript*, THE WASHINGTON POST (Feb. 2, 2012).

[xxxv] The only question posed to Jesus regarding taxation (about which we have any record) concerned not steeply progressive, graduated income taxes like those favored by Obama, but an Imperial Roman *poll tax*—a highly regressive per capitum tax in which every man paid the same amount whether rich or poor. *See* Matthew 22:15-22; Luke 20:19-26; Mark 12:13-17 (King James); *see also* speech against Jewish revolt by Marcus Julius (Herod) Agrippa II, as recorded in TITUS FLAVIUS JOSEPHUS (JOSEPH BEN MATITYAHU), THE WARS OF THE JEWS II.16:4-5 (pp. 182-184) (William Whiston trans., The Echo Library 2009) (c. 75 A.D.) ("'And indeed what occasion is there for showing you the power of the Romans over remote countries, when it is so easy to learn it from Egypt, in your [own] neighborhood? This country is extended as far as the Ethiopians, and Arabia the Happy, and borders upon India; it hath seven millions five hundred thousand men, besides the inhabitants of Alexandria, *as may be learned from the revenue of the* ***poll tax***; yet it is not ashamed to submit to the Roman government . . . .' To which Agrippa replied, that what they had already done was like such as make war against the Romans; 'for you have not paid the tribute which is due to Caesar . . . . You will therefore prevent any occasion of revolt if . . . you will but pay your tribute . . . .'") (emphasis added).

And the only record we have of Jesus' answer regarding taxation shows *he approved of that highly regressive Imperial poll tax* (!). Matthew 22:15-22 (King James). So long as we are using Jesus'

our creator, listening to him. *Avoiding phony religiosity*, listening to him."[72] (!)

Mainstream media outlets will tread ever so gingerly around the edges of an Incrementalist's "Christian faith." They will never corner him on the issue. They will never ask in what particular circumstances his faith can be expected to compel policy decisions. They will never question whether such beliefs put religious conviction before logic, before country, or before law. They will never inquire if such ardor constitutes, in the President, an unconstitutional admixture of federal power with religious fervor. They will never imply such beliefs are symptomatic of a breach in the sacred "separation of church and state." They will never investigate whether this deep-seated faith constitutes an unlawful imposition of majoritarian Christian beliefs upon atheist minorities. (And for their own part, implacable atheists will feign no offense.) They will never ask if this creed represents black liberation theology. They will never inquire whether Reverend Wright taught this doctrine. And they will never print an orthodox pastor's opinion that it is heretical.

No, if they cover such news at all, they will simply state that "Obama draws on faith at prayer breakfast."[73] Oooo, how very temperate! Or that, "President Obama connected his faith with his policies toward the poor at the National Prayer Breakfast on Thursday (Feb. 2), a subtle but sharp contrast to remarks made by presidential hopeful Mitt Romney the day before."[74] Who would begrudge him that? Perhaps they will state that, "President Obama outlined a *moral* case for some of his economic policies on Thursday, saying that his religious values drive his decision to push for tougher regulation, economic equality and changes to the healthcare system."[75] Well, that sounds sensible enough! Or perhaps that, "Obama used the platform in front of religious dignitaries and politicians to express his vision of how faith and government intersect and can work together. After his remarks, the president received a standing ovation from the crowd . . . ."[76] His comments were so well received! Or that, "Blending politics and religion, President Barack Obama said his Christian faith is a driving force behind his economic policies, from Wall Street reform to his calls for the wealthy to pay higher taxes. Obama's remarks Thursday at the National Prayer Breakfast

---

words to determine tax policy, regressive poll taxes are explicitly supported. (Not exactly what socialists have in mind!) And highly progressive, graduated income taxes are not. (Whoops!)

In any case, the *poll tax* about which the Herodians and Pharisees asked Jesus soon after featured prominently in a Jewish tax revolt which metastasized into the First Jewish-Roman War of 66-73 A.D. *See* TITUS FLAVIUS JOSEPHUS (JOSEPH BEN MATITYAHU), THE WARS OF THE JEWS II.8:1 (p. 144) (William Whiston trans., The Echo Library 2009) (c. 75 A.D.) (c. 75 A.D.) ("Under [Coponius'] administration it was that a certain Galilean, whose name was Judas, prevailed with his countrymen to revolt, and said they were cowards if they would endure to pay a tax to the Romans and would, after God, submit to mortal men as their lords."). Revolts of this sort are what Incrementalists hope to avoid. So perhaps they should take it easy on proving the "morality" of redistributive taxes using Jesus' teachings.

were his most explicit account of how his personal religious beliefs factor into his decision-making on the nation's pressing problems."[77] How very nice!

Yes, mainstream newsmakers are Incrementalists' biggest cheerleaders. And in this regard, the content of modern news is not so different from the content of Mayan ballgames: *It is carefully contrived so as to amplify the popularity, preeminence, and power of Incrementalist rulers.*

But what if a *non*-socialist should run for the same office within the same year? In such a case the same cheerleaders double as proctologists. Take, for example, Rick Santorum in 2012. Newsmakers will dig through every speech the man has ever made—public or private. Right Wing Watch, an Incrementalist advocacy group bent on muzzling Middle America, will take the lead. They will find the private speech he made; four years ago (in 2008); exclusively to devout Catholics at an orthodox Catholic University (Ave Maria); two-years removed from the Senate; not yet running for elective office; when he mentioned "Satan" and "America" in the same sentence:

> Satan is attacking the great institutions of America, using those great vices of pride, vanity, and sensuality as the root to attack all of the strong plants that have so deeply rooted in the American tradition. [78]

No, no, Christian crazy man—don't personify evil in traditional Christian terms! (At least, not unless you bat for socialism.) Do so and mainstream "news" outlets will have a field day. The headlines will read quite differently from those after President Obama's most pious and authentic Christian tax soliloquy: "*The Real Problem with Rick Santorum's 'Satan' Remarks*."[79] That doesn't sound too good! Whole articles will aggregate "Santorum's 'Satan' Comments and More of His Outlandish Statements."[80] Why, this sounds a tad extreme! Mainstream columns will explain how reasonable Americans are opposed to such extremism: "Santorum, a devout Catholic who is the most overtly religious candidate in the race, has startled many Americans with comments on matters of faith."[81] After all, "These comments were made by *radical* Rick Santorum . . . ."[82] Yikes! And other mainstream publications will detail how typical of Mr. Santorum this latest religious faux-pas is: "Another day, another controversy for Rick Santorum."[83] Is this man fanatical? Other outlets will explain how badly it hurts Mr. Santorum's electoral chances: "A comment Rick Santorum made four years ago may come back to haunt him during tomorrow night's GOP debate in Arizona."[84] Representatives of his own faith will be trotted out to tell us that such statements are un-Catholic: "Father Beck seemed very concerned [about Santorum's] understanding of Catholic theology."[85]

Mixing politics with religion will suddenly demand greater scrutiny. (And reports of Santorum's "Satan gaffe" will omit any mention of President Obama's remarks of *just nineteen days prior*: That Jesus taught highly-progressive, graduated income taxes. Now there is a sincere effort at impartiality!) Yes, sophisticated voters will be troubled by Mr. Santorum's use of Christian jargon: "Mr. Santorum may be sabotaging his chances of winning over moderate voters for whom *religion and politics do not necessarily belong in the same sentence*."[86] Indeed, by personifying evil in traditional Christian terms, "Mr. Santorum was drawing particular attention [to] *his radical Christian stripes*."[87] After all, "Santorum's belief in a satanic conspiracy is not a trivial matter. *It might well shape how he would govern, should he reach the White House*. . . . [W]hen the theological notions of a politician might fundamentally guide his or her actions and decision making, it ought not be out of bounds to examine those beliefs . . . ."[88] And damn his zealotry, "Rick Santorum is making no effort to distance himself from his 2008 remarks about Satan attacking America"![89] Why, this is "lunacy"![90] Here is a Christian madman![91] A fundamentalist nut job! How could a man so hopelessly entangled in his primitive faith lead our most secular States? How could such a man lead the free world?

Or observe mainstream newsmakers' coverage of politicians' extramarital dalliances. On one side of the ledger, you have presidential candidates who promise Incrementalist advances. Take John Edwards, for example. He is a man with an insatiable itch for extramarital recreation. He doesn't oppose a good romp on the campaign trail. He won't postpone an illicit frolic for his wife's chemotherapy, either. No, Mr. Edwards is quite content to establish a new romantic affair soon after his wife is diagnosed with breast cancer.[92] (The man has a sweet tooth, you understand.)

The National Enquirer—not a mainstream news publication—knows this very well. It takes pictures of Edwards' pregnant mistress on September 27, 2007, and on October 10, 2007 it publishes a story stating that Edwards is conducting an extramarital affair.[93] But mainstream newsmakers are conspicuously uninterested in the Enquirer's discoveries; they refuse to investigate, to inquire into, or to report on the Edwards affair.

On December 19, 2007, The National Enquirer publishes photographs of John Edwards' very pregnant mistress, claim the unborn child was the product of Edwards' affair, and name Edwards' mistress as Rielle Hunter.[94] Despite names and photographic documentation, mainstream newsmakers still obstinately refuse to report the story. Throughout the 2008 campaign season, John and Elizabeth Edwards publicly fight over John's affair. The Edwards' domestic spats are wild in the extreme: In a brilliant appeal to pathos, Elizabeth tears her shirt open to show John (and other campaign staffers in the vicinity) the scars from breast cancer surgeries. Disgruntled Edwards campaign staffers leave the campaign over Edwards' affair. But still, not a single mainstream newsmaker will touch the story.[95] Not even mainstream journalists assigned to cover Edwards' campaign. No—during the length of Edwards' 2008 presidential and vice presidential campaigns, no mainstream journalists will ever ask Edwards about the affair.

On January 30, 2008, Mr. Edwards drops out of the Democratic primaries. But there still remains a chance he could get onto the Democratic ticket as vice president. So mainstream newsmakers maintain their impenetrable reticence regarding the affair.

On July 21, 2008, The National Enquirer catches Edwards visiting his baby and mistress at the Beverly Hills Hilton.[96] Edwards calls personal aides, like Andrew Young, "bawling . . . 'I have been caught! I have been caught!'"[97] The National Enquirer publishes its discovery the very next day.[98] Still mainstream newsmakers refuse to notice or report the Enquirer's discoveries—despite the story's financial value.

On August 6, 2008, The National Enquirer publishes a photograph of John Edwards *holding his love child.* Only now—now that Barack Obama has clinched the Democratic Party nomination, and any possibility that Edwards might serve as a vice presidential candidate is finished—only now do mainstream newsmakers begin to ask questions![99] On August 8, 2008, Bob Woodruff finally interviews John Edwards for ABC News' *Nightline*—and finally asks whether Mr. Edwards has had an affair with Rielle Hunter. (Mr. Edwards admits to the affair with Rielle Hunter, but denies the child is his.) Then ABC and its peer networks bury the story for good. And dump the shovels at sea.

Only years later will information trickle out of mainstream news outlets: that Mr. Edwards admits paternity of Ms. Hunter's child (January 21, 2010);[100] that Elizabeth Edwards has died of cancer (December 7, 2010);[101] that Elizabeth's will never mentioned John and leaves him nothing (Jan. 5, 2011);[102] that an arrest warrant has issued for Mr. Edwards in connection with an indictment alleging his illegal use of campaign contributions during the 2008 campaign (June 3, 2011).[103]

But what if you bat for the wrong team? In that case, your candidacy inhabits the *other* side of the ledger. You will be judged by the *other* set of rules—the draconian ones. Mainstream newsmakers will strip search you. They will carefully comb through your body hair. They will find every louse that ever sucked your scalp. They will discover all the nits you sired. Not years after the election—oh, no! They will complete their investigation while you are your Party's front-running candidate. They will interview alleged lice. (Herman Cain.[104]) They will air unopposed interviews with your enraged ex-wife—immediately prior to primary debates. (Newt Gingrich.[105]) They will host press conferences alleging unrequited advances. (Herman Cain.[106]) They will open primary debates by asking you about your dalliances. (Newt Gingrich.[107]) They will derail your campaign. And they will accomplish all this in *mere weeks.*

(Do not misunderstand: We don't wish to discourage mainstream newsmakers from broadcasting information related to a candidates' moral fiber! On the contrary, we prefer solid investigative journalism. We just require it *for all candidates*. What we don't want is newsmakers pretending objectivity while waging a campaign of reticence to hide from us the truth about their favorites.)

An unending double-standard promoting Incrementalist revolution: This is the content of "news." And what is "news" but another facet of electronic entertainment? We ingest it daily by computer, smartphone, radio, and television; we use it to take breaks during work, during lunch, at the gym, and at home.

Whether we examine the artifice of mainstream films or modern journalism, the socialist content of entertainment has ossified into an undeniable feature of American culture. Mainstream films and journalism are no longer an expression of public opinion, but rather the organized creation of it.

Hitler would be proud.

* * *

And so, in the final analysis, modern electronic entertainment is not so very different from its ancient Mayan analogue.

Like the Mayan ballgame, modern electronic entertainment saps life quite effectively. (Though not so suddenly.) Like the Mayan ballgame, it tears out the soul. (While preserving physical stamina for the construction of "public" works!) Like the Mayan ballgame, it drowns out the inner voice. (And replaces it with "public opinion.") Like the Mayan ballgame, it distracts spectators from the irrepresentative business of government. (And the rulers who implement it!) Like the Mayan ballgame, it provides a captive audience for monolithic planners. (So long as spectators' right to entertainment is preserved.)

And like the Mayan ballgame, electronic entertainment does more than merely sap and distract: It is strongly didactic. It is measured not for art's sake, but for propagandistic effect. Its content is contrived so as to mold and to bend. It thus *promotes* a certain worldview and a certain value system among the entertained. That worldview is contrived, to be sure. Contrived by those at the top to entertain the hive—and to preserve a monolithic hierarchy.

Yes, in the technological explosion of the past century Incrementalism found another crack into which to insert its cultural maul. With the available programming, the increasingly transportive experience, and the ubiquitous reach of cyber-networks, time for private thought and sober reflection is choked out. With so many collegiate and professional sporting events to review, so many social networks to update, so much programming to survey, and so many images to inspect, Americans take less interest in real life than their Predecessors. So many are willing to tolerate Incrementalist usurpations so long as their "right" to watch *Glee* or *Modern Family* is not compromised. So few step back from the mural and think.

These have been entertained into submission. Hypnotized by kitsch, they are unresponsive to real life. Millions of them vote, though they have little idea of what they are voting for or against. And while they are sleepwalking through real life, in a cyber-, cell-, satellite-, or cable-induced haze, the Incrementalist Cultural Revolution marches on.

Miserable Americans!
You have achieved much.
But you relinquish your stupendous potential—
You live and die for entertainment.

Further Notes to Chapter 7

[1] Surveys show that some 45% of UK children, from eleven to eighteen years old, are "sometimes happier online than in their real lives." Liz Thomas, *Generation Net: The Youngsters Who Prefer Their Virtual Lives to the Real World*, MAIL ONLINE (Feb. 8, 2011). Granted, those are children in the UK. But really—is the situation so much different here in the U.S.? Why, here in the U.S., more than 90% of *adults* aged twenty-eight to thirty-five years old return calls and texts while sitting on the toilet. Neal Augenstein, *Toilet Texting on the Rise*, WTOP NEWS (Feb. 1, 2012).

[2] Sufferers believe themselves to have been given fake families, fake friends, fake jobs, all contrived as part of an elaborate set. Because they believe themselves to be unwilling participants, such delusions of grandeur are, of course, also delusions of *persecution*. Joel Gold & Ian Gold, *The "Truman Show" Delusion: Psychosis in the Global Village*, COGNITIVE NEUROPSYCHIATRY 1-18 (May 29, 2012).

[3] Indeed, it is difficult to imagine just how humans—which are completely unique—could progress without discovering the proper balance of entertainment for themselves.

[4] "Over the last few decades, huge advances in technology have allowed businesses to do more with less . . . . And many of you know firsthand the painful disruptions this has caused for a lot of Americans. . . . If you were a *bank teller* or a *phone operator* or a *travel agent*, you saw many in your profession *replaced by ATMs and the Internet*. . . . And if you're somebody whose job *can be done cheaper by a computer* or someone in another country, you don't have a lot of leverage with your employer when it comes to asking for better wages or better benefits, especially since fewer Americans today are part of a union." Barack Obama, *Remarks by the President on the Economy in Osawatomie, Kansas*, OFFICE OF THE PRESS SECRETARY, WHITE HOUSE (Dec. 6, 2011) (emphasis added).

[5] *Ibid.*

[6] *Ibid.*

[7] Paul Haven (AP), *Cuba Legalizes General Purchase and Sale of Cars*, ASSOCIATED PRESS (Sept. 28, 2011).

[8] *Ibid.*

[9] KIM JONG IL, ON THE ART OF THE CINEMA, 2 (Foreign Languages Publishing House, Pyongyang 1989) (1973) (emphasis added). Moreover, "The basic duty of the creative group is to create revolutionary films of high ideological and artistic value, which are [sic] effective contribution in equipping the people with the entire armoury [sic] of the Party's monolithic ideology and imbuing the whole of society with the great concept of Juche." *Ibid.* at 116.

[10] Daniel Wallis & Stacey Joyce, *Sean Penn Joins Chavez on Campaign in Venezuela*, REUTERS (Aug. 5, 2012).

[11] Quoting Jack Nicholson. Humberto Fontova, *Hollywood Loves Fidel—But Why?*, CANADA FREE PRESS (May 8, 2009).

[12] Sean Penn, *Video Interview re Article Written for The Nation*, THE NATION (Produced by Brett Story) (Nov. 24, 2008), http://www.youtube.com/watch?v= LrvRpIokeAg.

[13] *Ibid.*

[14] Humberto Fontova, *Hollywood Loves Fidel—But Why?*, CANADA FREE PRESS (May 8, 2009).

[15] *Wall Street* (1987), hospital room scene with Charlie and Martin Sheen.

[16] *Wall Street* (1987), monologue by Michael Douglas (Academy Award winner for his portrayal of conscienceless capitalist Gordon Gekko).

[17] Don't watch *Money Never Sleeps* if you know anything about finance, or else you will feel like an electrical engineer trying to watch an episode of Star Trek. Your practical knowledge of the contemporary state of the art will prove confounding.

[18] *Bolivian President Says Avatar Inspires Anti-Capitalist Struggle*, RIA NOVOSTI (Jan. 12, 2010). And yes, this is the RIA Novosti of Cold War fame: the very same state owned, Moscow "news agency" that began its life as the dreaded Sovinformburo (Soviet Information Bureau).

[19] *Evo Morales Praises 'Avatar'*, THE HUFFINGTON POST (Jan. 12, 2010).

[20] Roger Friedman, *James Cameron Will Film Three "Avatar" Sequels at the Same Time*, SHOWBIZ 411 (June 26, 2012).
[21] *I.e.*, voting members of the Academy of Motion Picture Arts and Sciences. And whom *exactly* does that consist of? Well, that "is closely guarded secret." John Horn, Nicole Sperling, & Doug Smith, *Unmasking the Academy: Oscar Voters Overwhelmingly White, Male*, LOS ANGELES TIMES (Feb. 19, 2012).
[22] As of May 18, 2012.
[23] As of May 18, 2012.
[24] As of May 18, 2012.
[25] *See, e.g.*, Michael Schauerte, *What Was He Fighting For?*, WORLD SOCIALISM No. 1281 (May 2011).
[26] As of May 18, 2012.
[27] As of May 18, 2012.
[28] As of May 18, 2012.
[29] As of May 18, 2012.
[30] As of May 18, 2012.
[31] As of May 18, 2012.
[32] Indeed, most critics are wannabe Hollywood writers and directors.
[33] *See, e.g.*, Paul Bond, *Study: 'Conservative' Movies Make More Money Than 'Liberal' Movies*, THE HOLLYWOOD REPORTER (Feb. 2, 2012); Billy Hallowell, *Report: Faith-Based Movies Brought In More Money Than Their Liberal Counterparts in 2011*, THE BLAZE (Mar. 8, 2012).
[34] KIM JONG IL, ON THE ART OF THE CINEMA, 52; 54 (Foreign Languages Publishing House, Pyongyang 1989) (1973) (emphasis added).
[35] "Lawmakers say she [i.e., Minority Leader Nancy Pelosi] is consulting marketing experts about building a stronger brand. The most prominent of her new whisperers is Steven Spielberg, the Hollywood director whose films have been works of branding genius." Rachel Weiner, *Steven Spielberg Advising Nancy Pelosi on Rebranding Democrats*, THE WASHINGTON POST (Dec. 22, 2010).
[36] *Ibid.*
[37] Abby Goodnough, *California Tries to Guide the Way on Health Law*, THE NEW YORK TIMES (Sept. 14, 2012).
[38] *Ibid.*
[39] *Ibid.*
[40] Quote by Peter V. Lee, executive director of the California Health Care Exchange—an administrative agency which, despite its title, is actually federal in nature. *Ibid.*
[41] Again, this is Peter V. Lee speaking. *Ibid.*
[42] Erik Wemple, *NBC To Do "Internal Investigation" on Zimmerman Segment*, THE WASHINGTON POST (Mar. 31, 2012).
[43] *Piers Morgan Tonight*, CNN (June 4, 2012).
[44] *Political Party*, NEW YORK POST (July 23, 2012).
[45] *See, e.g.*, BERNARD GOLDBERG, BIAS: A CBS INSIDER EXPOSES HOW THE MEDIA DISTORT THE NEWS (Harper Paperbacks 2003) (5th Printing); S. ROBERT LICHTER, THE MEDIA ELITE: AMERICA'S NEW POWER BROKERS (Hastings House 1990).
[46] Bill Dedman, *Journalists Dole Out Cash to Politicians (Quietly)*, MSNBC.COM (June 25, 2007). Ethical concerns over such clear conflicts of interest—in which news writers author "unbiased" articles in favor of a candidate and, unbeknownst to readers, also personally contribute money to campaigns—are minimized by socialists. As explained by Mark Singer, author of the New Yorker's Howard Dean profile during the 2004 campaign, and contributor to America Coming Together and its campaign to defeat President Bush,

> "Probably there should be a rule against [news people contributing to political campaigns]. But there's a rule against murder. If someone had murdered Hitler—a journalist interviewing him had murdered him—the world would be a better place. As a citizen, I can only feel good about participating in a get-out-the-vote effort to get rid of George Bush, who has been the most destructive president in my lifetime. I certainly don't regret it."

Ibid. So there you have it. It is quite right for newscasters to pretend objectivity yet practice propaganda. . . .

Occasionally you will see a mainstream media outlet fire a journalist for making campaign contributions to Incrementalist politicians. But this only happens in the most egregious of examples. Like Keith Olbermann, who was suspended by MSNBC for making the maximum individual campaign contribution ($2,400.00) to three different Incrementalist politicians (Representative Raúl Grijalva, Co-Chair of the Congressional Progressive Caucus, and Representative Gabriel Giffords, and Senate candidate Jack Conway), *making the donation to Grijalva on the same day Grijalva made a guest appearance on Olberman's show.* Simmi Aujla, *Keith Olbermann Suspended After Donating to Democrats*, POLITICO (Nov. 5, 2010); CNN Political Unit, *UPDATE: Olbermann Suspended for Dem Contributions*, CNN (Nov. 5, 2010).

[47] Yes, media sources influence public opinion *by choosing which stories to cover and which stories to bury*. Lisa M. George and Joel Waldfogel, *The New York Times and the Market for Local Newspapers*, vol. 96 no. 1 AMERICAN ECONOMIC REVIEW 435 (2006). A simple example of this phenomenon: When eight democratic city council members in Bell, CA were arrested for what the L.A. County District Attorney called "corruption on steroids," no major news outlets mentioned the fact that *all eight were Democrats.* Too many such examples exist to list them here. One web outlet that attempts to catalog such news media bias is Newsbusters.org, http://newsbusters.org/.

[48] More precisely, William Dean Singleton—Chairman of the Board of Directors for the Associated Press. Daniel Halper, *Associated Press Chief Offers Lavish Praise for Obama*, THE WEEKLY STANDARD (April 3, 2012).

[49] Here we are referring to Chris Matthews, host of MSNBC's *Hardball*—the same news host who told us, "I felt this thrill up my leg" when he heard Barack Obama deliver a 2008 campaign speech. Not exactly a paragon of journalistic impartiality. Still, he assures us that his latest comparison of President Obama to Henry V "has nothing to do with partisanship." Ian Schwartz, *Matthews: "So Proud" of Obama Addressing Troops in Afghanistan*, REAL CLEAR POLITICS (May 1, 2012). Meanwhile, reporters coordinate prejudicial questions prior to GOP presidential candidate's press conferences, so "no matter who [sic] he calls on we're covered on the one question." Daniel Halper, *Press Coordinates Question to Ask Romney*, THE WEEKLY STANDARD (Sep. 12, 2012).

[50] In producing her story about President Bush's alleged failures as a pilot in the Texas Air National Guard, Mary Mapes received un-vetted documents providing the main evidence from Lt. Burkett—someone "she knew many in the press considered . . . an 'anti-Bush zealot,' his credibility in question." Walter V. Robinson, *"Truth and Duty": A Distorted Lens*, THE BOSTON GLOBE (Dec. 11, 2005).

[51] Associate Producer Michael Smith emailed Producer Mary Mapes, "What if there was [sic] a person who might have some information that could possibly change the momentum of an election but we needed to get an ASAP book deal to help get us the information?" To which Producer Mary Mapes responded, "that looks good, hypothetically speaking of course." Dick Thornburgh & Louis D. Boccardi, *Report of the Independent Review Panel on the September 8, 2004* 60 MINUTES WEDNESDAY *Segment*, 61 (Jan. 5, 2005).

[52] Dick Thornburgh & Louis D. Boccardi, *Report of the Independent Review Panel on the September 8, 2004* 60 MINUTES WEDNESDAY *Segment*, 65 (Jan. 5, 2005).

[53] Executive Producer Josh Howard himself wished to hold the Bush Texas Air National Guard story until September—less than two months before the November 2004 election. *Ibid.* at 64.

[54] The listed anachronisms in the so-called Killian Documents were obvious to the casual observer. They were also noted by forensic document examiners like Peter Tytell, who concluded that "the Killian documents were produced on a computer in Times New Roman typestyle," and that "the Killian documents were not produced on a typewriter in the early 1970s and therefore were not authentic." *Ibid.* at Appendix 4.

[55] "Philosophers have hitherto only interpreted the world in various ways; the point is to change it." Karl Marx, *Theses on Feuerbach*, Thesis 11 (Institute of Marxism-Leninism, 1845). *See, e.g.*, http://www.marxists.org/archive/marx/works/1845/theses/index.htm.

[56] Alan Gerber, Dean Karlan, & Daniel Bergan, *Does the Media Matter? A Field Experiment Measuring the Effect of Newspapers on Voting Behavior and Political Opinions*, vol. 1 no. 2 AMERICAN ECONOMIC JOURNAL: APPLIED ECONOMICS 35, 47 (2009).
[57] *Ibid.* at 45 (emphasis added).
[58] As Public Editor of The New York Times, Arthur S. Brisbane, noted when stepping down: "Across the paper's many departments, though, so many share a kind of political and cultural progressivism—for lack of a better term—that this worldview virtually bleeds through the fabric of The Times. As a result, developments like the Occupy movement and gay marriage seem almost to erupt in The Times, overloved and undermanaged, more like causes than news subjects." Arthur S. Brisbane, *Success and Risk as The Times Transforms*, THE NEW YORK TIMES (Aug. 25, 2012). And I think you can guess what he soft-pedals as "a kind of political and cultural progressivism."
[59] Ed Schultz, *The Ed Schultz Show*, nationally syndicated by DIAL GLOBAL (May 24, 2011).
[60] *See, e.g.*, Melissa McEwan, *Unacceptable: Sexist Bill Maher Calls Sarah Palin the C-Word*, ALTERNET (March 29, 2011).
[61] *I.e.*, to "Priorities USA," the Super PAC backing President Obama's reelection efforts. *Bill Maher Gives $1 Million to Obama Super PAC*, REAL CLEAR POLITICS (Feb. 24, 2012).
[62] "It's misogyny, it's sexism, it's rampant all over talk radio!" Eric Boehlert, Senior Fellow at Media Matters, speaking on THE ED SHOW, *Rushing Away*, MSNBC (March 12, 2012).
[63] *Ibid.*
[64] Ed Schultz, THE ED SHOW, *Rushing Away*, MSNBC (March 12, 2012).
[65] *See, e.g.*, Toby Harnden, *Illegal Robocalls Accuse Republicans Over Rush Limbaugh and "Slut" Slur*, MAIL ONLINE (March 9, 2012).
[66] *See, e.g.*, *Ibid.*
[67] Socialist front groups like Media Matters will lead the boycott. David Bauder, *Radio Campaign Next Step Against Rush Limbaugh*, THE WASHINGTON TIMES (March 22, 2012).
[68] Min Jung Lee, *Gloria Allred Seeks Rush Limbaugh Prosecution*, POLITICO (March 9, 2012).
[69] Barack H. Obama, *Address at National Prayer Breakfast*, Washington, D.C., (Feb. 2, 2012), as transcribed in *National Prayer Breakfast: President Obama's Speech Transcript*, THE WASHINGTON POST (Feb. 2, 2012).
[70] "And so when I talk about our financial institutions playing by the same rules as folks on Main Street, when I talk about making sure insurance companies aren't discriminating against those who are already sick, or making sure that unscrupulous lenders aren't taking advantage of the most vulnerable among us, I do so because I genuinely believe it will make the economy stronger for everybody. But I also do it because I know that far too many neighbors in our country have been hurt and treated unfairly over the last few years, and I believe in God's command to "love thy neighbor as thyself."" Barack H. Obama, *Address at National Prayer Breakfast*, Washington, D.C., (Feb. 2, 2012), as transcribed in *Ibid.* (emphasis added).
[71] Barack H. Obama, *Address at National Prayer Breakfast*, Washington, D.C., (Feb. 2, 2012), as transcribed in *Ibid.*
[72] Barack H. Obama, *Address at National Prayer Breakfast*, Washington, D.C., (Feb. 2, 2012), as transcribed in *Ibid.*
[73] Scott Horsley, *Obama Draws On Faith At Prayer Breakfast*, NATIONAL PUBLIC RADIO (Feb. 2, 2012).
[74] Lauren Markoe, *At National Prayer Breakfast, Obama Says Faith Mandates Him To [sic] Care For The Poor*, HUFFINGTON POST (Feb. 2, 2012) ("Specifically, Obama said, they translate to policies that support research to fight disease and support foreign aid. His faith, he continued, inspires him 'to give up some of the tax breaks that I enjoy.' Romney has come under fire for telling CNN on Wednesday that 'I'm not concerned about the very poor,' but is instead focused on the middle class.").
[75] Kathleen Hennessey, *National Prayer Breakfast: Obama Says His Values Guide Policies*, LOS ANGELES TIMES (Feb. 2, 2012) (emphasis added).
[76] Eric Marrapodi, *Obama Reflects on Faith in Prayer Breakfast Speech*, CNN (Feb. 2, 2012). *See also* Mark Landler, *At Prayer Breakfast, Obama Ties Economic Message to Christian Values*, THE NEW YORK TIMES (Feb. 2, 2012) ("The president emphasized that his themes of economic equity and a fair shot for the middle class would reinvigorate the American economy. But he said they

were also product [sic] of his faith, noting, 'We're required to have a living, breathing, active faith in our own lives.'"); Kent Klein, *Obama: Religious Faith Helps Guide His Decisions*, VOICE OF AMERICA (Feb. 2, 2012) ("President Barack Obama says his religious faith and values help guide him in setting his policies.").

[77] Julie Pace, *Obama National Prayer Breakfast Speech: President Links Economic Policies With Faith*, THE HUFFINGTON POST (Feb. 2, 2012).

[78] Kyle Mantyla, *Santorum: Satan Is Systematically Destroying America*, RIGHT WING WATCH (Feb. 16, 2012); *see also Rick Santorum Defends Satan Comments*, THE HUFFINGTON POST (Feb. 22, 2012).

[79] Josh Barro, *The Real Problem with Rick Santorum's 'Satan' Remarks*, FORBES (Feb. 21, 2012).

[80] *Santorum's "Satan" Comments & More of His Outlandish Statements*, THE DAILY BEAST (Feb. 22, 2012).

[81] Jonathan Mann, *Will Satan Stop Rick Santorum?*, CNN (Feb. 24, 2012).

[82] Steve Frank, *Rick Santorum: 'Satan Has His Sights Set' on America*, MSNBC (Feb. 21, 2012).

[83] Kenneth T. Walsh, *Critics Set Sights on Rick Santorum's Satan Comments*, U.S. NEWS & WORLD REPORT (Feb. 22, 2012).

[84] *Santorum's 'Satan' Comment Resurfaces*, THE DAILY BEAST (Feb. 21, 2012).

[85] Frances Martel, *Catholic Priest Disowns Santorum's Satan comments as 'Not Catholic' to O'Reilly*, MEDIAITE (Feb. 22, 2012) (describing Father Edward Beck's opinion of Santorum's "Satan" comments on The O'Reilly Factor).

[86] David Usborne, *After Four Years, Speech Haunts the Republican Front-Runner as He Tries to Convert Moderate Voters*, THE INDEPENDENT (Feb. 23, 2012).

[87] *Ibid.* (emphasis added).

[88] David Corn, *Does Santorum Believe Obama is Part of a Satanic Plot?*, MOTHER JONES (Feb. 22, 2012).

[89] *Rick Santorum Defends Satan Comments*, THE HUFFINGTON POST (Feb. 22, 2012); *see also* Rebecca Kaplan, *Santorum: Satan Comments in 2008 'Not Relevant' Today*, NATIONAL JOURNAL (Feb. 22, 2012).

[90] *See, e.g.*, Hugh Kramer, *Attack Santorum on His Satan Remarks & You "Are Insulting Jesus Christ Himself"*, EXAMINER.COM (Feb. 26, 2012).

[91] "It would be hard, in fact, to invent things that better illustrate that *craziness* than what [the Religious Right and Rick Santorum] say themselves." Hugh Kramer, *Attack Santorum on His Satan Remarks & You "Are Insulting Jesus Christ Himself"*, EXAMINER.COM (Feb. 26, 2012) (emphasis added).

[92] John Edwards learned of Elizabeth Edwards' breast cancer in November, 2004. He began an affair with Rielle Hunter in February, 2006—with Elizabeth's cancer treatment ongoing. *See, e.g.*, Nadine Shubailat, James Hill, & Teri Whitcraft, *Timeline: Scandal According to Andrew Young*, ABC 20/20 (Jan. 28, 2010)

[93] Rick Egusquiza, *Presidential Cheating Scandal! Alleged Affair Could Wreck John Edwards' Campaign Bid*, NATIONAL ENQUIRER (Oct. 10, 2007); *see also, e.g.*, Nadine Shubailat, James Hill, & Teri Whitcraft, *Timeline: Scandal According to Andrew Young*, ABC 20/20 (Jan. 28, 2010).

[94] *Update: John Edwards Love Child Scandal!*, NATIONAL ENQUIRER (Dec. 19, 2007); Nadine Shubailat, James Hill, & Teri Whitcraft, *Timeline: Scandal According to Andrew Young*, ABC 20/20 (Jan. 28, 2010).

[95] Emily Miller, *Does The National Enquirer Deserve a Pulitzer for Breaking the John Edwards Scandal?*, POLITICS DAILY (Jan. 9, 2010).

[96] Nadine Shubailat, James Hill, & Teri Whitcraft, *Timeline: Scandal According to Andrew Young*, ABC 20/20 (Jan. 28, 2010).

[97] *Ibid.*

[98] *Sen. John Edwards Caught With Mistress and Love Child!*, NATIONAL ENQUIRER (July 22, 2008).

[99] Emily Miller, *Does The National Enquirer Deserve a Pulitzer for Breaking the John Edwards Scandal?*, POLITICS DAILY (Jan. 9, 2010).

[100] *See, e.g.*, Garance Franke-Ruta, *John Edwards Admits Paternity*, THE WASHINGTON POST (Jan. 21, 2010); *Edwards Admits Fathering Love Child, Reportedly Separates from Wife*, FOX NEWS (Jan. 21, 2010).

[101] Hari Sreenivasan, *News Wrap: Elizabeth Edwards Dies After Cancer, Personal Struggles*, PBS NEWSHOUR (Dec. 7, 2010); Adam Hochberg, *Elizabeth Edwards Succumbs to Cancer*, NPR (Dec. 7, 2010).
[102] Jessica Derschowitz, *Elizabeth Edwards' Will Released*, CBS NEWS (Jan. 5, 2011).
[103] Andrew Cohen, *The John Edwards Arrest Warrant and Indictment*, THE ATLANTIC (June 3, 2011); *John Edwards: "I Did Not Break the Law"*, CBS NEWS (June 3, 2011).
[104] Ginger White was the alleged louse. *See, e.g.*, Lucy Madison & Brian Montopoli, *Herman Cain Preemptively Denies New Sex Allegation*, CBS NEWS (Nov. 28, 2011).
[105] Marianne Gingrich was the enraged ex-wife. Brian Ross & Rhonda Schwartz, *Exclusive: Gingrich Lacks Moral Character to Be President, Ex-Wife Says*, ABC NEWS (Jan. 19, 2012).
[106] Sharon Bialek was the alleged harassee. *See, e.g.*, Juana Summers, Maggie Haberman, & Kenneth P. Vogel, *Sharon Bialek Says Herman Cain Made Inappropriate Advances*, Politico (Nov. 7, 2011); David Rothschild, *Accuser's Press Conference Cuts Herman Cain's Odds in Half*, YAHOO! NEWS (Nov. 7, 2011).
[107] At CNN's South Carolina Primary Debate. *See, e.g.*, Matt Negrin, *Newt Gingrich Turns Ex-Wife's Interview Into Attack on Media*, ABC NEWS (Jan. 19, 2012); Rachel Streitfeld & Paul Steinhauser, *Gingrich Delivers Show-Stopper at Beginning of South Carolina Debate*, CNN (Jan. 19, 2012).

8

Government In Your Panties

I consider the foundation of the Constitution as laid on this ground: That "all powers not delegated to the United States, by the Constitution, nor prohibited by it to the States, are reserved to the States or to the people." To take a single step beyond the boundaries thus specially drawn around the powers of Congress, is to take possession of a boundless field of power, no longer susceptible of any definition.

—Thomas Jefferson[i]

HAVE YOU EVER EXPERIENCED a social-anxiety nightmare?

You know, one of those dreams where you spend considerable time delivering a presentation at work; or strolling through the mall; or getting books out of your locker at school—and then you look down, and come to an abrupt realization that *you are unclothed?*

What horror!

Naked and alone in a public place. Nowhere to hide. And only then—only at the moment you realize you are unclothed—only then does everyone else in your dream *also realize* you forgot to dress today! Only at that instant do peers' eyes widen in disbelief. Only then do they begin to gawk and point. Only then—as you sprint down corridors, burst through doorways, vault over benches, scramble up fences, bound past astonished onlookers, dash through parking lots, all while flapping freely in the breeze—do onlookers begin to congregate in your wake, to giggle and to discuss your plight.

For shame!

[i] Thomas Jefferson, *Opinion on the Constitutionality of Creating a National Bank* (1791).

What sweet consolation to awaken in a warm morning's sunshine! To comprehend the absurdity and falsity of a long night's terror. To recognize the byproduct of an overactive REM cycle for what it is: the mere reprocessing of universal yet harmless anxieties!

How about this one:

You are leaving town to attend a wedding. You verify your luggage is faultlessly packed: Your tuxedo is there; dress shoes, too; freshly-washed socks and undergarments; toiletries packed snugly in little plastic baggies. Bundled in a smaller carryon are a freshly-printed boarding pass and a book to read on the plane. Everything appears to be as it should.

You load your bags into the car. You drive to the airport. You avoid traffic with assistance from your smartphone. You park your vehicle. You hop the shuttle to Terminal C. You check your suitcase at the airline counter, shoulder your carryon, make your way through security, and proceed to your gate. You have timed everything perfectly—just thirty-five minutes to takeoff!

As you stroll through the concourse toward your gate, you casually look down to avoid stepping on someone's laptop power cord.

Something strange and dark catches your eye;

You glance down again—

With mounting horror and disbelief you see and you comprehend:

You have wet yourself!

What, the . . . ?

You cannot imagine how this happened, but it has. Your pants are soaked. As the realization sinks in, you notice that everyone else has noticed, too. People are stopping and staring. Mothers shield young children's eyes. Men snigger under their breath and quietly shake their heads in disapproval. Youths openly point and laugh.

You will miss your flight—and the wedding—if you exit the airport and return to your vehicle. The clean clothes packed in your suitcase were checked with the airline some time ago, and will remain unavailable until your flight reaches its destination. There are no clothes in your carryon. You scour novelty vendors' shops for clothes, but no one is selling anything but t-shirts in this part of the concourse. Your hand is forced; there is no time for anything else:

You walk briskly through the crowded airport, soaked in urine like a naughty child. You must catch this flight to make the wedding. You are humiliated, and so upset you cannot speak. You weep as you approach the gate. You must board the plane with all the rest—reeking of that uric product which so obviously soaks your pants, your socks, your shoes. Even your shirt. You must wait in line, pancaked between travelers on the gangway.

Once onboard the airplane, you make your way to coach. You must sit practically on top strangers. And they know.

How could they not know? Within the sweaty cabin prior to takeoff, while air conditioning vents are inoperable, you try to conceal the vinegary, salty stench. But you cannot. It hangs in the air.

Once the plane reaches cruising altitude and the fasten-seat-belts sign switches off, you retreat to the cramped lavatory at the back of the plane. You try to clean up. (But what can you do in there, with nothing but a few paper napkins? There is no shower, and no clean clothes.) You return to your seat.

Everyone is looking.

Pretend you don't feel their eyes.

Synergy

Incrementalism wears many masks.

Cultural developments like political correctness, Incrementalist immigration, and entertainment submission provide independent stepping stones across which implicit socialism slinks. Monolithic techniques like the Fourth Head's obfuscation and lack of accountability, as well as consolidation of federal authority in general, are separately used to further Incrementalist revolution.

But all Incrementalist methods—whether cultural or governmental—are far more effective when employed *in combination*. Indeed, that is the subject of this chapter: The mind-boggling heights which Incrementalism can attain through a synergistic combination of (1) timing, (2) Incrementalist culture, and (3) Incrementalist institutions upon which we have previously touched. As we shall see, the Incrementalist whole far exceeds the sum of its parts!

Incrementalism is pleased to wait for synergistic opportunities. Such opportunities often present themselves during national crises—i.e., when citizens *fear*. The best crises are those which inspire visceral fear: terrors so compelling that, in the short run, citizens are willing to sell their birthright of liberty for a mess of security theater. (A trade which Incrementalism is happy to make, because Incrementalism's game is simply to maintain monolithic gains long, long after the cause of citizens' fear has passed.)

So many examples exist of the synergistic confluence of citizen fear with Incrementalist method that limiting our discussion to a single exemplar proves difficult. Examples of this phenomenon are quite familiar, and each possesses fantastic explanatory power.

Yet some examples are more tangible than others. As a result they are more memorable. And in this regard, it is difficult to find an example of Incrementalist synergy which trumps the tangibility and memorability of our experience within airports nationwide.

As everyone knows, foreign-born, Islamic terrorists hijacked four airplanes on 9/11, 2001. And thousands of Americans died.

In response to the newfound threat of American aviation terrorism, Incrementalist President George W. Bush signed into law the Aviation and Transportation Security Act of 2001. This law created a new federal agency, complete with a new bureaucracy of unelected officials, tasked with keeping air travelers and ground targets safe: the so-called Transportation Security Administration (TSA). The monolithic idea was that a single, federal agency—uniform in its screening protocols, comprehensive in its reach, and symmetrical in its simultaneous protection of all airlines and airports—could better defend against the threat of airborne terrorism than could private companies, under private agreements, contracting with one or more airlines at any given airport terminal.

Citizens, who were understandably panicked by the events of 9/11, submitted to TSA and its new screening procedures without a squeak.

At first the new agency didn't do very much. TSA barred non-passengers from passing through security and into airport terminals, thereby foreclosing most of the airport to all but ticketed passengers (and, of course, airport and airline employees.) You could no longer frequent airport shops or restaurants without a ticket. Nor could you greet loved ones at the gate. But this was a small price to pay for security.

TSA also updated the list of prohibited carryon items, conspicuously adding box cutters (after their successful deployment as weapons by the 9/11 hijackers). Then cigarette lighters, printer cartridges, and snow globes were banned. Later on fluids, syrups, gels, creams, oils, sprays, and pastes were prohibited unless housed in 100ml containers carried within a single, transparent, re-sealable plastic bag. And after the shoe-bomber incident TSA insisted passengers remove their shoes for security scanning, too. It was inconvenient. It was hard on one's socks. It was unhygienic. And like all government agencies, TSA considerably slowed the pace of formerly private activities (in this case, security screenings)—so more time was required to fly. But removing your shoes at the security check point was preferable to plunging thousands of feet to a fiery death, so citizens tolerated these changes, too.

TSA, however, was just warming up to its new airline security authority. In November, 2010, TSA began informing travelers that they had a choice to make. Travelers at airport security check points could opt for: (1) virtual strip searches (via backscatter X-ray or millimeter-wave Whole Body Imaging machines); (2) "enhanced pat-downs" (i.e., direct encounters between TSA and your genitals); (3) foregoing the flight altogether (yet still paying full ticket price); or instead of (3), and at TSA's sole discretion, (4a) arrest and (4b) formal banishment from the airport. These were the only options.

For the sake of those who fly infrequently, TSA's security options warrant further explanation:

Virtual strip searches using UBI machines create a detailed image of your naked body, down to the slightest dimple, crease, and pucker. The only part of your body invisible in the resulting image is any hair you might have—i.e., the last vestige of a more primitive privacy. (Yes, the darn millimeter-wave scanners use too long a wavelength to pick up human hair.) So you are on display for TSA agents as if you had just received a full Brazilian wax.

And you know those TSA employees—so respectful, so professional, so courteous, so well-cultured![ii] They would *never* abuse their access to nude images of air travelers! Besides, TSA assures us that images produced by such advanced imaging technology will never be stored, printed, transmitted, saved, or used for purposes other than security.[1] Indeed, TSA assures that "the image is *automatically deleted from the system*," as soon as individual security clearance is granted.[2]

(Yet whatever TSA's stated policy regarding saving those images, such nudy-scan images *can*, of course, be saved. And they *are* saved. For example, a Freedom of Information Act request turned up 35,000 images saved from a single screening checkpoint at a federal court in Florida.[3] Admittedly, they were not impeccably well-trained, highly-educated TSA employees doing the screening at the Florida Courthouse—they were *U.S. Marshals* . . . .)

As invasive as the nudy-scans are, they don't hold a candle to TSA's "enhanced" pat-downs. Some persons—those specially and "randomly" selected at the discretion of TSA agents; those who set off a metal detector; those whose medical devices or prostheses are exposed during nudy-screening; those who refuse a nudy-screening; and many others—have no choice but to submit to this latter approach.

What occurs during an "enhanced" pat-down? Well, just about anything *can* happen. What generally happens is: (1) the passenger spreads his legs; (2) a TSA agent approaches the passenger safely from the rear; (3) the TSA agent assumes a kneeling position behind the passenger; (4) the TSA agent runs his hands along the inside of the passenger's legs, groin, and crack from the back; (5) the passenger turns 180 degrees around, and again spreads his legs; (6) the TSA agent runs his hands along the inside of the passenger's legs and groin from the front; (7) the TSA agent stands and pats the passenger's hips and buttocks; (8) the TSA agent runs his fingers inside the beltline of the passenger's pants (inside or outside the passenger's undergarments, at the agent's option).

[ii] Actually, it seems every time one turns around there is another news story about TSA agents thieving passengers' effects. Pythias Brown, who as a TSA agent manned a luggage screening machine at the Newark Airport, estimates he *singlehandedly* stole $800,000-worth of passenger property over a four year period. Megan Chuchmach, Randy Kreider, & Brian Ross, ABC NEWS NIGHTLINE INVESTIGATES (Sep. 27, 2012). *See video published at*, *e.g.*, Megan Chuchmach, Randy Kreider, & Brian Ross, *ABC News Tracks Missing iPad to Florida Home of TSA Officer*, ABC NEWS (Sep. 27, 2012).

It is at times like these that men are forced to acknowledge the modern inconveniences of external genitalia.

But the foregoing outline is a mere guarantee—nay, a mere hors d'œuvre!—to what *may yet occur.* For example, and at the discretion of the TSA agent conducting the screening, (9) the TSA agent may also touch, grip, and/or strip the passenger in whatever additional ways he deems necessary to grant the passenger a federal security "clearance" to board his flight.

TSA counsels that we must not worry about agents touching our genitals. After all, enhanced pat-downs are generally (not always, but generally) conducted by a screener of the same gender as the passenger.[4] By which TSA means to insinuate that any touching performed during pat-downs is entirely professional, related only to security—and never, *never* of a sexual nature. No, no—TSA agents do *not* get their jollies handling genitals of the same make as their own during pat-downs! (But really—in modern America, what kind of a guarantee is this? We are to believe every TSA agent in America is exclusively heterosexual? Come, now!—let us be reasonable . . . .[iii])

While TSA declares it removes people to private rooms for actual strip-screenings, this is not always the case. Sometimes TSA fails to take you to a private room, and still insists you drop your pants in public—right there in front of the rest of the passengers lined up at the security checkpoint. Like the autistic man who was traveling through Boston's Logan International Airport: "They did not put him in a private area. Instead they insisted that he undress in public."[5]

That safely anonymous autistic man did not appreciate his overexposure in Boston.[6] But have no fear: When questioned about this incident, TSA spokeswoman Sari Koshetz responded reassuringly as follows: "TSA's policy is to treat everybody with respect. We train our officers to be sensitive to various types of needs and individuals."[7] Well, in that case—since TSA agents are so respectful, and since they are so well-trained, to sympathetically and tenderly service even the autistic—there is no cause for alarm!

Still, many women remain uncomfortable with TSA's "enhanced" pat-downs. Penny Moroney, a woman with artificial knees who was required to submit to an "enhanced" pat-down in St. Louis' Lambert International Airport, described her experience as follows:

> Then she went into the top of my slacks, inserted her hands between my underwear and my skin, then put her hands up on outside [sic] of my slacks, and patted my genitals. I was shaking and crying when I left that

[iii] "I got a security 'patdown' [sic] by a woman at the airport that made me feel very uncomfortable and left no doubt about her sexual preferences." Supermodel Bar Refaeli, as quoted in Jade Watkins, *'It Left Me No Doubt About Her Sexual Preference': Bar Refaeli Felt Violated After Airport Pat Down by Female Security Guard*, MAIL ONLINE (Apr. 17, 2012).

> room. Under any other circumstance, if a person touched me like that without my permission, it would be considered criminal sexual assault.[8]

Ah, but this is not under "any other circumstance"! This is a matter of *national security!* And within Hive America, as TSA informs us, "Security is not optional."[9]

After unilateral mastectomies, breast cancer surviving flight attendants (like Cathy Bossi at Terminal D of Charlotte's Douglas International Airport) are required to remove prosthetic breasts for TSA inspection.[10] In Cathy Bossi's words, "She put her full hand on my breast and said, 'What is this?' And I said, 'It's my prosthesis because I've had breast cancer.' And she said, 'Well, you'll need to show me that.'"[11]

And after *bi*lateral mastectomies, breast cancer survivors' tissue-expanding implants (a medical preparation for future breast reconstruction) are detected by full-body scanners. Those implants must be examined as well. Consider, for example, Lori Dorn: She was subjected at New York's JFK International Airport to an "enhanced" frisk of her post-bilateral-mastectomy, tissue-expanding implants during Breast Cancer Awareness Month—*despite offering to produce TSA-specified medical documentation in lieu of a frisk as specifically condoned by official TSA procedure.*[12]

Prostheses and tissue-expanders create security headaches for cancer-survivors and TSA agents alike. But TSA is not interested *only* in prostheses. TSA is also interested in the genuine article! Yes—women are apparently selected for nudy-scanner screening not entirely at random, and not entirely for the purpose of airline security. Indeed, *some women are selected by male TSA staffers based specifically on their prodigious and youthful breasts.*[13] In the words of Eliana Sutherland, who was singled out by male TSA staffers at Orlando International Airport based on her ample and youthful bosoms, "It was pretty obvious. One of the guys that was staring me up and down was the one who pulled me over. Not a comfortable feeling."[14] Such incidents have been reported across the country.[15]

But never fear: The head Administrator of TSA, John Pistole (yes, that really is his name!), reassures us that "the agency will look further into [these] allegations."[16] Well then, ladies, there's no reason to worry!

Sometimes even beauties like supermodel Bar Refaeli[17] or Miss USA Susie Castillo are "arbitrarily" selected for "enhanced" pat-downs. Speaking of her experience in a home video taken at the Dallas airport immediately after being frisked, Ms. Castillo tells us:

> She actually felt my—touched my—vagina. And so, I think that's why I'm crying, that's why I'm so emotional, because I'm already so upset that they're making me go, making me do this, making me choose, to either get molested, because that's what I feel like, and, or, or, go through this machine . . . . I do feel violated. I didn't think that I would,

> when I had to opt out of the machine, but I completely feel violated. This woman, she touched my vagina. Four times. 'Cause she went up my leg, up both legs, from behind, and then turn around, and did it in the front. That was my experience this morning at Dallas Airport.[18]

Women are also explored so roughly that they are occasionally lifted off their heels when TSA staffers run a hand up the inside of the thigh—and when that hand's momentum is inevitably stopped short by the groin. [19] Like Ella Swift, flying out of Grand Rapids' Gerald R. Ford International Airport, who complained of physical pain *for an hour* after the "pat down." And why was Ms. Swift selected for an "enhanced" pat down? Because she was wearing "bulky" clothing. Meaning *a skirt.*

But do not fret; do not agonize over others' misadventures. When asked about the karate-chop to the biscuit incident, TSA responded with a thorough, unbiased internal review, and "determined that the transportation security officers involved acted appropriately and respectfully."[20] If TSA performed an investigation upon itself, and found its agents had taken nothing but appropriate and respectful actions, then everything must have been kosher!

Still, if it should ever become necessary to take your ninety-five-year-old, 105 pound, wheelchair-bound, cancer-stricken, dementia-afflicted mother through security—be certain to pack some extra Depend® undergarments in your carryon baggage. No, no—don't pack the Depends in your checked luggage! Otherwise, you and your mother may find yourselves up the proverbial creek—without a paddle. Like Jean Weber and her ninety-five-year-old, 105 pound, wheelchair-bound, dementia-afflicted, leukemia-stricken mother at Northwest Florida Regional Airport, who were traveling for the purpose of admitting Jean Weber's mother to an assisted-living facility.

Ms. Weber's mother can barely stand.[21] Ah, but "Wheelchairs trigger certain protocols," according to Sari Koshetz, spokesperson for TSA—and those protocols include the full terrorist pat-down (and possibly swabbing for explosives).[22] So Ms. Weber's aged mother automatically qualified for a full, terrorist pat-down. During that pat-down, TSA screeners "felt something suspicious on (her mother's) leg and they couldn't determine what it was."[23] So they took Ms. Weber's mother to a closed room for strip search. They returned and told Ms. Weber that her mother's "Depend undergarment was 'wet and it was firm, and they couldn't check it thoroughly'" without removal.[24]

TSA's dictate was unequivocal: Remove the diaper so TSA can thoroughly inspect it.[25] Otherwise your mother is "not going to get on the plane."[26] So Ms. Weber was forced to take her sweet mother back to the lobby lavatory, remove her mother's Depend undergarment—and then come back through the screening checkpoint again. Extra Depends were packed in the checked luggage, so Ms. Weber's mother was *forced to fly commando*. After pat-downs all around, and inspection of Ms. Weber's mother's used Depend undergarment, Ms. Weber and her mother barely made their flight. Neither of them had anticipated having their undergarments confiscated by TSA—so Ms. Weber's 95 year-old mother was forced to walk through the terminal, board the plane, and fly from Florida to Michigan *without undergarments*—and under the constant and real threat of public incontinence within a confined space. Neither Ms. Weber nor her mother appreciated such treatment.[27]

But have no fear! TSA reviewed this incident after Ms. Weber made a formal complaint to DHS (the outer matryoshka doll in which TSA safely nests). In the heat of the imbroglio, TSA first denied that Ms. Weber's mother was asked to remove her diaper at all. But after further investigation, TSA admitted they had required Ms. Weber's 95-year-old, wheelchair-bound, leukemia-stricken mother to make a choice between removing her diaper and missing her flight to the assisted living facility. And after a thoroughgoing and perfectly unbiased review of this incident, TSA assures us: "TSA works with passengers to resolve security alarms in a respectful and sensitive manner. We have reviewed the circumstances involving this screening and determined that our officers acted professionally and according to proper procedure."[28]

Well, if TSA determined that its officers acted professionally and according to proper TSA procedure, what is there to worry about? All is well at the airports! At any rate, the Weber incident is quite run-of-the-mill: Strip search is what TSA does to hundred-pound, disabled grandmothers.[iv]

Besides, "TSA estimates that only 3% of [airline] passengers are subjected to pat-downs."[29] Now that's not too deep an impingement on liberty, right? (But even TSA admits that *every day an average of 2 million airline passengers fly*![30] So 3% of airline passengers actually means *TSA is patting-down 21.9 millions of airline passengers annually*.)

Ms. Weber, implacable cane beetle that she is, remains pitifully unconvinced. With a common sense uncommon to monolithic government, she tells us: "It's something I couldn't imagine happening on American soil. . . . I'm not one to make waves, but dadgummit, this is wrong. People need to know. Next time it could be you."[31]

[iv] "[85-year-old, 4-foot-11-inch] Lenore Zimmerman, who lives in Long Beach, says she was on her way to a 1 p.m. flight to Fort Lauderdale when security whisked her to a private room and took off her clothes. 'I walk with a walker—I really look like a terrorist,' she said sarcastically. 'I'm tiny. I weigh 110 pounds, 107 without clothes, and I was strip-searched.' TSA spokeswoman Lisa Farbstein said a review of closed circuit TV footage from the airport shows 'proper procedures were followed.'" *Cf.* Nicholas Hirshon, *TSA Strip Searches Granny in a Walker*, New York Daily News (Dec. 2, 2011).

Federal Pederasty

So far as I am aware, neither infants nor children have ever hijacked U.S. airliners.

And so far as I am aware, neither infants nor children have ever bombed U.S. airliners.

But TSA does not wish to appear lax.

(And really, would you put it past jihadis to sneak a bomb onto a plane within or upon a child? In this regard, head TSA Administrator John Pistole has advised us: "Unfortunately we know that terrorists around the world have used children as suicide bombers."[32] Here—while we dispute TSA's *methods* for detecting terrorist paraphernalia—we are forced to acknowledge TSA's *reasoning*. Allah only knows the bounds of jihadi ingenuity . . . .)

So, from the beginning, TSA has insisted upon "enhanced" pat-downs for children and infants as well.

As early as March, 2008, video was taken of TSA agents performing an "enhanced" pat-down on little three-year-old Mandy Simon (who is screaming, "Don't touch me!" while attempting to run away) at Chattanooga Metropolitan Airport.[33]

In November, 2010 a fellow passenger videoed TSA agents at Salt Lake City International Airport frisking a shy and retiring eight-year-old boy. By the time the film begins, the child is already naked from the waist up. The more the boy is touched, the further he tries to back away from the TSA screener. Especially when the TSA screener appears to go for the boy's pills.[34]

Subjecting innocents to TSA's "enhanced" pat-down procedures caused a furor among Middle Americans. TSA, administrative agency that it is, nevertheless recognized it had a public relations time bomb in its hands. So in an effort to diffuse the child-frisk PR bomb, Administrator John Pistole publicly announced: "*We've heard the concerns that have been expressed and agree that children under twelve should not receive that pat-down.*"[35]

That sounded like iron-clad policy! What else could such a bold announcement by TSA's top administrator possibly mean? Finally, TSA had gotten the message: Middle Americans do not appreciate their children being mishandled at the airport. Even when mishandled under the banner of national security.

But apparently Administrator Pistole was bluffing. Actually, TSA intended to continue frisking infants and children. And so a few months later, in April, 2011, TSA agents at the New Orleans' Louis Armstrong International Airport frisked little six-year-old Anna Drexel. Little Anna's pat-down made headlines not because it was unusual, but simply *because it was filmed*. (TSA had come to realize that videos illustrating actual pat-downs compromise TSA's public image, so TSA had implemented a policy of threatening travelers who film pat-downs with *arrest*. And that cut down on YouTube pat-down videos right away!)

TSA required the Drexel family to undergo nudy-scans. TSA staff thereafter selected little Anna for a further pat-down. When the Drexel parents asked why Anna had been selected for a follow-up pat-down, TSA refused to explain. When the Drexel parents suggested Anna be re-scanned, TSA agents "just refused and said that they were going to do what they were going to do."[36] TSA wanted to pat-down little Anna, so stand back! A TSA supervisor approached, and hovered over the scene. The TSA supervisor did not utter a word (being on camera and all), but nevertheless made his presence felt. According to Mrs. Selena Drexel, "Not verbally, but in no uncertain terms—apparently the TSA supervisor is very skilled at nonverbal communication—[he let] me know that there would be trouble if I caused a fuss."[37] So despite ongoing parental protests, little Anna's pat-down proceeded without pause.

Anna was devastated by the pat-down. In the words of her father, Dr. Todd Drexel, "She broke down crying, because she really didn't understand what she had done wrong."[38]

After the pat-down, the Drexel parents were left wondering just how to balance the admonition "No one can touch you there" with the exhortation "Strangers at the airport can." In the words of Mrs. Drexel,

> We felt that it was inappropriate. You know, we struggle to teach our child to protect themselves, to say "No," to say it's, you know, "it's not OK for folks to touch me in this way in these areas," yet here we are . . . saying it's OK for these people. We feel that for children, especially, the answer should always be "No," that there needs to be different screening procedures, especially for children, and if we don't find other ways we're then making them more vulnerable to people who would harm them in that manner.[39]

But have no fear! As DHS Secretary Janet Napolitano affirms, little Anna Drexel's pat-down "was done *professionally according to the protocols*."[40] (And Secretary Napolitano is keenly sensitive to the Drexel family's situation! After all, she has raised numerous children of her own.) Besides, little Anna had flinched during the nudy-scan, so TSA agents couldn't see if she had hidden a bomb in her clothing or not. (Which suggests the obvious question—why not just re-scan Anna as her parents originally implored?)

In case the foregoing justifications were insufficient to allay public anxieties, TSA has investigated their own actions in the forced pat-down of little Anna Drexel, and TSA has determined that its agents specifically followed "the proper procedures":

> A video taken of one of our officers patting down a six year-old has attracted quite a bit of attention. Some folks are asking if the proper procedures were followed. Yes. TSA has reviewed the incident and the security officer in the video followed the current standard operating procedures.[41]

Which is to say that TSA did nothing wrong *because TSA followed its own, current operating procedures.* In other words, the governed are not to judge whether government is doing right by patting down six-year-old girls. The governed are not to concern themselves with such incidents, aside from confirming that government follows the rules it writes for itself in patting down six-year-old girls. No standard of right and wrong exists aside from monolithic whim. Whether citizens consent to government policy is immaterial. Government is in charge of airport security; *please move along.*

After the Anna Drexel debacle, TSA again announced it had heard the People—and had (again) changed its procedures to resolve screening *sans pat-down* for children under twelve years old. At a Senate Homeland Security and Government Affairs Committee meeting on June 22, 2011, TSA Administrator Pistole specifically answered questions about the Anna Drexel incident, and announced: "*We have changed the policy to say that there'll be repeated efforts made to resolve that* [i.e., child screenings like Anna's] *without a pat-down.*"[42]

Middle Americans were left to ponder: After Administrator Pistole's previous pledge to lay off the children—and after TSA's subsequent resumption of child pat-downs—could Administrator Pistole's recent assurances be trusted?

In short, no. A few weeks after Administrator Pistole's announcement that TSA would avoid pat-downs of children, another six-year-old boy was subjected to two serial pat-downs at Sea-Tac ("Seattle-Tacoma") International Airport. The cause for alarm? The child's handheld video console (which was not on his person, and which had already received a separate x-ray screening). But perhaps this pat-down was less invasive after Administrator Pistole's announcement? Perhaps TSA pulled on the kid gloves for this child exploration?

Unfortunately, with TSA's policy of forbidding all video coverage of their work, we have no objective record of this frisk. We have only the family's word that the boy was—like most children and adults—unnerved by the involuntary touching. In the words of Jenine Michaelis, the boy's mother, "Immediately after this happened my son—I hugged him and he started crying, saying, '*I don't want to go to Disney Land anymore.*'"[43] (For agency administrators like Uncle Napolitano, who may be somewhat unfamiliar with children, the statement "I don't want to go to Disney Land anymore" signifies profound distress.) In the words of Alex Long, the boy's father, "They just treated him like he's a terrorist. He's a six-year-old boy."[44] So at least in the view of the boy's family, TSA is not standing down where child frisks are concerned. (And indeed, Administrator Pistole's latest promise to stop frisking children has proven to be an outright lie. Today TSA child-frisks continue apace![45])

And again Jenine Michaelis, mother to this identity-protected six-year-old boy at Sea-Tac, raises predator-child boundary concerns. "We all talk to our kids about improper touching, someone shouldn't touch you unless you want to be touched; you know, we didn't have any time to talk to him about what they were really doing."[46] But TSA does not trouble itself with private parenting conundra, or speculation that TSA pat-downs might permanently perforate child defenses against sexual predation. No, TSA's concern lies in how best to ensure child pat-downs take place in the first instance. And in that regard, TSA Regional Security Director James Marchand has a marvelous idea about how to make child pat-downs easier on everyone: Just present pat-downs as a *game* for the child:

> In reality, what we as an agency should be doing, or employees, is looking at that child with a little bit of, of difference in how we handle the child [no pun intended!] . . . You try to make it as best you can for that child to come through. You ask the child to put their arms up in some way, and if you can come up with some kind of *game* you're trying to play with the child, then it makes it a lot easier.[47]

What an excellent idea! *TSA should employ the modus operandi of experienced pedophiles!* "Let's play 'doctor,' little Johnny! This will be fun! First, 'doctor' touches Johnny—then Johnny gets to touch 'doctor'! In *special* places! Like this . . . ."

Even infants get in on the game. Yes, infants need pat-downs, too.[48]

But have no fear: TSA does not share the misgivings of viewers and distributors of photographs like the one linked in that last footnote. TSA illuminates us:

> The caption used with the photo is "TSA Looking for Poop Bombs?" We reviewed the screening of this family, and found that the child's stroller alarmed during explosives screening. *Our officers followed proper current screening procedures by screening the family after the alarm*, who by the way were very cooperative and were on the way to their gate in no time. The child in the photo was simply receiving a modified pat-down which doesn't even come close to what the headline implies.[49]

Well, if TSA officers followed "proper current screening procedures," then there is nothing for cane beetles to concern themselves with! Proper, current, TSA screening procedures were employed. And those procedures say eight-month-old Anglo-Saxons are fair game. Besides, *that* family *was* compliant!

So let's move along, fellow travelers; let's catch our flights without delay—there's nothing to see here!

Federal Satisfaction

If you haven't yet been molested by TSA, guarantees made by the most federal government of the United States of America—that pat-downs are flawlessly executed according to TSA protocols (and that pat-downs are therefore OK); that TSA agents are highly trained professionals (and that "enhanced" pat-downs thus respect travelers' dignity and privacy); that only 3% of air travelers are subject to "enhanced" pat-downs (and that's not too many!); that pat-downs are conducted by same-gender TSA screeners (and therefore the touching is *never* sexual in nature); that "security is not optional" (and therefore liberty must take a seat at the back of the bus)—may sound perfectly plausible. There are many reasons such guarantees sound plausible. And those reasons are amplified by Incrementalist *synergies.*

First, there are the synergies of *fear* and *crisis*. The crisis of domestic terrorism, the fear of another airline hijacking or bombing, cause many Americans to dial back their expectations for liberty. (Which is precisely what both jihadis and monolithicists desire.)

And if you rarely fly the answer is easy: "Enhanced" pat-downs must continue! After all, *national security* is at stake. (And as I myself don't fly, *you* can bear the cost of national security.) But in the Land of Incrementalism, this line of reasoning signifies nothing but submission to Incrementalist strategy. *Today the airline checkpoints, tomorrow mall shopping centers.* And football Stadia. And highways.[50] And hotels. And bus stations. And cruise ship gangways. And NASCAR arenas. And subways. And tennis venues. And ferry terminals. And train stations. And captive TV networks.[51] And . . . . (Yes, DHS has already reached out to such venues. It established more than 9,300 unannounced security checkpoints and searches at such venues in 2011 alone.[52] And it intends to increase such unannounced searches by approximately 48% in 2012.[53] After all, as air marshal Ray Dineen [head of Charlotte's TSA office] observes, "We are not the *Airport* Security Administration. We take that transportation part seriously."[54] And this is to say nothing of DHS' expansion into social network, online news, and blog monitoring[v]—wouldn't want to let a revolution get underway here at home!

---

[v] Since June 2010, DHS has been monitoring and keeping records of your visits and posts to Facebook, Twitter, YouTube, Hulu, Flickr, Drudge Report, WikiLeaks, Cryptome (one of the first websites to reveal DHS's Internet monitoring program!), multiple blogs related to border news (surprise there!), and blogs such as JihadWatch. Mark Hosenball, *Homeland Security Watches Twitter, Social Media,* REUTERS (Jan. 11, 2012). Moreover, every Tweet ever sent is now housed

Like what recently happened in Tunisia. And Egypt. And Libya.[vi] [But I thought the federal government *was in favor of those uprisings?*]) One can never assume that new extensions of monolithic authority will necessarily remain limited to those objects which they regulate today. Just give them time. It is their habit to *extend.*

But what if you *have* been molested by TSA? And what if you *have* put yourself through the wild goose-chase that is making a complaint to an unelected federal bureaucracy regarding performance of a federal "service" which you never wished to have performed? And what if you *have* followed up on that complaint? And what if you *have* spent hours on hold, hoping to talk to an actual administrator? And what if you *have* waited weeks for a reply?

You are free to complain to TSA, to DHS, and to any other agency you can think of about being mishandled. But you will not be heard.[55] At least, not in the long run. The Fourth Head is impenetrable. Yes, public relations officers and top administrators at TSA (and DHS) will occasionally make appearances to suppress news about public grievances like yours.[56] They will make a few seemly remarks; they will suggest that citizen-driven changes are currently being implemented.[57] But TSA and DHS will continue to do as they please.[58] That is, after all, their purpose: *to do socialists' bidding, while insulated from Middle American will.* (And here we have an Incrementalist synergy: Along with fear and crisis, the impenetrability of the Fourth Head strongly amplifies citizen submission to government procedure.)

But monolithic apologists cry out: *These are mere anecdotes!* You have named a few instances of dissatisfied travelers—yet TSA is servicing millions of people each day, and most people get along just fine with TSA pat-downs. Show me something real—*show me statistics!*

Fair enough: 61% of likely voters oppose both TSA nudy-scans and TSA enhanced pat-downs.[59] (In fact, citizens are so worked up about TSA screenings that States—more localized bodies than the federal government,

---

by the library of Congress—which is handy, because now the entire Twitter archive can be viewed "as a complete set of data, which [researchers] could then data-mine for interesting information." Michael O'Connell, *Library of Congress to Receive Entire Twitter Archive*, FEDERALNEWSRADIO.COM (Dec. 6, 2011).

[vi] You see, "The wave of uprisings across North Africa and the Middle East that have overturned three governments in the past year have prompted the U.S. government to begin developing guidelines for culling intelligence from social media networks, a top Homeland Security official said Monday. Department of Homeland Security Undersecretary Caryn Wagner said the use of such technology in uprisings that started in December in Tunisia shocked some officials into attention and prompted questions of whether the U.S. needs to do a better job of monitoring domestic social networking activity. 'We're still trying to figure out how you use things like Twitter as a source,' she said. 'How do you establish trends and how do you then capture that in an intelligence product?' Wagner said the department is establishing guidelines on gleaning information from sites such as Twitter and Facebook for law enforcement purposes." P. Solomon Banda, *Homeland Security Reviews Social Media Guidelines*, THE ASSOCIATED PRESS (Nov. 1, 2011).

and therefore more responsive to citizens' will—are forming coalitions to oppose TSA procedures.[60] States have even introduced legislation to prohibit TSA procedures or make TSA pat-downs a felony within their borders.[61])

Yet that very 61% majority which opposes both nudy-scans and enhanced pat-downs presents a riddle. If a 61% majority opposes TSA security protocols, then why—*within the airport*—do citizens *not act up?* Why do citizens not refuse "enhanced" pat downs and nudy-scans en masse? If they did so, even TSA—monolithic agency that it is—would begin hunting terrorists using other methods. Tomorrow.

Well, citizens don't refuse pat-downs or nudy-scans because citizens have seen what happens when you refuse. Fifty-six-year-old rape victim Claire Hirschkind's experience at the Austin-Bergstrom International Airport is illustrative: Due to her pacemaker, Ms. Hirschkind did not feel a nudy-scan would be safe. And by opting out of the nudy-scanner, she automatically opted into a frisk. But when TSA approached her breasts, Ms. Hirschkind refused access because—as a rape victim—she did not relish the idea of having her breasts (again) groped against her will. For refusing an all-encompassing frisk, Ms. Hirschkind received TSA's discretionary options 4(a) and 4(b): She was shoved to the airport floor, cuffed and arrested, dragged across the floor while bawling and in full view of onlooking passengers, and then *formally banned from the airport* (!).[62]

Most citizens don't want that kind of treatment. Besides, American citizens have been taught to grovel before uniforms in general. (Even mall-cop-looking uniforms like the ones TSA agents wear.) Civic courage—to stand up and be counted when uniformed government agents trespass, no matter the situation, and no matter who or how many are watching—is an antique from a bygone era. (And here we have another Incrementalist synergy—this time a cultural one—which further augments fear, crisis, and the impenetrability of the Fourth Head.)

So mass refusal of TSA's unwanted services does not appear to be an option. Citizens will not stand up for themselves and *act* when confronted by uniformed federal authorities. But here we have another riddle. If a 61% majority opposes TSA procedures, why—*within the airport*—do citizens not at least *speak up?* When accosted by TSA agents across the fruited plain, why do flyers not say, "Hey, stop manhandling my nonagenarian mother! Does she look like a jihadi to you?" or "Hey, get your hands off my twelve-year-old son's junk! He's no terrorist!"?

Is that too extreme? Alright, alright—we shall be meek and polite. Why do citizens not ask TSA agents to explain the particular grounds for selecting their three-year-old son for further screening? Why do they not at least ask TSA agents how family members "alarmed" TSA, and thereby merited more invasive screening procedures? Why do they not mutter heart-felt complaints *even under their breath* while lining up for pat-downs? And why do they not at least speak their mind *during the frisk?* Is there anything to lose at *that* point?! Why are citizens so compliant?

Listen carefully at security checkpoints: You won't hear many vocal protests. Instead—at this one location in an otherwise lively and audibly buzzing airport—you will perceive an eerie silence.

Look about you. Behold scores of fellow citizens, all taking the frisk of themselves and their little children, their elderly and their women, in silence. (Just hurry up and let this be over with! Please God—please let this be over! And let me get back to surfing the web; or watching my personal video console; or listening to my iPod; or texting on my mobile device. Let me detach from life and return to the comforts of electronic entertainment. So I can numb the pain. So I can forget . . . .) Like zeks at pre-dawn line-up in the Kolyma, they don't make eye contact with the convoy guards. Like zeks, they stare out blankly into the distance. Like zeks, they make no resistance. Like zeks, they humbly lift their arms and spread their legs for unlimited exploration of their persons. Like zeks, they wince—but only inwardly. Like zeks, they are mute unless spoken to; and when they are spoken to, they give one-word answers. Like zeks, they are patient in their humiliation. *They don't want trouble.* (Yet another Incrementalist synergy! What a worthy tool is culture.)

Not in the airport—do not make a scene at the airport! TSA possesses discretion to take as long as they please looking you and your baggage over. They can make you pay. They can make you miss your flight. Say something crazy like "I'm no terrorist!" or "I know my rights!" or "I'm not a convict and we're not at the State Penitentiary!" or "My four-year-old daughter doesn't have a *bomb*!" and you know you will get the full treatment. Probably they will take you to a windowless room somewhere so federal authorities can grill you at their leisure. Perhaps you will miss your flight. And maybe they will put your name in a database somewhere, so you get the full treatment every time you fly.

Americans aren't stupid. They know the drill: They know that *TSA agents specifically select those who complain about TSA security procedures for further and more invasive screenings.*[63] Yes—singling out complainers is part of TSA's most proper protocols! (And herein lies another Incrementalist synergy. The particular behavior which labels you a "high risk" passenger under TSA guidelines is as follows: "Very arrogant and expresses contempt against [sic] airport passenger procedures."[64] Now, I am no graduate of Langley's Farm, but this TSA rule appears aimed at harassing benign citizens who speak their mind—and, thereby, at also safeguarding TSA agents from traveler interrogation, vituperation, and insurrection. I mean, if you were a terrorist, and you were attempting to sneak a weapon or a bomb through security, would *you* complain about TSA or enhanced security measures? Would *you* make a scene? Of course not! You would act as meekly as a lamb. You would not wish to stick out from the crowd. Perhaps you might say something complimentary of the job TSA does, or mention the necessity of security to safe travel. But you would never bemoan TSA security procedures!)

Besides—and here is the rub—Americans have been instructed for decades *what not to say.* They know political correctness is lurking behind the smile of every fellow traveler, yes; but more importantly they know that cultural considerations embodied in the PC muzzle are *particularly important within specially federalized zones.* Like within the confines of The Most Federal Airports. And here we are greeted by a profound irony: It is only the *federal* government's authority which is circumscribed by the Constitution, to "make no law . . . abridging the freedom of speech."[vii] Yet it is precisely within zones of Federal power that one most fears the consequences of speaking freely. (Another synergy! And here we must also credit the federal government's skill in balancing so precariously on the *letter* of constitutional law: The federal government has conscientiously avoided making any *law* abridging the freedom of speech. Instead, the federal government simply allows uniformed federal agents to take you to a windowless room, to more thoroughly examine you and your belongings, to touch your children, to make you miss your flight, all at agents' discretion. Now as far as the *spirit* of the law goes . . . .)

If it were not for the ongoing suppression of politically incorrect speech (and therefore also the ongoing suppression of politically incorrect thought), millions of innocent citizens would ponder politically incorrect questions while having their giblets frisked for bombs. Like the following:

One generally assumes people have their own private reasons for continuing to work at exceptionally distasteful vocations—private, psychological reasons which go above and beyond salary and benefits. Otherwise, why not find other work? If you are daily repulsed by what you do it would seem an easy decision. Even if retraining and a pay cut were required, it would be a small cost for the benefit of switching to a job you can live with. Take executioners for instance: Most people wouldn't touch that line of work with a ten-foot pole. (Would you want to be the walk-down

---

[vii] U.S. CONST. amend. I. And to you self-styled constitutional scholars out there, who are in an uproar over this line, who scream, "But the First Amendment is incorporated also against the States through the Fourteenth Amendment!", I say:

(1) Read again the Tenth Amendment;

(2) Read again the Fourteenth Amendment (and note § 5 says "Congress shall have power to enforce, *by appropriate legislation*, the provisions of this article." The Fourteenth Amendment does not say the First Amendment is hereby incorporated against the States (which would have been a very simple, one-line addition if it were intended); Congress has not passed any legislation purporting to force States to abide by the limitations of the First Amendment; and even if Congress had passed such legislation, it would be void because Congress alone does not have power to amend the Constitution (i.e., to destroy the Tenth Amendment by unilaterally applying the First Amendment against the States. *See* U.S. CONST. art. V.); and

(3) The so-called "doctrine of incorporation" is nothing but a hoax to surreptitiously limit State power—and thereby consolidate monolithic federal authority.

officer? Would you want to be a member of the tie-down team? Part of the non-Hippocratic "medical" team? Would you wish to be the intravenous technician? The needle gal? The potassium chloride supplier? The death-pronouncement clinician? The death chamber janitor? The gurney washer? The deathhouse public relations officer? The witness gallery usher? The warden? Many would find such jobs distasteful. But none of these jobs are what we are discussing here. No, we are discussing *exceptionally* distasteful jobs: We are discussing the man who remains safely anonymous, who these days peers from behind a blue curtain instead of from behind a black hood—the very man who depresses three syringe plungers, thereby administering sodium thiopental, pancuronium bromide, and potassium chloride to the condemned.)

Because most people would never consider executioning as a vocation, most people are therefore left to assume that executioners tend either to (1) already be sadists or sociopaths when they take the job, or else (2) come to enjoy killing due to their proximity to and authority over death for a period of years. Surely there is some reason people stay on as executioners? And surely that reason has little to do with salary and benefits?

Having set aside our cultural blinders we are forced to ask: *What does this suggest about TSA crotch-handlers?* Might it not suggest TSA agents tend either to (1) already be perverts when they take the job, or else (2) come to like touching strangers' genitalia as a consequence of their duty to conduct thousands of "enhanced" pat-downs? One thing is certain: Handling male strangers' sweaty, travel-day junk day-in and day-out is not a job the average man would take. *No matter how excellent the salary and benefits.* (And from what I understand, TSA screeners are not pulling down the highest salaries or benefits out there.)

Which leads to a further query: If TSA fondlers tend to be perverts—whether before taking the job or through repetitive participation in TSA screenings thereafter—do we really want them touching our children?

And of course some TSA screeners *are* criminal perverts.[viii] Some of

---

[viii] *E.g.*, 41-year-old Michael Scott Wilson (*TSA Agent Charged with Possession of Child Porn*, ABC 2 NEWS BALTIMORE (Oct. 11, 2011) ("Wilson admitted to county police that he had downloaded images of children—some as young as toddlers—having sex with adults."); WBALTV 11 News, *Md. TSA Agent Charged with Child Porn*, WBALTV.com (Oct. 11, 2011) ("Neighbors said he's married with no children. They said they're stunned and disturbed by the charges, especially since most of them described Wilson as a straight-laced federal worker who took pride in his position and the trust that comes with it."); *Caught in Act, TSA Bomb Screener Declares Child Porn 'Not Right In a Legal and Moral Sense'*, THE SMOKING GUN (Dec. 28, 2011) ("After waiving his Miranda rights, Wilson. . . told investigators . . . that he 'sometimes masturbates to the images of child pornography.'"));

61-year-old David Ralph Anderson (Elko Daily Free Press Staff, *DA Charges Spring Creek Man with Lewdness*, ELKO DAILY FREE PRESS (Aug. 26, 2011) ("on seven to ten occasions between 2010 and this year, Anderson allegedly taught the victim about various sexual acts and had sexual contact in the form of touching each other's genitals. . . . In addition, the girl stated he would rub lotion all over her body, placed his hand up her shirt to touch her breasts, had her watch pornographic films with him, [and] encouraged her to consume alcohol . . . "));

them, like 52-year-old Harold Glen Rodman, wear full TSA uniforms and flash their TSA badges even *during* aggravated sexual batteries, forcible sodomies, object sexual penetrations, and abductions with intent to defile.[65] Others, like 46-year-old TSA screener Thomas Gordon, Jr., even post pictures of themselves dressed in TSA uniform *alongside their child pornography posts* (!).[66]

But TSA reassures us regarding pedophile employee arrests: "The TSA holds its security officers to the highest professional and ethical standards and aggressively investigates allegations of misconduct. The allegations against this individual *in no way reflect on the outstanding job our more than 50,000 security officers do every day* to ensure the security of the traveling public."[67] Monolithic apologists assure us that TSA perverts are mere statistical aberrations, and present at no more than the common rate among any population. (But really, why go to the trouble of establishing and funding a charitable foundation for disadvantaged boys to conceal your pederasty and provide access to

---

62-year-old David Rains (Jeff Weiner, *Former OIA TSA Employee Faces Child Porn Charges*, ORLANDO SENTINEL (Nov. 1, 2011) ("An Orange County man faces child porn charges, records show, stemming from *images authorities say he possessed while working as a TSA employee* at Orlando International Airport. . . . The images, the agent said, showed sex acts by children who appeared to be *between five and 11 years old.*") (emphasis added));

46-year-old Thomas Gordon, Jr. (John Shiffman, *Airport Passenger Screener Charged in Distributing Child Pornography*, PHILADELPHIA INQUIRER (April 23, 2011) ("Transportation Safety Administration Officer Thomas Gordon Jr. of Philadelphia, who routinely searched airline passengers, uploaded explicit pictures of young girls to an Internet site on which he also posted a photograph of himself in his TSA uniform."));

59-year-old Jose E. Salgado (Christine McConville, *TSA Agent Among 55 Caught in Kid Porn Net*, BOSTON HERALD (April 11, 2012) ("a Transportation Security Administration officer assigned to Logan International Airport who is just the latest embarrassment for the troubled federal agency. TSA agent Jose E. Salgado, 59, of Chelsea was suspended from his job after his employers learned that local law enforcement agencies are pursuing criminal charges against him for the possession and sharing of pornographic images of children."));

65-year-old Thomas Harkins (Editorial, *TSA Hires a Priest Excluded From Clergy for Child Molestation*, RT.COM (Oct. 2, 2012) ("In 2002, Thomas Harkins was permanently removed by the Catholic Church after 20-plus years of allegations that the former clergyman had molested children at parishes across the East Coast. Today, he's your friendly TSA agent. Despite being excommunicated and forced to pay around $195,000 to settle civil lawsuit[s] relating to a barrage of sex-crime charges in the greater Philadelphia area, Harkins, now 65, didn't have a problem finding a new job after being booted from the Catholic Church in 2002. Shortly after, he was hired by the Transportation Security Administration and assigned to a position that required him to routinely pat-down young children and subject them to the evasive [sic], hands-on body scans that have become a hallmark of post-9/11 America."); Barbara Boyer, *TSA Hired Defrocked Camden Priest Without Background Check*, THE PHILADELPHIA INQUIRER (Oct. 1, 2012) ("About four months after being defrocked by the Diocese of Camden in 2002, Thomas Harkins had a new job as a security officer, including patting down passengers, with the Transportation Security at Philadelphia International Airport. The TSA hired the former priest before completing a background check, the agency recently confirmed. According to a church document, the diocese revealed to the TSA in 2003 as part of the background check that Harkins had been removed from ministry because of allegations he had molested two grade-school girls. . . . The TSA took no action as a result of the disclosure. 'An allegation alone does not warrant dismissal or automatically disqualify applicants from employment with the TSA,' spokeswoman Ann Davis said.")).

victims—like Jerry Sandusky at Penn State—when joining an institution possessing the full weight of federal authority can put you in contact with boys' genitals every day?)

And so long as the cultural blinders are off, how about this:

Whenever a serial murderer is suspected, the first thing any self-respecting law enforcement agency does is hire a *criminal profiler*. Such an expert analyzes unsolved offenses and the ways in which they were committed, including the type of victims selected, modus operandi, geographic patterns, and detailed physical evidence discovered at crime scenes. The profiler then compares such evidence with evidence left by *other* criminals known to have perpetrated similar crimes. This comparison is used by the profiler to work up a report on *what type of criminal is likely committing the crimes in the ongoing and unsolved crime spree*: What age is the likely murderer? What sex? What race? What motivations? What interests? What neighborhood? What language? Law enforcement then focuses its limited resources on persons fitting the criminal profile—in order to prevent further carnage.

With cultural blinders removed, it is natural to ask why—in the context of preventing the next mass airline murders—TSA does not similarly *profile*. Let us be candid: With regard to airborne terrorism, an expert profiler is not even required. Everyone knows whom TSA should be looking for: The airborne terrorist is a young (say, 17 to 35-year-old); foreign-born; Third-World-raised; Arabic-speaking; man; fanatically interested in the Qur'an and in killing; and motivated specifically by the Islamic ideal of jihad. He likes to yell "!!!الله أكـــــبر" when engaged in murder.

Nope—native-born tax protesters are not hijacking airliners. Nor are aged grandmothers. Nor Hindu infants. Nor Christian children. Nor Jewish young women. Nor Zoroastrian grandfathers. Nor really any other group.

Now, TSA has never intercepted or prevented a single airborne terrorist attack—but it would sure improve its chances by looking more closely at those fitting the profile of past airborne terrorists! TSA spends hundreds of millions of dollars in an attempt to keep air travel safe—and it could sure save time and money by focusing resources on the source of past aviation terrorism threats. But Political Correctness is roused by our suggestion. Political Correctness recognizes another teachable moment, and immediately he assaults us—"Racist!" "Xenophobe!" "Bigot!" And all within earshot prostrate themselves before the shrine of Politeness. On the double. (Indeed, Incrementalists immediately subdue any TSA screeners accused of profiling[68]—another synergy! And for their part, cane toads demand religious exemptions *to pat themselves down in lieu of a TSA agent*![69] Now there is an idea TSA should explore further. . . .)

Political Correctness is not alone in demanding we turn a blind eye on 17 to 35-year-old, foreign-born, Third-World-raised, Arabic-speaking, men, motivated specifically by the Islamic creed of jihad, and yelling "الله أكبر!!!" There are further considerations:

Sit down Mr. Cane Beetle, and shut up!

You are being replaced!

And these are they who must replace you!

These are the special ones, destined by Incrementalist wise men to inherit Outopia: The foreign-born. The Third-World. The militant. The materially dependent. Those unwilling or unable to become Middle Americans.

(Yay! Another Incrementalist synergy!)

Oversight

Citizens oppose TSA's nudy-scans and enhanced pat-downs. Yet as we have seen, citizens dare not defy TSA *within* the airport—where their bodies, belongings, family members, and flight plans hang precariously in the federal balance. Where that balance can be overturned at the whim of a single government employee. Where *synergies* abound.

And so, *only outside* the airport do citizens dare ask questions of TSA, DHS, or the federal government which those agencies represent. Once safely outside the Most Federal confines of American airports, questions abound:

Isn't hands in panties excessive?

Do you handle children's genitalia, too? (Because people have accused TSA of that as well.[70])

But with monolithic government, *discretion* is the rule of the day. No hard and fast rules exist. No direct answers are required. TSA obfuscates: TSA screeners' "first priority is safety."[71] Well, sure! But the question remains: Isn't hands in panties excessive?

TSA's stated policy is to refuse "comment on individual screening procedures at checkpoints. . . . [We] use a less aggressive touch for children under twelve."[72] Yes, yes, that's all very well—but does *less aggressive touch* mean you do or do not plan to handle my children's genitalia? And if you plan not to, what should I do if I find the particular TSA agent at our checkpoint doing just that?—because I have been through numerous airports, and TSA agents on duty there claim varying degrees of authority and differing procedures on the very same day.

And while your "touch" of those under twelve is "less aggressive," where does that put me as a parent? As parents of touched children have already highlighted, one fortifies a child against sexual predation by emphasizing that *no one but you touches you there.* As any parent knows, young children respond well to clear-cut rules; exceptions and amendments create confusion. Yet now strangers at airports *can* and *must* touch you there! And contradicting what mommy and daddy said previously, mommy and daddy must now acquiesce to total strangers—and allow them to touch you there (or else forfeit the price of the entire family's airfare, and the family trip as well).

So next time you are at the airport, and you are forced to wait and watch while TSA staffers attempt to tactilely distinguish your twelve-year-old daughter's labia majora from a discreetly hidden lump of moldable, putty-like plastic explosives (remember, ages twelve and up receive fully "aggressive" touch!), consider this: Why are congresspersons not outraged with the current state of affairs? Why is the President not scandalized? They are *our* representatives, are they not? They represent *our* will, do they not?

Well . . . that was the idea. They were *intended* to live amongst us, to be subject to identical laws, to share our own experiences, and therefore to most naturally *represent our will.* But because our federal "representatives" have written special rules to insulate themselves from airport screenings, they cannot very well relate to the TSA experience. You see, while the President has been setting a presidential travel record, he flies Air Force One (at a cost of $181,757/hour)[73]. Which is to say, the President *does not fly commercial.* So he avoids TSA security checks.

Former Speaker of the House and current Minority Leader Nancy Pelosi doesn't like to fly commercial, either. Instead, under a policy implemented by George Bush II, she had a military jet fly her home for weekends in California. Current Speaker John Boehner prides himself in flying commercial (unlike his predecessor Ms. Pelosi), yet he nevertheless refuses TSA nudy-scanners, pat-downs, and even metal detectors.[74] So does Harry Reid.[75] You see, even when congressional leaders *do* fly commercial, they nevertheless *need not pass through airport security.*[76] Those are the rules! And not only congressional *leaders*, but in fact *any congressperson* escorted by an armed security detail walks right past TSA screening checkpoints (and the accompanying nudy-scanners, pat-downs, and lowly metal detectors).[77]

And *any cabinet member* escorted by an armed security detail also walks right past the TSA screening line.[78] Meaning Uncle Napolitano has not likely had a pat-down (unless she has unilaterally requested one). Treasury Secretary Timothy Geithner and FBI Director Robert Mueller also avoid TSA pat-downs in this manner. And Defense Secretary Robert Gates, Secretary of State Hillary Rodham Clinton, and Attorney General Eric Holder travel almost exclusively on military or government planes. So they avoid TSA security screenings, too.[79]

Who determines which of our federal overseers—or rather, representatives! Representatives!—receives a security pass to circumvent TSA screenings? Why, that is quietly "determined by the Capitol Police working with the Transportation Security Administration."[80] In other words, the federal police and the Fourth Head confer, and together they work out just who can step around TSA security checkpoints. And they determine that federal representatives can do so. (Out of sight, out of mind! And safely out of Middle American reach.)

So our federal "representatives" cannot really be said to represent the will of the People. At least not on issues like TSA security screenings, where our "representatives" hand themselves an airport security pass.

Yet some congresspersons still sit on committees claiming TSA oversight responsibilities, do they not? Some congresspersons still assert they hold the reins of federal agencies? Well yes, undoubtedly they do. Take for example Congresswoman Sheila Jackson-Lee, Texas Democrat and Chairwoman of the House Homeland Security Subcommittee on Transportation Security, who boldly proclaims: "My committee in particular has the oversight [over TSA]. . . . I'll be at my airport on Monday and Tuesday, ah, at Bush Intercontinental airport, both speaking to officials, watching what is going on. . . . [W]e are listening to the American public."[81]

So congresspersons *do* still claim oversight where agencies like TSA are concerned. And they *are* listening to the American public. In that case we are compelled to ask: Perhaps—though congresspersons themselves avoid TSA explorations—perhaps they might nevertheless oblige TSA to adopt security protocols more representative of citizen sensibilities?

But no. Congresswoman Jackson-Lee informs us that nudy-scanners remain the order of the day:

> Frankly, Anderson [Cooper], I'd like everybody to be reminded that we might have wanted to have this kind of equipment [i.e., nudy-scanners] on 9/11. We saw 3,000 or more Americans lose their lives. This is a different America and a different world. And so we have to confront issues head-on. . . .
>
> And so we're testing it, we're determining what is, ah, the best approach to best quality. [?] My understanding is that the viewers of this particular, ah, image are, ah, hidden away and there is, um, a way of protecting the privacy of those who choose to use the AIT [nudy-scanners].[82]

Now what would that "way of protecting privacy" be? We are discussing innocent citizens viewed nude and bikini-waxed!

And let us consider carefully the Chairwoman of Transportation Security's argument about nudy-scanners and 9/11. Would nudy-scanners have prevented the 9/11 attack? No, of course they would not: at that time, box cutters were approved carryon items! So even if nudy-scanners had been installed and had detected box cutters, the box cutters and the jihadis who carried them would have been shepherded right on through airport security to their respective flights. Just the same as when nudy-scanners detect house keys in your pocket today.

But the incisive wit of our "representative," the Chairwoman, continues. "Enhanced" pat-downs *also* remain the order of the day:

> Now pat-downs are limited: if you go to a metal detector or opt for an AIT [i.e., nudy-scan] you go through and you are fine. If it is necessary for a pat-down because you alarm or for other problems—I was traveling this morning, and one of the passengers said, "I need a pat down because I have a metal, ah, leg, or, eh, some form of metal on my personal body." That person volunteered that.
>
> So we have to be very much in context: what happened on 9/11; what happened on Christmas, 2009. It's very important to emphasize that.[83]

Well, no doubt 9/11 and the Christmas Underwear Bomber of 2009 were harrowing episodes. (And if not for the Flying Dutchman, the Christmas 2009 episode could have ended much, much worse.) Yet it does not follow that the only methods for preventing aviation terrorism are nudy-scanners and enhanced pat-downs! You know, TSA could pay better attention to an Islamic radical who overstays his student visa to train with Al-Qaida in Yemen. Or at least TSA could do so when the Islamic radical's father goes to the trouble of making reports to multiple CIA agents within a U.S. embassy, detailing that his son's religious views are extreme, that he might be a terrorist, that he might act, and that he is likely training for that purpose in Yemen. Or at least once the Islamic radical's name is placed on the Terrorist Identities Datamart Environment of the U.S. National Counterterrorism Center. Or at least when the Islamic radical purchases a one way ticket to America with cash (!). After all, *it was due to each and every one of these independent failings that the Christmas Underwear Bomber*[ix] *was allowed onboard Northwest Airlines Flight 253.*

Yes, it was in response to these embarrassing failings in the Christmas Underwear Bomber case that a mortified monolithic government introduced the nudy-scan/enhanced-pat-down dichotomy in the first place. But of course all terrorists are now on notice that TSA insists on either nudy-scans or "enhanced" pat-downs![x] Terrorists also know how to hide bombs in their butts (more specifically, their recta) and they have successfully detonated bombs while thus concealed.[84] And no x-ray backscatter or millimeter wave scanner can detect plastic explosives in there!—those types of radiation

---

[ix] I.e., Umar Farouk Abdulmatallab, who attempted to take down a passenger plane en route from Amsterdam to Detroit using plastic explosives hidden in his underwear (December 25, 2009).

[x] Terrorists also know—as any half-baked electrical engineer can tell you—that nudy-scanners cannot prevent metallic contraband from being carried through security. Just sew an extra pocket in the armpit of your shirt or jacket. Stow the contraband in the armpit pocket. When they tell you to raise your arms in the nudy-scanner, the contraband in the extra pocket swings out away from your body. On the nudy-scan its shows up as a matte black object. And because it has swung away from your body, it is positioned over the matte black background. Can't be seen at all. Bingo.

reflect off the first soft tissue they see. (Hence the nude pictures.) And no "enhanced" pat-down can detect plastic explosives in there, either. (Unless TSA really wants to go the extra mile.)

Besides, any terrorist worth his salt will bypass TSA checkpoints altogether. It is not difficult to do. You simply get a job as a TSA agent. Or an airline employee. Or an airport shoeshiner. Or an airport newsstand operator. Or any of a host of other airport jobs having high turnover rates and requiring few qualifications.

So perhaps the federal government made some mistakes in the Christmas Underwear Bomber incident itself, or in the resulting decision to implement the nudy-scan/enhanced-pat-down dichotomy? But no:

> Where we made our mistake, Anderson, was not providing the broad-based information, the emphasis on privacy [?], *and the right, ah, to explain to travelers just what they would be choosing.*[85]

The mistake was in not providing *government* with the "right" to explain to travelers just what travelers would be "choosing"? ("Rights" are now for government, and obligations are now for governed?) With all due respect, Congresswoman, the record makes travelers' choices perfectly clear: (1) nudy-scan; (2) "enhanced" pat-down; (3) foregone flight; (4a) arrest; and/or (4b) formal banishment from the airport.

But perhaps, with a majority of citizens outraged over current TSA screening protocols, congresspersons with TSA oversight might consider amending those protocols?

> The protocols I want to have changed is [sic] to articulate the privacy rights of our travelling public; to listen to the travelling public [TSA has not been listening to the public? But TSA says it has!]; and to be able to modify those protocols according to the needs of the travelling public [that is, total discretion to change TSA screening protocols any time at will]. When I say that, to make sure that those protocols are used, ah, when it is appropriate, meaning the more extensive one. [WTH?]
>
> But I don't want them to stop. I do want the public to be informed [i.e., of what TSA will do to the public]. I want to make sure that children are not, ah, pat-down [sic] in an incorrect manner [i.e., in a manner inconsistent with current TSA protocols]. And I don't believe the legislation by Congressman Paul is appropriate. Nor do I believe we need to go back to privatizing, ah, the Transportation Security Administration or TSO. [TS*O*? Does she mean the Trans Siberian Orchestra? Or Time Share Option? Or Texas State Optical? But surely she means TS*A*?] More professional training? Yes. More privacy information? Yes.[86]

While it is unclear from Chairwoman Sheila Jackson-Lee's response whether she understands what is meant by the term "protocol," the congresswoman nevertheless does claim ongoing oversight over TSA. And she wishes TSA's screening procedures to remain the same. She does *not* want nudy-scans or pat-downs "to stop." She does *not* wish to privatize security functions currently operated by the Fourth Head. She *does* want more money to train TSA agents. And she *does* wish to "articulate the privacy rights of our traveling public."

In parting, our "representative" to the federal government, our Chairwoman of the House Homeland Security Subcommittee on Transportation Security, leaves us with a thinly-veiled threat. Ask for a change to TSA's screening procedures, and you are asking for more terrorism:

> I don't think we want to go back to pre-9/11. . . . We don't want to go back to a privatized system of protecting the nation's airports and air travelers. We don't want, ah, to, if you will, ah, go back to the opportunity of more terrorism and terrorist acts. We've been lucky for the last eight years, or nine years, but let's not forget what happened on 9/11.[87]

Monolithic Reality

TSA overseers' ardent desire "to articulate the privacy rights of our traveling public"[88] make it easy to forget the obvious: *Our privacy rights have already been articulated.* They were articulated centuries ago by our Predecessors. And they were forever codified in our Constitution, which expressly defines federal search authority *by unequivocally limiting it.* Our privacy rights are unmistakable and unambiguous:

> The right of the people to be secure in their persons . . . against unreasonable searches and seizures, shall not be violated, and no Warrants shall issue, but upon probable cause, supported by Oath or affirmation, and particularly describing the place to be searched, and the persons or things to be seized.[xi]

I would be surprised to find that before I even arrived at the airport, the federal government, or DHS, or TSA, had actually uncovered evidence that I personally intend to wreak acts of airborne terrorism. I would be more surprised if such "evidence" were sufficient to support a claim of probable cause. I would be amazed to learn that TSA had gone to the trouble of obtaining a warrant to specifically search *my person*—meaning *my body*—based on probable cause, and sworn by a witness before a judge. And I would be truly flabbergasted to find that the warrant thus obtained particularly described the place to be searched, and the thing to be seized, as *my scrotum.*

But that is precisely what the Constitution requires TSA to do before searching me there.

[xi] U.S. CONST. amend. IV.

And until three-quarters of our respective State Legislatures approve a constitutional amendment obviating the liberties of the Fourth Amendment within airport terminals, the Constitution still requires TSA to jump through all those hoops before subjecting my scrotum to a search. (And of course that goes for your scrotum as well; and/or whatever other parts of your person you would prefer not to share with casual TSA acquaintances.)

I would be even more astonished to learn that TSA had uncovered probable cause and obtained individual bench warrants to search each and every one of the other tens of thousands of passengers travelling with me through the airport today. And their scrota as well. And warrants to search each and every one of the millions of other passengers travelling through other airports across the nation today. And their scrota. And especially warrants to search the children. And their scrota.

But this is precisely what the Constitution requires TSA to do before performing enhanced pat-downs.

It will be remembered that the protections of the Fourth Amendment were a direct response to the writs of assistance issued by our previous monolithic government, the British Parliament.[xii] It will be remembered that Parliament's writs of assistance functioned as *generalized* search warrants allowing customs officers to search all persons, places, and things; having no expiration date; being freely transferrable; and providing no compensation for damage done to searched persons or property.[xiii] (Admittedly, there were no *air*ports in 1767—but there were *ports*, and this is the domain in which writs of assistance most prominently featured.) And it will be remembered that writs of assistance catalyzed the Revolutionary War.[xiv]

Our federal government bestows identical powers on its agents today. It issues TSA agents a *generalized* search warrant to search all persons, places, and things (except Congresspersons and Secretaries of administrative agencies and *their* things); having no expiration date; freely transferable (e.g., to private security enterprises employed in lieu of TSA); and requiring no compensation for damage done to persons and property searched. It is difficult to contrive a hypothetical situation in which government action could more perfectly duplicate Parliament's writs of assistance, or more completely contradict the Fourth Amendment. We must speak plainly. We must come to terms with this fact: *Our federal government issues writs of assistance today.*

Whither the Fourth Amendment?

For a citizenry simultaneously frightened by the prospect of death in the skies, overwhelmed by federal agencies' ubiquity and power, thoroughly

---

xii Particularly under the Revenue Act of 1767. *See* TEA WITH SOCIALISTS, Book I (The Hive Mentality), chap. 10 *Our Predecessors' Paranoia.*

xiii *See* TEA WITH SOCIALISTS, Book I (The Hive Mentality), chap. 10 *Our Predecessors' Paranoia.*

xiv *See* TEA WITH SOCIALISTS, Book I (The Hive Mentality), chap. 10 *Our Predecessors' Paranoia.*

enculturated with silence, diluted by foreign dependents, and entertained into submission, the constitutional limits of federal search authority are not spoken. They are forgotten.

And soon they will disappear altogether.

Do not be fooled (like Congresswoman Sheila Jackson-Lee) into viewing arguments for constitutional liberty as promotions of aviation terrorism. I, at the very least, do not wish to do away with all airport security. But that is not the question. The question is whether, when attempting to prevent aviation terrorism, the federal government has the authority to paw my genitals without probable cause, oath and affirmation, and a properly-issued bench warrant. The answer to this question is "No." Such authority has never been ceded to the federal government. Indeed, the very charter granting all federal authority *specifically denies such power to the federal government.* The Constitution could not be plainer on this issue.

We must be perfectly clear on this point: *A government which can handle my genitalia in the name of security, when it has absolutely no reason to suspect me a danger, can do anything at all.* There are no restraints on such a government's power. Such a government has traded administrative restraint and personal liberty for coercive might and individual subjugation. It has taken possession of a boundless field of power, no longer susceptible of any definition. It has ceased to be a constitutional republic, and has reverted to operating as an unlimited parliament—a government of rulers' whims and not of laws. Its monolithic status can no longer be disputed.

Fellow travelers, we have wandered further than we expected down the path to federal coercion when we meekly set aside our shoes, our laptops, our clothes, and our dignity for TSA. The federal government has gotten away with warrantless nudy-scans and enhanced pat-downs for years. And however it may reform security procedures in the future, the precedent has forever been set: *Wherever the federal government asserts "security," the Fourth Amendment no longer applies.* The liberty embodied in the Fourth Amendment has been permanently compromised. Monolithic power has been successfully consolidated and repetitively asserted. Citizens have been prepared for deeper explorations of their persons and property. When the time is right—nay, when the *crisis* is right!—the hive is prepared to relinquish yet further liberties in exchange for a little security theater.

The fruits of Incrementalism are on display within every American airport. Decades ago the first pink shoots were grafted onto indigenous rootstocks. Inosculated saplings were carefully sheltered from native pests, and fastidiously insulated from the local climate. Maturing trees were diligently watered, fertilized, staked, pruned, and sprayed. They were nurtured in reserve—for a future season of synergistic opportunities. The harvest has required great patience; it has taken nearly a century to get this far—to reassert complete control over American (air)ports.

But for Incrementalists bent on establishing socialism in the United States, it has been very well worth the wait.

A government sufficiently powerful to administer socialism has arisen.

Nocturnal Enuresis

What about running through the airport concourse, and boarding your flight, and sitting practically on top of all the other coach passengers throughout your flight—*while soaked in urine like a naughty child?* A mere social-anxiety nightmare? A bad fantasy? A visit from the succubi? Have you been hagridden?

No, this is no dream. This is reality. It happened to Mr. Thomas Sawyer in the Detroit Metropolitan Airport.

And how did Mr. Sawyer wet himself in the middle of the airport? Well, that is the intriguing part of the story!

You see, Mr. Sawyer is a bladder cancer survivor. And like many bladder cancer survivors, Mr. Sawyer underwent a urostomy. Without a bladder, Mr. Sawyer's uric waste is collected in a bag sealed to an artificial stoma in his abdomen.

When Mr. Sawyer received a nudy-scan at the Detroit Metropolitan Airport, TSA agents immediately noticed his urostomy bag—and therefore summoned him for an "enhanced" pat-down. Aware that his urostomy bag would soon be subjected to TSA scrutiny, Mr. Sawyer requested a private room for his "enhanced" screening. TSA agents begrudgingly took him to a closed room. ("One officer looked at another, rolled his eyes and said that they really didn't have any place to take me. After I said again that I'd like privacy, they took me to an office."[89])

Mr. Sawyer was prepared. He had done his homework before arriving at the airport. He had read TSA's published procedures, and knew that TSA recommends "if you have a hidden medical device, you may want to bring it to the officer's attention before screening. We'll be better able to help expedite your screening that way . . . . [ellipsis original, though what they were intended to omit is anyone's guess]"[90] And so, for the purpose of full disclosure and the convenience of all persons involved, Mr. Sawyer repeatedly forewarned his TSA examiners of his medical condition and related medical device. But in Mr. Sawyer's words, and contrary to TSA's published procedures, "every time I tried to tell them about my medical condition, they said they didn't need to know about that."[91]

Once TSA agents removed Mr. Sawyer's clothes and saw his urostomy bag, then they *did* ask questions about his medical condition. But they didn't listen too much to the answers. "One agent watched as the other used his flat hand to go slowly down my chest. I tried to warn him that he would hit the bag and break the seal on my bag, but he ignored me."[92] Sure enough, the seal between the ostomy wafer and his abdomen was broken—and urine ran down Mr. Sawyer's belly, shirt, legs, pants, ankles, and socks.

After consummating the pat-down, TSA agents released Mr. Sawyer without further ado. "He told me I could go. They never apologized. They never offered to help. They acted like they hadn't seen what happened. But I know they saw it . . . ."[93]

Mr. Sawyer's clean clothes were naturally packed in his checked luggage. And so it was that Mr. Sawyer was presented with a dilemma: (1) miss his flight (and the wedding); or (2) march through the airport, board his flight, and fly in a cramped cabin and practically on top of other coach passengers—soaked in his own urine. Putting his loved ones ahead of himself, Mr. Sawyer chose the latter.

Those other details of Mr. Sawyer's travel are reality, too: Mr. Sawyer really was humiliated.[94] He really was so upset he could not speak.[95] He wept in the airport.[96] He really did try to clean up in the lavatory after takeoff.[97] It really didn't work too well.

Mr. Sawyer went through all the recommended procedures in response to that living nightmare. He filled out a formal TSA complaint card. And due to understandable media exposure, Mr. Sawyer's complaint was moved to the head of the line! TSA told Mr. Sawyer that it took his living nightmare at Detroit Metro very, very seriously; that TSA was sorry; that TSA wanted to make it right; and best of all, *that TSA believed Mr. Sawyer could help the agency brainstorm improved security procedures—procedures to treat persons presenting medical disabilities with greater dignity in the future*!

Mr. Sawyer took TSA at its word. Based on TSA's representations, Mr. Sawyer was "under the assumption that this would be an ongoing dialogue" between TSA and himself; a continuing operation to improve TSA procedures.[98] Mr. Sawyer believed himself well-placed to assist TSA, due to both his disability and his experience at Dallas Metro. And despite being so badly maltreated at their hands, Mr. Sawyer still wished to assist TSA in improving airport screening procedures. He hoped by so doing to help other travelers avoid his living nightmare. He sought security protocol reformation. He aspired to a Mr.-Smith-Goes-to-Washington moment.

So Mr. Sawyer attended a formal TSA meeting in Washington D.C.—the inner sanctum of the Fourth Head!—to share his ideas for improving TSA procedures, and treating the medically disabled in more dignified manner. In his own words, "I left the meeting feeling very good and I thought it was the government at its best in action. I really did."[99]

But weeks passed. And then months. The furor over Mr. Sawyer's TSA nightmare abated.

Mr. Sawyer was never invited back to Washington. And TSA has no plans to reconvene its disability dignity meetings. Eventually reality set in: Mr. Sawyer's meeting with TSA was "a dog and pony show."[100] It was an icy towel and nothing more, crafted by TSA to throw over a blazing media frenzy. Now that the media frenzy has cooled, so has TSA's interest in Mr. Sawyer's input.

Poor Mr. Sawyer, cane beetle that he is, is still attempting to make himself heard. He is still trying to make a point:

> I am a good American and I want safety for all passengers as much as the next person. But if this country is going to sacrifice treating people like human beings in the name of safety, then we have already lost the war.[101]

Who will break it to Mr. Sawyer? TSA never cared about his living nightmare in the first place. His loss of dignity was anticipated, appraised, and found wanting. His loss of dignity was Incrementalism's collateral damage.

And TSA never cared about Mr. Sawyer's "input." That was a public relations stunt intended to smooth over the wrinkles in an otherwise well-laid Incrementalist plan. TSA never inclined to change its protocols. TSA always wanted to maintain bodily control over citizens—both the able-bodied and the medically challenged. (Indeed, TSA's abuse of the medically challenged proceeds apace! Even after Mr. Sawyer's powwow with TSA.[102])

Mr. Sawyer, you are just one among hundreds of millions.

You are the governed.

Move along!

Further Notes to Chapter 8

[1] Transportation Security Administration, *Privacy: Advanced Imaging Technology*, TSA.GOV (no publication date given) (copy on file with author). http://www.tsa.gov/approach/tech/ait/privacy.shtm.
[2] *Ibid.* (emphasis added).
[3] *E.g.*, Joel Johnson, *100 Naked Citizens: 100 Leaked Body Scans*, WIRED (Nov. 16, 2010).
[4] "**Same-Gender Screening**: If you are asked to undergo a personal screening you will be provided a security officer of the same gender except in extraordinary circumstances. In some cases you may have to wait for a security officer of your gender to conduct the screening." Transportation Security Administration, *The Screening Process*, (as of Jan. 4, 2012) (copy on file with author). http://www.tsa.gov/travelers/customer/customer_service_procedures.shtm.
[5] Justin Moss, *Raleigh Man Angered by TSA Security Screening*, NBC17.COM (March 20, 2011).
[6] *Ibid.*
[7] *Ibid.*
[8] KMOV 4 St. Louis, *Woman Says her Lambert Security Screening was Sexual Assault*, KMOV MOBILE NEWS (Nov. 18, 2010).
[9] Jim Bergamo, *Woman Arrested at ABIA After Refusing Enhanced Pat Down*, KVUE NEWS (an ABC affiliate) (Dec. 22, 2010).
[10] Molly Grantham, *Cancer Surviving Flight Attendant Forced to Remove Prosthetic Breast During Pat-Down*, WBTV.COM (Nov. 19, 2010).
[11] *TSA Makes Cancer Victim Remove Prosthetic Breast*, CBS NEWS (Nov. 19, 2010).
[12] CBS New York & the Associated Press, *Breast Cancer Survivor Lori Dorn Says She Endured 'Humiliating' Pat-Down at JFK: TSA, JFK Security Apologize, Admit Proper Protocol Was Not Followed*, CBS NEW YORK (Oct. 4, 2011).
[13] WKMG Local 6, *Woman: TSA Agents Singled Me Out For My Breasts*, CLICKORLANDO.COM (Nov. 23, 2010).
[14] *Ibid.*
[15] *Ibid.*
[16] *Ibid.*
[17] Bar Refaeli, as quote in Jade Watkins, *'It Left Me No Doubt About Her Sexual Preference': Bar Refaeli Felt Violated After Airport Pat Down by Female Security Guard*, MAIL ONLINE (Apr. 17, 2012).
[18] *See, e.g.*, The Official Website of Susie Castillo (http://www.susiecastillo.net/), at entry (http://www.susiecastillo.net/blog/2011/4/25/my-tsa-pat-down-experience.html). Copies of this video all still abound elsewhere, *e.g.*, http://www.youtube.com/watch?v=X6hvUWv2CsY.
[19] Phil Dawson & Christa Graban, *Enhanced Pat Down Leaves Grand Rapids Airline Passenger in Tears*, ABC WZZM 13.COM (Nov. 19, 2010).
[20] *See* online video accompanying Phil Dawson & Christa Graban, *Enhanced Pat Down Leaves Grand Rapids Airline Passenger in Tears*, ABC WZZM 13.COM (Nov. 19, 2010). http://www.wzzm13.com/news/story.aspx?storyid=140233.
[21] Lauren Sage Reinlie, *Elderly Woman Asked to Remove Adult Diaper During TSA Search*, NEWS HERALD (June 25, 2011).
[22] *Ibid.*
[23] CNN Wire Staff, *TSA Stands By Officers After Pat-Down of Elderly Woman in Florida*, CNN (June 28, 2011).
[24] *Ibid.*
[25] CNN Wire Staff, *TSA Denies Having Required a 95-Year-Old Woman to Remove Diaper*, CNN (June 27, 2011) ("Weber said the agents made it clear that her mother could not board the plane unless they were able to inspect the diaper.").
[26] *Ibid.*
[27] *Ibid.*
[28] CNN Wire Staff, *TSA Stands By Officers After Pat-Down of Elderly Woman in Florida*, CNN (June 28, 2011).
[29] *Ibid.*

[30] TSA Blog Team, *TSA Myth or Fact: Leaked Images, Handcuffed Hosts, Religious Garb, and More!*, THE TSA BLOG (Nov. 18, 2010).
[31] Lauren Sage Reinlie, *Elderly Woman Asked to Remove Adult Diaper During TSA Search*, NEWS HERALD (June 25, 2011).
[32] John S. Pistole, Administrator, Transportation Security Administration, U.S. Department of Homeland Security, *See Something, Say Something, Do Something: Next Steps for Securing Rail and Transit*, Hearing before the United States Senate Homeland Security and Governmental Affairs Committee (June 22, 2011). http://hsgac.senate.gov/public/index.cfm?FuseAction= Hearings.Hearing&Hearing_ID=5cb4a10a-bfd0-4925-a254-de8589cb4745.
[33] The actual video was shot in March, 2008. It was re-aired in April, 2008: *see, e.g.*, Steve Simon, CW39 NEWS (April 9, 2008); Robert Dominguez, *Bad Timing: Video of TSA Pat-Down of 3-Year-Old Girl Resurfaces After Two Years*, NEW YORK DAILY NEWS (Nov. 17, 2010).
[34] *See* the original video and post on YouTube, *e.g.*, http://www.youtube.com/watch?v= Hnb9Vddbc3k. Federal authorities knew they had a serious problem on their hands with this video. It one was one thing to frisk children in the dark; it was quite another to have that frisking posted on YouTube for Middle Americans to see. So while the photographer of this incident attempted to talk to the 8-year-old boy and his father subsequent to the pat-down, a "man in a black suit" quickly approached and stopped the conversation. (*Ibid.*) The man in the black suit "interrogated" the photographer about why he "was videotaping the 'procedures of the TSA.'" (*Ibid.*) The man in the black suit repeatedly pressured the photographer to delete the video and, in his own words, tried to "intimidate me to obey." (*Ibid.*) Unfortunately for TSA, the passenger-photographer posted his video anyway.
[35] John Pistole in an interview on NBC's *Today Show*, as quoted by Jeremy Pelofsky, *U.S. Officials Defend New Airport Screening Procedures*, REUTERS (Nov. 15, 2010) (emphasis added).
[36] GMA Exclusive, *TSA Frisks Six-Year-Old: Taking Security Too Far?*, WFAA 8 (ABC NEWS) (April 13, 2011). *See* complete interview of Dr. and Mrs. Drexel at http://abcnews.go.com/ GMA/video/tsa-frisks-year-parents-speak-13363521.
[37] *Ibid.*
[38] *Ibid.*
[39] *Ibid.*
[40] Jeff Poor, *Napolitano Backs 6-Year Old's* [sic] *Pat-Down*, THE DAILY CALLER (April 20, 2011).
[41] TSA Blog Team, *Screening of 6 Year-Old* [sic] *at MSY*, THE TSA BLOG (April 13, 2011).
[42] John S. Pistole, Administrator, Transportation Security Administration, U.S. Department of Homeland Security, *See Something, Say Something, Do Something: Next Steps for Securing Rail and Transit*, Hearing before the United States Senate Homeland Security and Governmental Affairs Committee (June 22, 2011). *See* Administrator Pistole's remarks starting at minute 90:00: http://hsgac.senate.gov/public/index.cfm?FuseAction=Hearings.Hearing&Hearing_ID=5cb4a 10a-bfd0-4925-a254-de8589cb4745.
[43] Tanya Mosley, *Kirkland 6-Year-Old Patted Down by TSA Agents*, KING 5 NEWS (July 9, 2011).
[44] *Ibid.*
[45] *See, e.g.*, Noreen O'Donnell, *Exclusive: Does This Girl Look Like a Terrorist?*, THE DAILY (Apr. 25, 2012) (developmentally-disabled 7-year-old girl with cerebral palsy gets the full treatment at New York's John F. Kennedy International Airport; TSA has no comment); Hugo Gye, *Weeping Four-Year-Old Girl Accused of Carrying a GUN by TSA Officers After She Hugged Her Grandmother While Passing Through Security*, MAIL ONLINE (Apr. 24, 2012) (4-year-old girl accused of having a gun and declared a "high security threat" at Wichita Mid-Continent Airport; TSA "agents threatened to shut down the whole airport if she could not be calmed down" for her frisk; TSA spokesman responds that TSA reviewed the incident and determined that TSA officers followed proper current screening procedures in conducting the child pat-down); Editorial, *Father's Outrage as TSA Subjects His Wheelchair-Bound Three-year-Old Son to Humiliating Search. . . On His Way to Disney*, MAIL ONLINE (Mar. 19, 2012) (3-year-old boy swabbed at Chicago O'Hare International Airport).
[46] Tanya Mosley, *Kirkland 6-Year-Old Patted Down by TSA Agents*, KING 5 NEWS (July 9, 2011).
[47] James Marchand interview with Steve Simon, CW39 NEWS (April 9, 2008). This interview can still be found online; *see, e.g.*, http://www.youtube.com/watch?v=vT30LWH8p4E&feature=

related; *see also* Robert Dominguez, *Bad Timing: Video of TSA Pat-Down of 3-Year-Old Girl Resurfaces After Two Years*, NY DAILY NEWS (Nov. 17, 2010).
[48] See for yourself the now-famous infant-pat-down at: Christopher Elliot, *TSA Baby Pat-Down Photographer: 'I've Never Seen Anything Quite That Bad"*, Elliot.org (May 9, 2011). http://www.elliott.org/blog/tsa-baby-pat-down-photographer-ive-never-seen-anything-quite-that-bad/.
[49] TSA Blogger Team, *TSA Searching for Poop Bombs?: Headline Not Up to Snuff*, THE TSA BLOG (May 9, 2011) (emphasis added).
[50] *See, e.g.*, Marsha Blackburn, *The TSA Is Coming to a Highway Near You*, FORBES (Feb. 29, 2012); Adam Ghassemi, *Tennessee Becomes First State to Fight Terrorism Statewide*, NEWS CHANNEL 5.COM (Oct. 18, 2011) ("You're probably used to seeing TSA's signature blue uniforms at the airport, but now agents are hitting the interstates to fight terrorism with Visible Intermodal Prevention and Response (VIPR).").
[51] Barbara De Lollis, *Hotel Guests Recruited with Homeland Security TV Spots*, USA TODAY (Nov. 2, 2011).
[52] *E.g.*, Brian Benett, *TSA Screenings Aren't Just for Airports Anymore*, LOS ANGELES TIMES (Dec. 20, 2011). And DHS Secretary Janet Napolitano informs us: "We look at so-called soft targets—the hotels, shopping malls, for example—all of which we have reached out to in the past year and have done a fair amount of training for their own employees. . . . [W]e have enhanced measures going on at surface transportation, not because we have a specific or credible threat there, but because we know, looking at Madrid and London, that's been another source of targets for terrorists." Agence France-Presse, *'Homeland' Security Coming to Hotels, Malls*, THE RAW STORY (Dec. 26, 2010); *see also* Barbara De Lollis, *Hotel Guests Recruited with Homeland Security TV Spots*, USA TODAY (Nov. 2, 2011).
[53] TSA seeks to expand the number of its Visible Intermodal Prevention and Response (VIPR or "viper") teams—the extra-aviation, unannounced security checkpoints and searches—from 25 to 37 in 2012. *See* Brian Benett, *TSA Screenings Aren't Just for Airports Anymore*, LOS ANGELES TIMES (Dec. 20, 2011).
[54] As quoted in *Ibid.* (emphasis added).
[55] Cedra Mayfield, *Local Man Says TSA Broke Promise*, WLNS.COM (6 NEWS) (April 24, 2011).
[56] *See supra* n. 7, 16, 20, 22, 28, 29, 35, 40, 41, 42, 49, and accompanying text.
[57] *Ibid.*
[58] *Ibid.*
[59] Zogby Poll, *Zogby Interactive: 61% Oppose Full Body Scans and TSA Pat Downs; 48% Will Seek Alternative to Flying*, ZOGBY INTERNATIONAL (Nov. 23, 2010).
[60] For example, Michigan, New Jersey, Pennsylvania, Texas, Washington, Hawaii, Alaska, Montana, and New Hampshire have organized against TSA and also introduced legislation to modify TSA procedures within their borders. Sam Slom, *Hawaii, Other States, Form Caucus to Oppose TSA Intrusions*, HAWAII REPORTER (April 15, 2011).
[61] *Ibid.*; TX HB 1937 and TX HB 1938; Examiner Staff, *Texas State Law Would Have Made Invasive TSA Patdowns a Felony*, SAN FRANCISCO EXAMINER.COM (May 25, 2011).
[62] Jim Bergamo, *Woman Arrested at ABIA After Refusing Enhanced Pat Down*, KVUE NEWS (an ABC affiliate) (Dec. 22, 2010).
[63] *E.g.*, Mike M. Ahlers & Jeanne Meserve, *TSA Security Looks At People Who Complain About … TSA Security*, CNN (April 15, 2011); *see also* Statement of Stephen M. Lord, Director Homeland Security and Justice Issues, *Aviation Security: TSA Has Made Progress, But Additional Efforts are Needed to Improve Security*, before the Subcommittee on Oversight, Investigations, and Management, Committee on Homeland Security, House of Representatives (published by the U.S. Government Accountability Office in GAO-11-938T, pp. 7-11 (Sept. 16, 2011)).
[64] Mike M. Ahlers & Jeanne Meserve, *TSA Security Looks At People Who Complain About … TSA Security*, CNN (April 15, 2011); *see also* Statement of Stephen M. Lord, Director Homeland Security and Justice Issues, *Aviation Security: TSA Has Made Progress, But Additional Efforts are Needed to Improve Security*, before the Subcommittee on Oversight, Investigations, and Management, Committee on Homeland Security, House of Representatives (published by the U.S. Government Accountability Office in GAO-11-938T, pp. 7-11 (Sept. 16, 2011)).
[65] TSA representatives were quick to point out that Harold Glen Rodman had been suspended and/or put on administrative leave pending an investigation of his case; but that is not saying

much, being that Harold is being *held without bail.* It's difficult to pat down passengers at the airport while simultaneously being housed against your will in a Manassas, VA jail. Gail Pennybacker, *Harold Rodman, TSA Worker, Arrested for Sexual Assault*, WJLA ABC 7 (Nov. 21, 2011); Associated Press, *TSA Worker Accused of Sexual Assault*, 12 NEWS (Nov. 22, 2011).
[66] John Shiffman, *Airport Passenger Screener Charged in Distributing Child Pornography*, PHILADELPHIA INQUIRER (April 23, 2011); Kristal Roberts, *Airport Passenger Screener Faces Child Porn Charges*, ABC ACTION NEWS (April 24, 2011).
[67] WBALTV 11 News, *Md. TSA Agent Charged with Child Porn*, WBALTV.com (Oct. 11, 2011) (emphasis added).
[68] *See, e.g.*, Steve Strunsky, *U.S. Homeland Security Committee Demands TSA Explain Reports of Racial Profiling at Newark Airport*, THE STAR-LEDGER (June 17, 2011); Bart Jansen, *TSA 'Chat-Downs' Investigated at Boston's Logan Airport*, USA TODAY (Aug. 14, 2012).
[69] As recommended by the Council on American-Islamic Relations (CAIR) in a Travel Advisory to Muslim women who wear hijab, "Before you are patted down, you should remind the TSA officer that they are only supposed to pat down the area in question, in this scenario, your head and neck. They SHOULD NOT subject you to a full-body or partial-body pat-down. . . . [R]*equest to pat down your own scarf*, including head and neck area, and have the [TSA] officers perform a chemical swipe of your hands." *CAIR Travel Advisory: New Airport Pat-Downs Called Invasive, Humiliating*, CAIR.COM (Nov. 10, 2010) (emphasis added). http://www.cair.com/ArticleDetails.aspx?ArticleID=26681&&name=n&&currPage=1.
[70] *See, e.g.*, Leonard Greene, *TSA Pat-Down of Shirtless Boy, 8, Adds Fuel to the Ire*, NEW YORK POST (Nov. 22, 2010); Jeremy Pelofsky, *Pilots and Passengers Rail at New Airport Patdowns*, YAHOO!NEWS.COM (Nov. 11, 2010).
[71] *Woman Says her Lambert Security Screening was Sexual Assault*, KMOV MOBILE NEWS (Nov. 18, 2010).
[72] *Ibid.*
[73] According to the 89th Airlift Wing of the U.S. Air Force, which provides ongoing estimates of that cost. *See, e.g.*, Demian Brady, *Incredible Journey: How Barack Obama Became the Most-Traveled President His First Two Years in Office*, Issue Brief #161, NATIONAL TAXPAYERS UNION FOUNDATION (Nov. 23, 2010.
[74] Jeff Zeleny, *Incoming Speaker Takes Commercial Flight, But Skips the Pat-Down*, THE NEW YORK TIMES (Nov. 19, 2010) ("There was no waiting for Mr. Boehner, who was escorted around the identification-checking agents, the metal detectors and the body scanners, and whisked directly to the gate.").
[75] Eileen Sullivan, *TSA: Some Gov't Officials to Skip Airport Security*, MYWAY.COM (Nov. 23, 2010).
[76] Jeff Zeleny, *Incoming Speaker Takes Commercial Flight, But Skips the Pat-Down*, THE NEW YORK TIMES (Nov. 19, 2010).
[77] *Ibid.*
[78] *Ibid.*; Eileen Sullivan, *TSA: Some Gov't Officials to Skip Airport Security*, MYWAY.COM (Nov. 23, 2010).
[79] Eileen Sullivan, *TSA: Some Gov't Officials to Skip Airport Security*, MYWAY.COM (Nov. 23, 2010).
[80] Jeff Zeleny, *Incoming Speaker Takes Commercial Flight, But Skips the Pat-Down*, THE NEW YORK TIMES (Nov. 19, 2010).
[81] Sheila Jackson Lee, as interviewed by Anderson Cooper for *360° Degree Raw Politics*, CNN (Nov. 19, 2010).
[82] Sheila Jackson Lee, *Ibid.*
[83] Sheila Jackson Lee, *Ibid.*
[84] E.g., this is precisely how a Yemeni al-Qaida operative bombed the Assistant Interior Minister of Saudi Arabia. *See, e.g.*, Europol SC5 – Counter Terrorism Unit, *The Concealment of Improvised Explosive Devices (IEDs) in Rectal Cavities*, (The Hague, 18 Sept. 2010) (**Warning:** graphic photographs of aftermath on last page.). http://www.strategypage.com/downloads/iedsrectalcavities.pdf. Of course, where plastic explosives are concerned terrorists can just as well flatten the explosive into a thin pancake and tape it to their body—and nudy-scanners will not detect it.
[85] Sheila Jackson Lee, as interviewed by Anderson Cooper for *360° Degree Raw Politics*, CNN (Nov. 19, 2010).

[86] Sheila Jackson Lee, *Ibid.*
[87] Sheila Jackson Lee, *Ibid.*
[88] Sheila Jackson Lee, *Ibid.*; *see supra* n. 86 and accompanying text.
[89] Harriet Baskas, *TSA Pat-Down Leaves Traveler Covered in Urine*, MSNBC.COM (March 25, 2011).
[90] TSA Blog Team, *New TSA Pat-Down Procedures*, THE TSA BLOG (Nov. 11, 2010).
[91] Harriet Baskas, *TSA Pat-Down Leaves Traveler Covered in Urine*, MSNBC.COM (March 25, 2011).
[92] *Ibid.*
[93] *Ibid.*
[94] *Ibid.*
[95] *Ibid.*
[96] *Ibid.*
[97] *Ibid.*
[98] Cedra Mayfield, *Local Man Says TSA Broke Promise*, WLNS.COM (6 NEWS) (April 24, 2011).
[99] *Ibid.*
[100] *Ibid.*
[101] Harriet Baskas, *TSA Pat-Down Leaves Traveler Covered in Urine*, MSNBC.COM (March 25, 2011).
[102] For example: On a single day, within a single airport [John F. Kennedy International], three aged grandmothers were strip-searched so TSA could better examine their medical devices. (Post Newsweek, *3 Elderly Women Say TSA Agents Made Them Pull Down Pants, Underwear*, LOCAL 10 NEWS (Dec. 5, 2011); CBS News, *TSA Officials: Proper Procedures Were Followed In Cases of Elderly Strip-Searching*, CBS NEW YORK (Dec. 6, 2011).) Their tales of humiliation and emotional distress are familiar: "She said please pull down your pants. I was crying then. I couldn't believe it." (CBS News, *TSA Officials: Proper Procedures Were Followed In Cases of Elderly Strip-Searching*, CBS NEW YORK (Dec. 6, 2011).) In the words of 88-year-old Ruth Sherman, who was strip-searched for her colostomy bag, "It's degrading. It's like someone raped you. They didn't know how to handle a human being." (Post Newsweek, *3 Elderly Women Say TSA Agents Made Them Pull Down Pants, Underwear*, LOCAL 10 NEWS (Dec. 5, 2011).) 85-year-old Lenore Zimmerman had to lower her pants and underwear, too—so TSA could examine her back brace. (Post Newsweek, *3 Elderly Women Say TSA Agents Made Them Pull Down Pants, Underwear*, LOCAL 10 NEWS (Dec. 5, 2011).)

At the time these poor women were examined at JFK International, TSA's own protocols insisted that passengers with colostomy bags "will not be required to expose these devices for inspection," and ruled that passengers would not be asked to "lift, remove, or raise any article of clothing to reveal a sensitive area of the body." (CBS News, *TSA Officials: Proper Procedures Were Followed In Cases of Elderly Strip-Searching*, CBS NEW YORK (Dec. 6, 2011).) Obviously TSA sidestepped its protocols in the treatment of these three elderly women at JFK. Nevertheless, TSA has performed an unbiased internal review (Post Newsweek, *3 Elderly Women Say TSA Agents Made Them Pull Down Pants, Underwear*, LOCAL 10 NEWS (Dec. 5, 2011) (emphasis added)), and determined that:

> Our officers are committed to treating every passenger with dignity and respect and we take complaints seriously. TSA is currently reviewing recent allegations of passengers who flew out of JFK. *Our preliminary review of each of these claims indicates all screening procedures were followed.*

So fear not, fellow citizens—all is well! *See also, e.g.*, Noreen O'Donnell, *Exclusive: Does This Girl Look Like a Terrorist?*, THE DAILY (Apr. 25, 2012) (developmentally-disabled 7-year-old girl with cerebral palsy gets the full treatment at New York's John F. Kennedy International Airport; TSA has no comment).

9

Government In My Toilet

Each public department at Washington keeps a minor asylum of salaried inmates whose business it is to invent a meaning for laws that have no meaning; and to detect meanings, where any exist, and distort and confuse them. This process is called "interpreting." And sublime and awe-inspiring is this art!

—Mark Twain[i]

[T]he federal judiciary [is] an irresponsible body (for impeachment is scarcely a scare-crow), working like gravity by night and by day, gaining a little to-day and a little to-morrow, and advancing its noiseless step like a thief, over the field of jurisdiction, until all shall be usurped from the States, and the government of all be consolidated into one.

To this I am opposed; because, when all government, domestic and foreign, in little as in great things, shall be drawn to Washington as the centre [sic] of all power, it will render powerless the checks provided of one government on another, and will become as venal and oppressive as the government from which we separated.

—Thomas Jefferson[ii]

IT IS DIFFICULT TO TURN AWAY from the TSA nightmare.

Difficult to delete from the mind's eye images of the Fourth Head digitally raping citizens.

But there are so many sights left to see at the socialist menagerie—so many other monstrosities to inspect!

---

[i] Mark Twain, unpublished manuscript c. 1881, as published in MARK TWAIN, WHO IS MARK TWAIN? 96 (Regents of the University of California eds., HarperCollins Publishers 2009).

[ii] Thomas Jefferson, *Letter to Charles Hammond* (Aug. 18 1921). *See, e.g.*, THOMAS JEFFERSON, THE WRITINGS OF THOMAS JEFFERSON (Andrew A. Lipscomb & Albert Ellery Bergh eds., The Thomas Jefferson memorial Association 1903).

Besides, TSA's fondling of citizens unsuspected of any crime is only one (undoubtedly tangible) example of Incrementalism. To understand the method of socialism we must move on. We must avert our gaze. We must look in another direction. We must leave the TSA exhibit behind, and explore other wings of the socialist menagerie.

As we have seen, culture is of magnificent assistance to Incrementalists' tacit revolution. Culture remains largely unnoticed; yet it diligently softens citizens for ever-increasing impositions on liberty, and ever-denser consolidations of federal power.

But while culture is an essential Incrementalist tool, culture is not socialism's ultimate goal.

You see, Incrementalism intends to enthrone socialism in America as surely as any Bolshevik-style revolution, guns and all—it simply means to do so via *alternative technique*: quietly and carefully, so as not to waken Middle America. Incrementalism will not be satisfied until the American socialist revolution is complete. Until toppling American socialism requires resorting to "illegal" means. (Like another Declaration of Independence. And another, ahem, ...) For this reason Incrementalism aims much higher than culture alone: *Incrementalism aims at the imprimatur of American law.*

As we saw in Book I, socialism requires an unrestrained and centralized government to service its goals of redistribution, group rights, and "moral" government—and as a limitation on federal power, the Constitution has always gotten underfoot. Only when the Constitution is tamed will all persons and all States be required to participate in socialism's monolithic plans. Only then will the tacit socialist revolution be complete. And so Incrementalism aims not at just any old law; Incrementalism aspires to the sanction of American *constitutional law.*

Yes, the Constitution is critical to socialist revolution. For this reason we must explore the *legal* aspect of Incrementalism.

I know what you are thinking: *Ugh!* . . . *Abstract* . . . . *Boring* . . . .

But if you read this chapter and the next, you will witness Incrementalism's most magnificent magic trick: *You will see the Constitution pulled inside out!* You will see a limited Constitution of enumerated powers inverted—and made into a grant of monolithic central authority. You will see the meaning of words flipped upside down and backwards with a wink. You will see courts conjure federal powers our Predecessors never dreamt of. You will see States deposed and individuals locked in the stocks. You will see the federal government unshackled and enthroned. You will see all this accomplished with a few words by a single court—just a hushed "Abracadabra!" and it is done. You will see that expansions of federal power no longer require formal constitutional amendment. You will see with perfect clarity the patient, intentional work of Incrementalism. You will witness juridical sophistry at its best!

One must not be intimidated by legal subject matter. It is far easier to understand than any of the philosophical, logical, and moral arguments we have treated previously. Indeed, law schools themselves accept students from every background and discipline—even community organizers! (And if the smuggest of law schools award the title of Juris Doctor to students with no particular credentials, then you surely don't need any special preparation to understand this chapter or the next.)

The questions presented are few and simple. (1) Can the federal government tell individuals how much of which crops to plant on their own land for their own consumption? (2) Can the federal government bribe States to follow *federal* policy—on subjects over which the Constitution grants States exclusive authority? (3) Can the federal government tax individuals for *not* buying a product the government wishes they had?

Before we begin, a disclaimer is in order: Attorneys are rightly rebuked for overestimating the significance of past legal decisions. In part this overestimation stems from the (once important) concept of *stare decisis*, a legal doctrine requiring that current court rulings conform to prior ones in order to preserve predictability and stability of law. And in part this overestimation is merely an example of the vocational pride to which people of all fields are subject.

On both counts I deserve the rebuke.

However, there is an independent reason for which these chapters analyze historical legal decisions. It is simply this: If one wishes to examine Incrementalist drift in constitutional law then there are few other materials to which one can turn. Certainly there are few *better* materials: Legal decisions forever preserve the arguments of opposing parties on a single issue at distinct moments in time. Legal decisions thus furnish a ready timeline illustrating how constitutional restrictions on government have been viewed—and have been *changed without amendment*—over time.

"Interpreting"

The Federal Judiciary is the third head of federal government, after the Legislature and the Executive.[iii] Unlike other branches of government, the Judiciary's membership—i.e., federal judges—consists exclusively of attorneys.

[iii] U.S. CONST. art. III.

Federal judges are appointed from above, never elected from below.[iv] And after appointment, federal judges serve for life—unless impeached and removed *for cause* (e.g., they become clinically insane).[v] No matter what rulings they make, federal judges are never impeached and removed for cause. And federal judges never come up for reelection. So the structure of the federal judiciary closely resembles that of the Fourth Head.[1]

When the Constitution was proposed, the Federal Judiciary was given the crucial role of "faithful guardians of the Constitution" against legislative incursions upon individual and State liberties.[vi] In their role as guardians of the Constitution, federal courts were expected to compare laws with the text of the Constitution—and to *void laws wherever conflict was found*.[vii] The Judiciary was to strike down laws contradicting the Constitution in order "to keep the [federal legislature] within the limits assigned to their authority."[2]

The Judiciary has always been critical to the realization of limited government. Without independent judicial oversight, individuals and States' constitutional liberties could not be protected from federal usurpations: The Legislature would simply write laws giving itself powers never granted under the Constitution. The Executive would promulgate regulations giving itself powers never ceded in the Constitution. Without independent judicial oversight, constitutional "protections" against federal intrusion would not be worth the paper they were written on.

[iv] U.S. CONST. art. II, § 2, cl. 2 ("The President . . . shall nominate, and by and with the Advice and Consent of the Senate, shall appoint . . . Judges of the supreme Court, and all other Officers of the United States, whose Appointments are not herein otherwise provided for, and which shall be established by Law: but the Congress may by Law vest the Appointment of such inferior Officers, as they think proper, in the President alone, in the Courts of Law, or in the Heads of Departments.").

[v] U.S. CONST. art. III, § 1 ("The Judges, both of the supreme and inferior Courts, shall hold their Offices during good Behaviour [sic] . . . .").

[vi] *See, e.g.*, THE FEDERALIST No. 78, at 501 (Hamilton) (Robert Scigliano ed., Modern Library 2001) (1787). *See also ibid.* at 498, 500 ("[T]he courts were designed to be an intermediate body between the people and the legislature, in order, among other things, to keep the latter within the limits assigned to their authority. . . . [T]he courts of justice are to be considered as the bulwarks of a limited Constitution against legislative encroachments . . . .").

[vii] THE FEDERALIST No. 78, at 497-500 (Hamilton) (Robert Scigliano ed., Modern Library 2001) (1787) ("Limitations [on federal legislative authority] can be preserved in practice no other way than through the medium of courts of justice, whose duty it must be to declare all acts contrary to the manifest tenor of the Constitution void. Without this, all the reservations of particular rights or privileges would amount to nothing. . . . It must therefore belong to [the courts] to ascertain [the Constitution's] meaning, as well as the meaning of any particular act proceeding from the legislative body. If there should happen to be an irreconcilable variance between the two, that which has the superior obligation and validity ought, of course, to be preferred; in other words, the Constitution ought to be preferred to the statute, the intention of the people to the intention of their agents. . . . [W]here the will of the legislature, declared in its statutes, stands in opposition to that of the people, declared in the Constitution, the judges ought to be governed by the latter rather than the former. . . . [W]henever a particular statute contravenes the Constitution, it will be the duty of the judicial tribunals to adhere to the latter and disregard the former.").

Federal judges were therefore expected to be independent and courageous in the face of majority will to circumvent the Constitution without explicit and formal amendment—whether that will was expressed through the Legislature, by the people, or even by both Legislature and people at the same time.[viii] Indeed, in order to safeguard federal judges' role as guardians of the Constitution, "*The complete independence of the courts of justice is peculiarly essential in a limited Constitution*. . . . Without this, all the [constitutional] reservations of particular rights or privileges would amount to nothing."[3]

Our Predecessors knew it.[ix] (Which is why they provided independent federal courts to strike down unconstitutional laws in the first instance.) And socialists soon learned it. (Which is why they relish subordinating federal courts to legislative fashion.)

And here is where Incrementalists saw their constitutional opportunity: In order to determine whether a law or other government action is constitutionally permissible, federal courts are forced to "interpret" the Constitution—that is, to *say what the Constitution means.* (One can't very well compare laws to the Constitution without saying what the Constitution itself means!) Over the centuries federal courts have had to "interpret" every little clause of the Constitution—because in making any ruling, one must decide precisely *what the constitutional law is.*[x] Interpretation and reinterpretation of the Constitution by unelected federal judges over hundreds of years thus provided Incrementalists with a ready tribunal for step-by-step alterations to the Constitution. All Incrementalists had to do was remove federal courts' independence—so that instead of independently following the Constitution they dependently followed someone else. This was the key to Incrementalists' constitutional strategy.

Above all federal courts, one possesses extraordinary power: the United States Supreme Court. The Supreme Court consists of nine Justices, and a

---

[viii] THE FEDERALIST No. 78, at 501 (Hamilton) (Robert Scigliano ed., Modern Library 2001) (1787) ("Until the people have, by some solemn and authoritative act, annulled or changed the established form, it is binding upon themselves collectively, as well as individually; and no presumption, or even knowledge, of their sentiments, can warrant their representatives in a departure from it, prior to such an act. But it is easy to see, that it would require an uncommon portion of fortitude in the judges to do their duty as faithful guardians of the Constitution, where legislative invasions of it had been instigated by the major voice of the community.").

[ix] THE FEDERALIST No. 78, at 497-98 (Hamilton) (Robert Scigliano ed., Modern Library 2001) (1787) ("Without this, all the reservations of particular rights or privileges would amount to nothing. . . . [E]very act of a delegated authority, contrary to the tenor of the commission under which it is exercised, is void. No legislative act, therefore, contrary to the Constitution, can be valid. To deny this, would be to affirm, that . . . the representatives of the people are superior to the people themselves . . . .").

[x] *See, e.g.*, THE FEDERALIST No. 78, at 498 (Hamilton) (Robert Scigliano ed., Modern Library 2001) (1787) ("The interpretation of the laws is the proper and peculiar province of the courts. A constitution is, in fact, and must be regarded by the judges, as a fundamental law. It must therefore belong to them to ascertain its meaning, as well as the meaning of any particular act proceeding from the legislative body.").

majority opinion by five or more Justices determines the outcome of litigation. Unlike other courts, whose decisions can be appealed to (and potentially reversed by) a higher tribunal, the Supreme Court is the court of last resort.[xi]

At the risk of belaboring the point, let us reiterate: The Supreme Court's phenomenal power comes from the fact that *its decisions are never reviewed.* Not by the Legislature. Not by the Executive. And certainly not by citizens. Supreme Court rulings are (for legal purposes, anyway!) infallible. What the Supreme Court says stands—unless formal amendment is made to the Constitution.[4] (Which requires a two-thirds supermajority in both the House and Senate in order to propose an amendment,[5] and ratification by *three-fourths* of all State legislatures [i.e., a full thirty-eight of fifty State legislatures]). Needless to say, constitutional amendments are rare.[xii]

Like other federal courts, the Supreme Court is forced to "interpret" the Constitution in order to make rulings. (Again, one can't very well compare laws to the Constitution without construing the Constitution itself!) And because the Supreme Court always has the last say, its "interpretations" are special—indeed, its "interpretations" are *irrefutable!* In the daily course of business the Supreme Court interprets and reinterprets the Constitution—and it does so *without the possibility of review, yeehah!*

What does this mean?

In general it means the Supreme Court has the final say on which government actions are legal and which are not.

But for Incrementalists this state of affairs has a further and more cynical import. For Incrementalists it means that *through the medium of the Supreme Court, the Constitution can be rewritten time and again—without ever actually being rewritten!* With nary an amendment! Without the bother of attaining supermajorities in House and Senate! Without the trouble of gaining thirty-eight State legislatures' consent! Without support among Middle Americans! Why, the Supreme Court can snap its fingers and rule "the Constitution means Y, not X"—whatever the Supreme Court says goes. No matter if the Supreme Court's "interpretation" is right or wrong. One merely needs five Supreme Court Justices to agree to a new "interpretation," and that is the end of it: Constitution amended!

So the Incrementalist solution to eliminating limited, constitutional, American government manifested itself at once: *Remove Supreme Court independence!* Pressure the Court to validate the Legislature's laws and the Executive's wishes. Discover the most timid Supreme Court Justices and lean on *them.* Assemble a Supreme Court which "interprets" the Constitution no longer as a restraint on federal powers, but instead as a new pretext for them.

[xi] U.S. CONST. art. III, § 2.

[xii] U.S. CONST. art. V.

From the very beginning, Incrementalism has pushed socialist revolution through the Supreme Court. Incrementalism has emphasized the role of federal courts (and especially the Supreme Court) in governmental decisions. It has employed the Federal Judiciary in much the same way it employs the Fourth Head. And when Incrementalism has its way with the Judiciary, the Constitution is forever changed.

One Tiny Clause

Every little part—or "clause"—of the Constitution is assumed to have meaning. And that meaning is open to reinterpretation by the Supreme Court.

During Incrementalists' hundred-year magic show, scores of clauses having universally understood meanings have been turned inside out via Supreme Court reinterpretation. Some of these little clauses have been more helpful to socialist causes than others; through successive reinterpretation some clauses have taken on a life of their own. One of these is the so-called "Commerce Clause."

The Commerce Clause is found in the Constitution, Article 1, section 8, and states simply that Congress shall have the power "To regulate Commerce . . . among the several States . . . ."[xiii]

The meaning of the Commerce Clause is quite specific. As is clear from the text itself, it is a grant of power to Congress to regulate *commerce*—that is, *trade*: the buying and selling of goods. The Commerce Clause was *not* a grant of power to regulate *production*—that is, *creation of the goods themselves*. In other words, the Commerce Clause was never a grant of power over manufacturing, or mining, or farming. Nor was the Commerce Clause a grant of congressional power to regulate the *relations of production*—meaning the relationships between owner and employee, or between capital and labor.

Furthermore, the Commerce Clause grants Congress power only over commerce "*among the several States*"—that is, commerce *between* the several States; or what we now commonly call *interstate commerce*. The Commerce Clause never granted Congress authority to regulate commerce *within* a State, or to dictate labor policy *to* a State, much less reach down into individual households and regulate private production and consumption *by an individual*. (If the Commerce Clause had been intended to do so, it would have been simple enough to enumerate a power saying precisely that. But our Predecessors did not.)

Finally, the Commerce Clause was included in the Constitution for a limited purpose. Our Predecessors added it *to prevent trade wars between the States*. (Preventing interstate trade wars was important to our Predecessors' goal of liberty. Our Predecessors recognized that choice is possible only

---

[xiii] U.S. CONST. art. I, § 8, cl. 3.

where alternatives exist. In the political sphere, alternatives exist where there are independent, sovereign States from which to choose—regions in which the law differs from surrounding territories. And authentic independence was only possible if States were protected from intentionally coercive taxes levied by their brethren.)

If the text of the Constitution were not plain enough, our Predecessors were adamant about the limited function of the Commerce Clause. As the Constitution's primary author, James Madison, explained, the Commerce Clause was only a power to "provide for the *harmony and proper intercourse among the States*."[6] Our Predecessors' concern was curtailing scenarios in which a first, strongly commercial State possessing well-developed ports, navigable waterways, and strong trading partners levied special tariffs on a second, less-commercial State for use of the first State's ports. Because the second State had few ports, and because it still needed to import and export trade goods, it would be forced to pay the first State's tariff or find more expensive, alternative means to import and export goods. As Madison explained, the first, well-commercialized State would be unjustly enriched by collecting "an indirect revenue from their uncommercial [sic] neighbors," which would be "not less impolitic than it is unfair."[7] The second, un-commercial State would be economically injured, which "would nourish unceasing animosities [between the States], and not improbably terminate in serious interruptions of the public tranquillity [sic]."[8]

Yes, the Commerce Clause was an effort to prevent interstate trade wars from becoming interstate *real wars*. It was included to allow an ostensibly neutral arbiter—the federal government—to prevent one State from taking economic advantage of another. It was included to guarantee States' economic independence. That was all. As the primary author of the Constitution testifies, it was no more than "a superintending authority over the *reciprocal trade* of confederated States."[9]

The Commerce Clause was such a dinky little stretch of Constitution—just seven words in all!—and our Predecessors naturally expected it to play a valuable, albeit tiny, role. Normally it would lie dormant; it would be available if ever States began abusing one another economically.

But Incrementalists had other plans for the puny Commerce Clause. They would make the Commerce Clause a federal star. They would promote the Commerce Clause to king-maker!

The Guardians' Last Stand

For many decades the Supreme Court maintained a lofty independence from both the Legislature and the Executive. No matter how raucously the Legislature howled or how bitterly the Executive cursed, the Court struck down laws attempting to expand federal power beyond those enumerated in the Constitution—just as the Court was designed to do. Sometimes the Court performed this duty better, sometimes worse, but in general Justices remained politically aloof and fulfilled their solemn duty as guardians of the Constitution. And in particular, the Court limited the miniscule Commerce Clause to its actual meaning: superintedance over (1) *prejudicial* (2) *commerce* (3) *between the States*.[10]

In the early 1930s, however, Supreme Court independence faced a new challenge. Led by Franklin Delano Roosevelt (FDR), Incrementalists passed a new set of national laws consolidating tremendous power within the federal government. In the name of helping the helpless, these laws purported to administer aspects of economic and social life over which the federal government had never been given authority. Collectively, these one-size-fits-all laws were referred to as the "New Deal." And as is apparent from their very name, such consolidations of federal power were unprecedented: This was the *New* Deal, after all, not the *Old* Deal.

At first the Supreme Court resisted overreaching New (Socialist[11]) Deal legislation. Despite overwhelming majorities in Congress, unified by executive leadership in the person of FDR, the Supreme Court courageously maintained its independence from the Legislature and the Executive. Just as it was designed to do.

So, for example, in 1935 the Supreme Court invalidated the Railroad Retirement Act of 1934—a New (Socialist) Deal law purporting to establish compulsory retirement and pension plans for all railroad workers.[12] The Railroad Retirement Act pretended to compel nationwide participation under the tiny Commerce Clause. But an independent Supreme Court didn't buy it. In a sober and unbending opinion authored by Justice Owen Josephus Roberts, the Supreme Court declared that establishing a national, mandatory retirement and pension plan for railroad workers is "essentially related solely to the social welfare of the worker," and was "therefore remote from any regulation of commerce as such."[13] In other words, a national retirement and pension plan is *not even commerce*. Much less is it *interstate* commerce. (Much less still is it an *unfair commercial practice used by a well-developed State to disadvantage a less-developed one.*) Therefore Congress had no authority to regulate retirement and pension plans; much less to unilaterally publish one and compel participation in it. Justice Roberts continued without batting an eye: "*We think the answer is plain. These matters obviously lie outside the orbit of congressional power.*"[14]

The Supreme Court was independent. The guardians of the Constitution stood firm. The runty Commerce Clause remained small and inconsequential.

Again in 1935 the Supreme Court voided Title I of the New (Socialist) Deal's National Industry Recovery Act (NIRA).[15] The NIRA purported to set compulsory minimum wage, maximum hours, maximum price for chickens, and rules for the sale of sick chickens; assure workers the right to unionize;

and prohibit child labor in the poultry industry. The federal government argued that setting uniform wages, prices, and labor standards promoted economic recovery from the Great Depression.[16] The rub here was that instead of regulating *inter*state chicken commerce, the NIRA explicitly professed to regulate *intra*state chicken commerce as well. That is, the NIRA forced States and individual chicken industrialists to adopt minimum wages, maximum hours, chicken prices, chicken unions, chicken health rules—*whether or not chickens were being traded across State borders.*

Like the Railroad Retirement Act before it, the NIRA claimed federal power under the wee little Commerce Clause. And again, an independent Supreme Court's answer was simple:

> It is not the province of the Court to consider the economic advantages or disadvantages of such a centralized system. It is sufficient to say that the Federal Constitution does not provide for it. . . . [T]he authority of the federal government may not be pushed to such an extreme as to destroy the distinction, which the commerce clause itself establishes, between commerce "among the several States" and the internal concerns of a state.[17]

In other words, perhaps a centrally planned chicken economy *would* promote economic recovery. But that is not the Court's concern. The Court's concern is whether the Constitution provides the federal government with sufficient authority to tell States and individuals how to sell chickens—how long they can work each day, what prices they may charge, how they must inspect ill chickens, and whether chicken unions must be allowed. The Constitution does not. The very words of the Commerce Clause illustrate it consists merely in a power to regulate commerce *between States*—it is not a power to override State sovereignty and dictate internal State commerce.[18]

So again, the Supreme Court voided Title I of the NIRA. The court's decision was unanimous. The guardians of the Constitution stood firm. The tiny Commerce Clause remained as it was written: pint-sized and benign.

In 1936 the Supreme Court struck down the New Deal's Bituminous Coal Conservation Act of 1935 on similar reasoning.[19] The court concluded that *mining* is a type of *production*.[20] The Court ruled that as a type of *production*, mining is *not commerce*—and therefore cannot fall within the ambit of congressional authority.[21]

In 1936 the Court also struck down the Agricultural Adjustment Act of 1933.[22] It ruled that like mining, *farming* is a type of *production*—and because production it is *not commerce*, it cannot be regulated by Congress. In doing so the Court reaffirmed the distinction between *production* on the one hand, over which the Commerce Clause grants Congress no authority, and *commerce* on the other, over which the Commerce Clause grants congressional authority in *interstate* scenarios.[23] As Justice Owen Josephus Roberts noted in the majority opinion, "The [Agricultural Adjustment Act] invades the reserved rights of the states. It is a statutory plan to regulate and control *agricultural production*, a matter beyond the powers delegated to the federal government."[24]

The Supreme Court preserved its independence. The guardians of the Constitution held firm—albeit generally by a slim 5-4 majority. Five Justices repeatedly united to void laws which stretched federal power beyond its constitutional bounds: Justices A. George Sutherland, Pierce Butler, James Clark McReynolds, Willis Van Devanter, and Owen Josephus Roberts.

So the diminutive Commerce Clause continued as before: petite and innocuous.

Fireside Chat

President Roosevelt was not pleased.

After having his best-loved brain children repeatedly paddled by the Supreme Court, FDR became frustrated with the independence of Constitutional Guardians. He was tired of losing 5-4 rulings. He recognized New (Socialist) Deal policies would never be implemented so long as the Supreme Court retained its stubborn constitutional allegiance. So long as the Court maintained *independence* from the Executive (himself) and the Legislature.

FDR commanded loyal Democratic majorities in both houses of Congress. As President he wielded tremendous political power of a sort never seen before or since (he is our only three-term president!). So he trampled the Judiciary's independence in the most spectacular fashion imaginable. He threatened to do the very thing our Predecessors said must never be done: *He threatened to pack the Supreme Court with yes-men.* He threatened to just keep on adding Justices to the Court—not when they retired, but *now*!—until he obtained a loyal majority to rubberstamp his New (Socialist) Deal. Why, if the Supreme Court had to have *fifteen Justices* before FDR could get a loyal majority, so be it![25]

FDR announced his proposal to pack the court (euphemistically referred to as the "Judicial Procedures Reform Bill") on February 5, 1937. Of course, FDR's court-packing bill did not come right out and say "FDR is weary of Supreme Court independence—so he is going to pack the Court with socialist toadies." Instead, FDR's court-packing plan was couched in terms of judicial efficiency: The Justices at the Supreme Court are *too old to do their jobs*, you see—the Court is hopelessly bogged down with sickly geriatrics and needs some younger, more energetic Justices to pick up the slack. Instead of the life terms granted by the Constitution,[xiv] FDR proposed that Justices of the Supreme Court *ought* to retire at age seventy—and if they didn't, a younger

---

[xiv] U.S. CONST. art. III, § 1 ("The Judges, both of the supreme and inferior Courts, shall hold their Offices during good Behaviour [sic]. . . .").

Justice would "automatically" be appointed to "help" the older Justice with his work.[26] And that younger, newly-appointed Justice would be *senior* to the elder Justice to which he was assigned (!).

Conveniently, FDR was currently serving as President—meaning that he would personally handpick any "necessary" and "automatic" younger Justices. And in three months time, six of the nine current Justices would be seventy or older—so whether or not those six Justices retired, under his court-packing scheme FDR would be appointing six additional Supreme Court Justices *immediately* (!).[27] (If that didn't turn the tables on unfavorable 5-4 rulings, nothing would. Yes, FDR aspired to favorable 10-5 rulings at the newly dependent Supreme Court!)

On March 9, 1937, FDR spent an entire installment of his celebrated Fireside Chat radio series pushing his court-packing scheme. He argued that the only way to avoid another Great Depression was to give more authority to the federal government—"to prevent and to cure the abuses and the inequalities which had thrown that system out of joint."[28] (Yes, indeed: New Deal redistribution was required to cure former "inequalities.") He argued that the federal government had begun New (Socialist) Deal policies which would make American economy "bombproof" against another Great Depression, but that the country was "only partway through that program."[29] He threatened that further economic recession was just around the corner, and "To complete our program of protection in time, therefore, we cannot delay one moment in making certain that our national government has power to carry through."[30] By which he meant, of course, sufficient power to carry through his New (Socialist) Deal.

FDR argued that the Supreme Court was the only federal department pulling against the New (Socialist) Deal.[31] He argued that the Court's contrarian posture was evident from its rulings against New (Socialist) Deal legislation. He singled out the Court as the lone department preventing economic recovery. From this FDR concluded, "We have therefore reached the point as a nation where we must take action to save the Constitution from the Court—and the Court from itself."[32]

And what did FDR propose to save the Court from itself?

Well, FDR argued that a constitutional amendment authorizing New (Socialist) Deal powers *could not be waited for*. (If that didn't set off alarm bells, nothing would!) The economic situation was too dire, further economic disaster was imminent, a constitutional amendment would take months or years to implement, and besides—it really wasn't fair that just 13 States, possessing such a small proportion of the population, could prevent the rest of the nation from altering the Constitution![33] And so, he said, "We cannot rely on an amendment as the immediate or only answer to our present difficulties."[34]

Instead, FDR argued, we must "infuse new blood into all our courts."[35] In particular, "we must have judges who will bring to the courts a *present-day sense of the Constitution*."[36] In other words, we need judges who will bring to the courts *FDR's* sense of the Constitution. We need a *willing* Supreme Court; a *dependent* Supreme Court; one that will submit to the Legislature and the Executive—one that will find New (Socialist) Deal programs constitutional. We need more bootlickers on the Court.

And if we let FDR pack the Court, we had his promise: "it will provide a reinvigorated, *liberal-minded judiciary* necessary to furnish quicker and cheaper justice from bottom to top."[37]

In the end FDR's Judicial Procedures Reform Bill was unnecessary. FDR's menace was keenly felt at a Court that had been bullied by the Executive and the Legislature for years. The mere threat of packing the Court with six new sycophants was sufficient! The Court dumped its independence.

Because one man was timid. Because a single Justice lacked that "uncommon portion of fortitude" which our Predecessors demanded of all federal judges.[38] Because one Guardian cared more what the President and the Press thought of him than what the Constitution commanded. Justice Owen Josephus Roberts, one of the independent five, one who had consistently stood against New (Socialist) Deal legislation in the past, one who had authored many of the Court's most defiant decisions, finally turned. On a dime Justice Roberts switched sides—from upholding the Constitution to upholding new and un-enumerated federal powers. He jettisoned his philosophy of limited government based on a written Constitution for one featuring a monolithic parliament possessed of power to enact any laws it pleased. Yes, Justice Roberts relinquished his burdensome independence for a more comfortable loyalty. And by that same 5-4 margin which the Supreme Court had previously struck down New (Socialist) Deal legislation, the Court now upheld it—with Justice Roberts' unwavering support.

After Justice Robert's switch, FDR was able to implement his New (Socialist) Deal without constitutional interference. On March 29, 1937—only twenty days after FDR's radio address!—the Supreme Court began handing down decisions uniformly favorable to New (Socialist) Deal legislation. It began with *West Coast Hotel Co. v. Parrish*, 300 U.S. 379 (1937) (upholding Washington State's minimum wage law).[39] Justice Roberts cast the deciding 5-4 vote in *West Coast Hotel*, and New (Socialist) Deal wins at the Supreme Court continued like dominoes thereafter.[xv]

[xv] For example, *NLRB v. Jones & Laughlin Steel Corp.*, 301 U.S. 1 (1937) (5-4 decision upholding the National Labor Relations Act as constitutional); *NLRB v. Fruehauf Trailer Co.*, 301 U.S. 49 (1937) (5-4 decision upholding National Labor Relations Act); *NLRB v. Friedman-Harry Marks Clothing Co.*, 301 U.S. 58 (1937) (5-4 decision upholding National Labor Relations Act); *Associated Press v. NLRB*,

FDR had successfully flipped the Court—he needed only one Justice to switch sides, not all nine!—and Incrementalism was off to the races.

In constitutional terms, Justice Roberts' switch provided total revolution: No longer would the Court ordinarily limit federal power. No longer would it guard the Constitution from overreaching Legislatures and domineering Executives. No longer would it zealously defend individuals and States from unconstitutional federal encroachments. No longer would there be a strict separation of powers between Legislative, Executive, and Judicial branches. The floodgates were open: The federal government was to be a monolithic monstrosity of unlimited powers—precisely the sort our Predecessors had cast off! Precisely the type our Predecessors forbade under the Constitution.

So much for independence at the Supreme Court.

There is an old adage stating that "a stitch in time saves nine." Well, Justice Robert's about-face was popularly referred to as "*the switch in time that saved nine*." (Which is to say, because Justice Roberts switched sides in the nick of time, nine Justices were saved from FDR's court-packing scheme.) It's a catchy mnemonic, and one developed by contemporaries who perfectly understood what they were witnessing:

Incrementalists' constitutional magic show had begun!

The "Commerce" Beanstalk

With the Supreme Court firmly in hand—or rather, with Justice Roberts firmly in hand—juridical Incrementalism was ready to enslave the States to federal will. And once the States acquiesced to federal power, individuals would soon follow.

But first the Court required a constitutional hook upon which to hang New (Socialist) Deal powers. Incrementalists needed some actual, enumerated

---

301 U.S. 103 (1937) (5-4 decision upholding National Labor Relations Act); *Washington Coach Co. v. NLRB*, 301 U.S. 142 (1937) (yet another 5-4 decision upholding the National Labor Relations Act); *Steward Machine Company v. Davis*, 301 U.S. 548 (1937) (5-4 decision upholding unemployment compensation provisions of the Social Security Act of 1935 as constitutional); *Helvering v. Davis*, 301 U.S. 619 (1937) (5-4 decision upholding Social Security Act); etc.

Justice Willis Van Devanter retired on June 2, 1937, Justice Alexander George Sutherland retired on January 17, 1938, and Justice Pierce Butler died on November 16, 1939. FDR appointed loyalists Hugo LaFayette Black (ardent New Deal Senator who voted for all twenty-four New Deal programs, sponsor of the Black-Connery Bill seeking establishment of a national minimum wage, and outspoken champion of the Judiciary Reorganization Bill), Stanley Forman Reed (FDR's loyal Solicitor General, who personally litigated the government's position in watershed New Deal cases like *Schechter Poultry Corp. v. United States*, *United States v. Butler*, *West Coast Hotel Co. v. Parrish*, and others), and William Francis (Frank) Murphy (FDR's Attorney General, and former pro-labor governor of Michigan), respectively, in their stead—further accelerating the domino effect.

In all, FDR eventually appointed eight of the Court's nine Justices. So, yeah—his interest in assembling a servile and dependent Supreme Court was fully realized.

federal power which could be construed very broadly. Some tiny tidbit of Constitution which might be cited in support of federal powers that were never really granted. Some constitutional phrase which might provide Incrementalist jurists—and especially the newly-tamed Supreme Court!—with cover.

Before Justice Robert's Switch in Time the Supreme Court could find none. The Court was, after all, independent—and as such, it limited congressional and presidential authority to those bounds set in the Constitution.

After the Switch in Time, however, the Supreme Court became remarkably creative in "finding" constitutional pretexts for extending federal power.

One hook the Supreme Court settled upon was the Commerce Clause. True, the Commerce Clause was intended merely as a limited superintendence over unfair commercial practices between States. It had been understood as such from the beginning—for one hundred fifty years! But in the flexible soil of the Switch in Time Court that tiny, torpid little phrase would germinate overnight. It would climb over constitutional ramparts. It would scale fences between production, pricing, consumption, and labor relations. Its tendrils would lengthen to encompass noncommercial *intrastate* and even *intrafarm* activities. It would mature year by year into a beanstalk of unimaginable proportions: A towering and transcendent power by which Washington could dictate a centrally-planned economy.

And up that gigantic stalk the New (Socialist) Deal would clamber!

It didn't take long.

Less than four years after the Switch in Time, the Supreme Court upheld the New (Socialist) Deal's Fair Labor Standards Act of 1938.[40] In an abrupt about-face, the Supreme Court ruled that *production and manufacture itself*—in this case the production and manufacture of lumber—could be regulated under Commerce Clause authority.[41] In other words, the Court held that Congress' Commerce Clause power was *no longer limited to commerce* (i.e. trade, exchange, buying and selling) at all—instead, it extended also to *production and manufacture* of articles which might later be subjects of commerce.[42] Yes, yes! With Justice Roberts' timorous assistance, the Switch in Time Court now "interpreted" the Commerce Clause as giving Congress power to *direct the production and manufacture of all goods*. (Whatever happened to *stare decisis?*)

And the wee little Commerce Clause grew!

After "interpreting" the Commerce Clause as no longer limited to commerce it was easy to go further. So the Switch in Time Court now upheld mandatory, nationwide minimum wage, maximum hours, and other labor standards of the sort it had only recently stricken as unconstitutional extensions of Commerce Clause authority.[43] For the first time ever the Court "reinterpreted" the Commerce Clause as a grant of regulatory power over *labor relations*—i.e., relations between employer and employee. In so doing the Court was forced to overrule fresh precedent.[44] (Whatever happened to *stare decisis?*)

And the Commerce Clause grew larger still!

But the constitutional magic show was not over. The Switch in Time Court went right on and upheld the Agriculture Marketing Agreement Act of 1937, which authorized the Secretary of Agriculture to set minimum prices for milk.[45] In yet another u-turn the Court now "interpreted" the Commerce Clause as no longer limited to commerce *among the several States* (i.e., *interstate* commerce). Instead, the Court ruled that the Commerce Clause extended congressional oversight to *intrastate* activities which might possibly *affect* interstate commerce.[46] Yes, the Court came right out and said it: "*The power of Congress over interstate commerce is not confined to the regulation of commerce among the states* [!!!]."[47] So long as Congress could compose some lame excuse about how *intra*state production, or *intra*state manufacture, or *intra*state pricing, or *intra*state labor relations *affected inter*state commerce, it could now regulate those *intra*state activities, too. Even though the Constitution grants no such powers to Congress. (Whatever happened to *stare decisis?*)

And now the little Commerce Clause had grown enormous!

In 1942—barely five years after the Switch in Time—citizens witnessed the climax to Incrementalists' Commerce Clause trick. In *Wickard v. Filburn*, the Switch in Time Court clarified how completely it had inverted the Commerce Clause when it upheld the Agricultural Adjustment Act's quota on agricultural *production and consumption.*[48]

It went like this:

Family farmer Roscoe Filburn grew wheat on his own land. He cultivated it for use on his own farm. Farmer Filburn's wheat was never sold, but used instead to feed himself, his chickens, and a few dairy cattle.

But the federal government had other ideas for Mr. Filburn's farm. The federal government wanted to raise wheat prices, you see. The government knew enough economics to grasp that wheat prices could be raised by decreasing wheat supply. So the federal government set a quota for the maximum amount of wheat that could be grown nationwide. They implemented this plan under the New Deal's Agricultural Adjustment Act of 1938 which, as amended, purported to give the Secretary of Agriculture power to set a national wheat quota. The nationwide wheat quota was thereafter apportioned to States, which apportioned the quota to counties, and finally *to individual farms.* The federal government proudly alleged power to do all this under the Commerce Clause.

Farmer Filburn was served a homestead wheat quota. But he did not follow it. The government's fine for planting "excess wheat" seemed fair enough. So Filburn planted more wheat than the federal government wanted him to, and planned to pay the fine. He would eat the wheat himself, and feed it to his chickens and dairy cattle, as he had always done. There would be no buying, selling, or trade of "excess wheat." The chickens were not paying Filburn for his wheat, after all—so this was not *commerce!* And Filburn's chickens were not living across State lines—so there was no sense in which Filburn's wheat production could be considered *interstate*, either.

But the federal government knew better: it was not farmer Filburn's place to decide how much of what crops he should plant, harvest, and consume on his own property. So the federal government *increased the fine for "excess wheat" by 260% after Filburn planted his wheat but before he could harvest it* (!).[xvi] When Filburn planted his "excess wheat," the fine looked quite reasonable; but now it was time to harvest, the government levied a farm-ruining sum. (Thereby yielding a succulent 260% windfall for the federal government. The bait-and-switch never fails to catch harmless, honest simpletons!)

Besides, as the Switch in Time Court itself pointed out, keeping wheat prices high was a *national emergency*—and therefore must be subject to "control by the central government."[49] That means family farms, too.

The Court was well aware that by raising and consuming a few acres of wheat on his own farm, Farmer Filburn's "own contribution to the demand for wheat may be trivial by itself."[50] But by this point the Court had become quite adept at stretching the Commerce Clause into fantastical shapes and knotting its simple words into a skein no one could unravel. So without batting an eye, the Court ruled that whether or not Filburn ever sold that "excess wheat," the few acres he raised for himself would be wheat Filburn need not buy on the interstate open market—which, if Filburn *had* bought on the open market, would have had an infinitesimally small yet positive effect on the interstate price of wheat.[xvii] And if an entire nation of family farmers raised "excess wheat" for home consumption, that would be wheat they needn't buy on the interstate market, either—which, if they *had* bought in the interstate market, would have had, *in the aggregate*, a measurable positive effect on interstate wheat prices.[xviii] So in this hypothetical sense, at least, Filburn's production and consumption of wheat on his own farm without sale or barter *really was commerce!* And in this hypothetical sense grain that was planted, harvested, and consumed on a single farm was also *interstate* commerce! In which case telling Filburn how much wheat he could

---

[xvi] From 15¢ per bushel to 49¢ per bushel! *Wickard v. Filburn*, 317 U.S. 111, 131-32 (1942).

[xvii] "But if we assume that [Filburn's wheat] is never marketed, it supplies a need of the man who grew it which would otherwise be reflected by purchases in the open market. Home-grown wheat in this sense competes with wheat in commerce." *Wickard v. Filburn*, 317 U.S. at 128 (1942).

[xviii] "That appellee's own contribution to the demand for wheat may be trivial by itself is not enough to remove him from the scope of federal regulation *where, as here, his contribution, taken together with that of many others similarly situated, is far from trivial.*" *Wickard v. Filburn*, 317 U.S. at 127-28 (1942) (emphasis added).

produce and consume intrafarm was a legitimate exercise of the Commerce Clause. Ergo, the New (Socialist) Deal's Agricultural Adjustment Act of 1938 was indeed constitutional.

Quod erat demonstrandum!

And with that dash of rhetorical magic, the tiny Commerce Clause became omnipotent. It had begun its constitutional life as a dainty and dormant seed, yes; but under the Switch in Time Court's supervision it had grown into a colossal beanstalk—one which entwined every facet of material production, entangled private citizens' noncommercial consumption, choked American private property, and wrapped around the minutiae of social relations. One which Incrementalists could climb to heaven!

The Power of "No"

Sometimes the hand *is* quicker than the eye!

In case you missed the Supreme Court's sleight of hand, it now "interpreted" the Commerce Clause as granting Congress the power to tell you how much of which crops to raise in your own garden, for your own noncommercial, personal use. In combination the Court's decisions meant not only commerce could be regulated, but also manufacturing, and distribution, and consumption, and pricing, and labor relations. Federal power under the Commerce Clause was no longer limited to commerce at all.[51] And congressional power was no longer limited to the interstate level, but in every case extended to the intrastate level! And even the intra-homestead level. The Commerce Clause now reached down and applied itself directly against the individual.

With such an expansive new ambit for the Commerce Clause there was practically nothing Congress could be prohibited from regulating. The federal government was transformed from a limited, constitutional one into a plenipotentiary parliament.

And so, *without ever amending the Constitution*, Incrementalists managed to forever change its meaning. (At least within government and legal circles.) *Without ever consulting citizens or their States*, Incrementalists unilaterally gifted themselves the power they wished to possess. This is the extraordinary power of Incrementalism: It transforms a seven-word phrase from a limited federal power to regulate *commerce, between the States*, into an unlimited federal power to regulate *all economic activity*. Just like magic.

And while Justice Roberts' switch was as abrupt as a lightning-strike,[52] the constitutional revolution it supplied would be distinctly Incremental. Like other Incrementalist gains, the Commerce Clause revolution was accomplished one ruling at a time—here a little and there a little. Over months and years. No single Supreme Court decision made such a startling departure as to rouse Middle America. Each "interpretation" of the Commerce Clause built smoothly upon the last. And when Incrementalists were done, the adorable little Commerce Clause had matured into a federal leviathan capable of swallowing citizens and sovereign States alike.

Over the past seventy years the Incrementalist Commerce Clause has been used to justify most federal lawmaking. This is no exaggeration. And while we cannot explore all the thousands of federal laws it has spawned in this book, we can mention a couple:

For example, the now gargantuan Commerce Clause is said to allow the federal government to prevent Californians from growing, harvesting, and using their own cannabis solely for medicinal purposes under physician supervision, and pursuant to valid California State law.[53] No matter that Angel Raich's cannabis is never bought or sold, but merely grown and consumed on the premises. (I.e., there is no *commerce* here.) No matter that Raich's six cannabis plants, destroyed immediately by the DEA, have no demonstrable effect on the (undoubtedly illegal) interstate cannabis market; and no matter that Raich's cannabis never crosses State lines. (I.e., there is no *interstate* component here.) No matter that California State law permits cannabis to be used by terminally and chronically ill patients. No matter Raich's physician testifies that "forgoing cannabis treatments would certainly cause Raich excruciating pain and could very well prove fatal."[54] No matter! The federal government knows best. (And no surprise the Supreme Court cited *Wickard v. Filburn* twenty times in this case, as the "leading authority" on the Incrementalist Commerce Clause . . . .[55])

It is also under pretense of regulating "commerce among the several States" that Congress prevents citizens from building on their own land due to the alleged presence of unorthodox cave bugs.[xix] No matter that these cave bugs lack commercial value and are never bought or sold. (I.e., there is no cave bug *commerce.*) And no matter that these cave bugs are unique to Texas. (I.e., there can be no *among the several States* component to protected cave bugs that are never transported across State lines.) No matter. Today, if an entomologist on the federal payroll claims that your property harbors peculiar cave bugs, you can forget about building so much as a shed there. While the *actual* Commerce Clause does not allow the federal government such coercive power, the *Incrementalist* Commerce Clause does.[xx]

[xix] Well, properly speaking not "bugs," but a combination of small arachnids and insects: namely the Tooth Cave pseudoscorpion, the Tooth Cave spider, the Tooth Cave ground beetle, the Kretschmarr Cave mold beetle, the Bee Creek Cave harvestman (i.e., daddy long legs), and the Bone Cave harvestman (another breed of daddy long legs). Brief for the Respondents in Opposition as Amicus Curiae, 14, *GDF Realty Investments, Ltd. v. Norton*, 125 S. Ct. 2898, (2005).

[xx] The Supreme Court has no desire to soil its robes in cases with facts like these, where Commerce Clause abuse would come into such clear focus. Cases of this sort present the Court with a Hobson's choice: (1) Recognize Congress' power to enforce the Endangered Species Act under the guise of the Commerce Clause, in which case the unlimited scope of the Incrementalist Commerce Clause is exposed for all to see; or (2) Invalidate many provisions of

Cast your mind back and you may remember that Book I concluded with an unresolved conundrum: The Constitution outlaws monolithic impositions on liberty; the vast majority of citizens oppose them; yet the federal government nevertheless demands I use a 1.6 gallon-per-flush toilet.[xxi]

Only now are we prepared to answer the question: *How was a federal toilet-power added to the Constitution without the States' and their citizens' consent?* The answer is simply this:

Incrementally.

One baby-step at a time.

It requires only a single Justice Roberts.

Yes, it is under the pretense of regulating commerce among the several States that Congress purports to make it illegal to buy or sell a toilet using more than 1.6 gallons-per-flush.[56] And it doesn't matter if you manufacture a 1.6 *plus* gallons-per-flush toilet at home, and install it for use only within your own home, and never sell it. Congress rules you cannot do it. As with Filburn's wheat, and Raich's cannabis, and Texan cave bugs, so with private toilets: The Incrementalist Commerce Clause no longer regulates interstate commerce—it regulates all things!

So long as we are discussing toilets, it is only natural to point out that under the newly monstrous Commerce Clause there is no reason the federal government cannot also tell you how to wipe your butt.

This is no joke. All Congress need do is declare it will regulate paper products—including toilet paper—under the Incrementalist Commerce Clause. To justify the law Congress could note that it is concerned with the threat deforestation poses to anthropogenic global warming; or to endangered species of one sort or another; or it may settle upon any other of a host of pretexts. Congress will declare that the number of squares of toilet paper you use after each dump has an immeasurably small (yet hypothetically conceivable!) effect on the interstate toilet paper trade. Even if you plant the trees on your own property, chop the lumber, make the slurry, process the pulp, drain it over screens, and dry it into paper at home—for use exclusively within the home. The federal government will argue that your individual, home manufacture of toilet paper products still impacts deforestation, even if only in a "trivial" way. And in the aggregate, multiple households manufacturing their own toilet paper products would have an appreciable effect on interstate toilet paper commerce. Under *Wickard v. Filburn* the

---

the Endangered Species Act. So the Supreme Court quietly refused to hear the cave bug dispute, thereby making lower courts' holding—that Congress *did* have power under the Commerce Clause to prevent an owner from building on his own land due to the alleged presence of intrastate cave bugs lacking commercial value—into irrefutable constitutional law. *GDF Realty Investments, Ltd. v. Norton*, 326 F.3d 622 (5th Cir. 2003), *en banc hearing denied*, 362 F.3d 286 (5th Cir. 2004), *cert. denied*, 125 S. Ct. 2898 (2005).

[xxi] *See* TEA WITH SOCIALISTS, Book I (The Hive Mentality), chap. 10 *Our Predecessors Paranoia.*

Supreme Court will be forced to agree. Yes, under the Incrementalist Commerce Clause Congress can establish a national toilet paper quota tomorrow. *Congress can appoint the maximum number of toilet paper squares you use to clean up, on every occasion that nature calls.*

This is not rhetorical exaggeration. It is simply a natural consequence of the Incrementalist Commerce Clause.

What is the Commerce Clause? It is no longer a limited power to regulate prejudicial interstate commerce. Through reinterpretation after reinterpretation by the Supreme Court, the Commerce Clause has been transformed into something quite different. It has become today a universal Power of "No": A federal authority to tell States and individuals alike, "No—you cannot; you must not!" You cannot raise wheat for home consumption. You cannot self-medicate. You cannot build on your own property. You cannot use a 2.0 gallon/flush toilet.

The Supreme Court has spoken. The ruling is made final. The actual meaning of the Commerce Clause no longer matters; that the Commerce Clause has never actually been amended no longer has significance; and what the rest of the Constitution says is of no consequence, either. All that matters today is the Power of "No." To access this stupendous power, all the federal government need do is allege that a given action *may conceivably affect* commerce—in some cockamamie hypothetical scenario—and it is done. Which means for practical purposes, the federal Power of "No" can be (and is) applied to any action at all.

This is Incrementalist jurisprudence.

* * *

The aforementioned Federal laws may include some of which you are in favor. Perhaps you dislike cannabis, even for medicinal use by the terminally ill in States with laws allowing it. Perhaps you prefer cave bugs to buildings, whether or not you are convinced of their genetic novelty. Perhaps you fancy 1.6 gallon toilets for everyone, though it causes us to flush our toilets twice or more often. (For my own part, I despise cannabis—but of course, I am not terminally ill. And as an amateur entomologist I quite enjoy unorthodox cave bugs—but then again, I do not own real estate.)

But the point is not whether you agree with a particular law made and enforced by the federal government. The point is not even whether such subjects are better regulated by the States or by the Feds. The point is simply this: *Who decides how much power the federal government has?*

Do *We, the People* decide how much power government has?

Or does the *federal government* decide how much power government has?

If it is we who decide how much power government has, then we enjoy the benefits of *representative government.* In such a case government is based on the will of the People. Citizens are in charge, and government is merely a political servant which carries their wishes into effect.

But if it is the federal government who decides how much power government has, then we live *without law.* We live instead under the arbitrary rule of men. We live under a constitutional tyranny—a government of despots who do as they please without limit, yet shielded by constitutional cover.

Our Predecessors bequeathed to us a representative constitutional Republic in which We, the People, decide how much power the federal government possesses. Should we ever consent to limitless federal power under the Commerce Clause, we could amend the Constitution to that effect. We could amend it to give Congress a *universal Power of "No".* We might amend it to give Congress power to regulate *any and all activities which might conceivably have some economic effect.* Or, if we were a bit more jealous of our liberty, we might amend the Constitution to allow Congress to regulate *drugs, bugs, and toilets.*

But if we haven't amended the Constitution to grant Congress powers to regulate drugs, cave bugs, and toilets, then the federal government either (a) is lying that it possesses such powers, or (b) has usurped those powers from citizens when no one was looking. If we haven't amended—if supermajorities in Congress didn't propose, and 38 State legislatures didn't adopt an amendment granting such powers to Congress—then the federal government is no longer a government of, by, and for the People.

It has become a government of, by, and for the Government.

Further Notes to Chapter 9

[1] Perhaps the Judiciary inspired Incrementalists' invention of the Fourth Head? So far as I am aware, we can only guess.
[2] THE FEDERALIST No. 78, at 501 (Hamilton) (Robert Scigliano ed., Modern Library 2001) (1787).
[3] THE FEDERALIST No. 78, at 497 (Hamilton) (Robert Scigliano ed., Modern Library 2001) (1787) (emphasis added).
[4] At least, this was the intention of the Constitution (U.S. CONST. art. V) and the Founders (THE FEDERALIST No. 78, at 501 (Hamilton) (Robert Scigliano ed., Modern Library 2001) (1787)).
[5] Or, alternatively, a constitutional convention called by two thirds of the State legislatures may propose an amendment (U.S. CONST. art. V)—but this method has never yet been employed.
[6] THE FEDERALIST No. 42, at 269 (Madison); *see also* No. 41, at 256-57 (Robert Scigliano ed., Modern Library 2001) (1787).
[7] THE FEDERALIST No. 42, at 270 (Madison) (Robert Scigliano ed., Modern Library 2001) (1787).
[8] THE FEDERALIST No. 42, at 270 (Madison) (Robert Scigliano ed., Modern Library 2001) (1787).
[9] THE FEDERALIST No. 42, at 270 (Madison) (Robert Scigliano ed., Modern Library 2001) (1787) (emphasis added).
[10] *See, e.g., United States v. E. C. Knight Co.*, 156 U.S. 1 (1895) (ruling that *manufacturing*—in this case refining sugar—is necessarily a local activity, and therefore not subject to congressional regulation of *interstate commerce*); *Kidd v. Pearson*, 128 U.S. 1 (1888) (reaffirming the distinction between *manufacturing*, over which Congress has no authority, and *commerce*, over which Congress may have authority).
[11] As we have noted previously, *FDR's New Deal was socialism in America.* This was recognized by socialists at the time:

"The New Deal is plainly an attempt to achieve a working socialism and avert a social collapse in America; it is extraordinarily parallel to the successive 'policies' and 'Plans' of the Russian experiment. Americans shirk the word 'socialism', but what else can one call it? . . . There is a strong opposition on the part of great interests in America to the President [F. D. Roosevelt], who has made himself the spear-head of the collectivizing drive; they want to put the brake now on his progressive socialisation [sic] of the nation, and quite possibly, at the cost of increasing social friction, they may slow down the drift to socialism very considerably.") H. G. WELLS, THE NEW WORLD ORDER 61-62; 70 (The Mayflower Press, Plymouth England 1940).

And it is recognized by socialists today:

"[Y]ears of communist-led unemployed council campaigns and union activism put huge grassroots pressure on the New Deal government to enact far-reaching labor and social legislation. . . . Communists stood in the forefront of the working-class struggle for much of this [New Deal] legislation, from labor law reform to Social Security and assistance for the unemployed. . . . [W]ithout the CPUSA, the mass organizations it created and led, the campaigns it initiated, and its defeats and victories, these [New Deal] achievements would not have been possible." Norman Markowitz, *Fighting for Change: The Great Depression, the New Deal and the CPUSA*, POLITICAL AFFAIRS (Sept. 2, 2009).

"The Left's involvement in Popular Front activities both led and complimented the rise of the Americanism [LOL!] which accompanied the Roosevelt Administration's gains . . . . An indication of the impact of the Popular Front on radicals and on the Communist Party's support of President Roosevelt was the fact that Charles Seeger, by 1936, was already an employee of the federal government, director of the Music Unit section of the Resettlement Administration, aiding migrating Southerners as they moved up and out of the Dustbowl." John Pietaro, *Out of the Red Megaphone: The Modernist Protest Music of a Lost Age*, POLITICAL AFFAIRS (Dec. 14, 2010).

See also Marilyn Bechtel, *Jobs, Labor and WPA's Living Legacy*, PEOPLE'S WORLD (July 29, 2010); People's World Editorial Board, *New Deal 2.0*, PEOPLE'S WORLD (Dec. 11, 2009); John Wojcik, *Economic Meltdown: We Need a New, Green New Deal!*, PEOPLE'S WORLD (July 23, 2008); People's World Editorial Board, *Needed: a new New Deal*, PEOPLE'S WORLD (Mar. 21, 2008); Simon Rosenberg and Peter Leyden, *The 50-Year Strategy—Beyond '08: Can Progressives Play for Keeps?*, MOTHER JONES 67 (Nov., Dec. 2007).

New Deal socialism remains, however, a sensitive subject where Incrementalist public relations are concerned. To publicly speak of FDR's New Deal as socialist would frustrate the closeted purposes of Incrementalism! And so this fact remains painfully taboo. . . .

[12] *R.R. Retirement Bd. v. Alton R.R. Co.*, 295 U.S. 330 (1935).

[13] *R.R. Retirement Bd.*, 295 U.S. at 368 (1935).

[14] *R.R. Retirement Bd.*, 295 U.S. at 368 (1935) (emphasis added).

[15] *A.L.A. Schechter Poultry Corp. v. United States*, 295 U.S. 495 (1935).

[16] *A.L.A. Schechter Poultry Corp.*, 295 U.S. at 548-49 (1935).

[17] *A.L.A. Schechter Poultry Corp.*, 295 U.S. at 549-50 (1935).

[18] *A.L.A. Schechter Poultry Corp.*, 295 U.S. at 549-50 (1935).

[19] *Carter v. Carter Coal Co.*, 298 U.S. 238 (1936).

[20] *Carter Coal Co.*, 298 U.S. at 302-03 (1936) (quoting *Oliver Iron Co. v. Lord*, 262 U.S. 172, 178 (1922); citing *Chassaniol v. Greenwood*, 291 U.S. 584, 587 (1934)).

[21] "'Mining is not interstate commerce, but, like manufacturing, is a local business subject to local regulation and taxation.' . . . Production is not commerce; but a step in preparation for commerce." *Carter Coal Co.*, 298 U.S. at 302-03 (1936) (quoting *Oliver Iron Co. v. Lord*, 262 U.S. 172, 178 (1922); citing *Chassaniol v. Greenwood*, 291 U.S. 584, 587 (1934)). "A consideration of the foregoing, and of many cases which might be added to those already cited, renders inescapable the conclusion that the effect of the labor provisions of the act, including those in respect of minimum wages, wage agreements, collective bargaining, and the Labor Board and its powers, primarily falls upon production and not upon commerce; and confirms the further resulting conclusion that production is a purely local activity. It follows that none of these essential antecedents of production constitutes a transaction in or forms any part of interstate commerce." *Carter Coal Co.*, 298 U.S. at 304 (1936) (citing *Schechter Corp. v. United States*, 295 U.S. 495, 542 (1935)).

[22] *United States v. Butler*, 297 U.S. 1 (1936).

[23] *Butler*, 297 U.S. 1 (1936).

[24] *Butler*, 297 U.S. at 68 (1936) (emphasis added).

[25] The Judicial Procedures Reform Bill of 1937 proposed that FDR appoint up to a maximum of six additional Justices. Six (additional Justices) plus nine (original Justices) is fifteen. *See, e.g.*, Franklin Delano Roosevelt, *Fireside Chat Address No. 9 Proposing Reorganization of the Federal Judiciary* (March 9, 1937).

[26] "What is my proposal? It is simply this: Whenever a judge or justice of any federal court has reached the age of seventy, and does not avail himself of the opportunity to retire on a pension, a new member should be appointed by the President then in office, with the approval, as required by the Constitution, of the Senate of the United States." Franklin Delano Roosevelt, *Fireside Chat Address No. 9 Proposing Reorganization of the Federal Judiciary* (March 9, 1937).

[27] Franklin Delano Roosevelt, *Fireside Chat Address No. 9 Proposing Reorganization of the Federal Judiciary* (March 9, 1937).

[28] "We also became convinced that the only way to avoid a repetition of those dark days was to have a government with power to prevent and to cure the abuses and the inequalities which had thrown that system out of joint." Franklin Delano Roosevelt, *Fireside Chat Address No. 9 Proposing Reorganization of the Federal Judiciary* (March 9, 1937).

[29] "We then began a program of remedying those abuses and inequalities, to give balance and stability to our economic system, to make it bombproof against the causes of 1929. Today we are only partway through that program." Franklin Delano Roosevelt, *Fireside Chat Address No. 9 Proposing Reorganization of the Federal Judiciary* (March 9, 1937).

[30] Franklin Delano Roosevelt, *Fireside Chat Address No. 9 Proposing Reorganization of the Federal Judiciary* (March 9, 1937).

[31] FDR used the analogy of a team of horses, with the Legislature and the Executive united in pulling for New Deal policies which would save the nation, and the Supreme Court pulling in another direction. Franklin Delano Roosevelt, *Fireside Chat Address No. 9 Proposing Reorganization of the Federal Judiciary* (March 9, 1937).
[32] Franklin Delano Roosevelt, *Fireside Chat Address No. 9 Proposing Reorganization of the Federal Judiciary* (March 9, 1937).
[33] "I believe that it would take months or years to get substantial agreement upon the type and language of an amendment. It would take months and years thereafter to get a two-thirds majority in favor of that amendment in both houses of the Congress. Then would come the long course of ratification—by three-quarters of all the States. . . . And remember that thirteen States which contain only five percent of the voting population can block ratification even though the thirty-five states with ninety-five percent of the population are in favor of it." Franklin Delano Roosevelt, *Fireside Chat Address No. 9 Proposing Reorganization of the Federal Judiciary* (March 9, 1937).
[34] Franklin Delano Roosevelt, *Fireside Chat Address No. 9 Proposing Reorganization of the Federal Judiciary* (March 9, 1937).
[35] Franklin Delano Roosevelt, *Fireside Chat Address No. 9 Proposing Reorganization of the Federal Judiciary* (March 9, 1937).
[36] Franklin Delano Roosevelt, *Fireside Chat Address No. 9 Proposing Reorganization of the Federal Judiciary* (March 9, 1937) (emphasis added). Moreover, "This plan of mine is no attack on the Court; it seeks to restore the Court to its rightful and historic place in our system of Constitutional government, and to have it resume its high task of building anew, on the Constitution, a system of living law." *Ibid.*
[37] Franklin Delano Roosevelt, *Fireside Chat Address No. 9 Proposing Reorganization of the Federal Judiciary* (March 9, 1937) (emphasis added).
[38] THE FEDERALIST No. 78, at 501 (Hamilton) (Robert Scigliano ed., Modern Library 2001) (1787) ("Until the people have, by some solemn and authoritative act, annulled or changed the established form, it is binding upon themselves collectively, as well as individually; and no presumption, or even knowledge, of their sentiments, can warrant their representatives in a departure from it, prior to such an act. *But it is easy to see, that it would require an uncommon portion of fortitude in the judges to do their duty as faithful guardians of the Constitution, where legislative invasions of it had been instigated by the major voice of the community.*") (emphasis added).
[39] Socialists were very pleased to see that with Justice Roberts' help, *West Coast Hotel* overturned the hated *Adkins v. Children's Hospital*, 261 U.S. 525 (1923) precedent (which had struck down federal minimum wage laws for women as unconstitutional under the due process clause of the Fifth Amendment).
[40] *United States v. Darby*, 312 U.S. 100 (1941).
[41] More precisely, the Court ruled that *production and manufacture itself* could be regulated by Congress under the Commerce Clause *so long as the goods produced were to be sold in interstate commerce. United States v. Darby*, 312 U.S. 100 (1941).
[42] "While manufacture is not of itself interstate commerce, the [subsequent] shipment of manufactured goods interstate is such commerce and the prohibition of such shipment by Congress is indubitably a regulation of the commerce. . . . The obvious purpose of the Act was not only to prevent the interstate transportation of the proscribed product, but to stop the initial step toward transportation, production with the purpose of so transporting it." *Darby*, 312 U.S. at 113; 117 (1941).
[43] Specifically, the Court had recently stricken national child labor legislation as an unconstitutional extension of the Commerce Clause power in *Hammer v. Dagenhart*, 247 U.S. 251 (1918).
[44] "The conclusion is inescapable that *Hammer v. Dagenhart*, 247 U.S. 251 (1918) . . . has long since been exhausted. It should be and now is overruled." *Darby*, 312 U.S. at 116-17 (1941).
[45] *United States v. Wrightwood Dairy Co.*, 315 U.S. 110 (1941).
[46] "Congress plainly has power to regulate the price of milk distributed through the medium of interstate commerce . . . and it possesses every power needed to make that regulation effective. *The commerce power is not confined in its exercise to the regulation of commerce among the states.* It extends to those activities intrastate which so affect interstate commerce, or the exertion of the power of

Congress over it, as to make regulation of them appropriate means to the attainment of a legitimate end, the effective execution of the granted power to regulate interstate commerce. . . . [N]o form of state activity can constitutionally thwart the regulatory power granted by the commerce clause to Congress. Hence the reach of that power extends to those intrastate activities which in a substantial way interfere with or obstruct the exercise of the granted power." *United States v. Wrightwood Dairy Co.*, 315 U.S. 110, 118-19 (1941) (emphasis added).
[47] *Darby*, 312 U.S. at 118 (1941) (emphasis added) ("There remains the question whether such restriction on the production of goods for commerce is a permissible exercise of the commerce power. *The power of Congress over interstate commerce is not confined to the regulation of commerce among the states.* It extends to those activities intrastate which so affect interstate commerce or the exercise of the power of Congress over it as to make regulation of them appropriate means to the attainment of a legitimate end, the exercise of the granted power of Congress to regulate interstate commerce.") (emphasis added). It doesn't take a legal genius to identify the circular fallacy embodied by that last sentence—why, even a first year law student could identify it.
[48] *Wickard v. Filburn*, 317 U.S. 111 (1942).
[49] *See Wickard v. Filburn*, 317 U.S. at 125-26 (1942). The New (Socialist) Deal enforced not only a national quota on *marketable* wheat, but extended that quota to wheat fed to poultry or livestock. *Wickard v. Filburn*, 317 U.S. at 118-19 (1942).
[50] *Wickard v. Filburn*, 317 U.S. at 127 (1942).
[51] "Whether the subject of the regulation in question was 'production,' 'consumption,' or 'marketing' is, therefore, not material for purposes of deciding the question of federal power before us. . . . But even if appellee's activity be local and though it may not be regarded as commerce, it may still, whatever its nature, be reached by Congress if it exerts a substantial economic effect on interstate commerce . . . ." *Wickard v. Filburn*, 317 U.S. at 124 (1942).
[52] Socialists always pretend that Justice Roberts wasn't so threatened by FDR's court packing scheme; that Justice Roberts' switch does not match up temporally with FDR's fireside chat radio address; that Justice Roberts had his own, private reason—a profound, personal, philosophical epiphany—that caused him to turn. As proof of this, they point to a trumped-up and self-serving excuse for the Switch in Time, a memorandum which, if it was authored by Roberts at all (as socialists claim), was drafted many years after the fact, published for the first time eighteen years after the Switch in Time, and even then *only after Roberts' death.*[52] Certainly the "memorandum" appears contrived and ambiguous. Certainly it was favorable to FDR and Felix Frankfurter's legacies. And it sure was convenient that it appeared only after the death of its "author," who could never dispute its claims! Probably this "memorandum" was not written by Roberts at all, but rather by Justice Felix Frankfurter, who submitted it for publication by the University of Pennsylvania Law Review. (*See, e.g.*, Michael Ariens, *A Thrice-Told Tale, or Felix the Cat*, 107 HARV. L. REV. 620, 645-49 (1994).)

Don't be fooled: Unlike most every Justice who has ever served on the Supreme Court, *Justice Roberts burned all his judicial manuscripts shortly after leaving the Court*—precisely because he didn't want future generations examining when, or how, or why he switched. So it would be truly miraculous if, after burning every single judicial manuscript in his possession, a single judicial manuscript—the very one that bails out FDR and other Incrementalist Justices!—should suddenly turn up in the hands of Incrementalist Justice Felix Frankfurter after Justice Robert's death.

Finally, however Justice Roberts started, he definitely ended an Incrementalist. He spend his retirement from the Court doing things like convening a group of international socialists who penned the Dublin Declaration—an attempt to turn the United Nations into a *world parliament*!
[53] *Gonzales v. Raich*, 545 U.S. 1 (2005).
[54] *Raich*, 545 U.S. at 7 (2005).
[55] *Raich*, 545 U.S. 1 (2005).
[56] *See* Energy Policy Act of 1992 (H.R. 776), § 123 `(k) *et. seq.*

10

Disappearing Act

The taxing power of the federal government, my dear; the taxing power is sufficient for everything you want and need.

—Harlan Fiske Stone[i]

"I don't know what you mean by 'glory,'" Alice said.

Humpty Dumpty smiled contemptuously. "Of course you don't—till I tell you. I meant 'there's a nice knock-down argument for you!'"

"But 'glory' doesn't mean 'a nice knock-down argument,'" Alice objected.

"When *I* use a word," Humpty Dumpty said, in rather a scornful tone, "it means just what I choose it to mean—neither more nor less."

"The question is," said Alice, "whether you *can* make words mean so many different things."

"The question is," said Humpty Dumpty, "which is to be master——that's all."

—Lewis Carroll[ii]

THE REINTERPRETED COMMERCE CLAUSE was an Incrementalist triumph!

It worked particularly well for expanding federal power over individuals and States in situations where the Constitution was silent—like gardening, drugs, cave bugs, and toilets. (As also minimum wages, maximum hours, and minimum and maximum prices.) By "reinterpreting" the Commerce Clause as

---

[i] Supreme Court Justice Harlan Fiske Stone, at a dinner party, offering an unconstitutional advisory opinion (U.S. CONST. art. III § 2) to FDR's Secretary of Labor Frances Perkins—*suggesting how New Deal programs like Social Security could be pushed through the Supreme Court* (1934). *See, e.g.*, Jonathan Alter, *The 1934 Dinner Party That May Have Helped Save Obamacare*, THE DAILY BEAST (July 1, 2012).

[ii] LEWIS CARROLL, ALICE'S ADVENTURES IN WONDERLAND *AND* THROUGH THE LOOKING-GLASS AND WHAT ALICE FOUND THERE 186 (Hugh Haughton ed., Penguin Classics 1998) (1872) (this particular passage is taken from *Through the Looking-Glass*).

a general power to regulate Incrementalists obtained near absolute power to tell States and individuals alike, "No, you can't!"—you cannot do, you will not decide—whatever the rest of the Constitution might say. And to invoke the Power of "No," all Incrementalists had to do was allege that State or individual action *might possibly affect* interstate commerce. (At least in the hypothetical sense!)

But what about a complimentary power to tell States and individuals, "*Yes, you must!*"—you must affirmatively act, you must perform, you must do—just as federal policy dictates? And what about situations in which the Constitution *specifically forbade* the federal government from exercising control? What about instances in which the Constitution reserved power exclusively to the States?

In order to implement its monolithic program of "moral" government, socialism needed to extend federal domination over these areas as well. Socialism would do so by an ingenious and roundabout approach. Through a quiet, juridical demolition of constitutional limitations on federal taxation, it would devise a new sort of tax altogether: It would tax States and citizens for what they *did not do.* It would tax citizens for what they *did not buy.* It would tax States and citizens alike into compliance with unconstitutional federal wishes.

And it would culminate in Obamacare.

Another Nascent Clause

In their efforts to develop a complimentary Power of "Yes," Incrementalists were forced to find yet another constitutional phrase on which to hang their plans for federal mastery. In the end they settled on the so-called Tax and Spend Clause: A congressional power to "collect Taxes, Duties, Imposts and Excises, to pay the Debts and provide for the common Defense and general Welfare of the United States."[iii]

Now, the Tax and Spend Clause never granted Congress power to tax and spend however it pleased. Indeed, taxing in general was viewed with great suspicion by our Predecessors. As Chief Justice John Marshall famously opined, "[T]he power to tax involves the power to destroy."[1] For this reason the Tax and Spend Clause was carefully circumscribed.

First, the Tax and Spend Clause was limited to taxing and spending *solely to fulfill other enumerated federal powers.*[2] One can see the problem immediately: If Congress held unlimited power to tax and spend, then Congress would use that power to control matters over which it was never granted authority. The entire design of a limited Constitution of enumerated powers would be frustrated, and all constitutional limitations on the federal

---

[iii] U.S. CONST. art. 1 § 8, cl. 1.

government would be rendered meaningless.[3] As the author of the Constitution, James Madison, explained:

> If Congress can do whatever in their discretion can be done by money, and will promote the General Welfare, the Government is no longer a limited one, possessing enumerated powers, but an indefinite one, subject to particular exceptions.[4]

Which is to say, if Congress can do whatever they want with money, then Congress has unlimited power. A Congress of unlimited power was not the intent of our Predecessors or the Constitution they drafted. Unlimited authority was what our Predecessors had toiled eight bloody years to cast off: the omnipotent English Parliament.

Second, the Tax and Spend Clause was limited to taxing and spending "for the *general* welfare."[iv] In other words, federal taxation and spending must assist States and citizens *generally*—it must not be for the benefit of a *particular* State or locale only.[5] The general welfare limitation was intended to prevent pork barrel projects like Congress' $398 million Bridge to Nowhere—a bridge which, if it had any use at all, could be useful *only to Alaskans*. The general welfare limitation thus created a level federal playing field for citizens and their States.

It is critical to remember that the "for the general welfare" portion of the Tax and Spend Clause is a *limitation* on federal power. Because it is a limitation on congressional power, it must be enforced by an authority external to Congress: the federal courts. Otherwise, Congress could assert that every law it makes is "in pursuit of the general welfare"—and the Tax and Spend Clause would again devolve into a general power to tax and spend for whatever purpose Congress desired. And all constitutional limitations on federal power would again become worthless. As Madison foresaw:

> If Congress can apply money indefinitely to the general welfare, and are the sole and supreme judges of the general welfare, they may . . . establish teachers in every State, county, and parish, and pay them out of the public treasury; they may take into their own hands the education of children, establishing in like manner schools throughout the union; they may assume the provision for the poor; they may undertake the regulation of all roads other than post roads; in short, every thing, from the highest object of State legislation, down to the most minute object of police, would be thrown under the power of Congress; for every object I have mentioned would admit the application of money, and might be called, if Congress pleased, provisions for the general welfare.[6]

Today, of course, Madison's prophecy has been fully realized. Congress undertakes to regulate all these things—and more—under the Tax and Spend Clause. (Because today, as we shall see, Congress *has* become the "supreme judge of general welfare."[7])

[iv] U.S. CONST. art. 1, § 8, cl. 1.

When socialists hear the word "welfare," they become aroused. Their nostrils flare; their eyes bulge; their hides quiver in anxious anticipation. Like stallions downwind from a mare. Because for socialists, "welfare" can only mean one thing: *government redistribution of private wealth!* On this basis socialists would have us believe that the Tax and Spend Clause, *when paired with the "for the general welfare" limitation*, becomes in combination an even more potent federal power: A power to redistribute private wealth and fund national welfare programs.

Socialists' reading of the Tax and Spend Clause is comically anachronistic. Our Predecessors never understood the word "welfare" to connote government programs for the redistribution of private wealth; they would have called such programs "public charity." The redistributionist connotation of the word "welfare" is quite recent. Besides, the Constitution was expected to *prevent* "an equal division of property."[8] And in any event, the General Welfare Clause was understood by our Predecessors as a *limitation* on Congress' power to tax and spend—not an augmentation of it.[9] Indeed, our Predecessors were careful to explain that the "for the general welfare" portion of the Tax and Spend Clause is *also* limited to taxing and spending to fulfill enumerated powers.[v]

The Tax and Spend Clause is limited in other ways as well, but we shall spare the layman from all the gory details. (The curious student may peruse this endnote. [10])

And what of the purpose of federal taxation? Well, that is plain enough to see. The primary object was, as the Tax and Spend Clause itself declares, "to pay the Debts and provide for the common Defense . . . of the United States."[vi] Our Predecessors intended that the vast majority of federal taxes would be spent on national defense. As Hamilton (the federal banker himself!) calculated, more than fourteen-fifteenths of federal taxes should be expected to go to defense.[11] The "debts" referred to by the Tax and Spend Clause also indicated debts incurred for national defense—namely, the costs of prosecuting the Revolutionary War.[12]

---

[v] If this were not sufficiently clear, Madison explained:

> Money cannot be applied to the General Welfare, otherwise than by an application of it to some *particular* measure conducive to the General Welfare. Whenever, therefore, money has been raised by the general Authority, and is to be applied to a particular measure, a question arises whether the particular measure be within the enumerated authorities vested in Congress. If it be, the money requisite for it may be applied to it; if it be not, no such application can be made.

James Madison, *Report of 1800*. *See, e.g.*, JAMES MADISON, THE PAPERS OF JAMES MADISON vol. 17, p. 315 (University of Virginia Press 1991) (emphasis original).

[vi] U.S. CONST. art. 1 § 8, cl. 1.

Socialists did not like limitations on the Tax and Spend Clause. And they didn't like its underlying purpose, either. They had bigger plans. They hung their hopes of monolithic government upon the Tax and Spend Clause. They would remake it in their own image; they would fashion it into a transcendent power of "Yes"—a federal power to command States and individuals alike to take action in instances where they had chosen not to act.

No matter what the rest of the Constitution said.

Constitutional Archaeopteryx

It is unclear whether socialists hit upon the idea themselves, or if they realized only after reading Madison, that limitless federal authority could be had by reinterpreting the Tax and Spend Clause as a generalized money power. In any event, Incrementalism set right to work reinterpreting the Tax and Spend Clause.

As it had done with the Commerce Clause, the Supreme Court initially defended the actual meaning of the Tax and Spend Clause. It did so time and again through the centuries. Even as late as 1922 we find the Court striking down a 10% federal excise "tax" on child labor as an unconstitutional extension of Tax and Spend authority.[13] The tax's intent—to eliminate child labor in factories and mines—was salutary in the Court's view. But salutary purpose does not a constitutional law make. On the contrary, and as the Court recognized, the law's salutary purpose was precisely what made it "insidious," as "it leads citizens and legislators of good purpose to promote it without thought of the serious breach it will make in [the Constitution]."[14]

The Court found the child labor "tax" unconstitutional because, while ostensibly a means to raise federal revenue, it was actually aimed to (and did) regulate matters reserved to the States: in this case, labor relations. The federal government was never granted power to regulate labor; so by regulating mandatory minimum age and maximum hours in the name of a "tax," the federal government *invaded State sovereignty.*[15] The Court explained that if Congress could enforce its will upon the States via taxation where child labor was concerned, then Congress could enslave the States in other matters over which the States retained exclusive jurisdiction, too.[16] In the Court's words, "To give such magic to the word 'tax' would be to break down all constitutional limitation of the powers of Congress and completely wipe out the sovereignty of the States."[17]

Yes, "magic" is certainly the right word for federal "taxation" aimed at obliterating State sovereignty! But here we have travelled back in time: This was the understanding of independent Guardians of the Constitution—this was *before* new (Socialist) Deal pressure on the Court. This was 1922, *before*

Justice Roberts' Switch in Time.[18] So it comes as little surprise that the Court faithfully upheld constitutional limits on the Tax and Spend power.

But that would soon change.[19]

In 1936 the Supreme Court made its last effort to strike down federal legislation as being beyond the Tax and Spend power.[20] The case involved the Agricultural Adjustment Act of 1933 ("the AAA"), yet another portion of the New (Socialist) Deal. The AAA purported to levy a tax which would be used to pay farmers for *not* planting certain crops. The idea was to decrease supply of agricultural products nationwide, in order to increase their selling price. The federal tax and subsidy scheme was billed as a boon to the beleaguered farmer, who would receive some money for doing nothing at all, and also get higher prices for what he did produce.[21]

The AAA case came along just barely before the Switch in Time. So the Court clung precariously to its time-honored independence—and struck down the AAA as unconstitutional federal taxation. Good ole Justice Owen Josephus Roberts wrote the Court's majority opinion, ruling that the AAA's tax-and-subsidy scheme (1) invaded the reserved rights of the States; (2) provided a federal plan to control agriculture, which was beyond the powers delegated to the federal government; and (3) attempted to disguise this unconstitutional exercise of federal power by calling it a "tax."[22,vii] In conclusion, Justice Roberts and the Supreme Court execrated the AAA as follows: "*At best, it is a scheme for purchasing with federal funds submission to federal regulation of a subject reserved to the states.*"[23]

So far the Court's decision was both self-consistent and congruent with previous rulings.

But by 1936 the Supreme Court had been under pressure from a New (Socialist) Deal Legislature and Executive for three long years. True, the Court hadn't yet heard FDR's Fireside Chat; it had not been directly threatened with FDR's court-packing scheme; but Justice Roberts had already been strained to the breaking point. (Indeed, the very next year the Switch in Time would be accomplished!)

[vii] The Tenth Amendment had not yet gone out of fashion—this was before the Switch in Time, mind you!—so Justice Roberts and the Court confidently reiterated that "powers not granted [to the federal government] are prohibited. None to regulate agricultural production is given, and therefore legislation by Congress for that purpose is forbidden. . . . [*T*]*he attainment of a prohibited end may not be accomplished under the pretext of the exertion of powers which are granted.*" (*U.S. v. Butler*, 297 U.S. at 72 (1936).)

In other words, you can call the AAA's method "taxing and spending" all you want. But let's be honest here: With this tax and this conditional spending you are actually regulating agricultural production. The constitution does not grant you that power. The "general welfare" limitation cannot expand federal tax and spending powers to agricultural regulation, either. Therefore you cannot regulate agriculture—whether you do it by a tax-and-subsidy program or in any other way.

As a result, Justice Roberts did something very peculiar in the AAA decision. While striking down the AAA's crop-restricting tax and spend scheme as unconstitutional, Roberts simultaneously *unhinged the Tax and Spend Clause from its most fundamental limitation*: The requirement that federal taxing and spending be used *only* to fulfill other enumerated powers.[24] And he did so in a most curious way: He interpreted the general welfare limitation, for the very first time, as no limitation at all but rather a *separate and enumerated grant of power* (!). He openly suggested Congress could tax and spend however it pleased so long as it claimed to do so "for the general welfare."[25]

Justice Roberts was clearly confused. He was unsure what the Tax and Spend Clause signified. Was it limited to fulfilling other enumerated powers (as he held in striking down the AAA)? Or could it be extended to justify non-enumerated regulatory powers "for the general welfare" (as he stated in dicta)?[viii] Such interpretations are mutually exclusive—yet Justice Roberts insisted upon both within the very same ruling!

The man was under a great deal of stress, you understand. The Legislature menaced him. The Executive tormented him. Both wished to see the New (Socialist) Deal become reality. Poor Justice Roberts just wanted everyone to be happy! So he ruled one thing and reasoned another. He split the baby. (*Something for everyone!*)

And the Court joined Justice Roberts' decision.

By doing so the Court proclaimed its softening spine. The Court intimated a desire to drop limitations on the Tax and Spend Clause. The Court opened the door to future Incrementalist rulings. Rulings that would allow Congress to tax and spend however it pleased—so long as Congress claimed all was done "for the general welfare."

The evolution of the Tax and Spend Clause had begun.

The Power of "Yes"

The Court's conflicted AAA decision represents a whimsical transitional form: It bridges the gap between an independent Supreme Court requiring *some* limitation on the federal tax and spending power, and a dependent Court requiring *none at all.*

But after the Switch in Time, Supreme Court jurisprudence became perfectly distinct and brutally consistent. The Court would no longer examine federal taxation and spending from the perspective of an independent consti-

---

[viii] *Obiter dicta*, literally "incidental statements," or "statements in passing," are those portions of a court's decision which are unnecessary to reach the ruling in the case at hand. Formally, *obiter dicta* have no controlling effect on future cases—i.e., dicta have no precedential effect. However, past dicta make juicy opportunities for future Incrementalist Courts—and they are frequently cited as "authority" in future rulings.

tutional arbiter. Oh, no. From now on the Court would defer to Congress. From now on the Court would abandon limitations on the Tax and Spend power. From now on the Court would approve all federal taxes and disbursements. From now on the Tax and Spend Clause would grow!

So in 1937, just one year after the Court struck down the AAA's crop-restricting tax and subsidy scheme as an invasion of the reserved rights of the States,[26] the Court reversed course completely. It now reinterpreted the Tax and Spend Clause to allow Congress to *purchase State compliance with federal policy—and to do so even in matters over which the federal government has no authority.*

The case was *Steward Machine Co. v. Davis.*[27] At issue was another chunk of the New (Socialist) Deal: In this case, the Social Security Act's tax and spend scheme for inducing States to provide unemployment compensation.[28] You see, the federal government wanted to pay money to people who had lost their jobs. But the federal government had never been given authority to do so. State governments had constitutional authority to provide unemployment insurance if they wanted to, but forty-nine of the fifty States had never done it. So the federal government decided to *coerce* State governments into providing unemployment benefits—on the federal government's behalf, and according to the federal government's own, meticulous requirements.[29] To pressure States into providing unemployment benefits the federal government would tax everywhere—but spend only in those States implementing an unemployment insurance program.

The Social Security Act's tax and conditional spending scheme was convoluted, to say the least.[30] Behind so many steps it hid multiple inducements. And the main inducement was this: It conditioned the return of federal tax money—money *taken from citizens of a given State!*—on that State's capitulation to *federal* policy. In other words the federal government taxed a State's citizens as it pleased, and then told the State and its citizens they would never see that money again unless they submitted to federal policy. And not just *any* federal policy, but federal policy as dictated by the Social Security Board (a proud new branch of the Fourth Head!), on an issue over which the federal government has no authority whatsoever: unemployment benefits. To see a full return on citizen's federal tax money, the State in which citizens lived would have to establish a State-funded, federally-approved unemployment insurance program which neither States nor citizens wanted in the first place.[31]

It was ugly. But as long as Congress employed an "indirect" tax and conditional spending scheme, one ostensibly "for the general welfare," the Switch in Time Court declared it constitutionally justified in commandeering State governments to accomplish what the federal government itself had no authority to do. And really, Congress was doing no more than Justice Roberts had previously advised in the AAA case: When it wished to impose federal policies for which it had no enumerated constitutional authority, Congress was coercing States "indirectly"[32] via taxes and conditional spending in the name of "general welfare."[33] Under the Court's newly-reinterpreted Tax and Spend Clause, this was perfectly "constitutional." Besides, the Switch in Time Justices had begun to prefer their newfound role as Constitutional Reinterpreters to their traditional role as Constitutional Guardians. So by a 5-4 majority the Switch in Time Court upheld the Social Security Act—and its tax and spend scheme for compelling nationwide "State" unemployment insurance plans.

No matter that the Constitution fails to empower Congress to pay or insure unemployed persons![34] No matter that the Constitution reserves such power to the States.[35] No matter that the *Steward Machine Co.* ruling shattered a century and a half of Supreme Court precedent. No matter that it handed Congress control of internal State policy going forward.[36] (What a curious departure from Supreme Court precedent! Why, from the very beginning the Court had declared that *the power to tax is the power to destroy.*[ix] It was on that basis the Court ruled State governments could never, ever tax federal institutions.[37] But the Court no longer seemed to care that to tax is to destroy; at least not when State governments were being destroyed by federal taxes, instead of the other way round.)

And what was the Switch in Time Court's justification for doing all this? Why economic crisis, of course! The Supreme Court decided that economic depression was a fine reason to ignore the Constitution.[38] (In which case we must ask, what is the purpose of a Constitution, anyway? Merely to direct traffic when all is well?)

The result was an Incrementalist triumph. While the Court euphemistically called the Social Security Act's tax and conditional spending approach "indirect," it imposed federal policy just as effectively as any direct legislation could.[39] This is a matter of empirical fact. When the Social Security Act became federal law, only a single State in the entire nation (Wisconsin) had *any* unemployment compensation program at all. And while Wisconsin's unemployment compensation program was "generally deemed the best yet devised,"[40] Wisconsin nevertheless overhauled its unemployment compensation program in order to qualify as a federally-approved plan. Not only this, but 42 of the remaining 49 States—those which provided no unemployment benefits of any kind when the Social Security Act became law—had already implemented a federally-approved program by the time *Steward Machine Co.* was argued in 1937.[41] And the remaining seven States followed suit immediately after the Court's ruling.

[ix] "[T]he power to tax involves the power to destroy." *McCulloch v. Maryland*, 17 U.S. 316, 431 (1819).

So yes: The Social Security Act's "indirect" tax and conditional spending scheme drove 100% of the States to implement federal policy. A policy which 100% of the States pursue to this very day.

How was the Social Security Act's tax and conditional spending scheme so very effective? Well, States had become slaves to the lavish federal budget. Incrementalists realized this. And with the sweeping success of the Social Security Act's tax and conditional spending scheme Incrementalists confirmed it. Ever since *Steward Machine Co.*, federal taxation and conditional spending has been one of socialists' primary methods for consolidating federal power, and steamrolling States and individuals. The federal game is as simple as it is effective: Just tax the dickens out of citizens from all States. Tax them so hard that the federal government collects more of citizens' money than all of the States combined. (Today, for example, the federal government collects 88% more in taxes than *all the States combined.*[42]) Then spend more of citizens' money than all of the States combined. Offer to return a lot of federal tax money—money taken from a State's citizens—to the State from which it came. (Federal spending comprises roughly 30% of *State budgets!*[43]) But make that offer contingent on States' capitulation to federal policy: *Return citizens' federal tax money in full only where States kneel and kiss the federal ring.*

This is the legacy of the Switch in Time Court's *Steward Machine Co.* ruling. It uncaged the Tax and Spend Clause. It dropped the constitutional limitation requiring taxing and spending *only* in fulfillment of other enumerated powers. It allowed the federal government to aim its vast financial resources at the little States generally. Overnight the Tax and Spend Clause swelled into a gargantuan Power of "Yes": The authority to tell States "Yes, you must act—you must do—you must comply with federal policy—even though the Constitution grants us Feds no authority on this subject!"

It was a proud moment for socialism.

And while the Court continued to mumble about States remaining free to choose federal money or unemployment insurance independence; and how States were not coerced in the least by Congress' tax and conditional spending program;[44] still every State in the Union implemented a federally-approved unemployment insurance plan *on the double.*

So one is left to wonder If 100% federal compliance is liberty, what would federal compulsion look like?

Obamacare

The Power of "Yes" provided Incrementalists with a striking way to consolidate central authority, undermine State autonomy, and tame the Constitution.

Call it coercion, or bribery, or whatever you like. With the Incrementalist Tax and Spend Clause the federal government could openly purchase State submission to federal regulation. And it could purchase submission using federal funds taken from the State's own citizens. And it could do so even in areas over which the federal government had been granted no authority at all.

But still the Tax and Spend magic show was unfinished. True, over the years Incrementalists pulled off a number of exhilarating tricks using the Tax and Spend Clause. And none more daring than the one they pulled during the Reagan Administration! (See APPENDIX for full treatment of this charming episode.[45]). Yet there remained one last trick to bring the Power of "Yes" into its own: application *directly to the individual.* Only then could it mirror the Power of "No," which bound not only States but reached right down and hogtied Farmer Filburn, too.

Incrementalists waited decades for an opportunity to apply the Tax and Spend Clause directly against the citizen. And when that opportunity finally presented itself, circumstances were not so different from the 1930s: The economy was in the worst depression any living American could remember. A charismatic, Incrementalist President commanded loyal majorities in both House and Senate. Legislature and Executive worked hand in hand to pass a new set of national laws of unprecedented scope aimed at redistribution, group "rights," and "moral" government. And Justices at the Supreme Court were again making 5-4 decisions suggesting some measure of political independence.

This new set of national laws included the so-called "Patient Protection and Affordable Care Act of 2010," more commonly referred to as "Obamacare."[46] And among other obligations in this thousand-page federal "law" was the infamous individual mandate: A requirement that Middle Americans purchase a federally-approved quantity of private health insurance, or else annually pay the federal government a "penalty" euphemistically entitled a "[s]hared responsibility payment."[47] (Prisoners, congresspersons, undocumented aliens, those who meet certain poverty guidelines, those who receive Medicare or Medicaid, and members of Indian tribes, however, are happily exempt from this burden.[48]) The "penalty," or "shared responsibility payment," as Obamacare variously refers to the federal ransom for not purchasing health insurance, was to be assessed as 2.5% of individual's household income—and in no case less than $695.00.[49]

Obamacare's individual health insurance mandate was an unprecedented assertion of federal power. It (1) compelled individuals to (2) buy a product which (3) they did not want and (4) were not currently purchasing (5) from private companies.[x] Or else pay a significant financial penalty to the federal

---

[x] Whenever this issue comes up, ignorant socialists always cry: "But what about vehicular insurance? You can't legally drive unless you have insurance!" The solution to socialists' "conundrum" is quite simple—but then socialists have always had a hard time with the concept of Federalism. The solution is simply this: Vehicular insurance is compelled by *State* governments, not the federal government. States retain broad police powers, and can do anything they are not explicitly prevented from doing under the Federal Constitution and their

government. Of course, the Constitution grants the federal government no "health care" power. (Go look and you will see!) So twenty-six States, as well as a number of private individuals and businesses, sued the federal government on the basis that Obamacare and its individual mandate were unconstitutional. They filed suit mere *minutes* after President Obama signed the Patient Protection and Affordable Care Act into law.[50]

As the lawsuit wound its way through the federal courts, the federal government made its favorite argument: Obamacare and its individual mandate were constitutional *under the Commerce Clause*. If Congress could use the Commerce Clause to command Farmer Filburn not to raise wheat, and Mr. Raich not to grow cannabis, and everyone else not to build where unorthodox cave bugs dwell, then why couldn't it use the same authority to command citizens to buy health insurance? After all, health insurance was sort of related to commerce. People buying or not buying health insurance sort of *affected* interstate commerce. Especially since federal law requires hospitals to treat all cane toads (and other uninsured persons) who hop into emergency rooms for nonemergency care.[51] Why, the situation was untenable: Not everyone had health insurance. And as hospitals passed the cost of treating uninsured cane toads on to insurance companies—who in turn passed the cost on to consumers by raising insurance premia—health care was becoming too expensive for everyone! This was clearly a "commerce" issue; Obamacare and its individual mandate must be constitutional under the Commerce Clause.

This was the federal argument.[52]

(It never occurred to federal officials that they might be responsible for the health care cost explosion: That by encouraging cane toad immigration;[53] and by requiring hospitals to care for the uninsured;[54] and by paying for health care which people were unwilling or unable to purchase themselves;[55] federal policy necessarily inflates health care costs. The federal government didn't want to admit fault or disband Incrementalist policies. On the contrary, it wanted *more* redistributive policies. It wanted healthy, uninsured cane beetles to pay for the health care of others. It wanted Middle Americans to pay for socialism's unintended consequences.)

Congressional leaders uniformly espoused the Commerce Clause argument. As Speaker of the House Nancy Pelosi brazenly declared, "Since virtually every aspect of the health care system has an effect on interstate commerce, the power of Congress to regulate health care is essentially unlimited."[56] Yes, that was the ticket: Health care *has an effect* on interstate commerce, so Congress' power to demand citizens buy health insurance is *essentially unlimited!*

Senate Majority Leader Harry Reid, and much of the rest of Congress' leadership, agreed: This was a Commerce Clause issue if ever there was one,

---

own State Constitutions. So States are free to compel us to purchase vehicular insurance—and health insurance as well, if they like. *But the federal government is NOT.*

and under that power Congress had full authority to command citizens to buy health insurance.[57] In congressional leaders' own words, Obamacare and the individual mandate "exercise *the core* of Congress's Commerce Clause authority."[58]

Besides, the Affordable Care Act itself carefully couched the individual mandate in Commerce Clause lingo. It asserted that the individual mandate "is commercial and economic in nature, and substantially affects interstate commerce. . . . The requirement regulates activity that is commercial and economic in nature: economic and financial decisions about how and when health care is paid for, and when health insurance is purchased."[59]

Congress had learned to use the magic words!

In the federal courts, the individual mandate was repeatedly found to be unconstitutional. Because the Patient Protection and Affordable Care Act of 2010 contained no severability clause, those federal courts which cared for the rule of law struck down Obamacare as unconstitutional in its entirety.[60] Other federal courts cared less about law, and pretended that while the individual mandate was unconstitutional, it was magically severable from the rest of Obamacare—even in the absence of a severability clause (!). Such courts found the individual mandate unconstitutional, but upheld the remainder of Obamacare.[61] Someone would have to decide which federal courts were right, and which were wrong.

On November 14, 2011, after multiple cross-appeals by both plaintiffs and defendants, the Supreme Court granted certiorari: The Supreme Court would settle this dispute. It would have the final word on the constitutionality of Obamacare and its individual mandate. It would hear oral arguments on March 26 through March 28, 2012. On the books, this case would be called *National Federation of Independent Business v. Sebelius.*[62]

During oral arguments before the Supreme Court, the federal government based its case for Obamacare on the Commerce Clause. Just like it always had.

There was only one problem.

The Commerce Clause is the power to *regulate* commerce—i.e., existing commerce—not to *create* or to *compel* commerce.[63] Even in its most wildly unlimited and socialist form, the Commerce Clause is a Power of "No"—the power to command States and individuals *not* to do something. This presupposes States and individuals are *doing something*—some commercial activity or other which they can be commanded to *stop doing.*[64] Like growing wheat. Or erecting buildings. Or using 1.6+ gallon-per-flush toilets. But insofar as people are *not* buying health insurance, *they are taking no action at all.*[65] They are performing no action about which they could be told "No, you cannot! Stop!" So far as people who are not buying health insurance are concerned, there is no commercial activity "to regulate." On the contrary, there is a stark lack of commercial activity—which is precisely what Congress wanted to remedy with Obamacare's individual mandate.[66]

So the congressional geniuses' Commerce Clause argument fell headlong at the Supreme Court. Oral arguments were painful to watch.[xi] Solicitor General Donald B. Verrilli, Jr. was tasked with articulating the federal government's argument, and when questioned by Supreme Court Justices he stammered and paused. He cleared his throat time and again. He took frequent, long drinks of water to gather his thoughts. He coughed and spluttered. He affected awkward, extended pauses as he thought what answer he might give to impossible questions. He made an arse of himself before the Supreme Court and before the nation.

Left-leaning commentators agree: Verrilli's performance was a genuine horror.[67] As one prominent socialist publication put it, Verrilli's was "the worst supreme court argument of all time."[68] Those less prone to exaggeration preferred to use terminology like "disaster"[69] or "train wreck."[70] And whether pundits understood it or not, the "train wreck" wasn't Verrilli's fault: The fault was with overweening legislators who insisted Verrilli base his Obamacare defense on an impossible Commerce Clause argument.[xii]

After Verrilli's misadventure it was clear to Court-watchers—from legal scholars to the most ignorant of journalists—that at least five Supreme Court Justices would find Obamacare's individual mandate unconstitutional.[71]

Roberts' Resurrection

Court-watchers' prognostications proved correct.

On Friday, March 30, 2012, the nine Supreme Court Justices held secret convocation deep in the bowels of the Supreme Court Building. Just as they always did at the conclusion of oral arguments. They deliberated. As always, they voted. And as anticipated, five Justices found the individual mandate unconstitutional.[72]

So the Chief Justice began drafting a majority ruling striking down the individual mandate.[73]

And yet—despite the Justices' vote of unconstitutionality, and despite the Chief Justice's draft ruling—in the end, the Supreme Court *did not consign Obamacare or its individual mandate to the middens of American legal history.*

[xi] Well, you can't actually *watch* oral arguments at the Supreme Court. Not unless you are part of the legal team, or camp out on the Supreme Court Building steps the night before. Because cameras are forbidden within the inner sanctum. But you can *listen* to oral arguments. Just go to http://www.supremecourt.gov/oral_arguments/argument_audio.aspx. You will see—er, hear—what I mean. It was painful.

[xii] The problem was not messenger, but the message. Verrilli is brilliant. His difficulty was the argument he was forced to make: The argument that Obamacare's individual mandate is a constitutional exercise of the Commerce Clause. The argument was incompetent. And that incompetent argument was forced upon Verrilli by his client, the federal government.

No indeed—the *Sebelius* decision upheld both Obamacare and its individual mandate as "constitutional"!

How so?

Well, Incrementalist Executives and Legislatures had studied the lessons of FDR and his New (Socialist) Deal. They had learned the key to constitutional victory: A *meek and dependent Supreme Court.* They were undaunted by the text of the Constitution. They were undeterred by Solicitor Verrilli's calamitous oral argument. They were unimpressed with the Court's recent display of independence. Instead, they turned their attention to identifying the most fragile Justice: The one most concerned with how well he was liked by the Executive, by the Legislature, and by the Press. They started bullying.

The Executive openly threatened the Court:

> Ultimately, I'm confident that the Supreme Court will not take *what would be an unprecedented, extraordinary step of overturning a law that was passed by a strong majority of a democratically elected Congress.*[74]

An "unprecedented, extraordinary step"? But the Supreme Court has been overturning laws passed by strong majorities of democratically elected Congresses for over two hundred years! And really, are there any laws passed by Congress *without* majority congressional support? Or by congresspersons who are *not* democratically elected? And anyway, what purpose does the Supreme Court have if not to overturn unconstitutional laws? (While President Obama's statement may have been historically and legally incomprehensible, his point was exceedingly clear: Court, you had better approve this legislation. We other branches of government are elected. Not you. We have the support of the people. Not you. Just *do it.*)

The Legislature threatened the Court as well:

> The Chief Justice seemed to understand that deference to the elected branch [sic] is fundamental to the proper exercise of judicial review. . . . I trust that he will be a Chief Justice for all of us and that he has a strong institutional sense of the proper role of the judicial branch. . . .
>
> [I]t would be extraordinary for the Supreme Court *not* to defer to Congress in this matter that so clearly affects interstate commerce. . . .
>
> You may agree or disagree with parts of the Affordable Care Act. But the fact is Congress acted within its authority. And I hope and have faith that the Supreme Court will not overstep the Judiciary's role by substituting policy preferences for the legislative determinations of Congress.[75]

It would be "extraordinary" for the Court "*not* to defer to Congress in this matter"? But surely there was to be a separation of powers among the three heads of federal government! And "The fact is Congress acted within its authority"? But surely Congress cannot be trusted to determine the bounds of its own power! Isn't that what an independent Supreme Court was organized to do? Determine the constitutional bounds of congressional power?

The Press threatened the Court, too. Indeed, entire editorial boards at major periodicals took the time to chime in:

> If the conservatives decide that they can sidestep the Constitution to negate Congress's choices [?] on crucial national policies, the court's legitimacy—and the millions of Americans who don't have insurance—will pay a very heavy price. Chief Justice Roberts has the opportunity to avoid this disastrous outcome by forging even a narrow ruling to uphold the mandate and the rest of the law. A split court striking down the act will be declaring itself virtually unfettered by the law. [???] And if that happens along party lines, with five Republican-appointed justices supporting the challenge led by 26 Republican governors, the court will mark itself as driven by politics.[76]

What? By striking down federal legislation the Court would "sidestep the Constitution"? Ridiculous! On the contrary, only by striking down unconstitutional legislation can the Court fulfill the Constitution. In any case, the Court was never obliged to Congress; its obligation is exclusively to the Constitution. And what? By voiding Obamacare the Court would show "itself virtually unfettered by the law"? Absurd! Striking down Obamacare would illustrate just the opposite: It would show the Court *unfettered by Congress*, and *bound by law*.

The arguments were lame, but they were relentless. Throughout April and May the Court was pummeled with threats about court "legitimacy" being called into question if they should void Congress' favorite new law.[77] And as we have already seen, campaigns to destroy Supreme Court independence need not succeed with *every* Justice; they need only reach one ninny to swing a 5-4 decision.

In May of 2012—just like March of 1937—the Executive's threats, and the Legislature's harassment, and the Press' vituperation found their mark.

Because one Justice listens more to network news than the Constitution. Because one man "is sensitive to how the court is perceived by the public."[78] Because one "Guardian" prefers puff pieces in Incrementalist periodicals to constitutional veracity. Because a single Justice lacks that "uncommon portion of fortitude" which our Predecessors demanded of all federal judges.[79] Chief Justice John G. Roberts—one of the independent five, who stood against socialist legislation in the past,[80] who voted to strike down the individual mandate as unconstitutional, yes, the very one who had already begun drafting an opinion striking the mandate—switched his vote.

No, no—this is not the late Justice Owen Josephus Roberts, lily liver of the 1937 Switch in Time! That Roberts hadn't penned a Supreme Court ruling for nearly seventy years. This is yet *another* Justice Roberts—Chief Justice John Glover Roberts, Jr., engineer of the 2012 Switch in Time. (Staggering, isn't it?

In over two centuries worth of Supreme Court Justices, there have been only two Justices Roberts. And they are brothers as it were: Appointees of failed Republican Presidents, targets of Democratic ones, judges who junked constitutional restraints on federal power for a little praise from the Left. What are the chances? The Universe has a keen sense of humor! What would Langland say?[81] Or Ball?[82])

Like his namesake, *Chief* Justice Roberts switched at the last possible minute. He relinquished a laborious independence for a more relaxing loyalty. And by that same 5-4 margin which the Supreme Court had voted to strike down Obamacare's individual mandate, the Court now upheld it—by Chief Justice Roberts' own pen. (As Chief Justice, Mr. Roberts decides who will author the Court's opinion. In the Obamacare case, he chose to write the opinion himself. So after his switch, he *reworked* the opinion he had already started—he flipped it around to *uphold* Obamacare's individual mandate, instead of striking it down.)

How did Chief Justice Roberts find the individual mandate "constitutional"?

Well, that is the amusing part: Therein lies the constitutional wizardry!

Of course, Chief Justice Roberts knew the individual mandate could never be constitutional under the Power of "No."[83] So he abandoned the federal government's argument that the individual mandate was a "penalty" or a "[s]hared responsibility payment"[84] under the Commerce Clause.

Instead, Justice Roberts tried a different route. He picked up an argument uniformly rejected by the lower courts: That the individual mandate was not a penalty at all, but rather a *federal tax*. Yes, that was the best approach: Justify Obamacare via the Tax and Spend Clause—apply the Power of "Yes" *to individuals as well as States!*

Myriad difficulties attended Justice Roberts' tax justification of Obamacare. For example, nowhere does the Affordable Care Act call the individual mandate's penalty a "tax." Nor did the federal government ever wish the penalty to be deemed a tax. Justice Roberts openly confessed these obstacles.[xiii] But at Humpty Dumpty's Court, where words mean whatever Justices say they mean, such obstacles are easily avoided!

Chief Justice Roberts "reasoned" as follows:

First, in order to hear the case at all, Chief Justice Roberts had to rule that *for the purposes of the Anti-Injunction Act*, Obamacare's individual mandate

---

[xiii] "The most straightforward reading of the mandate is that it commands individuals to purchase insurance. After all, it states that individuals 'shall' maintain health insurance. 26 U.S.C. § 5000A(a). *Congress thought it could enact such a command under the Commerce Clause, and the Government primarily defended the law on that basis.*" *Nat'l Fed'n of Indep. Bus. v. Sebelius*, 183 L. Ed. 450, 482 (2012) (emphasis added).

is *not a tax*.[xiv] Then—within the very same opinion, just a few pages later—Chief Justice Roberts ruled that *for the purposes of the Constitution*, Obamacare's individual mandate *is indeed a tax*.[85] (?!) It is difficult to comprehend, but that is exactly what he ruled: The individual mandate simultaneously *is* and *is not* a tax.[xv] (Now there is a legal fiction that only a *Chief* Justice dares utter! But you can forgive Humpty: He was under tremendous pressure to find Obamacare constitutional. He had only recently cracked, and there was precious little time to think. He had to write the opposite of what he thought; he did the best he could in the time available.)

Second, there was the difficulty that Obamacare's individual mandate introduces a completely new type of tax: A tax for *not* purchasing something the government wishes you had. (Just take a minute and let that sink in—in Obamacare, we are dealing with a tax for *not* purchasing. How odd!)

Justice Roberts was aware that a completely new variety of tax, one that had never been tried in over two centuries of American history, might arouse suspicions regarding its constitutionality. So he deceitfully claimed this sort of "tax"—a tax for *not* purchasing what the federal government wants you to have!—was nothing new. Yes, he came right out and said it: "Congress's use of the Taxing Clause to encourage buying something is, by contrast, not new. Tax incentives already promote, for example, purchasing homes and professional educations."[86]

What Chief Justice Roberts meant was that the tax code provides home owners with a mortgage interest *tax deduction*, and the educationally indebted with a student loan interest *tax deduction*. But this is a false comparison! The federal government has never taxed people for *not* buying a home, or for *not* purchasing a collegiate education! And that was the issue at hand: Could the

---

[xiv] The Anti-Injunction Act provides that "no suit for the purpose of restraining the assessment or collection of any tax shall be maintained in any court by any person, whether or not such person is the person against whom such tax was assessed." 26 U.S.C. § 7421(a). In other words, you can't challenge a tax until you have actually paid it (!). After paying the tax, *then* you can sue the Government for a refund. (If possession is nine-tenths of the law, then . . . .)

Obamacare's individual mandate first becomes enforceable in 2014. No one had paid the "tax" in 2012, so no one could bring suit claiming the "tax" unconstitutional in 2012. Under the Anti-Injunction Act, the fact that no one had paid the "tax" barred any lawsuit on the issue.

But Chief Justice Roberts and the Incrementalist Court wanted to rule Obamacare "constitutional" *today*. They wanted to proceed to the merits. So *for the purposes of the Anti-Injunction Act only*, Roberts and the Court ruled that Obamacare's individual mandate is *not* a tax. "The affordable Care Act does not require that the penalty for failing to comply with the individual mandate be treated as a tax for purposes of the Anti-Injunction Act. The Anti-Injunction Act therefore does not apply to this suit, and we may proceed to the merits." *Nat'l Fed'n of Indep. Bus. v. Sebelius*, 183 L. Ed. at 472 (2012); *see further ibid.* at 470-72.

[xv] "It is of course true that the Act describes the payment as a 'penalty,' not a 'tax.' But while that label is fatal to the application of the Anti-Injunction Act, it does not determine whether the payment may be viewed as an exercise of Congress's taxing power." *Nat'l Fed'n of Indep. Bus. v. Sebelius*, 183 L. Ed. at 483 (2012).

federal government tax you for *not* buying health care? (And after Roberts' ruling that Obamacare is constitutional, the federal government now *can* tax you for *not* buying a home. And it *can* tax you for *not* buying an education, too. Roberts' decision demands it. Take a minute to let that sink in, too.)

Third, there were other, further, ghastly difficulties with Justice Roberts' tax justification of Obamacare. However, we shall spare legal laymen the gory details of these horrors; the curious legal student is invited to consult this endnote.[87]

After determining that Obamacare's individual mandate both *is* and *is not* a tax, after deciding a tax for *not* purchasing is nothing new, and after ruling that the rest of the Constitution doesn't count for beans,[88] composing the remainder of the ruling was easy. Chief Justice Roberts reasserted the Court's obsequious deference to Congress, specifically noting the Court's "limited role in policing" the boundaries of federal power (!).[89] He discussed the stupendous reach of the Incrementalist Tax and Spend Clause.[90] He openly admitted the "regulatory effect" of the Obamacare "tax."[91] He waxed eloquent about the "lawful choice" which remained with individuals: to purchase health insurance, or to pay the Obamacare "tax."[xvi] He even had the chutzpah to claim that the "power to tax is *not* the power to destroy while this Court sits."[92]

This is how Chief Justice Roberts upheld Obamacare's individual mandate.

The *Sebelius* decision represents the climax to Incrementalists' Tax and Spend magic trick. It required a second Switch in Time. It demanded thrilling equivocation. It called for rousing rhetorical flourish by a flaccid Chief Justice. And on June 28, 2012, it was finally complete. With Humpty's assistance, the Tax and Spend Clause was irreversibly transformed from a limited power to tax and spend in fulfillment of other enumerated powers into a tyrannical power of "Yes"—a comprehensive federal power to tell States and individuals alike, "Yes, you must do, you must act." No matter what the rest of the Constitution says.[93]

Roberts the Pigeonheart received his reward: He got the effusive puff pieces in Left-leaning publications which he so desperately craved.[94]

But immediately after his reprise of the Switch in Time, The Pigeonheart was again made uncomfortable: Now he felt unfriendly glances from those who knew he had traded constitutional independence for a congressional

---

[xvi] "But imposition of a tax nonetheless leaves an individual with a lawful choice to do or not do a certain act, so long as he is willing to pay a tax levied on that choice." *Nat'l Fed'n of Indep. Bus. v. Sebelius*, 183 L. Ed. at 489-90 (2012). But that is not liberty! That is not freedom of choice! One might as well say the imposition of a criminal law nonetheless leaves an individual with a lawful choice to do or not do a certain act—*so long as he is willing to do time in prison!*

rubberstamp. He joked that to avoid such criticism, he might slip away to an "impregnable island fortress."[95]

Then he did precisely that. He fled to Malta.[96]

And he hasn't returned since.[xvii]

Grande Finale

Like other Incrementalist triumphs, the Pigeonheart's Switch went unnoticed by most of the citizenry. Why, the resulting Obamacare ruling itself went unnoticed by half the country.[97] Even though it was the most anticipated Supreme Court ruling in over a decade. Which is exactly the sort of civic ignorance Incrementalism relies upon.

It's a wee bit discouraging.

But the difficulty is not Obamacare or its individual mandate; or what they will cost; or how few Americans want either; or what parliamentary shenanigans Congress used to pass Obamacare and its individual mandate in the first place; or how Humpty's Court ruled them "constitutional." Obamacare and its individual mandate are not permanent ills. They are mere congressional legislation. And as such, either or both could be written out of existence by a future Congress (as endorsed by some future Executive).

No, the difficulty is that constitutional precedent lasts forever. So Obamacare and its individual mandate may be overthrown, but the Court's Obamacare ruling cannot. The *Sebelius* decision will remain on the books forever: It can never be written out of existence by a future Congress. And it will never be overruled by a future Court.[98] So with the everlasting *Sebelius* decision, the new and tremendous Power of "Yes" will remain forever as well. *Even if Obamacare and its individual mandate should be overwritten by a future Congress.*

Yes, whatever should happen to Obamacare, Congress will henceforward wield the imprimatur of constitutional "law" to coerce citizens "indirectly" via the Tax and Spend Clause—to make citizens participate in federal initiatives, in areas over which the federal government has never had authority, and even in areas where federal interference is specifically forbidden.[99] The Constitution has been eternally amended—quietly, informally, without the consent of citizens or their sovereign States—and in such a way as to give the federal government even more power than it had before. No matter what the text of the Constitution says,[100] and no matter how it is formally amended in the future,[101] the *Sebelius* and *Steward Machine Co.* rulings will linger.[102]

[xvii] Presumably Chief Justice Roberts will return from self-imposed exile to preside over the following term at the Supreme Court. But he is not back yet. Or rather, if he is back, he is keeping a very low profile during the Court's summer recess! (This is written as of late August, 2012.)

As it stands today, this is the federal game:

If Congress wishes to tell a State or an individual "No," you cannot take a given action, you cannot behave in a certain way, you cannot do a certain thing, it cites the Incrementalist Commerce Clause. After decades of "interpretation" by a dependent Supreme Court, the Incrementalist Com-merce Clause allows Congress to say "No!" to any action—so long as Congress can conjure some half-baked story about how that action might conceivably, infinitesimally, hypothetically, *affect* interstate commerce. It makes no difference if the Constitution supplies authority to regulate such behavior or no. And with so loose a standard, "commercial" pretexts can always be invented.

If Congress wishes to tell a State or an individual "Yes," you must affirmatively act, you must do a certain thing, you must perform an action you have chosen not to do, it simply cites the Incrementalist Tax and Spend Clause. After decades of "interpretation" by a dependent Supreme Court, the Incrementalist Tax and Spend Clause allows Congress to say "Yes, you must!" to anything and everything—so long as Congress does so "indirectly," via taxing and spending. It makes no difference whether the Constitution supplies authority to demand such behavior or no. Indeed, it makes no difference what the rest of the Constitution says: Even explicit clauses and amendments forbidding federal interference are no match for the Incrementalist Tax and Spend Clause.[103]

And so Incrementalism found for the Power of "No" an appropriate mate: The Power of "Yes." With the Power of "Yes," non-actions which cannot be reached by the creeping tendrils of the monstrous Commerce Clause are strangled instead by those of the hideous Tax and Spend Clause. And vice versa. The beanstalks are perfectly complimentary, you see, and span the entire universe of human volition: They stretch from that finite class of activities which individuals and States *do* perform, to the infinite class of activities which individuals and States have chosen *not* to perform. Together the colossal beanstalks of "Yes" and "No" overrun every constitutional moat and wall; they splinter the city gates; they climb through every window; they search out every room; they press into every nook and cranny. Nothing escapes their grasp, and all limitations on federal power are crushed beneath them. They supply Washington with monolithic power to control all American people, governments, and things. They choke out the freedom to choose. (And here again we see the irony of socialism: While premised on a creed insisting that human free will cannot exist, in practice socialism operates to stamp it out.)

We have told the tale of The Brothers Roberts; we have chronicled the Court's venal dependence; we have described the resulting Incrementalist Powers of "Yes" and "No." No doubt "Yes" and "No" are the twin pillars of monolithic government in America: Like Jachin and Boaz, they support the entire temple of tyrannical government.

But when the Constitutional Guardians surrendered institutional independence, when they began their midrash on the Constitution, limits on federal power were abandoned *generally*. In other words, "Yes" and "No" are just the tip of the federal iceberg. We cannot examine the iceberg in full here; such a treatment would fill many volumes. For example, time would fail to tell of the Court's piecemeal "Incorporation" of the Bill of Rights' restrictions on federal power against *State* authority.[104] Or its reversal of the Contracts Clause[105] from a prohibition on laws "impairing the obligation of contracts" into a separate excuse to nullify them.[106] Or its conversion of the Necessary and Proper Clause[107] from a strict limitation on federal power into an express grant of further, unenumerated powers.[108] Or its inversion of the Ex Post Facto Clauses[109] from prohibitions on retroactive criminal legislation into exceptions for it.[110] Or its abdication of the Guarantee Clause,[111] and its consent to non-republican forms of State government.[112] Or its reinterpretation of the Takings Clause[113] from a limited power to seize private property for public use, into an unlimited power to redistribute private property as government pleases—so long as doing so offers a possibility of raising more taxes![114] Or its outrageous overstep of the Case or Controversy Clause,[115] and its assertion that Supreme Court decisions bind *not only parties to suit, but also all other States, Municipalities, and persons as well.*[116] Or its reinterpretation of the Composition Clause[117] from an admission of State power to manage elections into a grant of federal control over States' apportionment of votes (for State Legislatures,[118] and for the lower house of Congress, too).[119] And so long as it was going to the trouble of turning the Constitution inside out, the Court decided to go for the whole shebang: It went right ahead and ruled that the Tenth Amendment[120] itself "states but a truism," and was never an independent limitation on Congressional power (!).[121]

This is the grand finale to Incrementalists constitutional magic show: Not the magnificent beanstalks of "Yes" and "No" alone, but rather *the complete disappearance of the Constitution as a whole.* And really, this is what socialists had in mind from the beginning: A *Constitutional Disappearing Act.* In true Incrementalist form, it took seventy-five years to accomplish. It was quiet and careful. It never once provoked Middle Americans to squirrel hunting. It has been ruthlessly effective. It continues unabated today. And it continues not only through Supreme Court rulings like the *Sebelius* decision, but also through the Court's proactive neglect. (For example, a week ago [October, 2012], the Roberts Court quietly *refused to hear* a case challenging TSA's nudy-scanners and enhanced grab-downs as a violation of the Fourth Amendment.[122] By refusing to recognize even the most obvious and outrageous examples of unreasonable searches and seizures, the Court thereby ignores the Fourth Amendment into nonexistence. Henceforward hands in your panties will be the constitutional rule, not the exception.)

And so we have arrived at that fateful day, envisioned by our prescient Predecessors, when "all shall be usurped from the States, and the government of all be consolidated into one."[xviii] It is unpleasant to acknowledge, but it is true: "The Government is no longer a limited one, possessing enumerated powers, but an indefinite one, subject to particular exceptions."[xix] And to be honest, it is becoming increasingly difficult to discern the "particular exceptions." Because today, "The legislative department is everywhere extending the sphere of its activity, and drawing all power into its impetuous vortex."[xx] Today, "Congress [has taken] possession of a boundless field of power, no longer susceptible of any definition."[xxi]

* * *

We said last chapter that due to our Incrementalist Supreme Court, *there is no law.* And that is fair enough.

But socialists' victory is greater than that. Through the diligent toil of a dependent Supreme Court, socialists got their ultimate wish: *There is no Constitution.* And for socialists, having no Constitution is more liberating than even having no law. Because without a Constitution, socialists have free rein to build omnipotent central government: A comprehensive authority to force group "rights," proactive redistributive "justice," and "moral" government upon all.

Do not misunderstand: No one will ever remove the Constitution from its lofty ceremonial perch! The Constitution will never *explicitly* be abandoned, any more than Imperial Rome ever discarded the title of "Republic." The Constitution's physical remains will stay on public display in a cavernous hall of mirror-polished marble, under bullet and UV proof glass, in a hermetically-sealed, temperature and humidity regulated display, watched over by armed honor guard, in the National Archives' Rotunda for the Charters of Freedom. You will be granted permission to filter through in small groups and marvel at the original in hushed tones—in the same way you may view the corpse of

---

[xviii] Thomas Jefferson, *Letter to Charles Hammond* (Aug. 18 1921). *See, e.g.*, THOMAS JEFFERSON, THE WRITINGS OF THOMAS JEFFERSON (Andrew A. Lipscomb & Albert Ellery Bergh eds., The Thomas Jefferson memorial Association 1903).

[xix] James Madison, *Letter to Edmund Pendleton* (Jan. 21, 1792). *See, e.g.*, JAMES MADISON, THE PAPERS OF JAMES MADISON Vol. 14 (Robert A. Rutland et al. eds., University Press of Virginia 1984).

[xx] THE FEDERALIST No. 48, at 316 (Madison) (Robert Scigliano ed., Modern Library 2001) (1787).

[xxi] Thomas Jefferson, *Opinion on the Constitutionality of Creating a National Bank* (1791).

Mao[xxii] or Lenin.[xxiii] And that is how socialists hope the Constitution will remain: Reverently embalmed, lying in state. Innocuous and inert.

In this limited role the Constitution will continue to inspire patriotic fervor: It will remain the subject of policy debates and the punchline of moving political oratory for centuries to come. It will be praised for its vision and its genius. It will be employed as a federal alibi. It will be called the linchpin of our political Union. It will function as a pitiful marketing gimmick. It will provide a grim reminder of past freedoms. It will be hailed as a "living document."

But let us be clear: The Constitution is with us in body only. Its words no longer drive the machinery of government. The spirit of the Constitution departed long ago, and the time when it will be reawakened and removed from its sterile sarcophagus is not yet at hand.

How did we get here? How did we crawl into the constitutional crypt?

Inch by inch. Law by law. Ruling upon ruling. Until the written law became a figment of the oral. *Incrementally*—over a period of nearly a hundred years.

And why did no one do anything? Why didn't we turn back before arriving in this place?

Well, our great grandparents were distracted by the Great Depression. Our grandparents were busy bleeding to save the world. Our parents explored sex, drugs, and rock 'n' roll. And we distract ourselves with the wonders of the digital age.

Along the way, political prophets occasionally arose and warned us—and our parents, and our grandparents, and our great grandparents—that we were headed for the constitutional crypt. They cautioned of the perils of monolithic government every step of the way. But their warnings were difficult to take seriously: At that time we lived in peace, prosperity, and relative freedom. Those political seers were party-poopers during the greatest run of prosperity in the history of the world! They were embarrassing. So we laughed them out of legislatures and chased them from the most prestigious professorships. We mocked them and their alarums. We publicly stoned their admonitions.

Only now, in hindsight, can we see and understand what they warned us about: Under a hundred year flood of socialist Supreme Court decisions, the American *Grundnorm* has been washed away. The foundation of our Republic

---

[xxii] At Chairman Mao Memorial Hall in Tiananmen Square, Beijing.

[xxiii] At the Lenin Mausoleum in Red Square, Moscow. Then there is also the Ho Chi Minh corpse at the Ho Chi Minh Mausoleum in Hanoi; and the Kim Il-sung corpse at the Kumsusan Palace of the Sun in Pyongyang. As cults of personality go, those corpses (and their mausolea) are hard to beat, too.

has disappeared. We stand on sandy ground. Only now can we see that those constitutional seers were correct.

Only now that the Constitution is dead.

For some this realization will prove unsettling—they pine for a simpler time, when liberty under a limited Constitution reigned supreme. Many will deny it is true—some because they are frightened, and others because they have not looked into it. Others yet will deny that it matters—*life goes on*, they will tell us.

But we need not fear, and we need not close our eyes to the truth. Actually, we are the fortunate few: We are they who lived to see our Predecessor's predictions fulfilled. We are no prophets, but we can look backward as well as any—and in retrospect we, too, can see the truth. Sufficient time has passed; the dust of previous generations has settled; the steps can now be viewed in rapid succession; and what went before is conspicuously manifest.

Now we can see that the slow, quiet, steady work of Incrementalism—which for generations they told us would never tear down constitutional liberties!—has in fact dismembered the Constitution. There is no need to debate abstractions, hypotheticals, unintended consequences, or generalities. Discerning the future is no longer required. The Constitution's dismemberment is accomplished fact, as all who are willing to look can plainly see.

And because we live now—only because we live now, when these facts stand candidly before us!—*we are they who can do something about it.*

Further Notes to Chapter 10

[1] *McCulloch v. Maryland*, 17 U.S. 316, 431 (1819) (denying State governments any power to tax federal institutions).
[2] When you get the chance, read the definitive statement for yourself. The text is too long to reproduce here: THE FEDERALIST No. 41, at 263-65 (Madison) (Robert Scigliano ed., Modern Library 2001) (1787).
[3] One of the most cogent expositions of this political fact is provided by James Madison, in his veto of a congressional bill which purported to provide federal monies for the construction of public roads, waterways, and improvements thereto. *See* James Madison, *Veto of Federal Internal Improvement Bill of 1817* (March 3, 1817).
[4] James Madison, *Letter to Edmund Pendleton* (Jan. 21, 1792). *See, e.g.*, JAMES MADISON, THE PAPERS OF JAMES MADISON Vol. 14 (Robert A. Rutland et al. eds., University Press of Virginia 1984). *See also* U.S. CONST., amend. X
[5] Hamilton held a minority view, along with a very few others of the Founding generation, that the Tax Clause conferred a *general* power on Congress. *But even Hamilton understood the meaning of the general welfare limitation*:

> The only qualification of the generality of the [Tax Clause] in question, which seems to be admissible, is this: That the object, to which an appropriation of money is to be made, be general, and not local; its operation extending, in fact, or by possibility throughout the Union, and not being confined to a particular spot.

ALEXANDER HAMILTON, INDUSTRIAL AND COMMERCIAL CORRESPONDENCE OF ALEXANDER HAMILTON 293 (Arthur Harrison Cole ed., A. W. Shaw Co. 1968).
[6] James Madison, *Bounty Payments on Cod Fisheries* (Feb. 6, 1792) (opposing a congressional bill to subsidize cod fisheries under the guise of taxing and spending *for the general welfare*). *See, e.g.*, JAMES MADISON, THE PAPERS OF JAMES MADISON vol. 14 (Robert A. Rutland et al. eds., University Press of Virginia 1984).
[7] "The level of deference to the congressional decision is such that the Court has more recently questioned whether 'general welfare' is a judicially enforceable restriction at all." *South Dakota v. Dole*, 483 U.S. 203, 208 n. 2 (1987) (citing *Buckley v. Valeo*, 424 U.S. 1, 90-91 (1976) (per curiam). *See further* APPENDIX, *"Yes" Plus.*
[8] "A rage for paper money, for an abolition of debts, *for an equal division of property*, or for any other improper or wicked project, will be less apt to pervade the whole body of the Union than a particular member of it; in the same proportion as such a malady is more likely to taint a particular county or district, than an entire State." THE FEDERALIST No. 10, at 61 (Madison) (Robert Scigliano ed., Modern Library 2001) (1787) (emphasis added).
[9] *See supra* n. 5.
[10] The Tax and Spend Clause was limited by another part of the Constitution—the Direct Tax Clause. This latter clause demands that "No Capitation, or other direct, Tax shall be laid, unless in Proportion to the Census or Enumeration herein before directed to be taken." (U.S. CONST. art. I § 9.)

The Direct Tax Clause is a mouthful. But it means simply this: Federal taxes *cannot reach down and tax individuals directly*—not unless they are apportioned by State population. The Direct Tax limitation on the Tax and Spend Clause has always been understood (*see, e.g.*, THE FEDERALIST No. 36 (Hamilton) (Robert Scigliano ed., Modern Library 2001) (1787); *Pollock v. Farmers' Loan & Trust Co.*, 157 U.S. 429 (1895)) and, until very recently, enforced by the federal courts. (*See, infra*, n. 87 and accompanying text.)

Ah, but what about federal income taxes, you say? Are they not "direct" federal taxation of the individual? Yes, yes indeed they are. But federal income taxes are the exception that proves the rule: Federal income taxes are only constitutional under the Sixteenth Amendment, ratified in 1913, which provides that "Congress shall have power to lay and collect *taxes on incomes*, from whatever source derived, without apportionment among the several States, and without regard to any census or enumeration." (U.S. CONST. amend. XVI (emphasis added).) Under the narrow

exception of the Sixteenth Amendment, in the limited sphere of income, federal taxation may touch the individual directly. But aside from this narrow and explicit exception, it may not.
[11] THE FEDERALIST No. 34, at 204 (Hamilton) (Robert Scigliano ed., Modern Library 2001) (1787).
[12] THE FEDERALIST No. 34, at 204 (Hamilton) (Robert Scigliano ed., Modern Library 2001) (1787).
[13] *Bailey v. Drexel Furniture Co.*, 259 U.S. 20 (1922) (voiding Title XII of the Revenue Act of 1919).
[14] *Bailey v. Drexel Furniture Co.*, 259 U.S. at 37 (1922).
[15] *Bailey v. Drexel Furniture Co.*, 259 U.S. at 38 (1922). Labor law is *not* among the enumerated powers entrusted to the federal government. Therefore the Constitution reserves exclusive power to regulate labor law to the States. The Tenth Amendment is instructive on this point: "The powers not delegated to the United States by the Constitution, nor prohibited by it to the States, are reserved to the States respectively, or to the people." U.S. CONST. amend. X.
[16] "Grant the validity of this law, and all that Congress would need to do, hereafter, in seeking to take over to its control any one of the great number of subjects of public interest, jurisdiction of which the States have never parted with, and which are reserved to them by the Tenth Amendment, would be to enact a detailed measure of complete regulation of the subject and enforce it by a so-called tax upon departures from it." *Bailey v. Drexel Furniture Co.*, 259 U.S. at 38 (1922) (emphasis added).
[17] *Bailey v. Drexel Furniture Co.*, 259 U.S. at 38 (1922) (emphasis added).
[18] "Reinterpretation" of the Tax and Spend Clause began as early as 1928, when the Supreme Court held the federal government could use its taxing power not only to raise revenues for the federal government but also to implement protectionist trade policies. *J. W. Hampton & Co. v. United States*, 276 U.S. 394 (1928). At the time this expansion in federal power didn't seem too much of a stretch. The Court had previously allowed a few federal taxes possessing motives "incidental" to raising revenue, as they fulfilled other enumerated powers. *J.W. Hampton & Co.*, 276 U.S. at 412-13 (1928) (finding tariffs on foreign imports constitutional—of course, Congress had justification for such tax under the power to "To regulate Commerce with foreign Nations," U.S. CONST. art. I, § 8.). But the stretch would soon become apparent: Supreme Court "reinterpretation" of the Tax and Spend Clause from 1928 through 1937 was incredible.
[19] By 1934 the Court assumed an increasingly Incrementalist posture with regards to the Tax and Spend Clause. The Court began to bow down before Congress. In *A. Magnano Co. v. Hamilton*, 292 U.S. 40, 47 (1934), the Supreme Court upheld a variable tariff on foreign imports. Now, tariffs on foreign imports have independent justification under Congress' power to "To regulate Commerce with foreign Nations," U.S. CONST. art. I, § 8.

But the Court didn't stop there. The Court went far beyond tariffs, and inserted dicta addressing taxes generally and not specifying tariffs on foreign imports:

> From the beginning of our government, the courts have sustained taxes although imposed with the collateral intent of effecting ulterior motives which, considered apart, were beyond the constitutional power of the lawmakers to realize by legislation directly addressed to their accomplishment.

A. Magnano Co. v. Hamilton, 292 U.S. at 47 (1934).

As you can see, the Supreme Court suffers from an elitist verbosity. Let me translate the above statement into plain English: "We at the Supreme Court will allow you at Congress to do what you please—so long as you do it *indirectly*, by *taxation* rather than *direct legislation*."[19]

In so saying, the Court openly invited Congress to impose federal policies by taxation in those areas where Congress had no constitutional authority to legislate. In so saying the Court also dissembled, and denied a century and a half of constitutional precedent.
[20] *U.S. v. Butler*, 297 U.S. 1 (1936).
[21] Yes, this sounds quite familiar—as related in the previous chapter, the federal government soon got its way on national crop quotas using the Incrementalist Commerce Clause, instead.
[22] Specifically, Justice Roberts and the Court wrote that the AAA "invades the reserved rights of the states. It is a statutory plan to regulate and control agricultural production, a matter beyond the powers delegated to the federal government. The tax, the appropriation of the funds raised,

and the direction for their disbursement, are but parts of the plan. They are but means to an unconstitutional end." *U.S. v. Butler*, 297 U.S. 1, 68 (1936).
[23] *U.S. v. Butler*, 297 U.S. at 72 (1936) (emphasis added).
[24] *U.S. v. Butler*, 297 U.S. 1, 64-66 (1936).
[25] *U.S. v. Butler*, 297 U.S. 1, 65-66 (1936) (emphasis added):

> The Congress is expressly empowered to lay taxes to provide *for the general welfare*. . . . The necessary implication from the terms of the grant is that the public funds may be appropriated "to provide *for the general welfare of the United States*." These words cannot be meaningless, else they would not have been used. The Conclusion must be that they were intended to limit *and define* the granted power to raise and to expend money. How shall they be construed to effectuate the intent of the instrument? . . .
>
> The [for the general welfare] clause *confers a power separate and distinct from those later enumerated, is not restricted in meaning by the grant of them, and Congress consequently has a substantive power to tax and to appropriate, limited only by the requirement that it shall be exercised to provide for the general welfare of the United States. . . . It results that the power of Congress to authorize expenditure of public money for public purposes is not limited by the direct grants of legislative power found in the Constitution.*

[26] *U.S. v. Butler*, 297 U.S. 1, 65-66 (1936).
[27] *See Steward Machine Co. v. Davis*, 301 U.S. 548 (1937).
[28] Formally, the Social Security Act of 1935.
[29] In unemployment compensation, as in other matters, the federal government views the States as stubborn and uncooperative beasts of burden. Congress needed a clever way to cajole unwilling States into packing federal unemployment compensation policy through the Great Depression. To this end Congress devised the Social Security Act's tax and conditional spending scheme, which imposed upon States both carrots and sticks. *See infra* n. 30, 31, and accompanying text.
[30] The Social Security Act's tax and credit scheme worked as follows:

First (1) the federal government imposed a tax upon employers.

However, (2) if a *State* would *also* tax employers, for the specific purpose of implementing a State-sponsored unemployment compensation program, and (3) if that State-sponsored unemployment insurance program were approved by the federal government's new Social Security Board,

Then: (4) The federal government would (a) allow employers in the State to *credit up to 90% of State taxes they paid toward State unemployment compensation against the federal tax*, and also (b) *spend federal monies* for maternal and child welfare, public health, welfare for the elderly, and unemployment compensation administration costs within the State.
[31] This was the carrot: The return of federal tax money to the State from which it was taken. There was also a stick:

The Social Security Act's tax and credit scheme put State governments between the hammer of their own State constituents and the anvil of federal unemployment policy. Employers domiciled in the State would *insist* on receiving that 90% federal tax credit for contributions to any State unemployment compensation program. (*See supra* n. 30.) This would force State governments to make their own unemployment compensation programs conform to all the federal particulars—as dictated by the Social Security Board.
[32] Unfortunately, we are here using the term "indirectly" in a different sense than we have used it elsewhere to distinguish between "direct" federal taxes, which must be apportioned by population among the States, and "indirect" federal taxes, which need not. (*See supra* n. 10; *see also infra* n. 87.) Here we use instead the Supreme Court's euphemism for "conditional taxes and conditional spending," which the Court asserts are not "direct" legislation—in the limited sense that conditional taxing and spending does not require submission to federal policy. Instead one has the "option" of doing as one wishes, but paying the conditional tax. Or forfeiting the conditional rebate. Or foregoing the conditional subsidy. Or whatever. It is unfortunate that we must use terminology like "direct" and "indirect" in two different senses when referring to federal taxation—but this is the language the Switch in Time Court has given us to discuss such matters.

[33] *U.S. v. Butler*, 297 U.S. 1, 65-66 (1936). *See supra* n. 25.
[34] U.S. CONST. art. I, § 8. Check it out: You will find no federal unemployment insurance power.
[35] U.S. CONST. amend. X. Check it out: Powers not granted to the federal government and not prohibited to the States are reserved to the States.
[36] So much for State sovereignty. So much for a federal government of limited, enumerated powers. So much for the structure of the Constitution. So much for the Tenth Amendment. *See also Sonzinsky v. United States*, 300 U.S. 506, 514 (1937) (So long as a congressional regulation or deterrence "operates as a tax, it is within the national taxing power.") In other words, Congress may have no authority to pass legislation restricting an activity—but dog gone it, Congress can still tax and spend in any way they please to restrict that activity!
[37] *McCulloch v. Maryland*, 17 U.S. 316 (1819).
[38] "During the years 1929 to 1936, when the country was passing through a cyclical depression, the number of the unemployed mounted to unprecedented heights. Often the average was more than 10 million; at times a peak was attained of 16 million or more. . . . It is too late today for the argument to be heard with tolerance that in a crisis so extreme the use of the moneys of the nation to relieve the unemployed and their dependents is a use for any purpose narrower than the promotion of the general welfare." *Steward Machine Co. v. Davis*, 301 U.S. at 586-87 (1937).
[39] *See supra* n. 32.
[40] *Steward Machine Co. v. Davis*, 301 U.S. at 617-18 (1937) (Justice Butler dissent).
[41] *Steward Machine Co. v. Davis*, 301 U.S. at 618 (1937) (Justice Butler dissent).
[42] For example, the federal government collected $2.524 trillion in taxes compared to the States' collection of $1.343 trillion in taxes for 2008.
[43] Ilya Somin, *Closing the Pandora's Box of Federalism: The Case for Judicial Restriction of Federal Subsidies to State Governments*, 90 Geo. L.J. 461 (2002).
[44] *Steward Machine Co. v. Davis*, 301 U.S. at 585-87 (1937):

> The excise is not void as involving the coercion of the States in contravention of the Tenth Amendment or of restrictions implicit in our federal form of government. . . .
>
> Supporters of the statute say that its operation is not constraint, but the creation of a larger freedom [!], the States and the nation joining in a cooperative endeavor to avert a common evil.

[45] The APPENDIX, entitled *"Yes" Plus*, treats *South Dakota v. Dole*, 483 U.S. 203, 205 (1987). This is a delightful little morsel of case law, one which resonates with many people, and one that is easy to relate in narrative form. It really belongs in this chapter. But it has been removed with an eye to preserving the commercial reader's attention span: it has been my experience that the vast majority of lay readers tire quickly of case law. For the curious student, however, I can recommend the Appendix as highly-entertaining reading.
[46] Pub. L. 111-152, amended by the "Health Care and Education Reconciliation Act of 2010," Pub. L. 111-148. *See* 26 U.S.C. § 5000A *et seq.*
[47] 26 U.S.C. § 5000A; *see esp.* §§ 5000A(c) ("penalty") and 5000A(b)(1) ("shared responsibility payment").
[48] 26 U.S.C. §§ 5000A(d); 5000(A)(f); and 5000A(e).
[49] In 2016, after the "phase in" period of 2014 and 2015. 26. U.S.C. § 5000A(c)(3)(B); *see generally* 26 U.S.C. § 5000A(c); 42 U.S.C. § 18022.
[50] *Florida v. United States Dep't. of Health and Human Services*, 780 F. Supp. 2d 1256, 1263 (N.D. Fla. 2011).
[51] Emergency Medical Treatment and Labor Act, 42 U.S.C. § 1395dd.
[52] Brief of Senate Majority Leader Harry Reid, House Democratic Leader Nancy Pelosi, and Congressional Leaders and Leaders of Committees of Relevant Jurisdiction as Amici Curiae in Support of Petitioners (Minimum Coverage Provision), 13, *Dept. of Health and Human Services v. State of Florida*, No. 11-398 (Jan. 13, 2012). *See also ibid.* at 15. http://www.americanbar.org/content/dam/aba/publications/supreme_court_preview/briefs/11-398_petitioneramcuharryreidetal.authcheckdam.pdf.
[53] *See supra* Chapters 5 (*Diluting Middle America*) and 6 (*¡Si, Se Puede!*).

[54] Emergency Medical Treatment and Labor Act, 42 U.S.C. § 1395dd.
[55] For example, programs like Medicare and Medicaid.
[56] Nancy Pelosi, *Health Insurance Reform Daily Mythbuster: 'Constitutionality of Health Insurance Reform'*, DEMOCRATIC LEADER Press Release (Sept. 16, 2009). http://www democraticleader.gov/news/facts?id=0107.
[57] Brief of Senate Majority Leader Harry Reid, House Democratic Leader Nancy Pelosi, and Congressional Leaders and Leaders of Committees of Relevant Jurisdiction as Amici Curiae in Support of Petitioners (Minimum Coverage Provision), 8-18, *Dept. of Health and Human Services v. State of Florida*, No. 11-398 (Jan. 13, 2012). http://www.americanbar.org/content/dam/aba/publications/supreme_court_preview/briefs/11-398_petitioneramcuharryreidetal.authcheckdam.pdf.
[58] Brief of Senate Majority Leader Harry Reid, House Democratic Leader Nancy Pelosi, and Congressional Leaders and Leaders of Committees of Relevant Jurisdiction as Amici Curiae in Support of Petitioners (Minimum Coverage Provision), 16, *Dept. of Health and Human Services v. State of Florida*, No. 11-398 (Jan. 13, 2012) (emphasis added). *See also ibid.* at 3: "The central and dispositive fact in this case is that the Patient Protection and Affordable Care Act ('the Act' or 'ACA'), including the provision that individuals maintain minimum health insurance coverage, is a congressional regulation of the interstate health insurance market."
[59] 42 U.S.C. §§ 18091(1) and 1501(2)(A); *cf.* Patient Protection and Affordable Care Act §§ 1501(a)(1) and 1501(a)(2)(A).
[60] *Florida v. United States Dep't. of Health and Human Services*, 780 F. Supp. 2d 1256 (N.D. Fla. 2011).
[61] *Florida v. United States Dep't. of Health and Human Services*, 648 F.3d 1235 (11th Cir. 2011).
[62] *Nat'l Fed'n of Indep. Bus. v. Sebelius*, 183 L. Ed. 450 (2012).
[63] "The Constitution grants Congress the power to '*regulate* Commerce.' Art. I, §8, cl. 3. The power to *regulate* commerce presupposes the existence of commercial activity to be regulated. If the power to 'regulate' something included the power to create it, many of the provisions of the Constitution would be superfluous. For example, the Constitution gives Congress the power to 'coin Money,' in addition to the power to 'regulate the Value thereof.' *Ibid.*, cl. 5. . . . The language of the Constitution reflects the natural understanding that the power to regulate assumes there is already something to be regulated." *Nat'l Fed'n of Indep. Bus. v. Sebelius*, 183 L. Ed. 450, 474 (2012) (emphasis original).
[64] "Our precedent also reflects this understanding. As expansive as our cases construing the scope of the commerce power have been, they all have one thing in common: They uniformly describe the power as reaching 'activity.' It is nearly impossible to avoid the word when quoting them." *Nat'l Fed'n of Indep. Bus. v. Sebelius*, 183 L. Ed. at 475 (2012) (citations omitted).
[65] "The individual mandate, however, does not regulate existing commercial activity. It instead compels individuals to *become* active in commerce by purchasing a product, on the ground that their failure to do so affects interstate commerce. Construing the Commerce Clause to permit Congress to regulate individuals precisely *because* they are doing nothing would open a new and potentially vast domain to congressional authority." *Nat'l Fed'n of Indep. Bus. v. Sebelius*, 183 L. Ed. at 475 (2012) (emphasis original).
[66] "The individual mandate, however, does not regulate existing commercial activity. It instead compels individuals to *become* active in commerce by purchasing a product, on the ground that their failure to do so affects interstate commerce." *Nat'l Fed'n of Indep. Bus. v. Sebelius*, 183 L. Ed. at 475 (2012) (emphasis original).
[67] *See, e.g.*, Kevin Drum, *Donald Verrilli Makes the Worst Supreme Court Argument of All Time*, MOTHER JONES (Mar. 27, 2012) ("Virtually everyone agrees that today's arguments before the Supreme Court were a disaster for the Obama Administration."); Adam Serwer, *Obamacare's Supreme Court Disaster*, MOTHER JONES (Mar. 27 2012) ("Solicitor General Donald B. Verrilli Jr. should be grateful to the Supreme Court for refusing to allow cameras in the courtroom, because his defense of Obamacare on Tuesday may go down as one of the most spectacular flameouts in the history of the court. . . . Sounding less like a world-class lawyer and more like a teenager giving an oral presentation for the first time, Verrilli delivered a rambling, apprehensive legal defense of liberalism's biggest domestic accomplishment since the 1960s—and one that may well have doubled as its eulogy. . . . *If the law is upheld, it will be in spite of Verrilli's performance,*

not because of it.") (emphasis added); Jeffrey Toobin, live comments after oral arguments, CNN (Mar. 27, 2012) ("This was a train wreck for the Obama Administration; this law looks like it's going to be struck down."); Jeffrey Rosen, *One Simple Argument Could Have Saved Obamacare. Too Bad Verrilli Didn't Make It.*, THE NEW REPUBLIC (Mar. 30, 2012) ("Verrilli's error was substantive: He failed squarely to answer Roberts and Kennedy's repeated questions about what limits he envisioned to Congress's power to regulate interstate commerce. Verrilli's evasions weren't only unhelpful—they were also unnecessary."); Morgan Little, *For Government Lawyer Verrilli, Tough Week on Healthcare Case*, LOS ANGELES TIMES (Mar. 30, 2012) ("Verrilli, an accomplished lawyer who this week became known for his frequent pauses, awkward noises and lengthy water breaks during his defense of the Patient Protection and Affordable Care Act, has been widely criticized for what some deemed a sub-par performance in the nation's highest court."); Ben Jacobs, *Did Solicitor General Donald Verrilli Blow the Case on Obamacare?*, THE DAILY BEAST (Mar. 27, 2012) ("Verrilli seemed more like a nervous first-year law student than a respected advocate who had appeared before the court o 17 previous occasions. He started out so poorly that on several occasions, one or more of the court's four liberal justices, who are all expected to vote to uphold the law, seemed to feel they had to guide Verrilli back to his strongest arguments.").

[68] Kevin Drum, *Donald Verrilli Makes the Worst Supreme Court Argument of All Time*, MOTHER JONES (Mar. 27, 2012).

[69] Adam Serwer, *Obamacare's Supreme Court Disaster*, MOTHER JONES (Mar. 27, 2012).

[70] Jeffrey Toobin, live comments after oral arguments, CNN (Mar. 27, 2012).

[71] *See, e.g.*, Editorial, *Court Likely to Overturn ObamaCare After Hearings*, INVESTORS BUSINESS DAILY (Mar. 28, 2012); Peter Ferrara, *Why the Supreme Court Will Strike Down All of Obamacare*, FORBES (April 5, 2012); David R. Dow, *Impeach the Supreme Court Justices If They Overturn Health-Care Law*, THE DAILY BEAST (April 3, 2012); Amy Bingham, *Betting Markets Predict Supreme Court Will Strike Down Individual Mandate*, ABC NEWS (June 23, 2012); Sahil Kapur, *Reading the 'Obamacare" Tea Leaves as Ruling Looms*, TALKING POINTS MEMO (June 24, 2012); Ed Whelan, *My Prediction on Tomorrow's Obamacare Ruling*, NATIONAL REVIEW (June 27, 2012) ("the Court will invalidate the individual mandate by a 5-4 vote."); Michael Tomasky, *My Supreme Court-Health Care Prediction*, THE DAILY BEAST (June 27, 2012) (Court will overturn the mandate 5-4); Peter Suderman, *Why I'm Cautiously Optimistic That ObamaCare's Mandate Will Be Struck Down*, REASON (June 25, 2012) ("I'm on record as predicting that the mandate will go down . . . ."); Brian Beutler, *Top Legal Commentator Toobin Stands By Doomsday Prediction For Health Care Law*, TALKING POINTS MEMO (April 3, 2012).

[72] Jan Crawford, *Roberts Switched Views to Uphold Health Care Law*, CBS NEWS (July 1, 2012).

[73] *Ibid.*

[74] Barack Obama, speaking at a joint press conference with Mexican President Felipe Calderon and Canadian Prime Minister Stephen Harper (April 2, 2012). The president said, moreover, "I think it's important—and I think the American people understand, and I think the Justices should understand—that in the absence of an individual mandate you cannot have a mechanism to ensure that people with preexisting conditions can actually get health care. . . . We are confident that this will be upheld because it should be upheld." *See, e.g.*, Jeff Mason, *Obama Takes a Shot at Supreme Court Over Healthcare*, REUTERS (April 2, 2012); Jennifer Epstein, *Obama: Supreme Court Won't Overturn Health Care Law*, POLITICO (April 2, 2012).

[75] Senate Judiciary Committee Chairman Patrick Leahy, making a speech from the senate floor (May 14, 2012).

[76] Editorial, *The Roberts Court Defines Itself*, THE NEW YORK TIMES (Mar. 31, 2012). *See also* Jeffrey Rosen, *Second Opinions: Obamacare Isn't The Only Target of Conservative Judges*, The New Republic (May 4, 2012) ("Of course, if the Roberts Court strikes down health care reform by a 5-4 vote, then the chief justice's stated goal of presiding over a less divisive court will be viewed as an irredeemable failure. But, by voting to strike down Obamacare, Roberts would also be abandoning the association of legal conservatism with restraint—and resurrecting the pre-New Deal era of economic judicial activism with a vengeance.").

[77] "There were countless news articles in May warning of damage to the court—and to Roberts' reputation—if the court were to strike down the mandate. Leading politicians, including the president himself, had expressed confidence the mandate would be upheld. Some even

suggested that if Roberts struck down the mandate, it would prove he had been deceitful during his confirmation hearings, when he explained a philosophy of judicial restraint." Jan Crawford, *Roberts Switched Views to Uphold Health Care Law*, CBS NEWS (July 1, 2012); *see also* Senate Judiciary Committee Chairman Patrick Leahy, making a speech from the senate floor (May 14, 2012).

[78] Jan Crawford, *Roberts Switched Views to Uphold Health Care Law*, CBS NEWS (July 1, 2012).

[79] THE FEDERALIST No. 78, at 501 (Hamilton) (Robert Scigliano ed., Modern Library 2001) (1787) ("Until the people have, by some solemn and authoritative act, annulled or changed the established form, it is binding upon themselves collectively, as well as individually; and no presumption, or even knowledge, of their sentiments, can warrant their representatives in a departure from it, prior to such an act. *But it is easy to see, that it would require an uncommon portion of fortitude in the judges to do their duty as faithful guardians of the Constitution, where legislative invasions of it had been instigated by the major voice of the community.*") (emphasis added).

[80] *See, e.g.*, *Parents Involved in Comty. Schs. v. Seattle Sch. Dist. No. 1*, 551 U.S. 701 (2007); *United States v. Stevens*, 130 S. Ct. 1577 (2010); *Citizens United v. Federal Election Comm'n*, 558 U.S. 50 (2010).

[81] WILLIAM LANGLAND, PIERS PLOWMAN, passus v lines 461-76:

> Robert the Robbere on *Reddite* lokede,
> And for ther was noughte [wherwith], he wepe swithe sore.
> Ac yet the synful shrewe seyde to hymselve,
> "Cryst that on Calvarye uppon the Crosse deydest,
> Tho Dismas my brother bisoughte [the] of grace,
> And haddest mercy on that man for *Memento* sake,
> So rewe on this robbere that *Reddere* ne have,
> Ne nevere wene to wynne with crafte that I owe;
> But for thi mykel mercy mitigacioun I biseche:
> Dampne me noughte at Domesday for that I did so ille."
> What bifel of this feloun I can noughte faire schewe. . . .

See, e.g., WILLIAM LANGLAND, PIERS PLOWMAN 86 (Elizabeth Robertson & Stephen H. A. Shepherd eds., W. W. Norton & Co. 2006) (1370).

[82] John Ball, *Letter to the Essex Commons*, lines 4-5 (British Library, Royal MS 13.E.ix fol. 287r) (1381):

> [A]nd biddeth Peres Ploughman go to his werk,
> and chastise wel Hobbe the Robbere . . . .

See, e.g., THOMAS WALSINGHAM, CHRONICA MAIORA 163 (David Preest trans., James G. Clark ed., Boydell Press 2005) (1422).

[83] *See supra* n. 63 through 66 and accompanying text.

[84] 26 U.S.C. § 5000A; *see esp.* §§ 5000A(c) ("penalty") and 5000A(b)(1) ("shared responsibility payment").

[85] Why, Obamacare's individual mandate penalty "produces at least some revenue for the Government"—so in that sense, at least, it works sort of like a tax! *Nat'l Fed'n of Indep. Bus. v. Sebelius*, 183 L. Ed. at 483 (2012). Besides, the "penalty" is collected by the IRS—another tax similarity! *Ibid.*; *see further* at 483-90.

[86] *Nat'l Fed'n of Indep. Bus. v. Sebelius*, 183 L. Ed. at 488 (2012).

[87] For example, there was the terrible difficulty of the Direct Tax Clause: The constitutional prohibition on un-apportioned direct taxes. (U.S. CONST. art. I § 9; *see supra* n. 10.) After all, if Obamacare's individual mandate is a "tax," it "taxes" citizens *directly*—and it is *not* apportioned by State population as the Constitution requires.

This was a difficult one. Like a child caught with her hand in the cookie jar, Justice Roberts served up an infantile copout: *He played stupid.* He ruled that the Supreme Court wasn't really sure what the term "direct taxes" meant. And he went well beyond that—he ruled that, even historically, *no one had ever really known what the term "direct taxes" meant!* He said, "Even when the Direct Tax Clause was written it was unclear what else, other than a capitation (also known as a 'head tax' or a 'poll tax'), might be a direct tax." (*Nat'l Fed'n of Indep. Bus. v. Sebelius*, 183 L. Ed. at 487 (2012).)

Now this was an unqualified lie. "Direct tax" is not an elusive term. Certainly the *Old* Supreme Court understood the meaning of the term—it was for this reason that the Old Court struck down the federal income tax of 1895 as an unconstitutional, un-apportioned, direct tax. (*Pollock v. Farmers' Loan & Trust Co.*, 157 U.S. 429 (1895).) And it is why the Sixteenth Amendment was added in 1913: To change the Constitution, to allow Congress "to lay and collect taxes on incomes, from whatever source derived, without apportionment among the several States, and without regard to any census or enumeration." (U.S. CONST. amend. XVI. And for all you Incrementalists out there, to whom this might not be obvious, a tax *for not having healthcare* is not a tax on "income." It is quite the opposite, in fact: it is a tax for *not* having an accoutrement of wealth. So the Obamacare individual mandate "tax" does not fit into the Sixteenth Amendment's exception for un-apportioned federal taxes on income. It is something entirely different.)

Why, even Alexander Hamilton—the most rabid proponent of federal power during the Founding!—recognized that "taxes may be subdivided into those of the *direct* and those of the *indirect* kind." (Emphasis original.) The direct/indirect dichotomy was a complete partition of the federal taxing space. And even Hamilton defined indirect taxes as "duties and excises on articles of consumption"—leaving *everything else* a species of direct tax. And Hamilton commanded, "Let it be recollected that the proportion of these [direct] taxes is not to be left to the discretion of the national legislature, but is to be determined by the numbers of each State, as described in the second section of the first article. An actual census or enumeration of the people must furnish the rule, a circumstance which effectually shuts the door to partiality or oppression. The abuse of this power of taxation seems to have been provided against with guarded circumspection." (THE FEDERALIST No. 36 (Hamilton) at 215-17 (Robert Scigliano ed., Modern Library 2001) (1787).)

So Roberts' ruling that, even historically, *no one had ever really known what the term "direct taxes" meant*, was a complete lie. But it is what he ruled. And by reinterpreting the constitutional prohibition on un-apportioned direct taxes as unfathomable, Justice Roberts effectively made the Direct Tax Clause disappear. His sophistry on this point was quite sophisticated, worked as follows: (1) No one ever really knew what the term "direct tax" included; (2) We at the Supreme Court have assumed in the past that it included *at least* capitations [a complete redundancy!], taxes on personal property, and income from personal property; (3) A tax on going without health insurance doesn't fall in any of those categories; so (4) Obamacare's "shared responsibility payment" is not a direct tax that must be apportioned among the States. (*Nat'l Fed'n of Indep. Bus. v. Sebelius*, 183 L. Ed. at 487-88 (2012).)

Of course, what such an argument really does is (a) deny all responsibility for determining whether a new form of tax—a tax *for not having bought something*—is direct or indirect; and (b) thereby declare it an indirect tax that need not be apportioned.

You see, only the Tax and Spend Monster matters; it swallows all other parts of the Constitution whole.

[88] *See supra* n. 87.

[89] "In this case we must again determine whether the Constitution grants Congress powers it now asserts, but which many States and individuals believe it does not possess. Resolving this controversy requires us to examine both the limits of the Government's power, *and our own limited role in policing those boundaries.*" *Nat'l Fed'n of Indep. Bus. v. Sebelius*, 183 L. Ed. at 465 (2012) (emphasis added). "Granting the Act *the full measure of deference owed to federal statutes*, it can be so read [as a tax], for the reasons set forth below." *Ibid.* at 483 (emphasis added). "More often and more recently we have declined to closely examine the regulatory motive or effect of revenue-raising measures." *Ibid.* at 489.

[90] *Nat'l Fed'n of Indep. Bus. v. Sebelius*, 183 L. Ed. at 483-90 (2012).

[91] "None of this is to say that the payment is not intended to affect individual conduct. Although the payment will raise considerable revenue, it is plainly designed to expand health insurance coverage. But taxes that seek to influence conduct are nothing new." *Nat'l Fed'n of Indep. Bus. v. Sebelius*, 183 L. Ed. at 485 (2012).

[92] *Nat'l Fed'n of Indep. Bus. v. Sebelius*, 183 L. Ed. at 489 (2012) (citing *Oklahoma Tax Comm'n v. Texas Co.*, 336 U.S. 342, 364 (1949) (quoting *Panhandle Oil Co. v. Mississippi ex rel. Knox*, 277 U.S. 218, 223 (1928) (Holmes, J., dissenting))) (emphasis added).

[93] *See supra* n. 10; 87; *see also* APPENDIX, *"Yes" Plus.*
[94] *E.g.*, Thomas L. Friedman, *Taking One for the Country*, THE NEW YORK TIMES (June 30, 2012) ("In my mind, there are two lessons from the Supreme Court's 5-to-4 decision to support President Obama's health care plan: 1) how starved the country is for leadership that puts the nation's interest before partisan politics, which is exactly what Chief Justice John Roberts Jr. did; and 2) the virtue of audacity in politics and thinking big. . . . It was not surprising to hear liberals extolling the legal creativity and courage of Chief Justice Roberts in finding a way to greenlight Obama's Affordable Care Act. . . . [I]t has been so long since a national leader ripped up the polls and not only acted out of political character but did so truly for the good of the country—as Chief Justice Roberts seemingly did."); Andrew Sullivan, *The First Elite Conservative To Say Enough*, THE DAILY BEAST (July 2, 2012) ("Mulling over the Supreme Court ruling in favor of Obamacare this weekend, it occurred to me why this remains a BFD. . . . It is that a creature of the conservative movement, one of its youngest and most intelligent stars, saw the radicalism of the four dissenters—and balked."); Jeffrey Toobin, *To Your Health*, THE NEW YORKER (July 9, 2012) ("And here, alone and exposed, Roberts joined with the Court's four liberals to dash the Republican Party's most fervent wishes. It was a singular act of courage."); Charles Lane, *John Roberts's Compromise of 2012*, THE WASHINGTON POST (June 29, 2012) ("If anyone sees a parallel between today's polarized politics and those of Webster's time, it would be Roberts. No one understands the United States' constitutional strengths, and vulnerabilities, better than he.").
[95] Justin Sink, *John Roberts Jokes About Vacationing on an 'Impregnable Island Fortress'*, THE HILL (June 29, 2012).
[96] Melissa Jeltsen, *John Roberts Arrives in Malta (PHOTOS)*, THE HUFFINGTON POST (July 3, 2012); Meghan Keneally, *After Joking About Heading to Malta to Escape Criticism… Chief Justice Roberts Heads to Malta As It Emerges That He May Have Written For AND Against Opinions on Obamacare*, MAIL ONLINE (July 4, 2012).
[97] For example, 30% of the population openly admit they don't know anything about the *Sebelius* decision, and another 15% incorrectly believe the Supreme Court struck down most provisions of Obamacare! So a full 45% have no idea what is going on. *See, e.g.*, Pew Research Center Poll: *Division, Uncertainty Over Court's Health Care Ruling: Top One-Word Reactions 'Disappointed,' 'Surprised'* (July 2, 2012). http://www.people-press.org/2012/07/02/division-uncertainty-over-courts-health-care-ruling/.
[98] In theory a future Supreme Court could overrule *Nat'l Fed'n of Indep. Bus. v. Sebelius*, 183 L. Ed. 450 (2012). But that is extraordinarily unlikely: The Supreme Court takes great pains not to overrule its own precedent. Instead, when the Court wishes to have a different result, it simply distinguishes the current facts from those in prior cases, or qualifies prior rulings. It practically never overrules itself or its constitutional precedent. (Go check and you will see!) And thus bad constitutional precedent lives forever—to be dusted off and presented at some future date as a justification for further federal usurpations.
[99] *See supra* n. 10; 87; *see also* APPENDIX, *"Yes" Plus.*
[100] *See supra* n. 10; 87.
[101] *See* APPENDIX, *"Yes" Plus*
[102] And *South Dakota v. Dole* will linger, too. *See supra* n. 45; 99.
[103] *See* APPENDIX, *"Yes" Plus.*
[104] Over a period of roughly ninety years, the Supreme Court has "reinterpreted" certain—but not all of—the restrictions on federal power found in the Bill of Rights as equally binding on the States. This process began with *Gitlow v. New York*, 268 U.S. 652 (1925) (incorporating First Amendment rights to freedom of speech and freedom of the press against State governments), and has most recently been invoked in McDonald v. Chicago, 561 U.S. 3025 (2010) (incorporating the Second Amendment right to bear arms against State governments). Now there's a clever way to bind disempower the States: Subject them to constitutional limitations which only apply to yourself!
[105] U.S. CONST. art. I, § 10 ("No State shall . . . pass any . . . Law impairing the Obligation of Contracts.").
[106] *Energy Reserves Group, Inc. v. Kansas Power & Light Co.*, 459 U.S. 400 (1983) (articulating a loose "three part test" to determine when laws impairing the obligation of contracts *are* constitutional

(!)); *see also* the original Switch in Time version: *Home Building & Loan Ass'n v. Blaisdell*, 290 U.S. 398 (1934) (ruling that economic downturn makes laws impairing the obligation of contracts suddenly constitutional (!)).
[107] U.S. CONST. art. I, § 8 ("To make all Laws which shall be necessary and proper for carrying into Execution the foregoing Powers").
[108] *See, e.g.*, *Wickard v. Filburn*, 317 U.S. 111 (1942). But this particular slippery slope was exposed very early in our Republic's history. *McCulloch v. Maryland*, 17 U.S. 316 (1819).
[109] U.S. CONST. art. I, § 9 ("No . . . ex post facto law shall be passed."); U.S. CONST. art. I, § 10 ("No State shall . . . pass any . . . ex post facto Law.").
[110] *See, e.g.*, *Rogers v. Tennessee*, 532 U.S. 451 (2001) (while legislatures cannot make retroactive criminal laws, *courts can!*); *United States v. Emerson*, 270 F.3d 203 (5th Cir. 2001) (retroactive criminal laws can be made by the *Federal Legislature, too!*); *Smith v. Doe*, 538 U.S. 84 (2003) (retroactive criminal laws can be made by *State legislatures, as well!*).
[111] U.S. CONST. art. IV, § 4 ("The United States shall guarantee to every State in this Union a Republican Form of Government"). In other words, the Constitution requires *representative government*—and forbids *direct democracy*. Direct democracy was one of our Predecessors' primary fears. *See, e.g.*, THE FEDERALIST No. 10 (Madison) (Robert Scigliano ed., Modern Library 2001) (1787).
[112] *See, e.g.*, *Luther v. Borden*, 48 U.S. 1 (1949) (establishing the so-called "political question doctrine," under which the Court surrendered its duty to adjudicate disputes regarding whether State governments were republican in form or not).
[113] U.S. CONST. amend. V ("nor shall private property be taken for public use without just compensation.")
[114] *Kelo v. City of New London*, 545 U.S. 469 (2005). To watch the Incrementalist drift in real time, *see also Housing Authority v. Midkiff*, 467 U.S. 229 (1984) (eminent domain need not put seized private property into *actual* public use; private property may be taken simply for the purpose of redistribution); *Berman v. Parker*, 384 U.S. 26 (1954) (dropping "public use" limitation altogether for "public purpose," including alleged aesthetic, financial, and physical benefits; refusing to analyze individual properties apart from the neighborhood as a whole).
[115] U.S. CONST. art. III § 2 ("The judicial Power shall extend to all Cases, in Law and Equity, arising under this Constitution . . . .").
[116] *Cooper v. Aaron*, 358 U.S. 1 (1958).
[117] U.S. CONST. art. I, § 2, cl. 1 ("The House of Representatives shall be composed of Members chosen every second Year by the People of the several States").
[118] Reinterpreting the Equal Protection Clause of the Fourteenth Amendment as a requirement of *equal representation* in voting—something not ever previously entertained, and something obviously not contemplated by the Constitution (as the Constitution commands that each State, no matter how large or small its population, elects two U.S. Senators). *Reynolds v. Sims*, 377 U.S. 533 (1964) (ruling that *State* Senate districts must be practically equal in population, so that each vote for State Senator receives roughly the same weight—yet allowing U.S. Senate districts to go on apportioned by State boundaries (as demanded by the Constitution), so that votes for U.S. Senator in Wyoming have 66 times the potency of votes in California!)
[119] *Wesberry v. Sanders*, 376 U.S. 1 (1964) (ruling that States must also draw U.S. Congressional districts so that they are approximately equal in population, too); *see also Baker v. Carr*, 369 U.S. 186 (1962) (dumping the political question doctrine in the matter of redistricting, and ruling that the Court had jurisdiction to oversee the apportionment of State voting districts).
[120] U.S. CONST. amend. X ("The powers not delegated to the United States by the Constitution, nor prohibited by it to the States, are reserved to the States respectively, or to the people.").
[121] "Our conclusion is unaffected by the Tenth Amendment which provides: 'The powers not delegated to the United States by the Constitution, nor prohibited by it to the States, are reserved to the States respectively, or to the people.' The amendment states but a truism that all is retained which has not been surrendered." *United States v. Darby*, 312 U.S. 100, 123-24 (1941).
[122] *Corbett v. United States*, 458 Fed. Appx. 866 (11th Cir. Fla., 2012), *cert. denied*, 2012 U.S. LEXIS 7447 (Oct. 1, 2012) (No. 11-1413).

11

Faking It

Reader, suppose you were an idiot. And suppose you were a member of Congress. But I repeat myself. Simply suppose you were a member of Congress.

—Mark Twain[i]

We talk about [acting] being creative expression. And really, you're just a f—ing puppet. You're this dumb f—ing doll that wears what someone else tells you to wear, stands where someone else tells you to stand, says what somebody else tells you to say. That's not expression! That's not creativity!

—Joaquin Phoenix[ii]

FROM THE SUMMIT OF THE Socialist Ararat, we attain an unobstructed view of socialist method:

Incrementalism strips the Supreme Court of its independence, cows the Justices, and seizes the imprimatur of constitutional law. Incrementalism wields the newly-created Powers of "Yes" and "No" to swallow human choice, and to dictate every action taken by States and citizens. Because Incrementalism reinterprets the Constitution as a grant of monolithic federal power, it justifies rule by the Fourth Head. And the Fourth Head does socialism's dirty work: Insulated from Middle American votes, TSA fondles citizens at security checkpoints. The FCC expropriates the Internet in order to redistribute it. The FED shovels billions of American dollars into foreign banks. The NMIH redistributes millions of American dollars on sub-Saharan

---

[i] Mark Twain, unpublished manuscript c. 1881, as published in MARK TWAIN, WHO IS MARK TWAIN? 95 (Regents of the University of California eds., HarperCollins Publishers 2009).

[ii] Joaquin Phoenix, opening monologue, *I'm Still Here* (2010). Mr. Phoenix's declaration may well have been facetious. But the truth of his statement remains.

African penis-washing experiments, the NSF on sick shrimp marathons, NASA on Muslim outreach, the ATF on selling guns to Mexican narco-gangs, the SSA on stockpiling hollow-point bullets, and on and on.

In all these government actions, Incrementalism blocks participation by Middle Americans. And in all these matters Incrementalism makes irrepresentation of popular will into established federal procedure.

Incrementalism also furtively reorganizes American culture. It muzzles Middle American speech. It cultivates an environment in which people believe it their solemn duty to be offended by honest speech—and to excommunicate those who speak up. It proactively replaces Middle Americans with Third-World immigrants, and by so doing replaces Middle American self-reliance with Third-World dependency. It justifies domestic redistribution with the presence of the very underclass it imports. And it relies upon the allure of electronic entertainment to hypnotize, stupefy, and propagandize a dwindling Middle America.

In all these reorganizations, Incrementalism eviscerates Middle American culture. And so with culture, as in government, Incrementalism minimizes Middle American influence.

In the foregoing political and cultural modifications, Incrementalism accomplished exactly what it set out to achieve. It moved the socialist revolution carefully and methodically. It kept to the shadows. It was quiet most of the time, and silent when necessary. It inched along the slow road to revolution, and patiently consolidated gains over time. When detected it froze in place—until citizens looked away. Then it crept noiselessly forward again. Along the way it was unwittingly joined by numerous special interests. With their assistance Incrementalism constructed a monolithic government capable of fulfilling its redistributional goals *in spite of unwilling Middle Americans.* And in all this, Incrementalism avoided the horror of squirrel hunting.

Only now that we have seen Incrementalism in its fullness can we catch our first glimpse of the Tea Movement:

Tea Movement adherents are those who chafe at the irrepresentative nature of contemporary government and culture. These are they who believe that governments "deriv[e] their just Powers from the Consent of the Governed."[iii] These are they who know something of what the Constitution says, and do not appreciate it being "reinterpreted" into an alibi for further federal coercion. These are they who notice the Fourth Head controlling ever expanding swaths of American life, in increasingly irrepresentative ways, and who do not appreciate it. These are they who recognize American culture is

[iii] THE DECLARATION OF INDEPENDENCE ¶ 2 (U.S. 1776).

no longer the natural expression of majority Americana, but rather a social experiment forced upon citizens by a few at the top. These are they who have begun to say, "Enough is enough!"—and to demand that government, at the very least, represent popular American will. In short, *these are they who see the irrepresentative method of Incrementalism, who recognize it as the established procedure in Washington, and who consciously reject it.*

But while awakened to the irrepresentative nature of establishment politics, while recognizing Incrementalism as customary federal procedure, while focused on restoring a federal government premised on representing the will of the People, many Tea Movement adherents nevertheless fail to recognize Incrementalism's origins, motivations, strategy, and ultimate aim. They see powerful elites aligned against them; they see the role of citizen minimized in every possible way; they see these as undesirable and established patterns in Washington; yet many fail to see *why*. They do not see that Incrementalism's origin and endgame are *socialism*. They fail to recognize with precision the socialist thought and theory which undergird the Incrementalist process they denounce.

(In this regard, however, adherents to the Tea Movement are no more ignorant than many coastal establishmentarians in media, academia, and politics, who actively support Incrementalist government and culture—and *who also* fail to recognize Incrementalism's origins, first principles, and ultimate intent.)

And only now that we have examined socialist method in some detail can we define socialism itself:

In the Age of Incrementalism, deceit is the premise of socialist strategy and the currency of political and cultural reformation. Socialism cannot admit its ultimate aims because it fears Middle America. As a result, we can no longer trust what we are told: We cannot allow politicians or federal programs to define themselves.

No, for socialism must have a *functional* definition. A *recursive* definition. A socialist is a person who pursues socialism—whether or not he publicly admits it. The same holds true for socialist programs: A socialist program is one which pursues socialism—whether or not the text of the bill or regulation describes itself that way. In the Age of Incrementalism what matters is not what a person or program says, but what the person or program does: If it simultaneously aims at proactive redistributive injustice, at group "rights," at "moral" government, at the difference principle, at minimizing citizen oversight, at eliminating free choice, at attenuating American autonomy, at demolishing the concept of citizenship, and at overturning the Constitution—then there's a good bet it is socialist.

Socialists are like ducks. A duck never announces, "I am a duck." But that doesn't mean the duck is something else. Indeed, we do not call a duck otherwise when it fails to correctly and verbally define itself.

Similarly, if a man fails to identify himself as a socialist it means nothing. What matters is what he does. If he waddles like a socialist, paddles like a socialist, and quacks like a socialist, he is a socialist.

Whether he admits it or not.

Play Acting

To what can we compare a career politician?

A career politician is the screamer at your local gym. He wears a new sweat band, a new tracksuit, a new CamelBak® (gotta stay hands-free hydrated for those lifts!), new wrist wraps, new knee wraps. He swigs a creatine shake. He heaves like a colossus and screams like Hercules—*with almost no weight on the bar.*

He is overweight and understrong. He straps a broad, double-tongued leather belt around his considerable girth, and cinches it as tight as it will go. He so desperately wishes to be noticed. He so desperately wishes to be powerful. So he buys every accessory which could suggest he belongs.

But his uniform and manner are pretense: He rarely goes to the health club. At least, he rarely goes *to exercise.* Instead, he goes to masquerade. To be seen. To be heard. He is a tenacious pretender.

———

A career politician is a scrawny cracker in inner-city Detroit. He is apprehensive, shifty-eyed, and easily bullied. He keeps a low profile.

But once safely sworn into office, he is the same scrawny cracker *after having listened to a few hours of gangster rap.* He cocks his ball cap askew, un-tucks his shirt, drops his pants below his buttocks (keeping a hand in the waistband to avoid wardrobe malfunctions), puffs out his chest, and begins to swagger. A toothpick or a cigarette hangs loosely from the lips. Ambulant movements are grossly exaggerated and no longer conducive to locomotive efficiency: One side is strongly favored, effecting a limp. The arms are held nearly straight, and swing far wider than necessary for strolling; they extend personal space to give the (false) impression of greater size.

When the promenade is over, he begins to speak in dialect—a dialect foreign to himself, his family, and his audience; some mix between the grammatically backward language he grew up speaking and the Ebonics of power he attempts to imitate.

———

A career politician is a homecoming queen—the winner of a national popularity contest. He is a specialist of sorts. He does a few things very, very well: He makes you believe he is beautiful. He knows how to get attention.

He enjoys being recognized in a crowd. He makes you believe he is well-liked by others, if not by yourself.

He did not do so well in calculus. Or trigonometry. Or algebra II. Or geometry. Or arithmetic. Or—well, pick your class. But no worries—tonight he came out on top. Because for homecoming royalty, school is not about *intellectual* advancement. It is about *popular* advancement. (And, as they say, government is to career politicians as school is to homecoming queens.)

A career politician is, as a rule, a fantastic actor!

And really, this is the best analogy we can find: Career politicians are carefully crafted dolls who wear what someone else tells them to wear, stand where someone else tells them to stand, and say what somebody else tells them to say.

Career politicians are told by market research firms what to wear. And by political strategists what positions to take. And by speech coaches how best to pronounce "difficult" words; how to speak in a lower register and at a faster clip; when to gesticulate and how—so as to give the impression of profound sagacity.

Speech writers craft career politicians' every public word. Teleprompters hold their hands during public addresses. Publicists determine when to make public speeches and when to keep a low profile. Handlers select the forum and terms of engagement for interviews, and help navigate unscripted terrors with constituents. Pollsters are hybrid assistants: On the one hand they provide career politicians with authentic market research; on the other they manufacture support for their favorites come election time.[1]

Like actors, career politicians tend to be handsomer than average. (When was the last time you saw a movie or a presidency in which the lead was physically repulsive?) Males tend to have good hair for their age, and both sexes tend to have symmetrical faces with reasonably unobtrusive features. (Perhaps beauty is inherent to leadership; perhaps the civilized refuse to follow a brute. But it is also possible that the tendency to beauty represents yet another symptom of entertainment submission: That when choosing an actor for the big presidential play, we care more for our protagonist's looks than his ability.)

Also like actors, career politicians protect their investment in celebrity with regular touchups on the cosmetic surgeon's operating table. (How modern medical art stretches flaccid flesh across seasoned public servants' crania is a wonder to behold! How drooping eyebrows can be suspended so high above the orbital cavity is miraculous! How living mouths can be pulled taut—into sneers no less terrifying than the Greek tragedian's mask—is inspiring! How normal noses can be trimmed, filed, and molded to sharp, upturned, Jacksonesque points is marvelous to see! And while tired skin is stretched to the limits of tensile strength, expressive creases are simultaneously paralyzed and filled.) They are sentient mannequins: With eyebrows pinned to hairlines and smiles like Halloween masks, they work their pompous craft before bodily crowds and television audiences alike.[2]

Like actors, career politicians dress the part. You will rarely find them out of costume! They are always made up for the show (layered with high definition foundation, eye shadow, and contouring blush). They wear a fine suit (or pantsuit, as the case may be). Every hair must be in place (which is why you so rarely find them out of doors, in a stiff breeze), with sections carefully dyed to match both audience and occasion (sometimes hoary wisdom is required; othertimes dusky hues of a more exuberant youth; it all depends on the role-du-jour). If career politicians exercise, they do it in secret (you won't find pictures of them in sweaty gym shorts). If they go to the beach, it is a private one (unless they have connections to a photog who is willing to augment aging physiques with Photoshop).

And because the terms of The Big Popularity Contest are premised upon representing constituents' political will, career politicians are especially adept at *acting as though* they will implement constituents' political will after the election. So no—career politicians are never out of character! Especially during election years. They understand constituents' desires—and they will implement them! So long as we elect them just one more time . . . .

Academy Award

Some will say career politicians' performances as federal powerbrokers fall short of the standard set by real, Hollywood actors.

But really, career politicians do remarkably well. Particularly when a campaign appears to be in trouble. At such times career politicians pull out all the stops, and take their place among modern thespian virtuosi. Who can forget Hillary Clinton's masterpiece in January, 2008—choking back tears over the travails of a difficult campaign in New Hampshire?[3] (It really was masterful: Immediately after Ms. Clinton's melancholy performance, she vaulted ahead of candidate Obama as the surprise winner of the New Hampshire primary.)

Who can forget Newt Gingrich's performance in December, 2011—when, during a precipitous slide in Iowa polls, his eyes welled over his mother's health struggles?[4] (In November, too, Gingrich fought back tears describing a family friend's son who underwent brain surgery. But Mr. Gingrich's performance was less effective; Iowans failed to give him the caucus nod.)

Who can forget Herman Cain's theatrics in November, 2011—when he choked back tears while recalling *his own* health problems?[5]

Or John Boehner's stagecraft in December, 2010—when, during an interview on 60 Minutes, he blubbered pitiably about the American Dream?[6]

Or Mitt Romney's dramatization when recalling a soldier's casket?

Yes, career politicians are fine actors! Perhaps they lack the dexterity to take on major Shakespearean roles, but they are masters of midday melodrama: They can turn on the faucet at will. (They should really look into membership in the Screen Actors Guild; they might find they qualify for some union-wide award.)

Sometimes political actors' stagecraft is more subtle. Sometimes it consists in the art of acting *without acting*.

Take Candidate Obama in the 2008 election: For most of his adult life Mr. Obama has been a smoker of various herbs.[iv] Certainly this was true during his 2008 campaign.[v] But you'd be hard pressed to find a picture of him smoking. Go ahead—search for a picture of Candidate Obama smoking in the lead-up to the election. Or even now, as President.[vi] *You won't find a single one*. The man smokes, yes. And the mainstream news outlets know this. But does he always light up in a closet? There is not a shred of pictorial evidence illustrating his habit!

Instead of smoking photos, what you will find are innumerable images of a trim fifty-something playing basketball. He runs on the treadmill and stamps on an elliptical machine. He lifts weights. He tells us, "There's always a trade-off between sleep and working out. Usually I get in about 45 minutes, six days a week. I'll lift one day, do cardio the next."[7] Of course his preference "would be to work out for 90 minutes,"[8] but he is a busy man. Even on the campaign trail, "even during the busiest periods, Obama made it a priority to start the day with a workout."[9] If we are to believe the act, he's not skinny because he smokes; he's lean because he's an absolute fitness junkie! And because, if we are to believe the First Lady, he's also a lean dieter and nibbler of greens.

To be fair to the rest of the production crew, Mr. Obama's non-smoking act is not a one-man routine. Transforming Mr. Obama's fitness character into convincing shtick requires careful stage direction and cinematography, too. (Which is to say that when Mr. Obama lights up, friends, family, and mainstream photographers alike shutter their cameras. Apparently they have

---

[iv] In high school, for example, President Obama was a member of the "Choom Gang," a group of students dedicated to smoking marijuana and getting the most out of it. When smoking in vehicles, the Choom Gang was careful to roll the windows up—so they wouldn't miss a single particle of marijuana smoke. *See, e.g.*, David Jackson, *Book Cites Obama's High School Marijuana Use*, USA TODAY (May 25, 2012); Aaron Blake, *Obama Book Details Extensive Marijuana Use*, THE WASHINGTON POST (May 25, 2012).

[v] *See, e.g.*, Kate Barrett, *Obama Admits Smoking Cigarettes in Last Few Months*, ABC NEWS (June 10, 2008).

[vi] *Smoking: The President's Problem, Too*, CBS NEWS (May 7, 2010); Lawrence K. Altman & Jeff Zeleny, *President in 'Excellent Health,' Routine Checkup Finds*, THE NEW YORK TIMES (Feb. 28, 2010).

done so for years. Such adroit and disciplined camerawork contributes immensely to the art of acting *without acting.*)

We are left to wonder why mainstream newsmakers categorically refuse to photograph President Obama's habit. Is it because such a habit might turn off potential voters? Is it because addiction might reflect poorly on the man's character? Because chain smoking is not as stylish as it once was? Because he bats for the same team—the Incrementalist Team? Because it might seem odd to greet diplomats in a White House that smells like an ashtray?

While fascinating, such questions miss the point entirely. The takeaway here is that career politicians are such prolific actors (and mainstream newsmakers such complicit art directors!) that we have precious little idea what our elected representatives are really like. Like celebrity actors, career politicians are—in the minds of millions—only what they show us. They exist only as carefully packaged PR products.

Rudderless Thespian

Career politicians are—sad to say—not original thinkers. And like the great Hollywood celebrities, they tend also to be sorely undereducated. (Yet deft at rattling off prepared answers! Which assists newsmakers in painting their favorites as knowledgeable, reasonable—even insightful . . . .)

Go talk to Representatives on the Hill: You will be hard-pressed to find a modern Madison or Jefferson.

But you will find plenty of Hank Johnsons ("My fear is that, uh, the whole island [of Guam] will, uh, become so overly-populated that it will tip over and, uh, *capsize*."[10]). You will find many Maxine Waterses ("We do not have a crisis at Freddie Mac, and particularly Fannie Mae, under the outstanding leadership of Frank Raines."[11]). The Hill harbors a gaggle of Sheila Jackson Lees ("Today we have two Vietnams, side by side, North and South. Exchanging and working. We may not agree with all that North Vietnam is doing, but they are living in peace. I would look for a better human rights record for North Vietnam, but they are living side by side."[12]).

It is embarrassing.

But it is not federal representatives' ignorance that infuriates citizens. Indeed, the current extent of the franchise ensures illiterate, indifferent, and undereducated voting. The sheer volume of ignorant voters *guarantees* selection of some federal representatives embodying voters' naïveté. And while embarrassing, this is a tradeoff we are happy to make: At least we choose our rulers—be they idiots or savants.

No, career politicians' illiteracy is not the issue. All would be well if federal representatives—though idiots—consistently implemented the will of the constituents who elected them. (Let them remain mindless automata so long as they are obedient!) Or at the very least *if they regularly implemented the platforms upon which they campaigned.* (Let them be fools so long as they keep their word!)

This is the issue: *That once elected, career politicians rarely follow through on campaign promises.* As soon as they are safely ensconced in the endless corridors of Washington, they stop representing constituents' interests and begin pursuing their own. Like George W. Bush, who in 2000 famously campaigned as a "compassionate *conservative*"—then once in office pushed redistributive programs like the prescription drug benefit for seniors (Medicare Schedule D), No Child Left Behind, and TARP; oversaw creation of DHS, TSA, and multiple wars which Congress never declared; and by doing all this necessarily expanded the federal budget by 30% in only eight years. It was President George W. Bush, after all, who ended his presidency nonsensically proclaiming, "I've abandoned free-market principles to save the free-market system."[13]

Like Barack H. Obama, who in 2007 and 2008 campaigned as a "moderate" promising "hope and change" to citizens exhausted by the duplicitous Bush years. Remember? He promised to *reign in federal spending* through a specific "net spending cut."[vii] He specifically opposed federal mandates to buy health insurance.[viii] He promised greater government transparency by publishing bills online five days before signing them.[ix] He promised "the first thing I will do" is bring troops home from the Iraq War.[x]

[vii] October 15, 2008: "There is no doubt that we've been living beyond our means, and we're going to have to make some adjustments. Now, what I've done, throughout this campaign, is to propose a net spending cut."

[viii] January 31, 2008 CNN debate: "Senator Clinton has a different approach. She believes that we have to force people who don't have health insurance to buy it. . . . I think it is important for us to recognize that if in fact you're going to mandate the purchase of insurance and it's not affordable then there's going to have to be some enforcement mechanism that the government uses and they may charge people who already don't have health care fines, or have to take it out of their paychecks and that I don't think is helping those without health insurance, that is a genuine difference." February 26, 2008 MSNBC debate: "[T]hen you can have a situation which we're seeing right now in the State of Massachusetts, where people are being fined for not having purchased health care, but choose to accept the fine because they still can't afford it even with the subsidies, and they are then worse off: they then have no health care, and are paying a fine above and beyond that. That is a genuine difference between myself and Senator Clinton . . . ."

[ix] June 22, 2007: "I'll make our government open and transparent, so that anyone can ensure that our business is the People's business. . . . When I'm president, meetings where laws are written will be more open to the public, no more secrecy—that's a commitment I make to you as president. No more secrecy. When there's a bill that ends up on my desk as president, you the public will have five days to look online, and find out what's in it before I sign it, so that you know what your government's doing."

[x] October 27, 2007: "I will promise you this, that if we have not gotten our troops out by the time I am president, it is the first thing I will do, I will get our troops home, we will bring an end to this war, you can take that to the bank."

He promised to close the Guantanamo Bay military detention center.[xi] (And we wonder: Can our president possibly be the man who campaigned thus?)

Like Senator Scott Brown, the *Cosmopolitan* model who in 2010 campaigned as *the* vote to filibuster Obamacare in the U.S. Senate.[xii] Running as a Republican in a very blue State, the *Cosmo* model's odds looked slim—but by taking a stand against Obama, Obamacare, and Democratic hegemony, Mr. Brown won! And again, once safely in office, the *Cosmo* model (now *Senator* Brown) cozied right up with those very interests he was sent to oppose.[14]

Like Mitt Romney, who campaigns as a "severely conservative,"[15] small government,[16] pro-life,[17] pro-gun,[18] pro-Reagan,[19] anti-Obamacare,[20] anti-path-to-citizenship,[21] heterosexual-marriage-only[22] warrior. But what are we to believe? Not long ago he was a liberal, anti-gun,[23] anti-Reagan,[24] pro-choice,[25] pro-insurance-mandate,[26] pro-immigrant,[27] gay marriage[28] warrior. This is the very man who pioneered Obamacare at the State level! This is the man whose own advisors flew to Washington *to teach Obama's team how to implement the Obamacare health insurance mandate*! Like all the actors before him, we will only know on which side of the waffle he stands after a multi-year trial run.

Why do career politicians do this? Once elected and seated in Washington, why do they renege on campaign promises? How can they so quickly become part of the problem they were sent to fight?

The reason lies in career politicians' nature as *political actors*. It is in the dramatic arts that career politicians are trained; it is in the capacity of theatrical performer that they have won their greatest successes; it is through persuasive acting that they achieved positions of power. So career politicians stick to what has worked in the past: Once in Washington they continue to wear what they are told to wear. They continue to stand where they are told to stand. They continue to repeat the lines they are given. They continue to parrot the philosophies of others. They continue to seek applause.

And while doing so, they always play to the audience directly in front of them.

[xi] November 15, 2007 CNN debate: "We're going to lead by shutting down Guantanamo, and restoring habeas corpus in this country, so we offer them an example." November 16, 2008 60 Minutes interview: "I've said repeatedly that I intend to close Guantanamo, and I will follow through on that."

[xii] To break a filibuster, Senate rules require a 60-vote supermajority. While the late Ted Kennedy had served as U.S. Senator from Massachusetts, Democrats controlled exactly that: a filibuster-proof 60-member majority in the Senate. If Mr. Brown were to take Mr. Kennedy's place as a Republican opposed to Obamacare, however, he would reduce the Democratic Senate majority 59 votes—and Democrats would no longer be able to defeat an Obamacare filibuster. Democrats would never be able to achieve an up or down vote on the Obamacare legislation. This is the scenario Scott Brown promised.

Which is to say that precious few career politicians bring to Washington guiding philosophies, deeply personal morals, robust worldviews, or devotion to constituents' sacred trust. So few possess a philosophical rudder by which to steer. Or a moral compass by which to navigate. Or a worldview capable of catching atmospheric breezes, and drawing the politician against Washington's political currents. Or a bond with constituents to anchor their political positions. These are not "statesmen." Not in the traditional sense, anyway. These are actors playing a role. They require costume, script, and captive audience. And once in Washington they quickly adapt to the new costumes, scripts, and audiences they are handed.

In this sense—in their true nature as political actors—career politicians ride the currents of public opinion as a rudderless boat rides the sea: Without compass, sail, or anchor, they run hither and thither as the *present* audience demands. They ride the *immediate* currents, the currents *nearest themselves*, the currents *in which they now float.* Not currents thousands of miles from where they sit. Like any vessel, while at sea they do not—indeed, they cannot!—ride the currents of home port.

So we can hardly be surprised that after floating into Washington, D.C., career politicians are as little influenced by the opinion of their constituents at home as a boat adrift by the weather in its home port. Let us be honest: Career politicians rarely sail home! Perhaps once or twice a year they hold faux tele-town-hall meetings; otherwise they remain at a safe distance from constituents—within the federal enclave. Once in Washington career politicians play to the D.C. crowd. They adapt their shtick to garner D.C. ovations. They play for party bosses, national power brokers, and D.C. lobbyists now—so they wear the costumes, recite the scripts, and act the parts their Washingtonian directors give them.[xiii]

This situation cannot, of course, provide *representative* government. Indeed, by staying all year in Washington and rarely traveling home, career politicians are perfectly sequestered from constituents' influence.

It was not always so. In the beginning Congress met once a year. The Constitution's default rule required Congress to assemble in Washington on the first Monday in December—*and conduct all legislative business for the entire year before Christmas*![xiv] To assemble any sooner required Congress to specifically

---

[xiii] The political casting couch lives! Once established in Washington, career politicians forget constituents and home districts altogether. Because they know who funds reelection campaigns, and it isn't constituents from their home district. It isn't voters. No, it is Washingtonian overseers who foot the reelection bill: Party bosses disburse national party finances to fund politician's reelection campaigns. Lobbyists provide money, connections, and platforms. Campaign bundlers raise money, awareness, and favors.

[xiv] U.S. CONST. art. I § 4, para. 2.

pass a law to that effect—each and every year.[xv] So in the beginning congresspersons were carefully trammeled—and tied closely to their constituents. They knew very well what constituents expected them to do during a short, three-week stay in Washington. Why, aside from a few weeks in December, congresspersons lived all the year amongst their constituents. They got an earful! And they took that earful to Washington, and made their constituents' voices heard like bona fide representatives.

But waiting to assemble until the first Monday in December was inconvenient for career politicians and Incrementalists alike. Career politicians wished to remain close to Washington audiences and Washington directors (and far from bothersome constituents!) throughout the year. And they got tired of the constitutional hassle of passing a new law every year to allow them come to Washington early. Incrementalists, for their part, wanted to sever the ties between Representative and constituent. Incrementalists required a monolithic ruling body, unencumbered by the interests of Middle America.

So in 1933, at the beginning of the New (Socialist) Deal, career politicians and Incrementalists united to amend the Constitution.[xvi] Under the Twentieth Amendment, Congress would again assemble in Washington "at least once in every year."[xvii] But this time Congress would *assemble by default at noon on January 3rd*—just as soon as representatives recovered from New Years' hangovers!—*so they could conduct legislative business unabated for the entire year.*[xviii] Yes, once again Congress would continue their assembly until Christmas recess—but this time they would start eleven months earlier *by default!* And under the new constitutional default, assembling Congress any *later* than the third of January would require specific and annual passage of a law appointing a different day of assembly. (A rule with which Congress grudgingly manages to comply whenever the third of January falls on a weekend.)

So today the tables are turned: Instead of being moored at home port all but a couple weeks out of the year, our federal representatives float the Sea of Washington all but a couple weeks of the year. Instead of being blown by the breezes of home port, our federal representatives encounter nothing but the trade winds of an Incrementalist enclave. Without rudder, anchor, compass, or sail, they go with the flow. They ride the irresistible currents of The Establishment. They are not Representatives, but Irrepresentatives. They are Insiders. In short order they become indistinguishable from the rest of the Washington machine: a coterie of the most venal, vainglorious, power

---

[xv] *Ibid.*
[xvi] U.S. CONST. amend. XX, § 2.
[xvii] *Ibid.*
[xviii] *Ibid.*

hungry, politically correct, boot-licking, groveling, administrative-agency-loving, constitution-denying cowards.

And thus they become Incrementalists.

A few remain aloof from Washington's trend-setting Incrementalism. These are true representatives. We can even call them statesmen. But they are difficult to find.

And when we do find them, they are nothing special to look at. They tend to lag in those areas where their peers excel: In looks. In charisma. In fashionability. In the perfection with which they color and style their hair. In their talent to deceive. In their ability to blend into whatever surroundings they are presented.

Probably we could find a man dressed in a frumpy, ill-fitting suit—someone who cares less about how he looks, how much people adore him, and whether he "fits in" in Washington—to do the job of president. A thinking man. A man of action. A man who speaks for himself. A man who tells us precisely what he will do. A man who sticks to his word after the election. But we don't often find such a man. And when we do, we rarely vote for him. Such men do not fit the political mold. Such men do not win national popularity contests.

Actor for Man

Is it wise?

Is it wise to send an actor to do a president's job?

Is it wise to send an actor to do a congressperson's job?

Electing actors to high political office is the customary thing to do, of course. But it is worth considering: If you needed to win a heavyweight boxing match, would you send Sylvester Stallone? If you needed an off-duty cop who bangs with terrorists, would you phone Bruce Willis? If you required lessons in game theory, would you hire Russell Crowe? If you needed a sheriff, would you summon John Wayne? Kevin Costner? Robert Duvall? (There are options here!) If you needed an independent-minded archaeologist, would you appoint Harrison Ford? If you needed to assassinate a foreign diplomat, would you send Daniel Craig? If you needed a coronary bypass, would you solicit Hugh Laurie? If you needed a cyber-Savior, would you select Keanu Reeves? If you needed a madman, would you recommend Jack Nicholson? (I take it back—Nicholson would perform admirably. He's typecast.)

If the answer is no, we must ask a further question: Would you send an actor to Washington—*to play president?* To make treaties? To grant pardons?

To appoint federal judges? To command the military? To hold the reins of the unconstitutional Fourth Head? To receive foreign ambassadors? To propose federal budgets?

Would you send an actor to Washington *to play legislator?* To draft bills? To ratify treaties? To conduct congressional hearings? To declare war (or not)? To vote on bills, and judges, and executive appointees? To head congressional committees? To impeach the president? To reject moneyed minions' overtures? To balance the budget?

Because in most cases, we *are* sending actors to Washington to do those things.

We are sending performers who care more about immediate applause than whether the Republic still stands fifty years from now. We are sending pretenders who wouldn't know liberty from coercion if Liberty unshackled them, and Coercion stabbed them in the eye. We are sending actors who will whistle "Mack the Knife" all the way to the ovens.

It is perilous to send an actor to do the job of a surgeon or a statesman. The most obvious danger is that, while looking every bit the part, one cannot expect an actor to competently perform delicate surgeries upon a patient or a nation. In this regard, danger lies in the actor's lack of experience, knowledge, and skill in the task at hand.

But there is a less obvious danger in sending an actor to do the job of a surgeon or a statesman. And this is that we almost never get a glimpse of what the actor really believes, how exactly he reasons, or what he actually intends. Instead, we hear and see only what the actor has gleaned from the script. A script that someone else wrote for him.

Consider: When impersonating a surgeon, an actor perfectly mimics a physician's concentration, confidence, and movements. He shows a surgeon's intensity during stressful moments. He learns medical jargon from the script. He repeats the words without question or pause. But while he performs his surgical parody, we in the audience can only guess what is going through the actor's mind: Does our actor even know what myocardial infarction is? Or what causes it? Can he pronounce the phrase without resorting to a cue card? If he were presented with the term "atherosclerosis," could he tell us what it means? Could he distinguish atheroma from fibroatheroma? Does he *care* whether he can? Does he have an opinion on how best to diagnose arterial stenosis? Does he favor stress testing or angiography? Intravascular ultrasound or lipoprotein subclass analysis? Can he give us a principled explanation as to *why*? And when he calls "Line!" do we see it? Or is that part of the take dumped before the final cut is televised?

When playing surgeon, our actor holds an electric bone saw in one hand and a bipolar cautery tool in the other—and they are not props. He has arteriotomy scissors, scalpels, coronary shunts, silk sutures, and forceps of every description within arm's reach. He holds power over life and death. But really—Once the patient's sternum is sawn asunder; the ribs are winched apart with a thoracic retractor; the periosteal arteries cauterized; the sternopericardial ligaments divided; and the living heart beats before our very eyes—Does he know where to incise the pericardium? (It will require three major cuts, and possibly four.) Can he tell the left coronary artery from the right? (No, no, dear actor—the patient's left is your right, and vice versa!) Can he communicate with the perfusionist? (When he is ready for cardioplegia, what will he say?) Can he locate the saphenous vein he will use for the bypass? (Careful there—the saphenous vein is in the patient's *leg* . . . .) Now that the helpless patient is sedated, his thorax split open like a tomato, his viscera exposed to a 19° Celsius operating room draft—now that we have reached the moment of truth!—*what does he plan to do?*

We can only guess. Because the actor has a script, and he sticks to it. He never betrays his own thoughts. Not on camera, at least. Not in front of his audience.

And so it is with the career politician. He mimics the imperious brow, the confident gait, the gravelly voice of a man of power. He holds aging shoulders back and proud head aloft to indicate his elevated rank. When asked a question he raises one eyebrow and drops the other to suggest he anticipates seven moves ahead, and knows he has already achieved intellectual checkmate.

When speaking he gesticulates emphatically: he employs the hands palms up, palms down, and one of each. He utilizes the wagging, bony, finger so common in Washington. He grasps for justice and equality in the very air. He clutches a welling heart; he cups emotion within his hands; he mimes empathy pouring from his breast. He cranes his neck and points to imagined vistas. He makes gestures unseen outside political theater, and difficult to decipher: A loose fist, with the thumb extended prominently over the top, shaken gently yet firmly. (Is this intended as emphasis? Is it meant to imply conviction?)

He learns economic, legal, and political jargon from the script. He reads the teleprompter. He pronounces table after table of statistics. He takes pregnant pauses. He cracks jokes. He delivers his lines without a hitch. He looks the part.

Like the actor playing surgeon, this actor playing president also possesses the tools of the trade. He does not play with props. Press one button, and atomic bombs drop. Press another, and interest rates plunge. Press a third, and ICE stops deporting illegal aliens. Press a fourth, and new treaties are made. Press a fifth, and longstanding allies are abandoned. Before him the helpless body politic is anesthetized, its limbs strapped down to a cold operating table, its trunk split open like a frog in the dissection lab. The clock is ticking, and the time is short—*what does he plan to do?*

Again, we can only guess. The political actor, too, utters only the words others have written for him. He says—nay, he *reads*—exactly what his speech writers wrote for him. Neither more nor less. Even during debates he rattles off little more than market-tested phrases approved by his handlers. On those rare occasions when he speaks his mind, his statements are dismissed as "gaffes" and quickly forgotten by all but those with the longest of memories.

And though he never speaks for himself in public, it is he, the political actor—not his speechwriters, his strategists, his pollsters, his publicists—who will actually make the critical decision! It is *he* who will push this button or that! It is *he* who will save or kill the Republic. We citizens must decide whom to vote for to perform the vital operation: Should we send him or another? *Yet we hardly know who he is or what he thinks!* Neither he nor his handlers allow him to talk to us; he is an opaque and impenetrable mask! We can only infer his beliefs, his knowledge, his experience, his thought processes, and his plan, from the advisors with whom he surrounds himself.

It would be nice if, at some random and inconvenient moment, we could force the President to sit alone in a sealed, soundproof room, with nothing but a pencil and a pad of paper—to write *his own* speech. Just one speech! After letting him out of that room and hearing his solitary speech, then we could form an opinion about what he really believes; what he really knows; what he has experienced; how he reasons; and what he plans to do. The procedure would be even more revealing if we could ask him direct and detailed questions on policy matters. (And of course, we should treat our congressional overlords to the same experience.)

Such an authentic speech would come off like a post-production "making of" documentary—one of those sad interviews where off-stage actors are caught without a script and, though thrown the most banal of softballs, find it difficult to respond coherently. When let out of his soundproof room, the President would probably have the same deer-in-the-headlights look. He would stammer more than usual; he would avoid eye contact with audience or camera; it would be painful to watch how meekly and uncertainly he delivers his address. (Something like President Obama's performance in the first 2012 presidential debate.) But at least we would have a better idea of his qualifications. At least we should get an idea of what *he* thinks, and what *he* plans to do. At least we would know what we were voting for!

Electoral Futility

Elections are a bit like falling in love. Like falling in love with a very bad girlfriend. It starts *so well.* It feels *so right.* Here is someone who understands us *completely*. Here is someone who lives only to fulfill our needs and dreams!

Then you find your new lover is a thief, a liar, and a stalker. A good actress but a bad person. It never quite works out in the end.

Yes, when it comes to gaining trust and affection; when it comes to manipulation; when it comes to political relationships; when it comes to elections; career politicians are masters of their craft. They exude confidence and self-assurance. Their eyes sparkle. They are handsome and coy. Upbeat and articulate; warm and affectionate. They are engaging conversationalists and electrifying storytellers. They are fun to be around. On occasion they even make you feel special.

And they talk a very big game. They promise the world! But listen carefully: When something goes wrong they are quick to blame others. When asked a pointed question they never answer directly; their answers simultaneously shade all sides of the issue; they say everything and nothing at all—yet somehow how they say it *sounds so good.* They are the Ted Bundy's of Politics. And once we voters give them the keys to Washington, they do what all malignant narcissists live to do: To coerce. To control. To rule. To aggrandize. To rape the public treasury for their own near-term popularity. To murder liberty in exchange for just one more term in office.

In politics as in relationships, when it really seems too good to be true, it is.

How can one recognize them? How can one spot a career politician *before* casting one's ballot? How can one be sure one is being told the truth, and not merely what an actor believes his audience wants to hear?

Only by thoroughly examining the record. In order to gauge how invested somebody is in what they are saying at present, the trick is to survey what positions they have taken in the past. This is much easier in politics than in romance, because in politics almost all participants are narcissists—so their records are extensive! They are always spouting off. They love to hear themselves speak. They love to give a speech or dedicate a building site. They love the chief seats at press conferences, and greetings in the Capitol, and to be called by everyone Senator, President. They enjoy seeing their names in print, so they enjoy writing articles. They especially love looking back on their own lives, reliving their own triumphs, and commenting upon them ad nauseam. For this reason they love to pen memoirs—even in their early thirties![xix]

[xix] In this regard, it is tough to beat Barack H. Obama's *Dreams From My Father*, a memoir written before its subject had even entered politics. BARACK H. OBAMA, DREAMS FROM MY FATHER: A STORY OF RACE AND INHERITANCE (Crown Publishers 2004) (1995).

But if you have not performed due diligence on those candidates you plan to vote for, it is better to stay home on election day. To vote in ignorance is worse than not voting at all: For all you know you are making a terrible and permanent decision.[xx] It is not civic virtue to vote in ignorance—it is civic malpractice. It is willful blindness. And if you have voted for a presidential candidate without reading his best-selling memoir, you should feel ashamed. He has told you how he thinks, what he believes, what motivates him, what he has experienced, how he views the nation and the world—and you held your nose, closed your eyes, and plugged your ears.[xxi] You are no better than the millions of Germans who voted for Hitler without ever reading *Mein Kampf*.

And you should expect no better results.

Americans, like all other peoples of the world, are overawed by their rulers.

But strip politicians of the sacred vestments of their popular priesthood—deprive them of their teleprompters, their lectern emblazoned with the seal of the Presidency, their makeup, their speech writers, their hair stylists, their publicists, their Botox, their political strategists, their office on the Hill, their focus groups, their market research studies—and as surely as the cardinal in your archdiocese preparing for bed after mass, they show themselves as they really are: shriveled old men, grey and stooped with age.

They are impotent, yes—*but only after losing an election*; only after the relationship between citizen and representative has been severed. Once stripped of their civic vestments we find former rulers to be, like the once powerful Senator Majority Leader Tom Daschle, perfectly harmless. They take fellowships with Incrementalist advocacy nonprofits. They condescend to accept Incrementalist awards. They do a little lobbying. Once in a blue moon they write a piece for Politico. They may even author a book. But aside from such trivialities, they do little. They are nobodies.

In this limited sense—as opportunities to end unhealthy political relationships and send career politicians packing—elections have great utility. They humble the overbearing. And they create a healthy turnover in Washington: They periodically replace hardened Incrementalists with some new politicians who only recently sailed from home port. These new federal representatives remember—for a few months, anyway—what their constituents sent them to do.

[xx] Permanent because the Constitution does not provide for electoral recall—so your electoral decision remains; it cannot be retracted.

[xxi] True, these days such a "memoir" has probably been ghost-written; but at the very least it has been approved by the candidate. And it was approved before so much was on the line (i.e., before this election). So it likely offers a far more revealing picture of the candidate than what he says today.

So we approach another presidential election.

It is a grand affair. With dignified manner, we proudly select our team. We root for noble mascots: the elephant or the ass. We wave our team colors: red or blue. It's March Madness—but in November, with politics instead of basketball! We hit the polling booth. And we stay up all night long, to be sure of the final results in tight races.

This is the year, we tell ourselves—*this is the year we select a true statesman.* Someone who will speak and act in office as he campaigned. This election will be different from all the others. This is the lucky lottery ticket; this one will hit the jackpot!

When our team wins, we exult! We cannot wipe the smirk away; we walk on clouds for days. We high-five like-minded friends. We treat ourselves to a longer lunch break. We skip down the sidewalk; we notice the sunshine on our shoulders.

When our team loses, we despair. We drag ourselves to work—but we avoid the company of coworkers. And particularly those who cheer for the opposing team. We sulk. Even the weather seems glum. We let the voicemail answer phone calls.

It is a grand farce.

Because Incrementalism cares little for presidential elections.[xxii] As we stated from the beginning, Incrementalism is that strategy designed by socialists *to sidestep* U.S. elections. And it has been quite effective. Whoever wins, Incrementalism rolls along; sometimes in fifth gear, sometimes in third, but always along the same road. The road to federal control. To monolithic government. To coercion. To socialism. So far as Incrementalism is concerned, presidential elections are a festival for fools. (Particularly when career politicians present the only viable electoral options.)

How can presidential elections have so little impact?

Well, simply electing a new president cannot resurrect the Constitution. It is true that as chief executive a president could decide *not* to exercise unconstitutional powers which the federal government claims to possess. But a president cannot remove those unconstitutional powers from future administrations as well; he cannot overturn eternal Supreme Court precedents

---

[xxii] And so does full-flowered socialism! Once socialism becomes ossified within a state, one finds charming statements like the following: "I consider it completely unimportant who in the party will vote, or how; but what is extraordinarily important is this—who will count the votes, and how." Joseph Stalin, as quoted in BORIS BAZHANOV, THE MEMOIRS OF STALIN'S FORMER SECRETARY (Ill Tysiacheletie, 2002).

justifying unconstitutional federal powers he himself chooses not to exercise. The Powers of "Yes" and "No" rule on.

Besides, the Fourth Head dictates day-to-day governance; the Fourth Head makes federal law and directs federal policy. The Fourth Head's bureaucrats fear no election because they are appointed—never elected—to their posts. (And should they ever be removed, they will quickly find another post. They are apparatchiks.) They are unconstitutional intermeddlers, to be sure—but they run the show. It has been so for nearly a century. *And none of this will change with the election of a new president.* The Fourth Head will not wither because the White House lodges a new occupant. (Yes, Commissioners Genachowski, Rosenworcel, McDowell, and Pai will continue plotting how best to expropriate and redistribute the Internet no matter who wins in 2012.)

Nor can electing a new president overcome cultural inertia. Political correctness will not disappear just because we have chosen a new president. Cane toads will continue to leap across the border based on nepotism, diversity lotteries, and geographic proximity. Cane beetles and their culture of self-reliance will continue to be displaced in corresponding measure. Administrative agencies will continue to scan our naked bodies and digitally rape us at security checkpoints, in spite of the Fourth Amendment—and citizens will continue to get accustomed to such treatment. (And if security procedures should ever be altered to conform with the Constitution, the precedent is set, my dears!—Incrementalism will reinstate digital rape in the future, whenever and wherever it appears serviceable.) Meanwhile, most of the remaining cane beetles will continue their indentured servitude to electronic entertainments; they will not look up from their mobile devices.

You see, socialist method cannot be overthrown by electing one more actor to the presidency. This is the power of Incrementalism: It ushers American socialism into Washington in spite of majority opposition; it negates Middle American electoral reprisals; and by doing so it makes socialist gains last. This is not congenital cynicism speaking, this is an expression of hard experience—election cycle after election cycle.

No, we cannot expect a miracle of liberty to appear suddenly on the American horizon the moment a new president is elected. (And really, in the American scheme of government, presidents are place kickers: They cannot singlehandedly win the football game—but they can certainly lose it.[29])

Does the fact that a single presidential election cannot overthrow Incrementalism mean Middle Americans have lost their contest with socialism? Not at all. It simply means that in the Age of Incrementalism, socialists' conflict with Middle Americans has moved outside the confines of the polling booth. It means that in order to erase socialist gains, Middle Americans will be forced to do more than just cast a ballot once every four years. Just as the Socialist Ararat took decades to build, so it will require years to disassemble. It will take time to identify, to tourniquet, and to amputate each unconstitutional limb from the body politic. It will require many election cycles to explain what liberty is, how it was lost, and why an Incrementalist federal government is a burden to citizens. One barrow of dirt at a time.

Middle Americans are beginning to understand these truths.

Middle Americans are starting to understand that a single election will not—indeed, it cannot!—return liberties quietly embezzled by Incrementalism over decades.

Middle Americans hope for more than the installation of a new elephant or a new ass in the White House. They hope to cast off irrepresentative government altogether. They want to reestablish government premised on the consent of the governed. They intend to put the citizen back in the driver's seat.

Middle Americans are beginning to think that irrepresentative government can only be made representative when a majority of citizens are awakened to its existence and methods. They are beginning to understand that the political and cultural excesses of Incrementalism must be repealed *one citizen at a time.*

For this reason they have begun to unbuckle their muzzles and cast them aside. They have begun to take a timorous stand against political correctness, to take social and vocational risks for truth, to make their opinions heard in public and private, in spite of the precarious position in which it puts them.

They understand that actors cannot be expected to perform the jobs of statesmen.

They have begun to sniff out malignant narcissists who pretend to represent them.

They recognize that capturing the presidency for four years is a Pyrrhic victory.

They have remembered that the citizen is master, and government his servant.

They know they are viewed as troublesome pests in need of eradication.

They realize that liberty requires loyal representation not only in the White House, but also in Governors' mansions, in federal and State legislatures, in federal and State courthouses, in federal and State agencies. They know it requires participation in party primaries and caucus straw polls, in the neighborhood, at the workplace, and at home.

They have begun to disregard the brassy trumpeting of the elephant and the shrill braying of the ass. They have started to look beyond mendacious mainstream media for news. These are they who have begun to consider more desperate measures.

These are they who are turning away from traditional party politics.

These are they who organize from the bottom up.

These are the Tea Movement.

To be sure, they failed to position a presidential candidate this election cycle. They have no horse in this race. (Well, many would take Paul Ryan as their own.) Yet Tea Movement members will have a tremendous impact in the coming election. Just as they did in 2008 (by refusing to vote for the establishment candidate). Just as they did in 2010 (by changing the composition of Congress). Just as they did in dumping Senators Bennett (2010) and Lugar (2012) in party primaries. Just as they did in reinstating Governor Walker in the Wisconsin recall (2012). Just as they did by defeating establishment candidates for Congress during Republican primaries in Texas, Nebraska, Florida, and elsewhere (2012).

What will Tea Movement enthusiasts do in the 2012 presidential election? Will they stay home? Will they write in protest votes? Will they transform Congress yet again, yet fail to topple the incumbent president? Do they seek the pragmatism of federal gridlock? Do they prefer a Presidency and Congress at odds to an agreeable Washington which writes federal laws by the hundreds of thousands of pages? Or will they hold their noses, cast a vote for the lesser of two evils now, and worry about a better replacement later?

While interesting in the short term, such questions matter little over the long. Because in Incrementalist America, one popularity contest between actors matters little.

And that is how Incrementalism intends to keep it.

* * *

And now the disappointed reader screams: *Is that it? That's all you've got?* Incrementalism? The Fourth Head? Muzzling? Immigration? Entertainment submission? TSA pat-downs? Constitutional reinterpretation? Career politicians? But that is not what the Tea Movement is about! The Tea Movement is about *the economy*! The Tea Movement is about *jobs*! The Tea Movement is about *Obamacare*! The Tea Movement is about *federal bailouts* of the largest corporations and banks! The Tea Movement is about *exploding sovereign debt*! The Tea Movement is about *imploding home values*! The Tea Movement is about *federal taxes*! The Tea Movement is about *crumbling U.S. credit ratings*! The Tea Movement is about *debauchery of the dollar*! The Tea Movement is about *runaway inflation*! The Tea Movement is about federal *financial regulations*! The Tea Movement is about *energy dependence*! The Tea Movement is about *federalized mortgage relief*! The Tea Movement is about *unending unemployment benefits*! The Tea Movement is about dissatisfaction not only with the Democrat establishment, but equally with *the Republican establishment*!

Of course, the reader is perfectly correct to say that contemporary economic, fiscal, monetary, and regulatory issues provoked the Tea Movement backlash. But everyone knows that. Every establishment (*viz.* Incrementalist) politician, commentator, and professional recognizes as much. And every Tea Movement enthusiast is perfectly aware of it as well. To spend so much ink to say so little would be pointless. The real question is the *cause* of those irrepresentative economic, fiscal, monetary, and regulatory policies (and therefore also the underlying cause of the popular backlash called the Tea Movement). This is the question which has confounded establishment commentators and Tea Movement enthusiasts alike.

As was duly noted in the Prologue, the foregoing economic, fiscal, monetary, and regulatory policies—and the Tea Movement response to them—*can only be understood in light of American socialism.* It is for this reason that we have laid out, in Book I, the principles, aims, policies, and structure of socialism—and their rejection by Middle Americans. It is for this reason that we have laid out here in Book II socialism's *method* for implementing socialist policy in the face of Middle American resistance. Only now are we prepared to examine contemporary American economy—and the federalized bailouts, stimuli, health care, energy dependence, taxation, debt, monetary policy, and market regulations which have produced it—*and to see, with open eyes, that those polices are socialist both in origin and in method.*

Only now can we examine whether the conflict lies between monolithic coercion on the one hand and common liberty on the other.

And only now are we prepared to consider how this conflict will end.

Further Notes to Chapter 11

[1] *See, e.g.*, Josh Gerstein, *A Pollster Under Oath*, POLITICO (Oct. 2, 2012).
[2] Yes, we can tell the difference between a good night's sleep and an overzealous facelift, Nancy. We know hair plugs when we see them, Joe. We comprehend why an eighty-year-old's eyelids are too tight to close. We can spot Botox. We recognize fake tans, too; the raccoon effect produced by minimalist tanning bed goggles is a dead giveaway. (And here, perhaps, lies one benefit of our entertainment addiction: After decades scrutinizing the slightest adjustments to celebrities' features, we are perfectly competent to discern cosmetic surgery amongst our representatives as well.)
[3] *See, e.g.*, http://www.youtube.com/watch?v=N7vQA92XlnM; http://www.youtube.com/watch?v=pl-W3IXRTHU&feature=fvsr.
[4] *See, e.g.*, http://www.youtube.com/watch?v=yDju7UT-Fp8; http://www.youtube.com/watch?v=Lb9hisd60bE.
[5] *See, e.g.*, http://www.youtube.com/watch?v=5EX_HXGsAaU.
[6] *See, e.g.*, http://www.youtube.com/watch?v=ufYmnD3fhfk.
[7] President Obama, as quoted in Deanna Bellandi, *Michelle Obama's Arms Hard-Won With Exercise*, NBC NEWS (Nov. 19, 2008).
[8] *Ibid.*
[9] *Ibid.*
[10] Lecturing Admiral Robert Willard, U.S. Pacific Command, on the dangers of installing 8,000 marines on Guam during a House Armed Services Committee hearing (March 25, 2010). *See, e.g.*, http://www.youtube.com/watch?v=c7m6aewquco&feature=related.
[11] Speaking at the House Financial Services Committee Hearing (Sept. 25, 2003). *See, e.g.*, *What They Said About Fan and Fred*, THE WALL STREET JOURNAL (Oct. 2, 2008); http://www.youtube.com/watch?v=3sKpzmojjfU.
[12] Speech on the House Floor (July 15, 2010). *See, e.g.*, http://www.youtube.com/watch?v=XK3rTUgoQD4.
[13] George W. Bush speaking of TARP, Interview for CNN (Dec. 16, 2008). *See, e.g.*, Jacob Weisberg, *Bushism of the Day*, SLATE (Dec. 17, 2008).
[14] Elise Foley, *Scott Brown Ad Boasts of 'Great Experience' Standing With Obama*, THE HUFFINGTON POST (May 1, 2012); Meghan Neal, *Scott Brown Continues To Align Himself With Obama*, THE HUFFINGTON POST (April 4, 2012).
[15] February 10, 2012 CPAC speech: "I know conservatism because I have lived conservatism. . . . I fought against long odds in a deep blue State, but I was a severely conservative Republican governor."
[16] February 10, 2012 CPAC speech: "I'm going to dramatically reduce the size of the federal workforce. . . . And by the way, tax hikes—they're off the table."
[17] February 10, 2012 CPAC speech: "And let me also be clear on this: my presidency will be a pro-life presidency. On day one I will reinstate the Mexico City policy. I will cut off funding for the United Nations Population Fund, which supports China's barbaric one-child policy. I'll ensure that organizations like Planned Parenthood get no more support. And I will reverse every single Obama regulation that attacks our religious liberty and threatens innocent life in this country." May 21, 2007 Time interview: "It hit me very hard that we had so cheapened the value of human life in a Roe v. Wade environment that it was important to stand for the dignity of human life." Karen Tumulty, *What Romney Believes*, TIME (May 21, 2007).
[18] When asked if America needs stricter gun laws in the wake of the Aurora, Colorado shooting, Mitt Romney stated that he is a "Second Amendment advocate," and that he doesn't "happen to believe that America needs new gun laws." Callum Borchers, *Romney Says Gun Laws are Adequate*, BOSTON GLOBE (July 26, 2012). He said the same at the Second Presidential Debate of 2012. *Second Presidential Debate of 2012*, CNN (Hofstra University, Hempstead, New York) (Oct. 16, 2012). (Of course, the very rifle which was used to shoot most of the Aurora, Colorado victims was of the "assault weapon" type which Mr. Romney banned as governor of

Massachusetts—because such guns are "are instruments of destruction with the sole purpose of hunting down and killing people." *See, infra*, n. 23.)

[19] February 26, 2005: "Ronald Reagan is one of my heroes." *See* Michael Levenson, *Romney Links Gay Marriage, US Prestige*, THE BOSTON GLOBE (Feb. 26, 2005).

[20] February 10, 2012 CPAC speech: "And as I'm sure you know, that will start with the easiest cut of all: I will eliminate Obamacare."

[21] May 22, 2007, speaking on CNN's *The Situation Room*: "I think I'm best off to describe my own positions. And my positions, I think I've just described for you—secure the border, employment verification, and no special pathway to citizenship."

[22] "Ed Gillespie, senior advisor to Mitt Romney's presidential campaign, told Chuck Todd on MSNBC's *Daily Rundown* that . . . Romney will actively push for a constitutional amendment to take away the right of states to voluntarily extend marriage equality to same-sex couples." Josh Israel, *Top Romney Adviser: We'll Campaign on Constitutional Marriage Ban*, THINK PROGRESS (May 10, 2012).

[23] While unsuccessfully running for Senator of Massachusetts against Ted Kennedy in 1994, Mitt Romney expressly supported both the Brady Bill and the federal "assault weapons" ban. As Governor of Massachusetts in 2004, Mitt Romney signed a State-wide ban on so-called "assault weapons," ostensibly the first of its kind—and at that time Mitt Romney said, "Deadly assault weapons have no place in Massachusetts. These guns are not made for recreation or self-defense. They are instruments of destruction with the sole purpose of hunting down and killing people." Rebekah Metzler, *Mitt Romney and the NRA: Uneasy Bedfellows*, U.S. NEWS AND WORLD REPORT (April 13, 2012).

[24] 1994 campaign debate with Senator Ted Kennedy: "Look, I was an independent during the time of Reagan-Bush. I'm not trying to return to Reagan-Bush."

[25] October 29, 2002 gubernatorial debate: "I will preserve and protect a woman's right to choose, and am devoted and dedicated to honoring my word in that regard."

[26] Signed Massachusetts' RomneyCare into law, thereby requiring all Massachusetts residents to purchase health insurance.

[27] March 30, 2006: "Gov. Mitt Romney expressed support . . . for an immigration program that places large numbers of illegal residents on the path toward citizenship . . . . Romney said illegal immigrants should have a chance to obtain citizenship." Evan Lehmann, *Romney Supports Immigration Program, But Not Granting "Amnesty"*, THE LOWELL SUN (March 3, 2006).

[28] As Governor of Massachusetts, Mitt Romney of course issued gay marriage licenses. *See, e.g.*, *Goode: Romney 'Father of Homosexual Marriages'*, AUGUSTA FREE PRESS (May 12, 2012). In general, Mitt Romney has opposed discrimination against gays. For example, in 1994 Mitt Romney "wrote a letter promising a gay Republican group he would be a stronger advocate for gay rights than Ted Kennedy." Kathy Belge, *Lesbian Life: Mitt Romney—2012 Republican Presidential Candidate*, ABOUT.COM (2012). And since 1994 Romney has openly pushed for gays' unilateral prerogative to join the Boy Scouts. *See, e.g.*, Gregory Kelley, *Mitt Romney, Make Up Your Mind To Be For Or Against the Gay Community*, EXAMINER.COM (Aug. 7, 2012).

[29] For example, presidents cannot resurrect the Constitution—but they can cow the Supreme Court into further dismembering it. Presidents cannot unilaterally disassemble the Fourth Head—but they can use it as cover for unpopular Incrementalist policies. Presidents cannot individually restore Middle American culture—but they can destroy it in a moment of indiscretion (e.g., with an intern in the Oval Office).

APPENDIX

"Yes" Plus

The Power of "Yes" was a tremendous Incrementalist advance. Yet the Switch in Time Court's *Steward Machine Co.* decision did not complete Incrementalists' constitutional magic show: What about matters over which the federal government not only has no enumerated power, but over which the *States explicitly reserve exclusive jurisdiction*? Might the Tax and Spend Clause be of assistance here, too?

It seemed like a stretch at first.

But Incrementalism was willing to bide its time, and await the right opportunity.

Back in primitive, Pre-Incrementalist times citizens themselves decided what powers would be granted to the federal government, and which would be retained by the States or themselves.[i] Neither citizens nor their States tolerated Incrementalist inversions of the Constitution. When they wanted to confer more power on the federal government, they did so explicitly—by amending the Constitution. For example, the federal government had no enumerated liquor power. As a result, liquor law was the exclusive province of the States. In the early part of the twentieth century citizens decided they wanted to change all that. So the Eighteenth Amendment was proposed and ratified in 1919, granting "concurrent power" to State *and federal* governments in enforcing a prohibition on the manufacture, sale, and transportation of "intoxicating liquors."[ii] And the era of Prohibition began.

As many will remember, the Eighteenth Amendment was a disaster of epic proportions. Beneficiaries of the Eighteenth Amendment tended not to be wives and children of alcoholics, as intended, but rather members of organized crime syndicates. So in 1933 citizens and their States repealed the Eighteenth Amendment *by amending the Constitution yet again.* The Twenty-first Amendment revoked the "concurrent authority" recently granted to the

---

[i] U.S. CONST. amend. X.
[ii] U.S. CONST. amend. XVIII.

federal government to enforce Prohibition, and returned exclusive authority over liquor law to the States.[iii]

With the Twenty-first Amendment everything returned to normal: The federal government had no liquor authority, and liquor law was again exclusively a matter of State jurisdiction. By the mid-seventies, most States had set a minimum drinking age of eighteen. (Eighteen was the age of majority and voting under the Twenty-sixth Amendment, after all. The idea behind the Twenty-sixth Amendment was quite straightforward: If eighteen-year-old boys are old enough to decide when to pull the trigger in a bloody Southeast Asian jungle, then they are old enough to vote. The States took this logic one step further: If eighteen-year-olds are old enough to decide who runs the country, then they are old enough to make decisions about drink.) And while there remained some diversity among the States with respect to precise drinking age, the vast majority—a full thirty-eight States—set their minimum drinking age *below the age of twenty-one.*

The foregoing facts are not in dispute. Even the post-Switch in Time Court recognized that the Twenty-first Amendment reserves plenary power over liquor law to the States.[1]

But in 1984—half a century after ratification of the Twenty-first Amendment—the federal government decided it didn't like States determining drinking age. The federal government felt all State liquor laws should be the same. The federal government had its own minimum drinking age in mind: It favored the age of twenty-one. And it wanted all State liquor laws to conform to that.[2]

By 1984 there was no longer any need to formally amend the Constitution to obtain the federal government's desired result. No, indeed! Forget the Twenty-first Amendment and its history. Forget supermajorities in Congress and consent from thirty-eight State legislatures. There was a much simpler route to attaining federal liquor authority: *Just use the Incrementalist Tax and Spend Clause!* Yes, that was the ticket: Establish a financial penalty for States whose laws did not accommodate Congress' preferred drinking age, and call the penalty a "contingent *grant* of federal monies"! Get the lickspittle Supreme Court's blessing and *voilà*—Constitution amended!

And that is precisely what happened.

In 1987, South Dakota regulated liquor within its borders just like every other State. South Dakota law "permit[ed] persons 19 years of age or older to purchase beer containing up to 3.2% alcohol."[3] (For you teetotalers out there, a beverage containing 3.2% or less alcohol by volume is not hard liquor. Or wine.

[iii] "The transportation or importation into any State, Territory, or possession of the United States for delivery or use therein of intoxicating liquors, in violation of the laws thereof, is hereby prohibited." U.S. CONST. amend XXI, § 2.

Or a wine cooler. Or a "malternative." Or a beer. Or even a cider. It is a fruit cooler: Something pretty things hold just to be sociable.)

The federal government, of course, wished to make South Dakota—and every other State in the Union—adopt a drinking age of twenty-one. And the ironically-numbered Twenty-first Amendment clearly forbade Congress from writing any such law or making any such regulation. So Congress adopted an "indirect" tax and conditional spending scheme shamelessly entitled "The National Minimum Drinking Age Act of 1984."[4] It worked as follows: First the federal government taxed South Dakota citizens. Then the federal government allocated some percentage of South Dakota citizens' federal taxes for maintenance and repair of federal highways in South Dakota. Finally, the federal government *withheld* "a percentage of federal highway funds otherwise allocable" to South Dakota highway repair—and said it would keep on doing so until South Dakota changed its drinking age to twenty-one.

The federal government gave the same treatment to all States which allowed purchase or possession of alcohol by those under twenty-one years of age.[5] Again, the federal government's tax and conditional spending scheme held State governments between the hammer of their own State constituents (who wanted to see a full return on federal taxes) and the anvil of federal liquor policy (which conditioned the return of federal taxes on State capitulation to the federal drinking age).

And that was good enough for the Supreme Court! Because Congress regulated "indirectly" through a tax and conditional spending scheme, instead of "directly" by writing a law defining a national drinking age, Congress' actions were declared constitutional. As the Court insisted in *South Dakota v. Dole*, "Here, Congress has acted *indirectly under its spending power* to encourage uniformity in the States' drinking ages. As we explain below, we find this legislative effort within constitutional bounds *even if Congress may not regulate drinking ages directly*."[6]

And how exactly did the Court "explain below" that Congress could "indirectly" commandeer States—even in matters which Congress cannot regulate "directly"? *Even in matters expressly reserved by the Constitution to the States?* Well, that was the fun part! Therein lay the magic:

First the Court explained that even when the federal government has no constitutional authority to do a certain thing, it can still accomplish it under the Incrementalist Tax and Spend Clause—i.e., by federal taxation and conditional spending.[7] And this was nothing new—this was the Power of "Yes," first granted by the Switch in Time Court in 1937.[iv]

[iv] *Steward Machine Co. v. Davis*, 301 U.S. 548 (1937). *See supra* TEA WITH SOCIALISTS, Book II (Government In Your Panties), chap. 10 *Disappearing Act*, n. 35-50 and accompanying text for further treatment.

Second, the Court reinterpreted the "for the general welfare" limitation on the Tax and Spend Clause as empty words without meaning.[8] The Court meekly reaffirmed its newfound servility. The Court would no longer police the general welfare limitation, and instead entreated Congress to police itself. (Way to wear the mantle of Constitutional Guardian!)

It gets much better. In *South Dakota v. Dole* the Court ruled that *even explicit and independent limitations on federal power do not apply to the Tax and Spend Clause.* The Court ruled that so long as Congress employed an indirect tax and conditional spending scheme, the rest of the Constitution didn't matter. So third, the Court held that the Tenth Amendment—which declares States retain all powers not delegated to the federal government nor prohibited to the States—*didn't apply to this tax and spend case* (!).[9]

And fourth—most amazing of all—the Court ruled that the Twenty-first Amendment, which expressly commands that States possess exclusive powers to regulate liquor, *cannot limit federal Tax and Spend schemes aimed at regulating liquor* (!). Yes, the Court said, "Even if Congress might lack the power to impose a national minimum drinking age directly, we conclude that encouragement to State action found in [the National Minimum Drinking Age Act] is a valid use of the spending power."[10] Which is to say, Congress can do *anything.* The "reasoning" used by the Court to arrive at this last conclusion was truly magical.[11] But so long as Congress employs an "indirect" taxation and conditional spending technique, the Court ruled Congress possesses power over even those areas it is specifically *disempowered* to meddle under the Constitution.

In *South Dakota v. Dole* the Incrementalist Tax and Spend Clause underwent a singular growth spurt! This was more than the Power of "Yes," which allowed Congress to coerce States into adopting federal policies in areas over which Congress had no enumerated authority. This was something new; something special; the Power of "Yes" *Plus*: A new extension of federal power to coerce States *even in areas explicitly reserved to State authority and explicitly forbidden to the federal government!* No matter what the rest of the Constitution said, or how it was amended in the future.

As always after the Switch in Time, the Supreme Court was motivated more by Congress' desires than by the Constitution. Drinking and driving was, after all, an "interstate problem [which] required a national solution."[12] And the goal of interstate highway safety "had been frustrated by varying drinking ages among the States."[13] Besides, a "Presidential commission" (oooooh, a Presidential commission!) had "concluded that the lack of uniformity in the States' drinking ages created an 'incentive to drink and drive.'"[14]

So in 1987 the Court declared the National Minimum Drinking Age Act "constitutional."[15] And oh, how very effective Congress' Tax and Spend plan was at controlling the little States! By 1988, all thirty-eight States having lower minimum drinking ages suddenly reversed course and adopted the federal drinking age of twenty-one. All fifty States acquiesced to Congress' federal liquor regulatio—excuse me, excuse me, I mean Congress' tax and conditional spending plan. Indeed we may say that Congress' "indirect" tax and spend plan was just as effective establishing a national drinking age as any direct legislation could have been. And again, while the Court continued to mumble about States remaining free to choose federal money or liquor law independence, and how States were not compelled by Congress' tax and conditional spending program,[16] 100% of the States adopted the federal drinking age.

And again one is left to wonder: If 100% federal compliance is liberty, what would federal compulsion look like?

Further Notes to Appendix

[1] The "Twenty-first Amendment grants the States virtually complete control over whether to permit importation or sale of liquor *and how to structure the liquor distribution system.*" *California Retail Liquor Dealers Assn. v. Midcal Aluminum, Inc.*, 445 U.S. 97, 100 (1980).
[2] 23 U.S.C. § 158 (1982 ed., Supp. III).
[3] *South Dakota v. Dole*, 483 U.S. 203, 205 (1987).
[4] 23 U.S.C. § 158 (1982 ed., Supp. III).
[5] *See South Dakota v. Dole*, 483 U.S. at 205 (1987).
[6] *South Dakota v. Dole*, 483 U.S. at 205 (1987) (emphasis added).
[7] More precisely, "objectives not thought to be within Article I's 'enumerated legislative fields,' may nevertheless be attained through the use of the spending power and the conditional grant of federal funds." *South Dakota v. Dole*, 483 U.S. at 207 (1987).
[8] Or more precisely, as the Court ruled, "The level of deference to the congressional decision is such that the Court has more recently questioned whether 'general welfare' is a judicially enforceable restriction at all." *South Dakota v. Dole*, 483 U.S. at 208 n. 2 (1987) (citing *Buckley v. Valeo*, 424 U.S. 1, 90-91 (1976) (per curiam). In other words, the "general welfare" limitation is part of the text of the Constitution; and it presents a constitutional restriction on the federal government's taxing and spending authority—but we aren't going to enforce it any longer. (Have at it, Congress!)
[9] "We have also held that a perceived Tenth Amendment limitation on congressional regulation of state affairs did not comitantly [sic] limit the range of conditions legitimately placed on federal grants." *South Dakota v. Dole*, 483 U.S. at 210 (1987).
[10] *South Dakota v. Dole*, 483 U.S. at 212 (1987).
[11] The Court explicitly recognized that "other constitutional provisions may provide an independent bar to the conditional grant of federal funds." *South Dakota v. Dole*, 483 U.S. at 208 (1987). And the Court recognized that the 21st Amendment provided a very obvious "independent constitutional bar" to Congress' tax and conditional spending scheme to enforce a nationwide drinking age. *South Dakota v. Dole*, 483 U.S. at 209 (1987). Then the Court magically "interpreted" such independent constitutional bars *out of existence*:

> These cases establish that the "independent constitutional bar" limitation on the spending power is not, as petitioner suggests, a prohibition on the indirect achievement of objectives which Congress is not empowered to achieve directly. *Instead, we think that the language in our earlier opinions stands for the unexceptional proposition that the power may not be used to induce the States to engage in activities that would themselves be unconstitutional.* Thus, for example, a grant of federal funds conditioned on invidiously discriminatory state action or the infliction of cruel and unusual punishment would be an illegitimate exercise of the Congress' broad spending power.

South Dakota v. Dole, 483 U.S. at 210-11 (1987). Note first that the Court obtained this result by looking to its own case law instead of the Constitution itself.

And notice also the nonsensical result. *States are already barred from engaging in activities that are themselves unconstitutional.* So an "independent constitutional bar" preventing Congress from inducing States to engage in activities that are themselves unconstitutional is superfluous.
[12] *South Dakota v. Dole*, 483 U.S. at 208 (1987).
[13] *South Dakota v. Dole*, 483 U.S at 209 (1987).
[14] *South Dakota v. Dole*, 483 U.S. at 209 (1987).
[15] *South Dakota v. Dole*, 483 U.S. 203 (1987) (upholding 23 U.S.C. § 158 (1982 ed., Supp. III)).
[16] South *Dakota v. Dole*, 483 U.S. at 211-12 (1987):

> Our decisions have recognized that in some circumstances the financial inducement offered by Congress might be so coercive as to pass the point at which 'pressure turns into compulsion.' *Steward Machine Co. v. Davis, supra*, at 590. Here, however, Congress has directed only that a State desiring to establish a minimum drinking age lower than 21 lose a relatively small percentage of certain federal highway funds. Petitioner

contends that the coercive nature of this program is evident from the degree of success it has achieved. We cannot conclude, however, that a conditional grant of federal money of this sort is unconstitutional simply by reason of its success in achieving the congressional objective. . . .

[T]he argument as to coercion is shown to be more rhetoric than fact. . . .

Here Congress has offered relatively mild encouragement to the States to enact higher minimum drinking ages than they would otherwise choose. But the enactment of such laws remains the prerogative of the States not merely in theory but in fact.

Author Bio

Blaine Brown holds a B.S. in Electrical Engineering from a large private university, where he attended as a Presidential Scholar and a National Merit Scholar. He holds a J.D. *magna cum laude* from the University of Michigan Law School, where he served as an editor of the Michigan Law Review.

After practicing patent litigation and prosecution at Fish & Richardson for several years, Mr. Brown opened his own law firm. Today he practices patent law, and—when the fancy strikes him—he writes.

Afterword

Books embody a strange and solitary form of communication: First, the author composes his words alone, outside the presence of his intended audience. At some later date, the reader reads some or all of those words. Like the author before him, the reader reads in solitude. And for this unilateral, temporally-displaced, and incomplete communication, the reader most often pays a price. That is, the reader actually *purchases* the author's words—whether he will read them or not. Whether he will find anything of value or not. He pays regardless.

In this odd and solitary communication—the book—paying the purchase price is generally considered the end of the reader's obligation, and the end of the author/reader encounter. In many ways the volume you have just read follows the same pattern. It, too, was composed in solitude. It, too, was read alone. And before it was read, it, too, was purchased.

However, in one respect this volume is different. In this case paying the purchase price is *not* the end of the reader's obligation. It is not the end for a very specific reason: for the *idea* this volume contains.

You see, most other books you read contain ideas that are largely unopposed. Whether you are reading vampire romances or mathematical textbooks, you will be hard-pressed to find a plurality who oppose the very *idea* of such books. Most people are indifferent. They do not feel threatened by such books because they view the underlying idea as unreal and therefore harmless (vampire romances) or quite real yet perfectly harmless (mathematical textbooks). In any case because they do not feel threatened, they do not oppose the idea—and they do not attempt to quash it.

The idea of this volume, on the other hand, is both very real and very threatening to the most powerful persons—to The Establishment. Because the idea of this volume exposes The Establishment, pulls it down, and raises in its place the traditional sovereignty of the common American citizen. For this reason it will be uniformly condemned by the most powerful voices in government (from *both* parties), media (from *both* sides), professional societies (*without* parties), and academia (*The* Party). And because The Establishment condemns the idea, it will also be condemned by an uninformed public (who parrot whatever they hear the Establishment say).

And so the reader's engagement with this volume does not end with payment of the purchase price. Because the reader has a relationship not only with the author but also, in this case, with the *idea*—an idea which will be attacked from all sides by the powerful and the ignorant alike. If the reader has benefited by being informed, or awakened, or touched, by the content of this volume then it is up to the reader to cast aside the muzzle buckled upon him by the Establishment, and to defend the idea. There will be no others to do so.

Ways abound in which a reader can discharge his duty to defend the idea. Some of them take very little time, no money, and are safely anonymous: Simply reviewing this volume at Amazon, or Goodreads, or Barnes & Noble defends the idea in a way that neither The Establishment nor its ignorant minions can ever erase or refute. Other ways are less anonymous, but equally effective: Sharing one's own copy of the volume with a friend, or adopting the arguments of the idea in political conversation, or hosting a book club treating the volume.

These latter, less-anonymous ways require a measure of civic gallantry seldom expressed in modern America. But you must do something, be it large or small. You owe it not to me as author (you already paid the purchase price!), but to *the idea.*

Otherwise you betray the very idea which set you free.

Dallas, Texas
October 31, 2012

www.ingramcontent.com/pod-product-compliance
Lightning Source LLC
Chambersburg PA
CBHW031145270326
41931CB00006B/152

* 9 7 8 0 9 8 8 5 1 9 9 4 7 *